GROWING UP AND G
International Perspe
Childhood and Youth ir

Edited by
John Horton, Helena Pimlott-Wilson
and Sarah Marie Hall

P

First published in Great Britain in 2022 by

Policy Press, an imprint of
Bristol University Press
University of Bristol
1-9 Old Park Hill
Bristol
BS2 8BB
UK
t: +44 (0)117 374 6645
e: bup-info@bristol.ac.uk

Details of international sales and distribution partners are available at
policy.bristoluniversitypress.co.uk

JH: For Bentley Library, for Northampton's statutory youth service, for Northampton Women's Aid, for Walsall Illuminations, for Northampton Meals on Wheels, for Northampton YMCA, for Croyland Sure Start, for Spencer Bridge food bank, for Ambrose, for Hero Ben, for Pelsall community centre, for my mother's walking group ...

HPW: For the children and young people getting by in hard times; the educators, youth workers and services wrestling the impacts of austerity; the communities and futures touched by inequalities.

SMH: For L, L & K, Lostock Youth Centre, Kids of Colour, RECLAIM, and all young people for whom austerity and hardship is their everyday normal ...

Contents

List of figures and tables

Figures

All the photographs in this volume are copyright to the contributors and are reproduced with their permission.

Tables

Notes on contributors

Dena Aufseeser is Assistant Professor at the Department of Geography and Environmental Systems, University of Maryland, Baltimore County, USA. She does research in social policy, geography and urban studies and poverty studies. Her current projects include 'Child migration, rights and inequality in Peru' and 'Child poverty and inequality in Baltimore, historically and today'. She also does research on motherhood and housing instability.

Anki Bengtsson holds a PhD in Education from Stockholm University, Sweden. She currently works as a senior lecturer at the Department of Education, Stockholm University. Her research interests concern policy, politics of education as well as the geography of education. Among other things, Anki has done research about teachers who recently migrated to Sweden and their studies in a supplementary, teacher training programme.

Michael Boampong is Lecturer in Childhood and Youth Studies at the Open University, UK. His most recent research explored the impact of the 2008 financial crisis on young people's everyday life within Ghanaian transnational households. His research interest concerns how globalisation and international political economy impacts childhood, transnational childhoods and youth transitions as well as creative and participatory research methods. Previously, he served a migration and youth policy specialist to several United Nations agencies and the Commonwealth Secretariat. Michael is the author of the United Nations flagship publication *Youth and Migration* (2013). He is currently the lead consultant to the Government of Ghana in the review of Ghana's National Youth Policy.

Jacob Breslow is Assistant Professor of Gender and Sexuality at the LSE Department of Gender Studies, UK. His primary line of research is on contemporary social justice movements in the US, and the ways in which the idea of childhood works within and against them. His book, which explores childhood's relation to blackness, transfeminism, queerness and deportability, is entitled *Ambivalent Childhoods: Speculative Futures and the Psychic Life of the Child* (2021) and is being published with the University of Minnesota Press. His research has been published in *Comparative American Studies* (2020), *American Quarterly* (2019), *Porn Studies* (2018) and *Transgender Studies Quarterly* (2017). Currently, he is extending his research on trans★ childhood, and he is working on a special issue tentatively entitled *Queer and Trans Geographies of Accommodation and Displacement*.

Chiung-wen Chang is Assistant Professor at the National Dong Hwa University, Taiwan. Her work has focused upon geographies of alternative economies with special concern about the ways that people situated in marginal areas/status act collectively in response to capitalist hegemony of neoliberalist economy. Her previous study was to look at knowledge transfer systems of organic farming among smallholders. She is now engaged in practices of post-capitalist communing. One programme is the initiation of credit union movement on campus. It aims at enhancing financial literature and encouraging young people to help each other through a campus-based credit union. Another is cooperative-informed participation in eastern Taiwan. An on-going project is to co-work with activists of animal welfare to support the elders to develop backyard poultry by setting up micro-businesses in a cooperative form. It is to connect community practices of solidarity economy to ideas of active aging and animal welfare at a community level.

Caroline Day is Senior Lecturer in the School of the Environment, Geography and Geosciences at the University of Portsmouth, UK. Caroline's research interests focus on a number of issues that fall within the wider discourse of International Development. These include children, young people and families, HIV and AIDS, disability and caregiving and the wider role that gender plays in the development of the global South. Caroline's work has most often focused on vulnerable children and young people in both the UK and Africa, examining how issues such as caregiving, bereavement, poverty, disability and special needs, substance misuse, sexual exploitation and homelessness can socially exclude young people from mainstream society.

Denise Goerisch is Assistant Professor and Assistant Chair in the Department of Integrative, Religious, and Intercultural Studies at Grand Valley State University, Michigan, USA. She received her PhD in Geography from San Diego State University and University of California, Santa Barbara. Her research focuses on the socioeconomic lives of children and young people, care ethics, and geographies of education. She has published on topics related to emotional labour and girlhood, children's work and play, leadership in informal education spaces, popular geopolitics and care, faculty labour, mentoring practices in higher education, college affordability and feminist methodologies.

Carlie Goldsmith is Visiting Research Fellow at St Mary's University, Twickenham, London, UK. Carlie previously worked as a senior lecturer in criminology for six years before founding the research organisation and consultancy North RTD in 2013. Over her career, Carlie has managed local, regional and national research and evaluation in criminal justice, offending, public health, community engagement, bereavement, financial capability and suicide prevention.

Sarah Marie Hall is Reader in Human Geography at the University of Manchester, UK. Her research sits in the broad field of feminist political economy: understanding how socio-economic processes are shaped by gender relations, lived experience and social difference. Recent research projects focus on everyday life and economic change, including empirical work in the context of austerity, Brexit and devolution. She is currently Co-Editor of the international academic journal *Area*.

John Horton is based in the Faculty of Education and Humanities at the University of Northampton, UK. His research explores the spaces, cultures, politics, playful practices and social-material exclusions of contemporary childhood and youth in diverse international contexts. John is currently one of the editors of the international academic journal *Social & Cultural Geography*, and previously edited the international academic journal *Children's Geographies*. John is also Series Editor of a new major book series on Spaces of Childhood and Youth for Routledge.

Vicky Johnson is Director of Centre for Remote and Rural Communites, Inverness College, University of the Highlands and Islands, Scotland. Vicky's research interests include understanding how marginalised people can be supported as agents of change in rapidly changing environmental, political and cultural contexts. She has developed and published papers on a 'change-scape' approach. This supports inclusive, gender sensitive and child and youth centred research that takes into account intergenerational dynamics in communities and their changing landscapes. Vicky's recent research projects include: 'Mapping child rights in community driven development' (Wellspring Philanthropic Foundation); 'Youth uncertainty rights (YOUR) world research with marginalised youth in Ethiopia and Nepal' (ESRC-DFID's Poverty Alleviation Fund); 'Engaging young children in research' (across global contexts for the Bernard van Leer Foundation); 'Youth sexual and reproductive health', with case studies in Africa, Asia and Latin America (IPPF); 'Education in informal settlements in Nairobi' (UN Girls' Education Initiative). She has also led action research processes funded by local and regional authorities and regenerational programmes across the UK.

Ruth Cheung Judge is a lecturer at the University of Liverpool, UK. Her contribution to this volume is based on her PhD research, funded by a ESRC studentship based at University College London. She is currently working on research about young people's 'homeland' educational mobilities within the Nigerian diaspora.

Philip Kelly is Professor in the Department of Geography at York University, Canada. Philip's recent research has examined the labour market trajectories of Filipino immigrants and their children in Toronto, the transnational linkages forged with communities and families in the Philippines, and the process of socio-economic change in sending areas. Conceptually, Philip's work addressed the interface between political economy approaches to class and labour markets, and cultural approaches that explore the intersection of class and other bases of identity. Philip's current research examines the potential of migrant social networks in the development of transnational alternative economic practices between Canada and the Philippines.

Eric Larsson holds a PhD in education from Stockholm University, Sweden. He currently works as a lecturer at the Department of Special Education at Stockholm University. His research interest concerns the intersection between sociology of education and the geography of education. More precisely, it focuses on themes such as educational strategies, elite education and educational markets.

Jonghee Lee-Caldararo is a PhD candidate in the Department of Geography at the University of Kentucky, USA and earned her master's degree at the Ewha Women's University, South Korea. As a cultural and political geographer, she has explored taken-for-granted urban spaces, including cafés and Mongolian enclaves in Seoul. With her research interest in urban night and everyday politics, she published 'Buy a cup of coffee, you will get your space' (forthcoming) and 'Dark side of the 24-hour society: focusing on night-time part-timers in Seoul' (co-authored). Her paper 'Micropolitics of sleepless in Seoul' won the Student paper award in 2020 from the PGSG, American

Association of Geographers. The award-winning paper was modified for her chapter in this book.

Aura Lehtonen is Senior Lecturer in Sociology at the University of Northampton, UK. Aura's primary area of research focuses on dominant narratives, representations and regulation of sexuality within broader cultural, political and economic formations – spanning political sociology, gender and sexuality studies and cultural studies. Her current project explores the limitations and possibilities of sexual politics within austerity and neoliberalism, interrogating the intersections of sexuality and gender with class and racial formations, work and welfare, and the state. She is also interested in pedagogy, with a research focus on feminist and queer pedagogical engagements with narratives and practices of inclusion, resistance, and employability in Higher Education.

Sonja Marzi is LSE Fellow in the Department of Methodology and the Department of International Development, LSE, UK. Sonja's research is interdisciplinary and focuses on urban issues in Latin America cutting across the fields of international development, urban geography and sociology. Sonja is particularly interested in socio-spatial mobility within urban space and place. Her current and recent research asks questions of how the neighbourhood, a sense of place, issues of societal insecurity, the built environment and urban development interrelate with women's and young people's aspirations and social mobility opportunities.

Hao-Che Pei was Chairman of Dong Hwa Campus Credit Union in Taiwan from 2016 to 2019. Now he is a PhD Student in Geography and Environmental Science at the University of Southampton, UK. His research interest is focused on alternative economy practices, based on participatory methods, to explore how marginalised groups, who are excluded due to neoliberal governance, achieve independent living by collective participation and collaboration. His previous study was to explore the possibility of financial independence with college students through participating in campus-based credit union operations, and indeed, to discover how young people cultivate their financial literacy and capacity collectively for responding to youth poverty caused by neoliberal discipline in Taiwan. Now he is carrying out a geographical research project on social enterprises, to explore political, cultural and economic dynamics among actors, including people, institutions and space, and moreover, to know how marginalised groups perform post-capitalist commons for changing subordinate status by social enterprise operations in post-industrial societies.

Heather Piggott is Strategic Lead for Access and Participation at Edge Hill University, UK. Her work includes ensuring the university's widening participation initiatives that seek equity of opportunity in higher education are strategically planned, research informed and effectively evaluated. Prior to this, Heather worked in local government in a policy and research role to support the creation and implementation of children and young people's policies and strategies. Heather has a PhD in Human Geography from the University of Manchester, her mixed methods research explored social attitudes, social norms and lived experiences of women in the rural labour markets of Bangladesh and India. This research was a collaboration between the University of Manchester, BIGD at BRAC University in Bangladesh and Varanasi Hindu University in India.

Helena Pimlott-Wilson is Reader in Geography at Loughborough University, UK. Her research focuses on the shifting importance of education and employment in the reproduction of classed power. Recent work investigates the aspirations of young people from socio-economically diverse areas in the UK, international mobility of students for higher education and work placements, and the alternative and supplementary education industries.

Peter Squires is Emeritus Professor in Criminology and Public Policy at the University of Brighton, UK. Since the early 1990s Peter has helped develop the teaching and research specialism in criminology and criminal justice at the University of Brighton, and his academic work has ranged across a wide range of themes and topics including youth crime and disorder, anti-social behaviour, weapons, crime and violence, gun crime and community safety. Peter has undertaken a great deal of research and consultancy addressing these topics with, among others, Sussex Police, the Metropolitan Police, London boroughs, the European Forum for Urban Safety, the East Sussex Fire and Rescue Service and the Youth Justice Board – as well as with colleagues in other universities.

Carl Walker is a community psychologist based at the University of Brighton, UK. Carl is on the British Psychological Society National Community Psychology section committee. Carl recently co-founded the national group 'Psychologists against Austerity' and his recent research involves action research projects on wellbeing drawing on statactivist techniques. Carl's main research interests include exploring the relations between debt, inequality and mental health and the use of community initiatives to work toward addressing mental health needs.

Andy West is an independent international researcher and development work adviser on childhood and youth, and Visiting Senior Fellow in International Development and Youth Studies at the University of Suffolk, UK. Andy has worked with children and young people and related issues, practices and policies for over 30 years, especially on rights, participation and protection, mainly in Asia and the UK for local, national and international organisations; he has also worked in the Middle East, Africa and the Pacific. His work has been focused with marginalised children and young people. Andy has been particularly interested in approaches taking account of local social and cultural settings, and concerned with the engagement with practice issues, dilemmas and ethics.

Catherine Wilkinson is Programme Leader for Education Studies at Liverpool John Moores University, UK. Catherine is a senior lecturer, teaching across at Education Studies and Early Childhood Studies degree programmes. Prior to this, Catherine worked as a lecturer in Children, Young People and Families in the Faculty of Health and Social Care, Edge Hill University. Catherine also previously worked as a postdoctoral research associate at Durham University in the School of Education. Catherine completed her PhD in Environmental Sciences at the University of Liverpool, funded by an ESRC CASE award. Catherine works at the intersection of a range of research approaches, including: mixed methods, ethnographic and participatory research. Catherine's primary research interests are: children, young people and identity; young people and community radio; and children and young people-friendly research methods. Catherine uses this research to inspire the teaching which she delivers.

1

Introduction

John Horton, Helena Pimlott-Wilson and Sarah Marie Hall

Introduction

We wish this book was not necessary

This collection gives voice to children, young people and families at the sharp end of contemporary processes of neoliberalisations, austerities and economic crises in diverse global contexts. We wish this book was not necessary or timely. However, as three geographers who have worked with many children, young people and families in different settings over the last 15 years, we are writing from a deep sense of sadness and urgency. This book has developed out of our anger and concern that the lives and prospects of so many of our research participants have demonstrably been adversely affected by manifestations of neoliberalisations, austerities and economic crises. The book is also written from heartbreak that our own communities, families and lifecourses have been profoundly affected by the same horrible processes. So as a point of departure, the following three vignettes from our research introduce some key terms, processes and deeply affecting encounters which echo throughout the following chapters.

John's research: just getting on with austerities, or 'we're fucked'?

During the global financial crisis of 2007–08, John was in the middle of several research projects based in spaces of play, youthwork and social care in the English Midlands. These spaces and communities were radically transformed by subsequent public sector funding cuts. Literally all of the youth organisations John worked with back then have now closed, literally all of the youthworkers and practitioners he worked with were made redundant. Within a few years entire, taken-for-granted categories of work/space ('the public library', 'the statutory youth service') were downsized, decommissioned and – apparently permanently – deemed unviable. John has written about some of these experiences (Horton, 2016; 2020) but, to be honest, finds it a bit too difficult. John holds on to the way many young people from these contexts demonstrated such tenacity, care and solidarity: 'a kind of modest, resigned, sometimes-determined acceptance' and capacity to 'just get on' with their lives and communities (Horton, 2017: 287). On the other hand, John can still hear a research participant talking about the probable closure of a particular service: they simply said 'we're fucked' and walked away. John was reminded of this when, in a recent project with Brazilian young people, a participant described the impacts of municipal funding cuts on local water supply: 'we are always waiting for water. Things are fucked'.

Helena's research: neoliberal subjectivities in play, education and parenting

Through a range of projects about play, education and parenting in economically diverse communities, Helena has traced some of the ways in which 'the self-reliant, entrepreneurial citizen-worker has become the epitome of the ideal neoliberal subject, as paid work has become the corner-stone by which social inclusion and successful citizenship are measured for those of working age' (Pimlott-Wilson, 2017: 289). Across diverse UK contexts, Helena's work reveals how 'this shift to an aspirational politics which normalises and mainstreams practices associated with a narrow, middle-class conception of aspirations marginalises those who do not, or cannot, conform to … ideals of neoliberal citizenship' (Pimlott-Wilson, 2017: 289). Helena has been struck by the people she has met who 'get by' and 'grow up' in 'hard times': young people who 'get in trouble' at school because they can't sleep well in their cold, damp homes and thus struggle to concentrate; families who experience food poverty when social welfare benefits are cut with little warning following work capability assessments; children unable to participate in after-school activities because they can't afford a 50p fee. Nevertheless, her research also shows that the material basis of these 'hard times' is often overlooked in political and policy contexts, and those who face the greatest challenges are unjustly blamed, in unguarded and stigmatising terms, for their perceived failure 'to support their children's learning … evading their responsibilities and … not putting children's needs first' (Holloway and Pimlott-Wilson, 2012: 645–646).

Sarah's research: everyday austerities and the complicated business of care

In 2013–15, Sarah undertook an in-depth programme of longitudinal ethnographic research with families in Greater Manchester, UK, exploring real, felt, lived experiences of austerity. One key finding from this study was the extent to which austerity in the UK must be understood as 'a distinctly *gendered* ideology, process and condition' (Hall, 2019a: 5) in two senses. On the one hand, 'women have been disproportionately affected by these cuts as a result of structural inequalities which mean they earn less, own less and have more responsibility for unpaid care and domestic work' (Hall et al, 2017: 1; see also Greer Murphy, 2017). On the other hand, Sarah also notes that most theorisations of austerity have been done by white, male, metatheoretical 'big boys' (after Katz, 1996) working in a very particular, self-assured political-economic tradition. There is an artwork in one of Sarah's creative outputs from the ethnographic research that gets John every time: entitled 'caring is a complicated business', it features a research participant talking about friends, family and different ways they care for one another (Hall, 2017), beautifully evoking relational and reciprocal communities of care in hard times.

With these kinds of encounters very much in mind, this book brings together new work by multidisciplinary researchers who have explored the ongoing consequences of neoliberalisations, austerities and economic crises for children, young people and families. As we explain in the following sections, we use the term 'hard times' to connect and think through the multiple, compound, challenging and deeply affecting situations that emerge through the book.

Hard times? Neoliberalisations, austerities and economic crises

The following chapters are all framed by concepts and contexts of economic crisis, austerity and neoliberalism. Here, we begin with a definitional and critical discussion of each of these terms, before offering the idea of 'hard times' as a provocative way of opening up new kinds of discussion about these interrelated processes.

Economic crises – and specifically the global financial crisis of 2007–08 – casts a dark shadow over all the chapters in this book. By now, the causes and form of the global financial crisis have been extensively historicised (Sorkin, 2009; Konings and Somers, 2010; Mason, 2010).

3

There are many comprehensive accounts of the crisis as a political-economic event, narrating the toxic and overwhelming coming-together of deregulated banking industries (Crotty, 2009), byzantine financialised commodity markets (Martin, 2011) (that we cannot even claim to understand), callous and shady banking practices (French and Leyshon, 2010), hubristic and inflated housing markets, vastly expanding sub-subprime mortgage and 'buy-to-let' sectors, lending defaults, property foreclosures, devalued mortgage bonds, crashing mortgage-backed securities (Aalbers, 2009), ineffective regulatory safeguards, panicked banking and financial institutions, contractions in closely interdependent banking/financial/manufacturing industries (Derudder et al, 2011), declining consumer confidence, runs on banks, multi-scaled economic shocks, shrinking GDPs, rising unemployment, and profound strain on often-risk-exposed public sector finances (Blažek et al, 2020). In many parts of the world, these complexly-intertwined crises and spaces of private and sovereign debt (see Langley, 2008; French et al, 2009) ultimately constituted the most severe economic recession since the Great Recession of the 1930s. This was manifest in, for example, a 4.5% decline in per capita GDP across the EU in 2009, and an increase in EU unemployment levels from 7.1% in 2008 to 10.5% in 2012 (Crescenzi et al, 2016; Eurostat, 2014). In developing this book, our aim has never been to contribute another neat narrative of the political-economic causes and consequences of the global financial crisis. Indeed, we will argue that principally theorising the global financial crisis as a political-economic event has led to personal, everyday, affecting lived experiences of economic crisis being overlooked in a great deal of major research in this area. Against this grain, we foreground the experiences of children, young people and families actually living-with economic crises in practice – and the messy, traumatic, nightmarish scenarios that this still entails, even more than a decade after the supposed end of the global financial crisis. Note, too, that we refer to economic *crises* in the plural here, to decentre normative Anglo-American accounts of *the* global financial crisis and acknowledge the existence of multiple, diversely-situated economic crises in the past, present and future (that's capitalism, sadly) (see also Larner, 2011). By pluralising crises, we also highlight the diversity, and gross inequity, of experiences of the global financial crisis: there is no universal experience of economic crisis – and it would be inaccurate to suggest that now is universally worse than some imaginary past time for all – but this book explores how, for some, the 2007–08 global financial crisis has intensified and compounded inequalities in diverse ways and settings.

Many of the following chapters also explicitly deal with children, young people and families living in situations of **austerity**. As Hall (2019a: 2) notes, 'austerity' has a twofold meaning being both a popular term denoting frugality or 'a condition of severe simplicity and self-restraint' and, latterly, a descriptor for 'a specific set of actions and policies by the state: the reduction of spending on public expenditure with the precise aim of reducing governmental budget deficit'. In particular, through this book, austerity is widely used to characterise a repertoire of ideological and policy responses to the 2007–08 global financial crisis and the recessions it later prompted. In this context, many state and federal governments in Europe and North America were quick to adopt severe public sector austerity programmes (see Hall et al 2020). This austerity politics was typified by very substantial and rapid cuts to budgets for welfare, local government, social care, civic spaces, public transport, and cultural, community, educational, heritage and leisure services. Although ideologically justified as a 'necessary' process of 'balancing the books' and reducing government indebtedness by cutting spend on 'non-essential' services, there is now considerable evidence that this vast roll-back of public spending has extended and compounded economic crises and constituted new social-political crises in diverse settings. In the UK, for example, the right-wing Conservative-led government's HM Treasury Spending Review of 2010 instituted an unprecedented programme to cut public spending in England by £81bn by 2015, including a 51% cut in the budget of national government departments, a £7bn cut in national welfare budget, and a 27% cut in the budget for Local Authorities, while devolving responsibility for implementation of these cuts to local agencies and actors (HM Treasury, 2010). The consequences of this round of multimillion spending cuts are still, at this time of writing, emerging. As with the 2007–08 global financial crisis, academic research primarily figured and theorised austerity as a political-economic event via important concepts, like 'austerity urbanism' (Peck, 2012), which foreground the impacts of 'rolling back' public expenditure for cities, regions, economic systems and governance thereof (Aalbers, 2009; Kitson et al, 2011). It is only relatively recently that sustained scholarly research has begun to evidence the substantial impacts of austerity for lived and local experiences (O'Hara, 2014), charting the increased prevalence of forms of food poverty (Garthwaite, 2016a), child poverty (Ridge, 2013), social isolation (Cross, 2013; Power and Bartlett, 2019), community breakdown (Jones et al, 2015), social care crises (Loopstra et al, 2016), and populist exclusionary ideologies (Vasilopoulou et al, 2014). Against this backdrop, this book collates new evidence about the haunting impacts of austerity for children, young people and families in diverse contexts. It is our hope that the following chapters will help to open up new kinds of research and conversations about austerity, beyond the political-economic, recognising the profound personal, everyday and intersectional harms constituted by recent austerity politics. Note, again, that we pluralise *austerities* to acknowledge diverse instances of austerity – past, present and future – and to recognise people's diverse orientations towards, and experiences of, public funding cuts in practice.

Underpinning all of the following chapters is a concern with longer-run processes of **neoliberalism**. This contested label critiques a series of linked, decades-long processes through which logics of individualism, free marketeering, cost-effectiveness, competitiveness, self-governance, managerialist reform, and rationalisation have come to be normatively embedded in all manner of workplace, organisational and policy contexts (Newman, 2013; Peck and Tickell, 2002). It is argued that, through these shifts, tactics of organisational 'leanness', 'flexibility', budgetary efficiency, competitiveness, outsourcing, 'doing more with less', the erosion of solidarities, and 'marketisation and privatisation, whether frontally or incrementally introduced' (Hall 2005: 322; Garrett, 2009; Shaw, 2009) became default operating principles of diverse organisational-institutional spaces in many post-1945 economies and policy contexts. It is thus argued that neoliberal reforms over the last half century created preconditions of vulnerability and risk which were profoundly exposed by the global financial crisis (Crescenzi et al, 2016). Or, somewhat differently, it is argued that recent austerity policies should be understood as intensified moments of neoliberalism, where neoliberal claims for deregulation, state roll-back and efficiency measures advanced dramatically after, or even *through*, the global financial crisis (Harvey, 2007, 2017). In this book, we do not intend to frame our discussion solely in terms of these political-economic theorisations of neoliberalism: instead, the following chapters focus on children, young people and families who find themselves in diverse *neoliberalised* settings. Indeed, we share concerns about the totalising, daunting metanarrative of neoliberalism (Barnett, 2005; Peck, 2013; Roy et al, 2012). However, we have found critical work around this concept important in diagnosing multiple forms of individualism, competitiveness and cost-effectiveness (Larner, 2003) which surface in all kinds of ways in the following chapters. We thus write in terms of *neoliberalisations* to highlight processes which are demonstrably affecting children, young people and families encountered in our research, without necessarily claiming it as a coherent, singular, stable or uncontested -*ism*. Again, we prefer to think in terms of plural neoliberalisations to recognise the multiple processes and experiences going on within this term.

After much discussion, we settled on **hard times** as a focal concept for the book. We use 'hard times' as a figure of speech – encompassing neoliberalisations, austerities and economic crises – for four reasons. First, we want to emphasise *hardness*. Through our research, we have witnessed first-hand the *hard*, hurtful, bruising, crushing, distressing, inequitable and inflexible impacts of neoliberalisations, austerities and economic crises for children, young people and families. The chapters in this book are full of experiences of painful, strain-filled, horrible, stressful situations: truly hard times, although the nature and severity of this hardness varies from context to context, shaped by all manner of structural inequalities, longstanding exclusions and power imbalances. In preparing this book, we therefore wanted to allow space for voices that speak of the sheer hardness of growing up in situations of social injustice and marginality that are being constituted or intensified by neoliberalisations, austerities and economic crises. There are clear resonances between our 'hard times' and Cloke et al's (2016) coining of *the mean times* to describe austerity-era Britain, or Loach's (2015) powerful evocation of the *conscious cruelty* inherent in contemporary neoliberal welfare regimes. Likewise, our 'hard times' are closely related to notions of *precariousness* ('an ontological condition common to all life') and *precarity* (how certain lives and spaces experience markedly and structurally greater exposure to risks, harms and traumas) (Harker, 2012; after Butler, 2009). However, second, in talking of 'hard times', we wanted to write and think in a register that children, young people and families might relate to. We wanted this book to centre the actually-existing, personal, everyday, emotive experiences of children, young people and families living with neoliberalisations, austerities and economic crises. Rather than totally impose a grand, inaccessible scholarly language – of neoliberalisations, austerities, economic crises or precarities – onto those experiences, we want to explore the critical potential of more colloquial understandings that come more from children, young people and families themselves: hence 'hard times'. Third, in particular 'hard times' helps us think about how complexly relational and interrelated processes are lived and experienced. We use 'hard times' to encompass neoliberalisations, austerities and economic crises and the ways in which these processes are always already materially, experientially, ideologically and affectively intertwined in practice. Thus, while a cool scholarly reading might enforce a nuanced distinction between neoliberalisations, austerities and economic crises, in this book we want to recognise how these processes are lumped together, materially and spatially (Katz, 2004; 2018) and in people's everyday experiences. Fourth, we like 'hard times' precisely because it feels a little colloquial, indefinite and conditional. We want our slightly flip notion of 'hard times' to serve as a point of critique of singular metanarratives of neoliberalisation, austerity and economic crisis. We worry about using terms like 'neoliberalisations', 'austerities' and 'economic crises' because (even with our pluralisation and critique) they feel *proper* and seem to denote quite intractable, permanent, inevitable, implacable situations. They also risk perpetuating crisis-led discourses of childhood and youth, wherein children, young people and families are overwhelmingly defined and shaped in terms of crises and related moral panics (O'Toole, 2015). Constantly writing about neoliberalisations, austerities and economic crises can feel overwhelming and hope-less. Thinking in terms of 'hard times' feels a little more hopeful: it contains a sense that hard times might, sometimes, hopefully, be endured, survived, eased and moved-beyond; it allows us to breathe a little easier; it allows the possibility that hard times might pass, and that some sort of tenacity, solidarity, care, reckoning or resistance (see Askins, 2015; Jupp, 2017) might, somewhere, be possible ...

Children, young people and families in hard times

In developing this book, we wanted to advance understandings of neoliberalisations, austerities and economic crises in three key ways. First, we wanted to make space to recognise and better understand the distinctive experiences and constitutive presence of children, young people and families within these contexts. We are really troubled by the way that children, young people and families are overwhelmingly absent from chief scholarly accounts of neoliberalism, austerity and the global financial crisis. There are just so many landmark accounts of these processes in which children/childhood, young people/youth and families/family *do not appear once* (for example, Peck and Tickell, 2002; Crotty, 2009; Martin, 2011; Peck, 2012; Blažek et al, 2020). These kinds of accounts have been critically important in shaping understandings (including our own) of contemporary political-economic processes. But these agenda-setting narratives have consistently declined to acknowledge the everyday experiences of children, young people and families. Their modus operandi – typically starting with slick city-, state-, or corporately-scaled case studies – seems to disallow any encounters with diverse, personal, or more raw lived experiences of those at the sharp end of these processes. Even where these kinds of analyses mobilise data around, for example, child poverty or youth unemployment, we would argue that children and young people themselves are rarely given voice. The authors of the following chapters redress this absence via work which explicitly foregrounds the experiences, lives, fears and hopes of children, young people and families in diverse hard times. The chapters do not just 'fill a gap' in extant accounts of neoliberalisations, austerities and economic crises: rather, as we argue later, these accounts require a more radical rethinking of how these hard times matter, how they cause harm and intensify marginality, and how they are lived-with and lived-through (or not).

Second, conversely, the book stands as an argument that more multidisciplinary researchers working with children, young people and families should directly consider neoliberalisations, austerities and economic crises. We are struck by how few scholars from, for example, Children's Geographies and interdisciplinary Childhood and Youth Studies have directly engaged these political-economic contexts (thus further perpetuating the absence of children, young people and families from normative scholarly accounts of these processes). There are important exceptions to this, and certainly our own work has been inspired by the exceptional, haunting work of scholars like Cindi Katz (2004; 2011), Sue Ruddick (2007a; 2007b) and Karen Wells (2015) on global neoliberalised childhoods, as well as studies by Jupp (2016), France (2016), Wilkinson and Ortega-Alcázar (2018), Stenning (2018) and van Lanen (2017; 2020) who vividly evoke youth and/or family in diverse austerity contexts. However, we suggest that this work has often been situated as a somewhat substantive, specialist concern within Children's Geographies and interdisciplinary Childhood and Youth Studies, in a way which seems vastly out of proportion to the profound impacts of global neoliberalisations, austerities and economic crises for children and young people's lives. Certainly, it seems remarkable that searching for 'austerity' or 'economic crisis' in titles/abstracts/keywords of research published in leading subdisciplinary journals currently only turns up one paper in *Childhood* (Filho and Neder, 2001), one paper in *Children's Geographies* (Cairns, 2017) and seven papers in *Journal of Youth Studies* (McDowell, 2012; Cairns et al, 2014; Gateley, 2014; Bendit and Miranda, 2015, Allen, 2016; Michail and Christou, 2016; Nikunen, 2017). In this context, the following chapters signpost many ways in which multidisciplinary researchers could do more to address the impacts of neoliberalisations, austerities and economic crises for children and young people's lives (Pimlott-Wilson and Hall, 2017), particularly inasmuch as they intersect with gendered, classed, ableist, post-colonial, heteronormative, and cis-normative modes of marginality and social exclusion.

Third, more broadly, we worry that too much is lost in normative accounts that figure neoliberalisations, austerities and economic crises in primarily political-economic terms. To us, assured, well-worn, important political-economic narratives of neoliberalism, austerity and economic crisis have a peculiar, distancing effect. City- and state-scaled critiques of these problems can inure us to lived experiences and impacts, as all manner of traumatic effects/affects go unseen and undocumented (Stenning, 2020). In preparing this collection, our central concern was to constitute a space where often-overlooked experiences of hard times as lived, as felt, as endured, as intimately experienced and as *personal* (Hall 2019a) could be articulated. As a counterpoint to normative political-economic analyses, the following chapters offer multiple instances of hard times 'lived in, through, and punctuating everyday life ... shaping lifecourses, biographies and imaginaries' and as 'lived, intimate, and so very personal' (Hall, 2019b: 480, 490).

Our aim, then, has been to bring together new work which (re)connects scholarly research with everyday spaces and experiences, to address how diverse hard times 'bleed into the very fabric of everyday geographies – the spaces in which people live, meet, work, play – in different ways and at a range of magnitudes' (Hall, 2019c: 770). We also wanted contributors to write about/with a wider emotional-affective register than has typically been the case, to acknowledge raw, visceral feelings of trauma occasioned by austerity's 'diffusive cruelties' (Hitchen, 2019) and more ambiguous, quiet or gentle and more hopeful, less lurid, less grandly narratable kinds of stories (Pottinger, 2017; Horton, 2020), and anything inbetween. Moreover, by juxtaposing these globally-located accounts, we hoped to suggest something of the complexly-relational, co-incident, always-multiple social-material processes which have often been hidden in normative political-economic analyses of neoliberalisations, austerities and economic crises (Lee et al, 2009; Hitchen, 2016). In so doing, we want the following chapters to act as a series of challenges to (re)frame understandings of hard times in terms of critical theorisations of everydayness, care, homes, families, intimacies, intersectionalities, injustices and activisms and via encounters with children, young people and families themselves.

Growing up and getting by: new perspectives on neoliberalisation, austerities and economic crises

Through encounters with diverse, globally-situated children, young people and families, the following chapters develop new understandings of 'hard times' around three key themes. The sections deliberately juxtapose chapters which are globally located, multi-method and multidisciplinary to bring different kinds of research, participants and hard times into dialogue.

In Part 1, chapters share a concern with **transformations**. Authors present new qualitative and quantitative evidence of the transformative impacts of hard times for contemporary experiences of childhood, youth and family in diverse international contexts (Horton, 2016; Ribbens et al, 2013). The chapters highlight some of the substantial, but unevenly experienced and locally experienced, transformations constituted by neoliberalisations, austerities and economic crises. Chapters will explore the interconnected, but geographically-differentiated, regionally-distinctive and personally-experienced nature of these transformations, via case studies from different states, regions, localities, cities and communities. Case studies as diverse as Swedish educational settings, Peruvian youth migrations, South Korean cafés, North American college campuses and British-Ghanaian households, evidence emergent new conditions of precarious, neoliberalised, austere, indebted or in-crisis childhood, youth and family lives. These chapters provide compelling evidence of some of the harms, anxieties and uncertainties constituted by these contexts. In particular, chapters note the way in which hard times are transforming everyday communities, ecologies and infrastructures and also the discursive formations of childhood, youth and family per se (France, 2016; Pimlott-Wilson, 2017).

In Chapter 2, for example, Eric Larsson and Anki Bengtsson show how multiple waves of neoliberal educational marketisation are transforming Swedish schools, student experiences and family prerogatives. The chapter explores some of the impacts of educational marketisation becoming normalised within institutional and urban spaces. Larsson and Bengtsson show how successive educational neoliberalisations in Stockholm since the 1990s have radically transformed schools in this region, not least via a major proliferation of schools funded by for-profit venture capitalist investors. The chapter also shows how aspirational discourses and architectures thus constituted are impacting upon young people's everyday experiences, creating and hardening classed social exclusions. Larsson and Bengtsson thus call for more careful, participatory understandings of actually-existing neoliberalisations in the lives of children, young people and families.

Dena Aufseeser's chapter (Chapter 3) highlights the complex, intersecting nature of transformations in contemporary children, young people and families' lives. Through participant observation with young people who migrate from rural Peruvian villages to Lima for work during school vacations, Aufseeser notes how young migrants are caught between a range of differently-paced transformations. On the one hand, the lives of these young people and their families are being profoundly affected by rapid and relentlessly uneven economic change in Peru as well as accelerating anthropocenic environmental degradation. Young people display considerable resourcefulness and tenacity to support their families despite such precarious and changing conditions. On the other hand, however, young migrants' lives are also being shaped by remarkably static and obdurate Peruvian media/policy discourses which cast them as vulnerable 'victims' and call for migration to be 'prevented' via criminalisation or education programmes. Aufseeser shows how this combination of rapidly-worsening economic-environmental risks versus only-slowly-evolving social norms is placing young migrants in profoundly challenging situations of isolation and marginality. Aufseeser thus suggests that enduring social norms about idealised childhood and family need to be critiqued and expanded to better understand and support children, young people and families in rapidly transforming political-economic situations.

In Chapter 4, Jonghee Lee-Caldararo shows how the transformational impacts of neoliberalisations, austerities and economic crises are felt at intimate, bodily scales. Through interviews and participant observation with young people at a selection of Seoul's '24-hour cafés' Lee-Caldararo argues that a highly competitive neoliberalised education system in South Korea, coupled with anxieties about post-recessionary unemployment and job insecurity, have led to 'laziness' being stigmatised. In this context, Lee-Caldararo suggests that sleeplessness, chronic fatigue, anxiety and stress have come to be normalised bodily conditions for many young people. This is evidenced by the preponderance of '24-hour cafés' in Seoul, where many young people regularly study, work and doze through the night, in lieu of going to bed. Through this haunting chapter, Lee-Caldararo vividly evokes the way in which neoliberalisations, austerities and economic crises are lived and deeply felt as personal, corporeal conditions, every day and every night.

Denise Goerisch's chapter (Chapter 5) also shows how processes of neoliberalisations and austerities result in profound forms of strain, tension and anxiety for many young people. Goerisch explores the transformative impacts of educational neoliberalisation and austerian budget cuts within North American Higher Education, particularly emphasising the proliferation of student debt. Through ethnographic research with students at a Wisconsin college the chapter charts some of the troubling, complex ways in which debt has come to be closely entangled with many young people's lives, at the same time that sources of support for indebted students have been significantly dis-invested. Goerisch suggests that experiences of debt pervade practically every aspect of young people's experiences, homes, education and family lives. However, Goerisch also argues that media and political discourses about student debt in the USA remain wedded to an idealised, rosy imaginary of student lifestyles, plus aspirational expectations of students as future workers/consumers, overlooking young people's own, present-day experiences as 'indebted subjects'. The chapter thus makes a compelling case for taking greater care to understand young people's own personal, present lived experiences.

In Chapter 6, Michael Boampong explores how neoliberalisations, austerities and economic crises have reshaped families and households in diverse and profoundly uneven ways. Through qualitative research with British-Ghanaian young adults, Boampong considers the ambivalent and unequal impacts of migration and labour market policies in the wake of the global financial crisis and decades of transformative neoliberalisations. Boampong argues that neoliberalised and austerity social welfare systems in Europe and North America have increasingly required families to care for themselves, while removing protections that would previously have supported them. The chapter shows that experiences of British-Ghanaian families differ markedly depending on their economic and social capital, with wealthier families experiencing unprecedented freedoms while other less wealthy British-Ghanaian families increasingly experience profound constraints, barriers and marginality within migration and social care contexts. Boampong argues that these polarised experiences each require young people to 'do family' in new ways, setting in motion new kinds of transnational flows of migrants, capital and ideas. The chapter thus suggests that understandings of youth and family in hard times must apprehend the diversity of kin, household and family-like networks through which family is being *done* in practice.

The chapters in Part 2, deal with what we are calling **inequalities/intersections**. Through diverse case studies, the chapters explore how hard times intersect with wider social-cultural geographies (for example, notably, here, of age, gender, ethnicity and social class) to produce new or intensified forms of poverty and inequality (see also Donald et al, 2014). A number of chapters explicitly use the term 'intersectionality' – which originated in black feminist scholarship (Crenshaw, 1991) – to denote 'the simultaneous, intersecting, inseparable, coterminous and multiple forces of oppression acting on individuals/groups' (Chadwick, 2017: 2). In juxtaposing these chapters, we invite reflection on how these forces of oppression are constituted via particular comings-together of social-cultural differences and inequalities, but also via intersecting discourses, norms, materialities and institutions (see Horton and Kraftl, 2018). Thus through international case studies encompassing Indian and Bangladeshi migrations, Ethiopian child labour, UK child poverty policies, corporate financial education, Filipino-Canadian masculinities, and international youth voluntarism, the chapters evidence the multiple forms of harm, vulnerability and precarity that are constituted by these inequalities/intersections. Authors consider how normative concepts of poverty, gender, stigma, parenthood and social class are being rethought or entrenched in and through the everyday lives of children, young people and families in diverse, global contexts. The chapters thus consider how the 'diffuse and extended events' of neoliberalisations, austerities and economic crises are materialising in practice (Hitchen and Raynor, 2020) and intersecting with diverse other forms and discourses of marginality (Garthwaite, 2015; 2016b).

For example, in Chapter 7, Heather Piggott explores how experiences of poverty in rural Bangladesh and North India intersect with experiences of motherhood and family caregiving. Piggott notes that previous research on women's labour market participation in the global South has overwhelmingly taken the form of nationally- or regionally-scaled quantitative economic analysis, overlooking families' lived experiences of poverty and work. Through rich mixed methods research with families in rural Bangladesh and North India, the chapter explores how experiences of poverty, inequality and marginality are compounded by neoliberal labour market restructurings and traditional patriarchal gender roles. The chapter suggests that subtle shifts in social attitudes may be allowing some hopeful, affirmative futures for women and girls in this context, but these attitudinal shifts remain uneven in terms of religion, class and caste norms. In so doing, Piggott calls for further intersectional work exploring intra-household and intra-familial labour relations and negotiations and their impacts for young people and families.

In Chapter 8 Vicky Johnson and Andy West reflect upon participatory research with street-connected young people in Addis Ababa and Kathmandu. The chapter shows how these young people's experiences of profound marginality intersect with, and are patterned by, the very uneven provision of institutional support offered by government and non-governmental agencies. Johnson and West's work with these young people reveals multiple, compound forms of marginalisation that remain hidden from public perceptions and government policymaking in both Ethiopia and Nepal. In particular, Johnson and West highlight how experiences of poverty intersect with young people's experiences of genderfluidity and disabilities. In so doing, they call for further youth-centred research and 'living rights' advocacy to better understand and address children, young people and families' bodily and relational experiences of poverty intersecting with gender, ethnicity, sexualities, caste, family situations, exploitative work and disabilities.

The chapter by Aura Lehtonen and Jacob Breslow (Chapter 9) considers how the lives of children and families intersect with, and are adversely affected by, contemporary policy and media discourses of 'childhood' and 'family' per se. Lehtonen and Breslow focus on the UK government's deployment of normative discourses of childhood in relation to austerity policies. They argue that harsh, neoliberalising policies have been advanced precisely through discursive appeals to normative concepts of 'childhood'. Specifically they evidence how key policy programmes have simultaneously 'infantilised' poor parents and 'adultified' poor children to justify austerity policies which – with dark irony – have the most severe impact on poorer families with children. Lehtonen and Breslow thus show how intersecting policy and media discourses should be folded into relational understandings of children, young people and families' lives in the current political-economic moment.

In Chapter 10, Carl Walker, Peter Squires and Carlie Goldsmith offer a further example of the discursive positioning of children, young people and families in the contexts of economic crises, austerities and neoliberalisations. They consider how the everyday lives of young people intersect with the instrumentalised, commercial imperatives of for-profit financial institutions. Walker, Squires and Goldsmith provide an analysis of recent UK financial education tools produced by financial institutions for young people. In so doing, they explore how 'financialisation' has become a taken for granted, everyday part of many young people's lives. They argue that neoliberalised financial institutions seek to craft financialed subjectivities through increasingly sophisticated pedagogic practices and interventions in educational policies and school curricula. The chapter thus suggests a need for more careful and critical understandings of the interfaces between young people's everyday lives and financial services, institutions, money, credit and debt.

The chapter by Philip Kelly (Chapter 11) explores how Filipino-Canadian families' experiences of precarity intersect with gendered, and particularly masculinist, norms and inequalities. Reporting new findings from a major study of Filipino youth transitions in Canada, Kelly explores how Filipino-Canadian young people's lives are framed by gendered disparities in intergenerational social (im)mobility. Kelly notes that normative trends in social reproduction (whereby university-educated parents typically support degree-gaining children) do not seem to apply for many Filipino-Canadian families. Instead, the chapter shows how Filipino-Canadian families are distinctively shaped by gendered impacts of foreign worker programmes in Canada. Through this analysis, Kelly draws attention to the often-overlooked intersectional impacts of masculinities for migrant families' lives and experiences.

In Chapter 12, Ruth Cheung Judge considers how politics of charity in the global South intersect with politics of austerity in young people's lives in the global North. Through rich qualitative research with young people from low-income UK backgrounds undertaking volunteering trips to sub-Saharan Africa, the chapter examines the different imaginaries of poverty circulating between these contexts. In particular, the chapter highlights the prevalence of imaginaries of the supposed 'grateful, happy poor' of the global South vis-à-vis the supposed 'undeserving poor' of UK urban neighbourhoods. The chapter insists that contemporary pressures on young people to adopt aspirational, responsible subjectivities under neoliberal austerity often constitutes a stigmatisation of lived poverty in diverse settings. The chapter thus calls for further research which adopts a multi-site, multi-scalar approach transcending either nation-state- or locally-scaled analyses.

The third Part of the book brings together chapters focusing upon **futures**. Here, authors explore how children, young people and families are negotiating the transformations and inequalities discussed in the preceding sections, constituting new orientations towards their futures. Chapters consider how aspirations, fears, imagined futures and hoped-for communities from these case studies may suggest affecting, hopeful or critical ways on/in/through/beyond hard times (see Brown 2011). In some senses, at least, authors signal how children, young people and families may offer more hopeful ways of thinking, caring and living which contest, or offer alternatives to neoliberalisations, austerities and economic crises. A wide range of ambiguous and ambivalent orientations to the future are evident in these chapters, but there is ample evidence here that children, young people and families live with hard times in diverse, sometimes hopeful ways (Horton 2016; 2017), that moral and crisis-led panics about contemporary childhood and youth need not always apply (McDowell, 2012), and that affirmative socio-political futures may yet be possible in the middle of profoundly troubling hard times.

For example, in Chapter 13, Sonja Marzi considers the ambivalent, complex aspirations of young, urban Colombians in Cartagena. On the one hand, Marzi shows how young people's aspirations are profoundly constrained by intersecting inequalities relating to class, race, gender and neo-colonial structural inequalities. However, despite these inequalities and exclusions, Marzi finds that young people show creative ways of sustaining hopes and constituting opportunities for social mobility. The chapter tracks these ambivalences through evocative accounts of independence day celebrations and beauty pageants. Marzi ultimately argues that care is needed to critique commonplace assumptions that many young people 'lack aspirations' and that their social immobility is a consequence of this lack. Instead, Marzi shows how young people manage to carve out aspirational opportunities for aspirational social mobility despite countervailing structural barriers. Nevertheless, the chapter shows how young people's everyday lives and hopes are profoundly affected by pervasive inequalities and discrimination on bases of race, class, gender and neo-colonial inequalities.

In Chapter 14, Catherine Wilkinson critiques the prevalence of individualised notions of aspiration in austerity UK. Through participant observation and qualitative research at a community youth radio station, the chapter considers the nature and content of young people's imagined futures. The chapter provides a close engagement with the variously witty, moving and hopeful aspirations of young people in this setting, witnessing the fabulous richness of young people's own 'storied selves' and futures. However, Wilkinson is critical of the emphasis on individualisation within neoliberal and austerity contexts, arguing that the fulfilment of 'possible selves' is relational and contingent on social and community bonds rather than solely the actions and desires of individuals. In particular, Wilkinson writes movingly of the direct impacts of austerity cutbacks of community support mechanisms for young people's aspirations and orientations to the future.

The chapter by Hao-Che Pei and Chiung-wen Chang (Chapter 15) offers a case study of young people working collaboratively to provide an innovative, affirmative support network to sustain hopeful futures in hard times. Pei and Chang contextualise this project by evidencing severe experiences of precarity for many Taiwanese Higher Education students. They show how increasing graduate unemployment rates, rising living costs, and growing inequalities have required many students to take on precarious, exploitative work and finance. In this context, Pei and Chang report on a collaborative, youth-led action research project to 'reinvigorate economic imaginations' and 'enact alternative economies'. They note the considerable regulatory and institutional barriers to enacting affirmative alternative futures, but also show how the project has been successful in constituting organisational change and new, more hopeful personal and collective orientations to the future. They note, however, the considerable work involved in making this kind of alternative space and future possible: all this was only possible because of significant *collective* actions.

In Chapter 16, Caroline Day considers the role of aspiration among caregiving and non-caregiving young people in Zambia. Day notes that youth-centred policymaking is relatively new and under-developed in Zambia, as in many other contexts. Day argues that better understanding of young people's aspirations and senses of the future is crucial in formulating policies and programmes that support, or impact upon, young people. Drawing on a significant programme of qualitative research, the chapter explores the nature of the future aspirations of diverse, and often extremely marginalised Zambian young people. We draw considerable hope from Day's key conclusion that, even in profoundly hard times, these young people's aspirations were rarely selfish and individualised: instead, Day's research participants overwhelmingly talked about aspirations in terms of caring relationships and responsibilities. These aspirations are full of care and love: for family members, friends, communities and older and young people. This sense of aspiring to care provides a hopeful and deeply affecting end point for the book.

In our concluding chapter we offer a series of reflections on the chapters and prompts for future research, reflection and practice. We hope, too, that the multiple, interrelated hard times witnessed through this collection will prompt readers to develop their own reflections, responses and ways forward with/in hard times.

Postscript: childhood and youth in COVID-19 times

We submitted this book manuscript in late February 2020. We were unaware that, within days, our lives, families, communities and workplaces would be radically transformed by the spread of the global COVID-19 ('Coronavirus') pandemic. This book is therefore an accidental record of time-spaces *just before* the impacts of COVID-19. All of the children, young people and families in this book are encountered in moments *just before* the pandemic. We cannot help but wonder how they are doing. We worry, profoundly, about how their lives, experiences and life-chances are being affected by COVID-19. Here and now, as we review the typescript in August 2020, this worry crystallises around five questions about childhood and youth in the context and aftermath of COVID-19.

1) How has COVID-19 affected children and young people's everyday lives?

Here and now, it is too early to attempt a comprehensive overview of the impacts of COVID-19 for children and young people in diverse global contexts. (And, to be frank, our experiences of living and working through the COVID-19 pandemic are just *too* raw and *too* close right now for that kind of thinking; it feels important to record that we are not in particularly great places – emotionally, personally, professionally – as we write this, trying to make academic writing happen in spite of the familial, educational, workplace and emotional impacts of COVID-19.) But evidence is just starting to emerge of the complex, compound, poignant and wide-ranging ways in which COVID-19 has touched – and often profoundly impacted – children and young people's everyday experiences (see the repository collated by RCPCH, 2020). We hope that future research and policy will notice, and empathise with, the many ways that COVID-19 has transformed children and young people's everyday relationships, disrupted their routines, institutions and support networks, constituted new anxieties, precarities and caring responsibilities, and radically refigured families, friendships, work, education, technologies and everyday spaces in so many ways and in so many contexts.

2) How are impacts of COVID-19 intersecting with multiple inequalities and exclusions?

It is important to state explicitly that there has been no universal experience of childhood and youth in COVID-19 (maybe we should think about COVID-19s to signal the many lived experiences of this virus). Rather, children and young people have been differentially affected by COVID-19, in ways which map onto existing inequalities in ways that are only just becoming clear. In England, for example, deeply affecting statistics showing that COVID-19 mortality rates have been twice as high in deprived communities compared to affluent areas (Pidd et al, 2020), and disproportionately high among black, Asian and minority ethnic communities (BBC, 2020a), reveal a stark 'hierarchy of precarity' during the pandemic (Langford, 2020). Similarly, controversies over the UK government's initial calculation of English school leavers' attainment in lieu of exams, using an algorithm which manifestly advantaged smaller class sizes and schools' previous exam results, have galvanised discussion about the extent to which experiences of COVID-19 have been patterned by structural inequalities (BBC, 2020b). Evidently, young people who were already diversely marginalised, precarious and at risk have been disproportionately exposed to COVID-19 risks and personal-political-economic fallout. It will be important for future research and policy to consider how multiple inequalities and exclusions have been compounded and hardened through COVID-19. We wonder, and worry profoundly, about how impacts of COVID-19 are intersecting with the kinds of gendered, classed, ableist, post-colonial, heteronormative, cis-normative and globally uneven modes of marginality and social exclusion evidenced through this book (see WBG, 2020; Brewer and Handscomb, 2020; European Commission, 2020). We fear that the complexly intersectional 'hard times' discussed through this book just got a lot harder, in all kinds of ways.

3) How are children and young people represented in media and policy discourses of COVID-19?

From our English perspective, we worry about the ways in which young people have repeatedly been represented in very particular, prominent ways in media and policy discourses of COVID-19. It seems to us that many media, political and social media discourses have fallen back on a default assumption that young people – particularly teenagers, perhaps particularly young men – are feckless, feral, amoral, irresponsible and anti-social. These kinds of discourses have been widely perpetuated via representations of, for example, young people defying 'social distancing' and 'lockdown' restrictions in pursuit of lairy, boozy, promiscuous, lawless, care-less lifestyles. (At this point, we had lined up some illustrative examples from outlets including *The Sun*, *MailOnline*, *Daily Telegraph* and Twitter. But we find that, right now, we are not really minded to give the oxygen of publicity to this sort of grim, divisive, exclusionary, trolling, culture war clickbait). These kinds of representations seem weirdly callous and toxic, and efface the precisely contemporaneous prominence of young people in community volunteering, familial and neighbourhood care work, and campaigning in support of social and environmental justice, LGBTQ+ rights and the *Black Lives Matter* movement. So we wonder, what can be learnt from representations of children and young people and COVID-19 in diverse contexts, beyond our UK media bubble, and what other, more hopeful cultural discourses and norms about contemporary childhood and youth might be possible?

4) How have neoliberalisations, austerities and economic crises been compounded by COVID-19?

It is with considerable anxiety that we try to anticipate the impacts of COVID-19 for the processes of economic crises, austerities and neoliberalisations that have framed this book. The outlook is not good. Economically, global and national forecasts suggest that COVID-19 will have significant and enduring consequences which will haunt every one of the contexts described in this book (European Commission, 2020). At time of writing, the World Bank baseline forecast predicts a 5.2% contraction in global gross domestic product (GDP) for 2020: 'the deepest global recession in decades ... the deep recessions triggered by the pandemic are expected to leave lasting scars through lower investment, an erosion of human capital through lost work and schooling, and fragmentation of global trade and supply linkages' (World Bank, 2020, unpaginated). In the UK for example, the Office for National Statistics GPD figures report a state of 'significant shock ... the economy is in a technical recession, falling by 20.4% during Quarter 2 (Apr to June) 2020, compared with Quarter 1 (Jan to Mar) 2020 ... the largest decline since quarterly records began' (ONS, 2020: unpaginated). The consequences of these economic shocks for communities *already* experiencing economic crises and austerities are unfathomable and deeply anxiety-inducing. In England, for example, emergent evidence suggests the extent to which COVID-19 has intersected with resented geographies of austerities. On the one hand, COVID-19 has resulted in a significant acceleration of cuts to local government budgets for many cultural, community, educational, heritage and leisure services; on the other hand, there is evidence that impacts of COVID-19 have been most profound in communities which previously experienced the deepest cuts to health, social care and community facilities (Gillespie and Hardy, 2020; Flesher Fominaya, 2020). In this context, it remains to be seen how unprecedented government spending on furlough schemes, subsidies for leisure and hospitality sectors, public health messaging, and emergency healthcare facilities will be balanced through future multi-sectoral spending cuts. A parallel strand of critical debate has begun to consider the intersection of COVID-19 with processes of neoliberalisations. It is argued that decades of neoliberalisation effectively depleted the capacities of states, institutions and systems to act with resilience and compassion in the face of a challenge like COVID-19; moreover, it is argued that COVID-19 is precisely the kind of systemic shock through which neoliberal claims for yet more deregulation and efficiency measures can be expected to advance dramatically (Saad-Filho, 2020).

5) Do any aspects of childhood and youth in COVID-19 times offer hope for more progressive and equitable futures?

Against these backdrops of entrenched economic crises, austerities and neoliberalisms it will be necessary for many of us to commit to renewed forms of community-mindedness, collegiality, care, support, activisms and progressive politics to safeguard the kinds of communities, spaces and precarious lives witnessed in the following chapters. And we want to conclude this chapter on a hopeful, affirmative note by asking: wherever and whenever you read this, can children and young people's everyday hopes, solidarities and care offer hopeful ways forward in contexts of economic crises–austerities–neoliberalisms–COVID-19s? We want to recognise that, sometimes, children and young people can role-model hopeful and progressive ways of being in spite of the 'hard times' of COVID-19. In our own communities and lives, we have been struck by children and young people's creativity, humour and play during this time, their community-minded actions, their intimate attunement to local spaces and natures, their gestures of inter- and intra- generational care, and their moral-political leadership in calling out issues of social and environmental injustice locally and globally. Maybe all of us could remember and learn from that …

As we prepare to submit this postscript, the COVID-19 situation continues to change daily, and will almost certainly have shifted further as the book goes to print, constituting new inequalities, new anxieties and new 'hard times'…

References

Aalbers, M. (2009) 'Geographies of the financial crisis', *Area*, 41(1): 34–42.

Allen, K. (2016) 'Top girls navigating austere times: Interrogating youth transitions since the "crisis"', *Journal of Youth Studies*, 19(6): 805–820.

Askins, K. (2015) 'Being together: Everyday geographies and the quiet politics of belonging', *ACME*, 14(2): 461–469.

Barnett, C. (2005) 'The consolations of "neoliberalism"', *Geoforum*, 36(1), 7–12.

BBC (2020a) 'Why are more people from BAME backgrounds dying from coronavirus?', https://www.bbc.co.uk/news/uk-52219070

BBC (2020b) 'A-levels and GCSEs: How did the exam algorithm work?', https://www.bbc.co.uk/news/explainers-53807730

Bendit, R. and Miranda, A. (2015) 'Transitions to adulthood in contexts of economic crisis and post-recession: The case of Argentina', *Journal of Youth Studies*, 18(2). 183 196.

Blažek, J., Hejnová, T. and Rada, H. (2020) 'The impacts of the global economic crisis and its aftermath on the banking centres of Europe', *European Urban and Regional Studies*, 27(1): 35–49.

Brewer, M. and Handscomb, K. (2020) *All together now? The impacts of the government's coronavirus income support schemes across the age distribution*, London: Resolution Foundation.

Brown, G. (2011) 'Emotional geographies of young people's aspirations for adult life', *Children's Geographies*, 9(1): 7–22.

Butler, J. (2009) *Frames of war: When is life grievable?*, London: Verso.

Cairns, D. (2017) 'Migration and tertiary educated youth: A reflexive view of mobility decision-making in an economic crisis context', *Children's Geographies*, 15(4): 413–425.

Cairns, D., Growiec, K. and de Almeida Alves, N. (2014) 'Another missing middle? The marginalised majority of tertiary educated youth in Portugal during the economic crisis', *Journal of Youth Studies*, 17(8): 1046–1060.

Chadwick, R. (2017) 'Thinking intersectionally with/through narrative methodologies', *Agenda*, 31(1): 5–16.

Cloke, P., May, J. and Williams, A. (2017) 'The geographies of food banks in the meantime', *Progress in Human Geography*, 41(6): 703–726.

Crenshaw, K. (1991) 'Mapping the margins: Intersectionality, identity politics, and violence against women of color', *Stanford Law Review*, 43(6): 1241–1299.

Crescenzi, R., Luca, D. and Milio, S. (2016) 'The geography of the economic crisis in Europe', *Cambridge Journal of Regions, Economy and Society*, 9(1): 13–32.

Cross, M. (2013) 'Demonised, impoverished and now forced into isolation: The fate of disabled people under austerity', *Disability & Society*, 28(5): 719–723.

Crotty, J. (2009) 'Structural causes of the global financial crisis: A critical assessment of the "new financial architecture"', *Cambridge Journal of Economics*, 33(4): 563–580.

Derudder, B., Hoyler, M. and Taylor, P. (2011) 'Goodbye Reykjavik: International banking centres and the global financial crisis', *Area*, 43(2): 173–182.

Donald, B., Glasmeier, A., Gray, M. and Loboa, L. (2014) 'Austerity in the city: Economic crisis and urban service decline?', *Cambridge Journal of Regions, Economy and Society*, 7(1): 3–15.

European Commission (2020) *2020 European semester: Country-specific recommendations*, Brussels: European Commission.

Eurostat (2014) *National GDP and unemployment accounts*, http://ec.europa.eu/eurostat/data/database

Filho, G. and Neder, G. (2001) 'Social and historical approaches regarding street children in Rio de Janeiro (Brazil) in the context of the transition to democracy', *Childhood*, 8(1): 11–29.

Flesher Fominaya, C. (2020) 'How austerity measures hurt the Covid-19 response', *OUPblog*, https://blog.oup.com/2020/04/how-austerity-measures-hurt-the-covid-19-response/

France, A. (2016) *Understanding youth in the global economic crisis*, Bristol: Policy Press.

French, S. and Leyshon, A. (2010) '"These f@#king guys": The terrible waste of a good crisis', *Environment and Planning A*, 42(11): 2549–2559.

French, S., Leyshon, A. and Thrift, N. (2009) 'A very geographical crisis', *Cambridge Journal of Regions, Economy and Society*, 2(2): 287–302.

Garrett, P. (2009) *'Transforming' children's services: Social work, neoliberalism and the 'modern' world*, Maidenhead: McGraw-Hill.

Garthwaite, K. (2015) '"Keeping meself to meself": How social networks can influence narratives of stigma and identity for long-term sickness benefits recipients', *Social Policy & Administration*, 49(2): 199–212.

Garthwaite, K. (2016a) *Hunger pains: Life inside foodbank Britain*, Bristol: Policy Press.

Garthwaite, K. (2016b) 'Stigma, shame and "people like us": An ethnographic study of foodbank use in the UK', *Journal of Poverty and Social Justice*, 24(3): 277–289.

Gateley, D. (2014) 'What alternatives post-austerity? Importance of targeted employment advice for refugee young people in London', *Journal of Youth Studies*, 17(9): 1260–1276.

Gillespie, T. and Hardy, K. (2020) 'All in this together? How a decade of austerity cleared the way for Covid-19 in deprived urban areas', *Global Development Institute Blog*, http://blog.gdi.manchester.ac.uk/decade-of-austerity-cleared-the-way-for-covid-19-in-deprived-urban-areas/

Greer Murphy, A. (2017) 'Austerity in the United Kingdom: The intersections of spatial and gendered inequalities', *Area*, 49(1): 122–124.

Hall, S. (2005) 'New Labour's double-shuffle', *Education, Pedagogy and Cultural Studies*, 27(4): 319–335.

Hall, S. (2017) *Everyday austerity*, https://e.issuu.com/anonymous-embed.html?u=everydayausterity&d=everyday_austerity_full_zine

Hall, S. (2019a) *Everyday life in austerity: Family, friends and intimate relations*, London: Palgrave.

Hall, S. (2019b) 'A very personal crisis: Family fragilities and everyday conjunctures within lived experiences of austerity', *Transactions of the Institute of British Geographers*, 44(3): 479–492.

Hall, S. (2019c) 'Everyday austerity: Towards relational geographies of family, friendship and intimacy', *Progress in Human Geography*, 3(5): 769–789.

Hall, S., McIntosh, K., Neitzert, E., Pottinger, L., Sandhu, K., Stephenson, M-A., Reed, H. and Taylor, L. (2017) *Intersecting inequalities: The impact of austerity on black and minority ethnic women in the UK*, London: Women's Budget Group.

Hall, S., Pimlott-Wilson, H. and Horton, J. (eds) (2020) *Austerity across Europe: Lived experiences of economic crises*, London: Routledge.

Harker, C. (2012) 'Precariousness, precarity, and family: Notes from Palestine', *Environment and Planning* A, 44(4): 849–865.

Harvey, D. (2007) *A brief history of neoliberalism*, Oxford: Oxford University Press.

Harvey, D. (2017) *Marx, capital, and the madness of economic reason*, Oxford: Oxford University Press.

Hitchen, E. (2016) 'Living and feeling the austere', *New Formations*, 87: 102–118.

Hitchen, E. (2019) 'The affective life of austerity: Uncanny atmospheres and paranoid temporalities', *Social & Cultural Geography* online early.

Hitchen, E. and Raynor, R. (2020) 'Encountering austerity in everyday life: Intensities, localities, materialities', *Geoforum*, 110: 186–190.

HM Treasury (2010) *Public Spending Review*, London: HMSO.

Holloway, S.L. and Pimlott-Wilson, H. (2012) 'Neoliberalism, policy localisation and idealised subjects: A case study of educational restructuring', *Transactions of the Institute of British Geographers*, 37(4): 639–654.

Horton, J. (2016) 'Anticipating service withdrawal: Young people in spaces of neoliberalisation, austerity and economic crisis', *Transactions of the Institute of British Geographers*, 41(4): 349–596.

Horton, J. (2017) 'Young people and debt: Getting on with austerities', *Area* 49(3): 280–287.

Horton, J. (2020) 'For diffident geographies and modest activisms: Questioning the *ANYTHING-BUT-GENTLE* academy', *Area* online early.

Horton, J. and Kraftl, P. (2018) 'Rats, assorted shit and "racist groundwater": Towards extra-sectional understandings of childhoods and social-material processes', *Environment and Planning D*, 36(5): 926–948.

Jones, G., Meegan, R., Kennett, P. and Croft, J. (2015) 'The uneven impact of austerity on the voluntary and community sector: A tale of two cities', *Urban Studies*, 53(10): 2064–2080.

Jupp, E. (2016) 'Families, policy and place in times of austerity', *Area*, 49(3): 266–272.

Jupp, E. (2017) 'Home space, gender and activism: The visible and the invisible in austere times', *Critical Social Policy*, 37(3): 348–366.

Katz, C. (1996) 'Towards minor theory', *Environment and Planning D*, 14(4): 487–499.

Katz, C. (2004) *Growing up global: Economic restructuring and children's everyday lives*, Minneapolis, MN: University of Minnesota Press.

Katz, C. (2011) 'Accumulation, excess, childhood: Toward a countertopography of risk and waste', *Documents d'Anàlisi Geogràfica*, 57(1): 47–60.

Katz, C. (2018) 'The angel of geography: Superman, Tiger Mother, aspiration management, and the child as waste', *Progress in Human Geography*, 42(5): 723–740.

Kitson, M., Martin, R. and Tyler, P. (2011) 'The geographies of austerity', *Cambridge Journal of Regions, Economy and Society*, 4(3): 289–302.

Konings, M. and Somers, J. (eds) (2010) *The great credit crash*, London: Verso.

Langford, N. (2020) 'Governing through insecurity: what COVID 19 tells us about precarity under (neo)liberalism', http://speri.dept.shef.ac.uk/2020/05/05/governing-through-insecurity-what-covid-19-tells-us-about-precarity-under-neoliberalism/

Langley, P. (2008) *The everyday life of global finance: Saving and borrowing in America*, Oxford: Oxford University Press.

Larner, W. (2003) 'Neoliberalism?', *Environment and Planning D*, 21(5): 309–12.

Larner, W. (2011) 'C-change? Geographies of crisis', *Dialogues in Human Geography*, 1(3): 319–35.

Lee, R., Clark, G., Pollard, J. and Leyshon, A. (2009) 'The remit of financial geography – before and after the crisis', *Journal of Economic Geography*, 9(5): 723–747.

Loach, K. (2015) '"Conscious cruelty": Ken Loach's shock at benefit sanctions and food banks', https://www.theguardian.com/film/2015/nov/23/ken-loach-benefit-sanctions-jeremy-corbyn-food-banks

Loopstra, R., McKee, M., Katikireddi, S.V., Taylor-Robinson, D., Barr, B. and Stuckler, D. (2016) 'Austerity and old-age mortality in England. A longitudinal cross local area analysis, 2007–2013', *Journal of the Royal Society of Medicine*, 109(3): 109–116.

Martin, R. (2011) 'The local geographies of the financial crisis: From the housing bubble to economic recession and beyond', *Journal of Economic Geography*, 11(4): 587–618.

Mason, P. (2010) *Meltdown: The end of the age of greed*, London: Verso.

McDowell, L. (2012) 'Post-crisis, post-Ford and post-gender? Youth identities in an era of austerity', *Journal of Youth Studies*, 15(5): 573–590.

Michail, D. and Christou, A. (2016) 'Diasporic youth identities of uncertainty and hope: Second generation Albanian experiences of transnational mobility in an era of economic crisis in Greece', *Journal of Youth Studies*, 19(7): 957–972.

Newman, J. (2013) 'Landscapes of antagonism: Local governance, neoliberalism and austerity', *Urban Studies*, 51(15): 3290–3305.

Nikunen, M. (2017) 'Young people, future hopes and concerns in Finland and the European Union: Classed and gendered expectations in policy documents', *Journal of Youth Studies*, 20(6): 661–676.

O'Hara, M. (2014) *Austerity Bites*, Bristol: Policy Press.

ONS (Office for National Statistics) (2020) 'Coronavirus and the impact on output in the UK economy: June 2020', https://www.ons.gov.uk/economy/grossdomesticproductgdp/articles/coronavirusandtheimpactonoutputintheukeconomy/june2020

O'Toole, T. (2015) 'Beyond crisis narratives: Changing modes and repertoires of political participation among young people', in: K. Kallio, S. Mills and T. Skelton (eds) *Politics, Citizenship and Rights*, Singapore: Springer, pp.225–242.

Peck, J. (2012) 'Austerity urbanism: American cities under extreme economy', *City*, 16(6): 626–55.

Peck, J. (2013) 'Explaining (with) neoliberalism', *Territory, Politics, Governance*, 1(2): 132–57.

Peck, J. and Tickell, A. (2002) 'Neoliberalising space', *Antipode*, 34(3): 380–404.

Pidd, H., Barr, C. and Mohdin, A. (2020) 'Calls for health funding to be prioritised as poor bear brunt of Covid-19', https://www.theguardian.com/world/2020/may/01/covid-19-deaths-twice-as-high-in-poorest-areas-in-england-and-wales

Pimlott-Wilson, H. (2017) 'Individualising the future: The emotional geographies of neoliberal governance in young peoples' aspirations', *Area*, 49(3): 288–295.

Pimlott-Wilson, H. and Hall, S.M. (2017) 'Everyday experiences of economic change: repositioning geographies of children, youth and families', Editorial introduction, *Area*, 49(3): 258–265.

Pottinger, L. (2017) 'Planting the seeds of a quiet activism', *Area*, 49(2): 215–222.

Power, A. and Bartlett, R. (2019) 'Ageing with a learning disability: Care and support in the context of austerity', *Social Science & Medicine*, 231: 55–61.

RCPCH (Royal College of Paediatrics and Child Health) (2020) *COVID-19 – research studies on children and young people's views*, https://www.rcpch.ac.uk/resources/covid-19-research-studies-children-young-peoples-views

Ribbens, J., Hooper, C. and Gillies, V. (eds) (2013) *Family Troubles? Exploring changes and challenges in the family lives of children and young people*, Bristol: Policy Press.

Ridge, T. (2013) '"We are all in this together"? The hidden costs of poverty, recession and austerity policies on Britain's poorest children', *Children & Society*, 27(5): 406–417.

Roy, A., Larner, W. and Peck, J. (2012) 'Book review symposium: Jamie Peck (2010) Constructions of neoliberal reason', *Progress in Human Geography*, 36(2): 273–281.

Ruddick, S. (2007a) 'At the horizons of the subject: Neoliberalism, neo-conservatism and the rights of the child. Part one: From "knowing" fetus to "confused" child', *Gender, Place and Culture*, 14(5): 513–526.

Ruddick, S. (2007b) 'At the horizons of the subject: Neo-liberalism, neo-conservatism and the rights of the child. Part two: Parent, caregiver, state', *Gender, Place and Culture*, 14(6): 627–640.

Saad-Filho, A. (2020) 'From COVID-19 to the end of neoliberalism', *Critical Sociology*, 46(4–5): 477–485.

Shaw, E. (2009) 'The meaning of modernisation: New Labour and public sector reform', in: J. Callaghan, N. Fishman, B. Jackson and M. McIvor (eds) *In search of social democracy*, Manchester: Manchester University Press, pp.147–67.

Sorkin, A. (2009) *Too big to fail: Inside the battle to save Wall Street*, London: Penguin.

Stenning, A. (2020) 'Feeling the squeeze: Towards a psychosocial geography of austerity in low-to-middle income families', *Geoforum*, 110(10): 200–210.

van Lanen, S. (2017) 'Living austerity urbanism: Space-time expansion and deepening socio-spatial inequalities for disadvantaged urban youth in Ireland', *Urban Geography*, 38(10): 1603–1613.

van Lanen, S. (2018) 'Encountering austerity in deprived urban neighbourhoods: Local geographies and the emergence of austerity in the lifeworld of urban youth', *Geoforum*, 110: 220–231.

Vasilopoulou, S., Halikiopoulou, D. and Exadaktylos, T. (2014) 'Greece in crisis: Austerity, populism and the politics of blame', *Journal of Common Market Studies*, 52(2): 388–402.

WBG (Women's Budget Group) (2020) 'Crises collide: Women and COVID-19', https://wbg.org.uk/analysis/reports/crises-collide-women-and-covid-19/

Wells, K. (2015) *Childhood in a global perspective*, Cambridge: Polity.

Wilkinson, E. and Ortega-Alcázar, I. (2018) 'The right to be weary? Endurance and exhaustion in austere times', *Transactions of the Institute of British Geographers*, 44(1), https://doi.org/10.1111/tran.12266

World Bank (2020) 'The global economic outlook during the COVID-19 pandemic: A changed world', https://www.worldbank.org/en/news/feature/2020/06/08/the-global-economic-outlook-during-the-covid-19-pandemic-a-changed-world

PART I

Transformations

2

Reconceptualising inner-city education? Marketisation, strategies and competition in the gentrified city

Eric Larsson and Anki Bengtsson

Introduction

This chapter highlights how far-reaching educational marketisation and the uneven geography of the Stockholm region together affect the strategies deployed by young people, their families and schools. Drawing from a Bourdieusian framework, we explore geography as a symbolic asset and how the gentrified and wealthier inner-city of Stockholm (Lilja, 2011; Clark, 2013) has become a 'melting-pot' (Webber, 2007) to the forces of marketisation. In an era of choice and competition this creates social, symbolic and educational division, as many well-resourced students leave their local school settings. At the same time, schools located in stigmatised areas struggle to keep up and still provide a good educational environments for students (Bunar, 2009; 2011).

The chapter begins with a summary of educational marketisation in Stockholm and Sweden from 1992 to 2019, outlining the various regulations that existed during this period. Among other things, we illustrate that some public post-16 schools were regulated by proximity zones until 2011, while students could apply to any independent school already in 1992. Next, the theoretical framework and methodological approach is explained. This is followed by an empirical exploration of the various ways that schools appropriate and profit from the inner-city. Next, we discuss students' perceptions of the inner-city and inner-city schooling. Finally, we will show that the term 'inner-city school' is more than a name in Stockholm. It is a consecrated and hierarchical title, that is given to a certain group of elite schools. This title is used by students, teachers and principals at these schools as a sign of distinction. By providing this analysis, we argue that the definition of inner-city schools is contextually linked to national education systems and geographical hierarchies. As shown in a socio-historical article by Gamsu (2015), when the geographical foundations of the city changes, so do the possibilities for schools to attract students.

A transforming, urban educational market

Swedish students usually start compulsory education at the age of 7 and graduate from secondary school at the age of 16. These nine years of school are mandatory. Following secondary education, around 98% of students then continue directly to post-16 school. In 2018, this meant a transition of 352,286 students nationwide (Swedish National Agency of Education, 2019). These students are spread throughout the country, yet a large proportion attends schools in the urban regions.

Of all regions Stockholm provides the largest post-16 educational market. Today it delivers education to approximately 77,000 students, and a prognosis states that the amount will increase to about 97,000 before 2027 (Storsthlm, 2019). At the same time, the number of schools have increased considerably in recent decades and will continue to do so. In 2019 the number of post-16 schools encompassed more than 200. Of these, 74 were public schools and 133 were independent schools (Larsson, 2019). This includes schools with a wide range of profiles, ownership and possibilities. Besides the public schools, which are run by the municipality, there are ideas-driven and non-profit schools, schools owned by private firms and large-scale educational enterprises governed by for-profit capitalists (Erixon Arreman and Holm, 2011a; 2011b). The latter has expanded vastly and continuously incorporates smaller educational firms throughout the country. One example is Academedia – a venture capitalist firm that provide education for about 56,600 secondary and post-16 students throughout the country. Among other things, this includes approximately 143 post-16 schools (Academedia, 2020[1]). The idea-driven and non-profit schools are often run by foundations. Some of these provide pedagogics such as Montessori, others offer more conventional education, but make a point of not capitalising on vouchers.

The surge in independent schools (free-schools as they are called in the Swedish context), is linked to a range of socio-historic and political processes. By the early 1990s the number of older private schools had been reduced to nearly non-existent and when the first wave of marketisation was initiated in 1992 the number of post-16 independent schools nationwide totalled 42.[2] While there had previously been a larger number, few had survived the post-war regulation of private welfare institutions (Blomqvist, 2004). Additionally, due to the interplay of policies aiming to limit the social boundaries of education, it became harder for families to rely on schooling as a means of reproducing social status (Hultqvist, 2017). Widening participation, heightened levels of education among the population and a lower degree of differentiation within the educational system all contributed to this change. As Hultqvist writes: 'The transition from an elite school to a more inclusive and democratised school system, where both the external differentiation (parallel school types) and internal differentiation (programme division, alternative courses) have disappeared or been abolished raises interesting questions' (Hultqvist, 2017: 80).

Accordingly, before the early 1990s there were few possibilities to surpass regulations and explore the potential 'profits' of school choice. Similar to other countries (Bridge, 2006; DeSena and Ansalone, 2009; Butler and Hamnett, 2011), one way was to live near to sought-after schools. Another was to attend any of the fee-paying private schools or to use resources and networks to 'beat' the regulations (Broccolichi and van Zanten, 2000). Therefore, most post-16 students attended schools close to home and applied for preferable programmes.[3] Usually this meant either choosing the theoretical natural or social science programmes, semi-theoretical programmes such as technical or child and recreation programme or vocationally orientated programmes such as construction or electricity. Among students with high grades and higher levels of capital, the natural science programme became the more prestigious path (Palme, 2008). Despite this, there was an increasing demand for a more diverse educational system.

One of the arguments behind restructuring the educational system was the acclaimed benefits of independent schools and parental choice. These two characteristics, it was argued, would reduce the lack of progress and financial inefficiency in Swedish schools (Lundahl et al, 2013). Furthermore, it was suggested that independent schools and parental choice would decrease the effects of residential and educational segregation (Söderström and Uusitalo, 2005). Under the reforms enacted in 1992, parents/guardians, regardless of their social position, were expected to engage in the process of school choice since it was assumed to optimise the wellbeing of the child. To produce such a foundational change, a universal voucher was provided to parents/guardians. However, at the post-16 level, the voucher was not enough. To keep a system of 'equal opportunities', grades from secondary school are a key element of entrance requirements. Grades are seen as an indicator of quality, and schools could thus be judged in accordance with entrance requirements and the number of applicants.

The voucher also functioned as an incentive to motivate progress and development in schools, as it stipulated the financial underpinning of the organisation. This meant that there was a continuous need to attract students to stay afloat, since the number of students (that is, vouchers) provided the economic basis of the school. Swedish scholars have analysed the impact of this competitive environment and the strategies deployed to attract students. Among other things, they have shown the variation of strategies that schools owned by different stakeholders use (Lundahl et al, 2014). The strategies used by schools to attract pupils is also shown to be dependent upon the perceived hierarchy of schools (Palme, 2008; Forsberg, 2015). While prestigious schools can attract students with minor efforts and a low-key profile, others have relied more profoundly on marketing and gifts (Lund, 2007). The latter is often visible at promotional events such as school fairs and open houses (Harling, 2017).

The particularity of Stockholm's expanding educational market is connected to the political and public support for pro-choice policies. Another reason is the increasing number of inhabitants. An equally important factor has been the emergence of a regional educational market between 2008 and 2011. The regional educational market consists of a collaboration between 28 different municipalities (Storsthlm, 2019). It includes all post-16 schools and produces competition at the regional level. However, competition existed before 2008. The difference resides in the size, sprawl, form and regulations of the educational market. The first generation of independent schools included ideas-driven schools with specific pedagogic visions and, furthermore, old private schools. These schools were predominantly placed in affluent areas and metropolitan regions. While the proximity zones of public schools were not fully eradicated until 2011, from 1992 young people could attend any independent school in the region. This led to an uneven competition and an advantage for many independent schools. As a consequence, independent schools continued to expand – often in profitable geographical areas.

When the regional educational market was introduced in 2008, regulation changed, and thus some public schools attracted an increasing number of students. Continuous changes in 2011 expanded the opportunities for school choice further. This means that young people are able to apply to any school in the Stockholm region and compete for a position based on grades. That is to say, higher grades equal more options and a greater probability to attend prestigious schools. The regional collaboration has fostered increasing possibilities for geographical mobility among young people. However, as research has suggested, social and educational differences persist (Söderström and Uusitalo, 2005; Forsberg, 2015). From this perspective, it becomes interesting to discuss the current state of schools in Stockholm, particularly, the phenomenon of inner-city schools.

Inner-city schools: a short introduction

Whereas the term 'inner-city school' typically insinuates something unfavourable, the opposite can be said for Stockholm and other major Swedish cities. This has, among other things, become obvious in the increasing number of post-16 schools situated in inner-city areas and the students attending these schools. Of the large number of post-16 schools in Stockholm, 59 are located within the inner-city area. This number has increased from 16 in the early 1990s. The same goes for students attending post-16 inner-city schools, which more than doubled between 1997 and 2017. Although many students still attend school close to home, this trend follows the general pattern of increasing geographical mobility among students in larger urban regions (The Swedish National Agency of Education, 2019). As Butler and Hamnett noted in 2007, 'neighbourhood social solidarity' has been 'important' in the Swedish context, however, 'this is changing' (p.1167). Nevertheless, as we will illustrate in this chapter, not all post-16 inner-city schools are equally prestigious. In fact, many rely on the profits of being located within wealthier areas to attract students. This ought to be contrasted with the post-16 inner-city elite schools, which rely on additional characteristics than just the geographical placement.

Theory: for a relational understanding of educational marketisations

Theoretically, our research takes inspiration from the scholarship of Pierre Bourdieu and successors. It includes concepts such as strategies, recognition and capitals (assets[4]) (Bourdieu, 1996). Analytically these concepts provide a relational foundation for understanding social phenomena. In our case, this relates to the hierarchical struggles of positions and positioning in the socially and symbolically uneven geography of Stockholm. The concepts of strategies, recognition and symbolic capital are useful to understand the notion of 'profits of localization' (Bourdieu, 1999) and how the inner-city schools are to be understood. But they also provide an analytical point of departure when analysing students' perceptions.

In this chapter we have also been inspired by contemporary Bourdieusian scholars such as Mike Savage and colleagues in particular, and their work that concerns 'emerging cultural capital' and the city (see Prieur and Savage, 2013; Savage et al, 2018). That is to say, how the transformation and continuous gentrification of certain urban areas has made some cities areas of emerging cultural capital and with a certain cosmopolitan position. This could be seen in the awareness of urban aesthetics, but also in the social dynamics of gentrified cities such as transnational investment and segregation. As discussed before, there is a need to link the geographies of education to socio-political processes. When the city transforms, so do the possibilities to arrange education. This is particularly the case when dominant groups such as middle-class, upper middle-class and upper-class families are affected by these transformations and decide to move on to other places (Gamsu, 2015). But also, it change the possibilities for schools and students who stay behind and struggle with fewer resources and harder conditions (Bunar, 2009).

Research methods

This chapter draws from data collected in different stages between 2012 and 2019. It is predominantly based on a one-year ethnography in three post-16 elite schools. This combines interviews with 119 agents, such as students, teachers, principals and other staff members with observations in classrooms, meetings, hallways, open houses and several other events and locations. Furthermore, the data include secondary statistics, marketing pamphlets, school documents, year books, school papers and different artefacts. We have also complemented the dataset with a broader spectrum of school webpages, marketing pamphlets, photos,[5] 24 interviews with students from 2012 to 2013 and secondary statistics to illustrate the expanding sector of post-16 schools in Stockholm.

The ambition has been to gather an extensive dataset, to be able to map, analyse and understand the different segments of the post-16 inner-city schools. However, we are especially interested in the elite segment. This means that we have mainly focused on understanding the intersection of students' educational strategies and schools' institutional strategies. For us, it means a focus on recognition, positional struggles and variations in symbolic assets. Consequently, this work illuminates how the hierarchies of geography within Stockholm affects the inner-city schools and the regional educational market. We also explore the hierarchical differences between a small number of recognised 'inner-city schools' and the larger number of schools located in the inner-city area. In other words, between the elite segment and the other segments of schools.

A school situated in the 'right place'

To grasp the expansion of post-16, inner-city schools, there are two important analytical features that need to be understood. The first of these are the 'socio-symbolic' boundaries (Wacquant, 2015) of the city. These boundaries define differences within the Stockholm region and affect all schools. As such, schools situated in the urban periphery become discredited by their proximity to low-income groups, the number of migrants and other social characteristics. If we also account for student group composition, elevated in- and outflow of students and performance rated struggles, peripheral schools are dually punished in the contemporary educational markets (Bunar, 2009; 2011). On the other hand, schools situated in affluent areas may 'profit' (Bourdieu, 1999) from locational advantages. While this is usually discussed in the literature about suburbia (Jellison Holme, 2002) and rural boarding schools (Gaztambide-Fernández, 2009), less has been written about wealthier urban areas.

Schools situated in the inner-city of Stockholm clearly illustrate how locational profits are accumulated. Besides profiting from the proximity to socio-economically well-off residents, many inner-city schools strategically appropriate the immediacy of the vibrant city as a competitive advantage. This includes references to lifestyles, shopping culture and outdoor eating on webpages and marketing pamphlets (Larsson and Hultqvist, 2017). As we will discuss later, these references echo the excitement of urbanity that some students long for. Nevertheless, these strategies differ, and the latter is generally referred to by recently established for-profit independent schools and in some cases also non-profit independent schools.

> Our beautiful school is located in the corner of Kungstensgatan/Drottninggatan [two main streets], close to The Stockholm School of Economics. With Stadsbiblioteket [Stockholm city library] around the corner and restaurants, coffee houses and shops nearby, we have a perfect and central location. [Kungstensgymnasiet, 2019][6]

> Our school is located on a calm street, a stone's throw from Odenplan [a central hub for commuters] and

in proximity to Stockholm's entire cultural supply. [Tillskärarakademin, 2019][7]

Stockholm International School is located in the centre of Stockholm next to a park, on a hilltop near the main business/shopping area. [Stockholm International School, 2019][8]

Additionally, the proximity to cultural and historical landmarks are used as references. In contrast to the vibrant city, the latter could more often be found amid elite schools. Among the older elite schools, it is manifest in anniversary books, documents, webpages and pamphlets where tradition is displayed as a sign of distinction and legacy. These schools frequently integrate their geographical, architectural and scholarly past with other historical events – drawing attention to their difference to more recently-established schools. The historical legacy of public elite schools is among other things demonstrated by references to the foundation of the school, followed by the key persons, the architectural layout and the inauguration. As one school states, 'Östra Real's current building was commissioned in 1910, but the official inauguration took place with the opening ceremony of Gustav V [Swedish king] in January 1911' (Östra Reals gymnasium, 2019).[9] Together with famous alumni, prestigious awards and stories of success, the historical legacy becomes an important institutionalised asset. As Rizvi (2014) shows, history can be an advantage when competing with schools that offer more contemporary assets. To continue this discussion in detail, we want to elaborate on the importance of architecture and school buildings, and, in particular, how these buildings are used strategically.

The strategic use of architecture and school buildings

The strategic manifestation of architecture and school buildings has been analysed before. Brooks and Waters (2015: 91), for instance, illustrate the use of images by elite schools and how these 'support a narrative stressing tradition, stability and reliability'. Similar results could be found in the Swedish context, yet, in the contemporary Swedish system, the strategic use of architecture and school buildings varies substantially. Some schools put much effort into 'the right location', including the school buildings, whereas others rely more specifically on the geographical placement.

While many pre-1992 independent schools are housed in ordinary school buildings dating back to the late 1800s and early 1900s, recent schools either have to purchase or rent office and residential buildings. These buildings vary in age, appearance and location. In some cases, they have been thoroughly converted into schools. In other words, little separates them from the regular outline of the city. This makes it hard to define what constitutes a contemporary school building. There are several reasons for this development. Mostly it is related to limited opportunities due to restricted space and real estate prices within the inner-city. As a consequence, whereas public schools – with a few exceptions – have a permanent address, independent schools do occasionally re-locate.

The construction of a historical legacy

Schools and educational firms that are able to purchase or rent centrally located, historical buildings, regularly use the term 'ancient' as an imaginative description. It is a term with symbolic connotations, which is used to create a feeling of authenticity (Zukin, 2008) and security. Therefore, it is especially interesting when it is used by schools that have a limited history. One recent example comes from the re-location of Jensen Södra which is one of two hierarchically low–mid segment[10] (Forsberg, 2015) inner-city schools, owned by a for-profit firm that provides education from pre-school level to adult extension studies. When Jensen Södra strategically re-located from a modest inner-city office building in 2017 to its current location in Gamla stan ('Old town'), the term *ancient* became a signum. The webpage states 'You can find us in ancient premises in the old town in the city centre of Stockholm' (Jensen Södra, 2019[11]). To a certain degree, the present building (Figure 2.1) does have a historical legacy and it is located in one of the older regions of Stockholm. Still, education has not been the primary use of the building. Rather, the location and building are used as a way to emulate older schools and gain prestige.

In contrast, some prestigious independent schools have been able to purchase buildings that were once used as schools or converted houses that architecturally resemble schools. Accompanied by the 'right' symbolic assets, such as networks and renowned board members, these schools have grown to become prominent agents on the contemporary educational market. A further asset, and significant difference to other independent schools, is the non-profit marker. In other words, rather than capitalising on students and redistributing capital to shareholders, money is relocated into the organisation. This means a less commercialised brand, that mainly appeals to students from the higher social stratum. One example is centrally located

Figure 2.1: Jensen Södra school

Campus Manilla, with 88% of the students having highly educated parents (Swedish National Agency for Education, 2019). The school offers primary, secondary and post-16 education and has in recent years attracted the attention of well-known families – among others, the royal family. Today, Campus Manilla inhabits the premises of the historical institution, Manilla, a former school for children with hearing loss. To illustrate the importance, the building is firmly centred in the school insignia (Campus Manilla, 2019[12]).

Another example is the Viktor Rydbergs School Foundation, with four sought-after post-16 schools in the Stockholm region. Two of these are located in the inner-city area. One of these two schools, Viktor Rydbergs gymnasium Odenplan is located in a former hospital building. The building has experienced substantial renovation and today looks strikingly similar to the prestigious public schools in Stockholm. As seen in Figure 2.2, both the architectural design with red bricks and the inscription over the main entrance of Viktor Rydbergs gymnasium Odenplan (on the right) emulates the design of public Norra Real (on the left) and Södra Latin, both dating back to the 1890s. Viktor Rydbergs gymnasium Odenplan even refers to the school as a 'cultural landmark' and continues by mentioning the construction date of 1885 (Viktor Rydberg Odenplan, 2019),[13] creating a similar historical legacy as older elite schools.

Something new, something borrowed

Most recently established inner-city independent schools do not have historical buildings. Typically, they provide educational settings in centrally located, residential or office buildings. As Figure 2.3 displays, sometimes store fronts are used as access points and entrances. Distinct from older inner-city elite schools or more recent schools inhabiting historical buildings, these schools also claim the profits from being centrally located. Consequently, there are several differences in how profits are made from the symbolic assets of geography and architecture.

One other interesting strategy could be found in the appearance of certain independent schools. For instance, the effort to capitalise from locational profits leads some post-16 schools to share a common space. When the concentration is this intense, students can choose to attend one of several comparable schools in the same area. In fact, schools owned by the same or competing companies occasionally share the same building. These agglomerations are often used by for-profit enterprises who provide smaller educational settings, often supply specific educational programmes and attract fewer high-achieving students. An illustrative example is provided in Figure 2.4 where three different post-16 schools share an office building from the 1970s. Two of the schools, Snitz and Cybergymnasiet are owned by Swedish Education Group AB and the third school, NTI Handelsgymnasiet, is owned by formerly mentioned Academedia.

As these examples suggest, the use of school buildings varies substantially among the different post-16 schools. The point we want to make, is that these schools profit from being located within the inner-city. At the same time, schools located in low-income areas and so on, struggle to provide educational opportunities. This is related to the socio-symbolic boundaries of the city. Still, as we will show later,

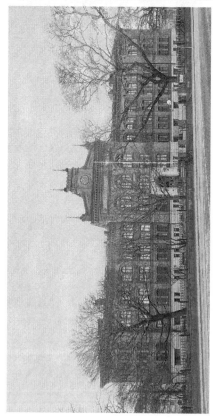

Figure 2.2: Norra Real and Viktor Rydbergs gymnasium Odenplan

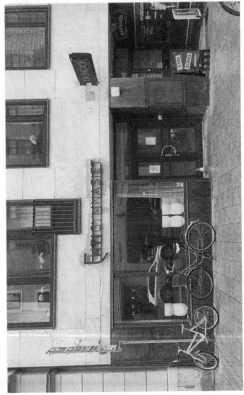

Figure 2.3: Two independent schools inhabiting office and residential buildings

Figure 2.4: Three independent schools using a former office building

besides the variations in how schools appropriate space, there are also differences in the degree that schools are recognised as prestigious/ sought-after inner-city schools.

Getting a 'feeling' for the city

To understand the strategies deployed by the different schools in the city centre of Stockholm, and the process of appropriating space, it is necessary to recognise students' perception of the city. That is to say, there is a relationship between students' strategies and opinions of preferable schools and the institutional strategies deployed by schools.

The geographical location of the school is not the only important feature for students. If it were, hierarchies between schools would be less observable. However, a large proportion of the interviewees make reference to their willingness to attend centrally located schools. For many students, the inner-city represent a hub, or the centre of the region and it delivers preferable schools within a reasonable distance due to the possibilities of public transport. There are many reasons for students' willingness to be geographically mobile and these reasons could usually be summarised by the term 'melting-pot' (Webber, 2007).

'Melting-pot' includes both the previously mentioned socio-symbolic boundaries and characteristics such as historical legacy. Equally important are features of meeting, culture and consumption. That is to say, a transformative city that simultaneously represents intermingling, possibilities and prosperity (Franzén, 2007). These categories are often inseparable and encapsulate a place where interesting things occur while it also refers to the distinction between home and away. Or in other terms, the difference between attending a familiar neighbourhood school or parting with the comfort of the accustomed and exploring new things. One important factor here is the rhetoric of 'freedom of choice'. Students often refer to school choice as a facilitator of mobility and pluralism. This does not necessarily mean a social pluralism, rather a geographical mixture. Therefore, they cite this as a reason for attending inner-city schools rather than neighbourhood schools (Larsson and Hultqvist, 2017).

> 'Then when I thought about it, it was like this: why exactly the inner-city? … Then it was like this: yes, but maybe because it is in the middle – so it is in the city, that is simply where you have mostly central Stockholm. So, you have people from everywhere come here all the time and it is so mixed. It won't be this kind of people from just the red [metro line] or people from just the green line but it's so mixed up so it's so fun getting to know other people than just the ones you've known in your [residential] area.' (Male, working-class)

The term 'melting-pot' also includes the cultural-consumption dimension of the city. Students often recognise the importance of the proximity to opportunities such as shopping culture, coffee houses and restaurants. It is the added experience of what occurs outside of school and differences from routine, that become crucial. As a student explains:

> 'But [attending a school in the city] is something different. I think just when school ends on a Friday. Then you can go out and do something fun instead of going home to someone. But when you go to where I live – then it is like this … Yes, but everyone meets up at someone's home. Here [in the city] you can go to a café or walk around town. Thus, make more stuff as well. It is another thing; you feel more grown up as well.' (Female, upper middle class)

In summary, there are a range of external forces that influence the process of choosing a school. These forces might not be directly accounted for when analysing the relationship between educational marketisation and segregation, for instance.

For students attending elite schools, pluralism and diversity are often perceived as an important feature. It is perceived to produce character, experience and insight and, as such, a cultivating part of adolescence (Khan 2011). Hence, school and the vibrant city become places for gathering awareness of the 'other'. It follows the outlook of the urban as a cosmopolitan space where people have the possibility to meet and exchange ideas. This resembles what Guilluy (2019, p.5) calls 'the myth of the open and egalitarian society of the cosmopolitan urban centres'. However, there are also social variations and limits to this openness. Arguably there are social boundaries that differ from the rhetorical emphasis of intermingling, experience and exchange. These boundaries are controlled with 'a skilful game of control and proximity' (Andreotti et al, 2015: 181). The willingness to meet and explore the experience of others is related to specific lifestyles and governed by a version of what Butler (2003) calls 'people like us'. This applies to which schools to attend, which people to socialise with and how the city is perceived. In other words, it is affected by the social limits of familiarity and linked to the place of residence. Among students residing outside the inner-city, those with larger assets tend to be more acquainted with the dynamics of the city. For these students, the city provides more than shopping and restaurants. The same goes for students residing in the inner-city. They have more intensive knowledge about the different schools and the difference between neighbourhoods. Furthermore, they are often not that impressed by the typical features of the inner-city as those residing outside.

Recognition and entitlement

To conclude this empirical section, we want to illustrate how the term 'inner-city school' differs and highlight that there are multiple hierarchies included in it. To do so we will focus on the elite school segment.

The best way of understanding the hierarchy of inner-city schools is perhaps to start with a retrospection of Swedish grammar schools. Grammar schools were often placed centrally in larger cities and, before the 1960s, provided education to a small section of the Swedish population. However, due to the geographical placement, they also functioned as hubs and gathering points for local discussions and meetings (Florin and Johansson, 1993). Consequently, they operated beyond the limits of formal educational settings. Even though grammar schools no longer exist and have either been converted into post-16 or disassembled, they still endure a certain social standing. For instance, because of the architectural style, some schools have been transformed into hotels and conference centres. More importantly, 'converted' grammar schools are among the more sought-after post-16 schools in the Stockholm region. Regardless of problems with smaller student cohorts during the 1980s, the latter have continued to be a well-regarded option for families living nearby. This means that, while widening participation and low levels of differentiation broadened the social spectrum of students (Hultqvist, 2017), geographical zoning and limited numbers of private schools kept the student group composition relatively intact. As a consequence, when the competition increased from the 1990s and onwards, these prestigious public schools became even more selective. Together with a small group of non-profit independent schools, they now represent the elite segment of post-16 schools. With exceptions, the same segment also constitutes the recognised inner-city schools.

The particularity of the recognised 'inner-city school' could be located in what some scholars call 'circuits of schooling' or 'circuits of education' (Ball et al, 1995; Butler and Robson, 2003; Popeau et al, 2007; Gamsu, 2017). More specifically, they represent the demarcated school choices students or families consider. In this study, circuits of schooling refer to the numerical order that students with different social and educational backgrounds use to classify their choices of schools and educational programmes.[14] With number one being the preferable option, most students attending post-16 elite schools choose from a limited segment of characteristically similar institutions. However, students from higher social classes and/or those who have attended prestigious secondary schools, are more often familiar with and aware of the norms regarding post-16 elite schools. This is also the reason why these schools could rely on a low-key profile and still attract the 'right' social and academic clientele; in a sense, making it harder for those less familiar to notice, recognise and identify them in the same way, even if they have grades that are good enough. Thus, these circuits create boundaries of belonging and exclusion. As one student describes: "I mean the big inner-city schools, the classics. Kungsholmen, Östra Real, Norra Real and Södra Latin. And there are some others who are quite popular, for example EG [Enskilda gymnasiet] or Viktor Rydberg, who just got bigger. They are very popular" (male, upper middle class). A second but related indication is the limited circuits of rivals and collaborators that elite schools have. In other words, there are schools that both compete for the same students and at the same time share commonalities. One example is that students who transfer between schools during the first year often change to other schools within the elite circuit (Larsson, 2019).

Another is collaboration is the different sports events and contests that are engaged in by similar schools.

The elite segment of inner-city schools could be described by a spectrum of characteristics. Geographical location is only one such feature. First, for students attending these schools, the term 'inner-city school' represents selectivity and legacy. Thus, composition, or the social and academic configuration of former and contemporary students, are crucial. To simplify it further, it is important to be part of a collective that has similar ambitions and skills, or to put it in the vocabulary of Bourdieu, symbolic assets. Additionally, it includes lifestyle choices and educational achievements. This is also why merits or grades from secondary school become an important measure. When students argue for plurality and diversity, they do it in the name of being chosen. In other words, as a statement of equal opportunity and that privilege has little to do with educational success.

> 'Well, I think it's very important, especially with free choice. So, there is some talk about not being allowed to go to inner-city schools, if you do not live in the inner-city and I think that is bad, since I would not have the opportunity attend this school then. Because I do not live in Stockholm County ... So, I think it is great that you have the chance to choose for yourself and because it creates a competition that makes the best students get in ... from all over Stockholm.' [Female, lower middle class]

Hence, middle-class, upper middle-class and upper-class students celebrate the possibilities of school choice, since it enables geographical mobility. For them, it usually means mobility due to academic ability even though social class differences remain a strong influence due to different opportunities at home and in secondary school. As one upper-class student argues, concerning possibilities of limiting school choice in Stockholm, "It would only contribute more to this kind of segregation and such things, as if not everyone is allowed 'to show their feet' kind of." He continues "But in any case, I think [school choice] is great for post-16 schools, because it is an awakening for some as well, that you have to take school seriously. If you do not [take school seriously] then sorry, but then, you just have to learn [it] the hard way."

As discussed before, new schools can also become accepted as inner-city schools. It is typically a question of being able to recruit students from higher social classes and/or with certain academic abilities. However, it also depends on the ability to mobilise enough other institutional assets. One such asset is legacy. Legacy does not necessarily mean a heritage, although recently established elite schools try to construct an authentic feeling of historical belonging. Rather, it means the possibility to create linage. A school needs to be up to date and continue to deliver knowledgeable students to high-status positions. One such way is to deliver students to prestigious universities. For students, this offers what Larsson (2019) has called 'exchange potential' or a hypothetical future. Bourdieu (1996) correspondingly describes how relationships between successful alumni and hypothetical futures foster a collective belief and therefore become an asset. This collective belief is important to be able to preserve the boundaries and hierarchies between inner-city schools. It provides a feeling of entitlement and more importantly, distinctively not being one among the others.

Conclusion

Educational marketisation is a significant part of Swedish society and is often taken for granted, especially in metropolitan regions such as Stockholm. This also means that the educational market is constantly changing and developing, and that there are continuous hierarchical struggles between schools. As new schools emerge, others change direction, re-locate, upscale, downsize or in some cases become obsolete. In this context, students and parents/guardians orientate between the different options and possibilities. They visit open houses and school fairs, gather information, consult friends, read webpages and are approached with marketing pamphlets containing a diverse array of promises. The latter might include offers to go abroad during the school year, gifts and prospects which have little to do with formal education. Prestigious schools often do the opposite and maintain a low-key profile with little explicit promotion. To navigate the educational market, students deploy various sets of strategies. These strategies are not rationally intentional (Bourdieu, 1990), rather class-based and governed by social factors such as familiarity, networks and lifestyle preferences. Schools on the other hand deploy strategies to attract students. This is done to keep up with competitors and avoid financial struggles. Except for the immediate marketing, schools compete by the means of institutional assets. Such assets include student group composition, respected teachers, specific educational programmes and successful alumni. Additionally, institutional assets could be related to the geography of the school. That is to say, where the school is situated, the history of the school and the architectural outline of the building.

This chapter has explored the phenomenon of post-16 inner-city schools. More specifically, how the uneven geography of the Stockholm region affects the strategies deployed by schools and students. The main theme has been related to the gentrified and wealthier inner-city of Stockholm and how it is used as a symbolic asset in the competition between schools. Our analysis shows that there are several hierarchies to account for. First of all, the socio-symbolic (Wacquant, 2015) boundaries that separates geographical regions and provides relational advantages for schools located in wealthier areas. Thus, schools placed in the inner-city profit from the locational setting. This is one significant reason for the growing number of inner-city schools since 1992. The same goes for the increasing number of students attending inner-city schools.

Besides the possibilities of public transport, inner-city schools profit from the proximity to a range of characteristics. Similar to what students argue, the city centre of Stockholm is portrayed as a melting-pot. Students see it as a place to meet, exchange ideas and consume. This is also why post-16 schools use the assets of geographical proximity as a comparative advantage (Larsson and Hultqvist, 2017). Some recent independent schools promote the vibrant city as an option with lots to offer while prestigious elite schools rely more heavily on culture and history. Simultaneously, school buildings and architecture also become important assets to attract potential students. Here, some older elite schools benefit by having history on their side. They can profit from a recognised legacy and stories that relate the school building to a history of education. More recent schools are forced to emulate a similar history to secure legitimacy. With the support of other institutional assets, some elite, independent schools have been able to do so with success. Others have not received the same amount of recognition. Most of the contemporary independent schools, however, are not able to obtain spacious and historical buildings. Instead, they are situated in regular office or residential buildings. Still, these schools profit from the location in the city and maintain a better position than they would elsewhere.

Yet, as we have shown in this chapter, there are also hierarchies among the post-16 inner-city schools. The term 'inner-city school' is socially and historically constituted and related to the circuit of post-16 elite schools. This means that not all schools are recognised or considered to be inner-city schools in spite of their placement in the city. For students attending schools within the elite circuit, the term 'inner-city school' indicates more than a geographical location and entails specific distinctive properties. Mostly these are related to the social, historical and academic foundation of the schools. As discussed earlier, the low-key profile of post-16 elite schools also means that they attract specific groups of students, often with higher levels of cultural capital. These students are aware of the hierarchies among the various post-16 schools in Stockholm and follow the norms created within the family, secondary school and among friends.

To conclude, the title inner-city school needs to be contextualised and related to the dynamics of the city. Furthermore, as shown in this chapter, it also needs to be discussed in relation to the hierarchies that exists among schools. When a city changes, so do the strategies of schools and students. For young people, these changes can be hard to evaluate which leads to some or them being marginalised by the system.

Notes

1   https://fakta.academedia.se/kortfakta/
2   By the late 1980s it was calculated that only 0.2% of students attended privately managed schools (Blomqvist, 2004: 142).
3   Swedish students both apply for schools and programmes. Different schools might have different programmes. However, the majority offer the natural or social science programmes.
4   In this chapter we have choosen to use the term 'assets' instead of 'capitals'. For discussion see Savage, Warde and Devine (2005).
5   All the photos in this chapter are by Staffan Larsson.
6   https://www.folkuniversitetet.se/Skolor/gymnasieskolor/Kungstensgymnasiet/Om-KSG/
7   https://www.tillskararakademin.com/gymnasiet/om-skolan/
8   https://intsch.se/about-sis/school-profile/
9   https://ostrarealsgymnasium.stockholm.se/om-oss
10 To illustrate, in 2018, 49% of the students at Jensen Södra had highly educated parents, which is 8% below the average in Stockholm (Swedish National Agency for Education, 2019).
11 https://www.jensengymnasium.se/sodra
12 http://campusmanilla.se/om-skolan/
13 https://vrskolor.se/alla-skolor/vrg-odenplan/
14 Dependent on grades, number of positions and number of requests, students are sorted in relation to this list of choices. The first school and programme on the list is the primary choice. The opportunity to attend an elite school and secure the primary choice depends on the grades from secondary school. Higher grades equal better options.

References

Andreotti, A., Le Galès, P. and Moreno-Fuentes, F. J. (2015) *Globalized minds, roots in the city: Urban upper-middles classes in Europe*, Oxford: Blackwell.

Ball, S. J., Bowe, R. and Gewirtz, S. (1995) 'Circuits of schooling: A sociological exploration of parental choice in social class contexts', *The Sociological Review*, 43(1): 52–78.

Blomqvist, P. (2004) 'The choice revolution: Privatization of Swedish welfare services in the 1990s', *Social Policy & Administration*, 38(2): 139–155.

Bourdieu, P. (1990) *The logic of practice*, Cambridge: Polity.

Bourdieu, P. (1996) *The state nobility: Elite schools in the field of power*, Stanford, CA: Stanford University Press.

Bourdieu, P. (1999) 'Site effects', in: P. Bourdieu, A. Accardo and P. Ferguson (eds) *The weight of the world: Social suffering in contemporary society*, Stanford, CA: Stanford University Press, pp.123–129.

Bridge, G. (2006) 'It's not just a question of taste: Gentrification, the neighbourhood and cultural capital', *Environment and Planning A*, 38(10): 1965–1978.

Broccolichi, S. and van Zanten, A. (2000) 'School competition and pupil flight in the urban periphery', *Journal of Education Policy*, 1(1): 51–60.

Bunar, N. (2009) *När marknaden kom till förorten. Valfrihet, konkurrens och symboliskt kapital i mångkulturella områden*, Lund: Studentlitteratur.

Bunar, N. (2011) 'Multicultural urban schools in Sweden and their communities: Social predicaments, the power of stigma, and relational dilemmas', *Urban Education*, 46(2): 141–164.

Butler, T. (2003) 'Living in the bubble: Gentrification and its "other" in north London', *Urban Studies*, 40(12): 2469–2486.

Butler, T. and Hamnett, C. (2007) 'The geography of education: Introduction', *Urban Studies*, 44(7): 1161–1174.

Butler, T. and Hamnett, C. (2011) 'Location^3 Education^3: place, choice, constraint in London', *Children's Geographies*, 9 (1): 35–48.

Butler, T. and Robson, G. (2003) 'Plotting the middle classes: Gentrification and circuits of education in London', *Housing Studies*, 18(1): 5–28.

Clark, E. (2013) 'Boendets nyliberalisering och sociala polarisering i Sverige', *Tidskriften Fronesis*, 42–43: 151–170.

DeSena, J. N. and Ansalone, G. (2009) 'Gentrification, schooling and social inequality', *Educational Research Quarterly*, 33(1): 60–74.

Erixon Arreman, I. and Holm, A.-S. (2011a) 'School as "edu-business": Four "serious players" in the Swedish upper secondary school Market', *Education Inquiry*, 2(4): 637–657.

Erixon Arreman, I. and Holm, A.-S. (2011b) 'Privatisation of public education? The emergence of independent upper secondary schools in Sweden', *Journal of Education Policy*, 26(2): 225–243.

Florin, C. and Johansson, U. (1993), *'Där de härliga lagrarna gro ...'. Kultur, klass och kön i det svenska läroverket 1850–1914*, Stockholm: Tiden.

Forsberg, H. (2015) *Kampen om eleverna. Gymnasiefältet och skolmarknadens framväxt i Stockholm 1987–2011*, Uppsala: Uppsala universitetsbibliotek.

Franzén, M. (2007) 'Partly Stockholm: The city synopsis', in: S. Gustavsson (ed) *Stockholm – Belgrade: Proceedings from the third Swedish-Serbian Symposium in Stockholm, April 21–25, 2004*, Stockholm: Kungl. Vitterhets historie och antikvitets akademien.

Gamsu, S. (2015) 'Moving up and moving out: The re-location of elite and middle-class schools from central London to the suburbs', *Urban Studies*, 53(11): 2921–2938.

Gamsu, S. (2017) *A historical geography of educational power: Comparing fields and circuits of education in Sheffield and London*, London: King's College London.

Gaztambide-Fernández, R. (2009) *The best of the best: Becoming elite at an American boarding school*, Cambridge, MA: Harvard University Press.

Guilluy, C. (2019) *Twilight of the elites: Prosperity, the periphery, and the future of France*, New Haven, CT: Yale University Press.

Harling, M. (2017) *Välja vara. En studie om gymnasieval, mässor och kampen om framtiden*, Norrköping: Institutionen för samhälls- och välfärdsstudier.

Hultqvist, E. (2017) 'Educational restructuring and social boundaries: School and consumers of education', in: E. Hultqvist, S. Lindblad and T. S. Popkewitz (eds) *Critical analyses of educational reforms in an era of transnational governance*, Cham: Springer.

Jellison Holme, J. (2002) 'Buying homes, buying schools: School choice and the social construction of school quality', *Harvard Educational Review*, 72(2): 177–205.

Khan, S. (2011) *Privilege: The making of an adolescent elite at St. Paul's School*, Princeton, NJ: Princeton University Press.

Larsson, E. (2019) *Innerstadsgymnasierna. En studie av tre elitpräglade gymnasieskolor I Stockholm och deras position på utbildningsmarknaden*, Stockholm: Stockholms universitet.

Larsson, E. and Hultqvist, E. (2017) 'Desirable places: Spatial representations and educational strategies in the inner city', *British Journal of Sociology of Education*, 39(5): 623–637.

Lilja, E. (2011) *Den segregerade staden. Tre kvarter i Stockholms innerstad*, Stockholm: Stockholmia.

Lund, S. (2007) 'Valfrihet och konkurrens. Utvecklingstendenser inom gymnasieutbildningen', *Pedagogisk forskning i Sverige*, 12(4): 281–300.

Lundahl, L., Erixon Arreman, I., Holm A.-S. and Lundström, U. (2013) 'Educational marketization the Swedish way', *Education Inquiry*, 4(3): 497–517.

Lundahl, L. Erixon Arreman, I., Holm A.-S. and Lundström, U. (2014) *Gymnasiet som marknad*, Umeå: Boréa.

Palme, M. (2008) *Det kulturella kapitalet. Studier av symboliska tillgångar i det svenska utbildningssystemet 1988–2008*, Uppsala: Uppsala universitetsbibliotek.

Poupeau, F., Francois, J.-C. and Couratier, E. (2007) 'Making the right move: How families are using transfers to adapt to socio-spatial differentiation of schools in the greater Paris region', *Journal of Education Policy*, 22(1): 31–47.

Prieur, A. and Savage, M. (2013) 'Emerging forms of cultural capital', *European Societies*, 15(2): 246–267.

Rizvi, F. (2014) 'Old elite schools, history and the construction of a new imaginary', *Globalisation, Societies and Education*, 12(2): 290–308.

Savage, M., Warde, A. and Devine, F. (2005) 'Capitals, assets, and resources: Some critical issues', *British Journal of Sociology*, 56(1): 31–47.

Savage, M., Hanquinet, L., Cunningham, N. and Hjellbrekke, J. (2018) 'Emerging cultural capital in the city: Profiling London and Brussels', *International Journal of Urban and Regional Research*, 42(1): 138–149.

Söderström, M. and Uusitalo, R. (2005) *Vad innebär införandet av fritt skolval i Stockholm för segregeringen i skolan*, Uppsala: IFAU.

Storsthlm (2019) *Gymnasiebehovet 2019: Trender och kunskap om Stocholms läns gymnasieregion*, Stockholm: Storsthlm.

Swedish National Agency of Education (2019) *Skolmarknadens geografi. Om gymnasielevers pendling på lokala och regionala skolmarknader*, Stockholm: The Swedish National Agency of Education.

Wacquant, L. (2010) 'Crafting the neoliberal state: Workfare and prisonfare in the bureaucratic field', in: M. Hilgers and E. Mangez (eds) *Bourdieu's theory of social fields: Concepts and applications*, London: Routledge, pp.197–220.

Wacquant, L. (2015) 'For a sociology of flesh and blood', *Qualitative Sociology*, 38: 1–11.

Waters, J. and Brooks, R. (2015) ' "The magical operation of separation": English elite schools' on-line geographies, internationalization and functional isolation', *Geoforum*, 58: 86–94.

Webber, R. (2007) 'The metropolitan habitus: Its manifestations, locations, and consumption profiles', *Environment and Planning A*, 39(1): 182–207.

Zukin, S. (2008) 'Consuming authenticity: From outpost of difference to means of exclusion', *Cultural Studies*, 22(5): 724–748.

3

Youth migration to Lima: vulnerability or opportunity, exclusion or network-building?

Dena Aufseeser

Introduction

'The National Governmental "Program [Yachay]"[1] sees that boys and girls develop in a good state and are not on Lima's streets where there are many dangers, much violence, many robberies and many kidnappings … You should keep in mind that in Lima there are bad people that take advantage of these boys and girls and send them to work in the street and on top of that, they can kidnap them to obligate them to continue working. Further, in the street there is a lot of pollution, there are no trees, there are many vehicles, a lot of smoke, and also people who take the little they [the children] have. These boys and these girls, to travel, they miss classes and do not finish the school year. Do you want that for your children or not? Do you love them? Yes? And how do you want them to be when they grow?' – Program Yachay staff talking to mothers of child migrants. (Chavarray Valiente, 2015: 27)[2]

In 2015, Peruvian media sources brought attention to the 'plight' of children who migrated from rural villages during their school vacations to work in Lima and earn money to pay for their school fees.[3] Reports highlighted the risks children faced on the streets and the need to prevent such movements through educating, and if need be, criminalising, the children's parents. Yet, the reports did not examine young people's own assessments of their migration experience or analyse the ways in which migration may simultaneously address and reinforce social exclusion. This chapter explores the experiences of young people who migrate from rural provinces in Peru to Lima,

Peru's capital, to earn money to pay for their school fees, help their families, or create other opportunities for themselves. I argue that although migration potentially allows young people to expand their social networks and earn money, changing economic conditions, climate change and static narratives about 'global childhood' hinder the effectiveness of migration as a strategy to address poverty and inequality. Furthermore, young people's aspirations and views of poverty may change through migration and in the context of social marginalisation in Lima.

Reports and conversations, like the one quoted earlier, frame children's migration as detrimental to their wellbeing and a direct hindrance to their education. Yet, tropes of migrants as 'victims' not only fail to consider some of the benefits that come from migration but may actually limit young people's ability to cultivate and access the social supports that improve experiences of migration. After outlining my research methods and some contextual background, I discuss three main themes. First, campaigns against children's work contributions and efforts to limit young people's movement can limit the openness with which young people discuss challenges linked to migration, therefore decreasing some of the material and socio-emotional benefits that can potentially occur. Second, despite assumptions that children's migration hinders education, in many situations, young people are specifically migrating to earn money to further their education (or the education of their siblings). They are also able to cultivate networks and 'learn' more about Lima, factors that may help them if they migrate more permanently as adults. Finally, young people recognise that while Lima may be imagined as a place of growth and opportunity, the situation is complicated by discrimination and a lack of community. While migration is not always beneficial for young people, uneven economic opportunities, combined with increased climate challenges, make it likely that young people will continue to seek opportunities on Peru's urban coast.

Context and research methods

This chapter focuses on the experiences of children and adolescents who migrated without their parents to Lima from other provinces of Peru. In some situations, young people migrated during school vacations, and then returned to their provinces. In other situations, they migrated for more indefinite periods of time. Three of the young people interviewed initially migrated over school vacations, before moving to Lima more permanently.[4] They engaged in a variety of activities, including shining shoes, selling candy, working in shops and restaurants, and engaging in domestic work.

The data cited in this article are based primarily on in-depth interviews with 15 young people between the ages of 11 and 18, three focus groups (two with female adolescent domestic workers at a night school, and one at a dining hall for working children), and participant observation conducted in Lima in 2014. However, multiple research trips between 2009 and 2019 inform this research. I also draw on interviews with NGO staff and educators, and analysis of government reports and media sources. Young people were contacted through a night school, a dining hall for child workers, a school in an informal community on the outskirts of Lima, and an NGO that works with children and adolescent domestic workers. Of those participating in more in-depth interviews, seven were girls and eight were boys. The majority migrated from the highlands, with three young people from jungle regions, and one from a rural part of a northern coastal city.

In the past 15 years, Peru has experienced significant economic growth. Official poverty rates declined from 42.4% in 2007 to 20.5% in 2018 (INEI, 2020). However, Peru is still a highly centralised and unequal country. As of 2018, 42.1% of the population in rural areas lived in poverty compared with 14.4% of the population in urban areas (INEI, 2020). Further, economic opportunities and health and educational services are concentrated in coastal cities, especially Lima (Cueto et al, 2011). The quality of schools in rural areas is significantly worse than public schools in urban areas (Castro and Rolleston, 2015). In 2016, for example, 36.6% of second graders (who are usually around 7- or 8-years old) in urban areas demonstrated proficiency in mathematics, compared with 17.3% of second graders in rural areas.[5] Such inequalities drive rural-to-urban migration.

Peru has a long history of internal migration. In the 1980s, migration intensified due to conflict between Peru's armed forces and Shining Path, an insurgent terrorist group. Peru's rural indigenous population was especially affected, with around 600,000 people displaced. Rural populations also migrated in search of economic opportunities and because of imagined geographies of Lima. Existing studies link the idea of 'progress' with urbanisation and migration to cities (Crivello, 2015). Yet, there have been some notable shifts in recent years. In the words of a consultant for Save the Children, "Lima is saturated." Regional economic growth has increased the attractiveness of other areas, including other coastal cities and Madre de Dios, a jungle region which is now the wealthiest state in Peru due to mining. However, in areas such as Madre de Dios, many communities do not have the same established social networks, nor is there a comparable presence of NGOs and government social services, which can increase the risks to which young people are exposed.

Studies focusing specifically on the migration of young Peruvians under the age of 18 are limited (for exceptions, see Crivello, 2015), and the Peruvian government does not keep detailed data on the short-term migration of children, which makes it difficult to formally monitor changes and trends. Yet, general reports indicate that youth from the highland and jungle regions of Peru have been migrating to Lima for decades. Among youth followed as part of a longitudinal study on childhood and poverty, one in five had migrated at least once by the time they turned 15 (Crivello, 2015). A government study of children working in public spaces in Lima during the summer vacation (December 2014–March 2015) found that more than half were from Huancavelica, a highlands region that at the time was the poorest region in Peru (Chavarray Vicente, 2015).

Thus, there is some recognition of links between poverty and migration. However, media headlines primarily focus on the vulnerabilities to which young people are exposed through migration,[6] as evidenced in the report quoted at the beginning of this chapter. I suggest that frameworks that depict young migrants as in need of rescue, and their movement as problematic, fail to recognise the lived realities of young people's everyday lives (see Boyden and Howard, 2013). In Peru, the 'circulation' of young people has been an important strategy to address inequalities and strengthen relationships between families for decades (Leinaweaver, 2007). Even when young people migrate alone, referred to as independent child migration, their migration is often part of complex family strategies and depends on significant support from extended family networks (Crivello, 2015; also see Hashim and Thorsen, 2011).

At the same time, in practice, young migrants do experience risks that potentially detract from the benefits of migration. Part of the ability to mitigate these risks has been hindered by campaigns against child labour, which limit young people's ability to access protection or better paying jobs. A 16-year old reported difficulties in finding work because of her age and because of assumptions that people have about young people from the provinces. "I can't find work because I am young. People do not want to give us jobs. They say we know nothing, that we are very *chibola* [Peruvian slang for youth]." Moreover, the municipal police conduct sporadic roundups to remove children who are working in public spaces of the city, focusing on commercial areas in the historic centre of Lima and in other wealthy neighbourhoods. These roundups do not specifically target migrants. However, to be released from detention, young people need a guardian who can come to the police station. As a result, children from the provinces may remain in detention for weeks or even months as the government tries to locate relatives to whom they can release the children. When relatives are not found quickly, children are temporarily sent to state-run children's institutions. Such detention can be highly detrimental to young people's wellbeing, self-esteem and family relationships (Aufseeser, 2014a). The director of an NGO working with children on the streets explained,

'They start to lose confidence that their parents care about them. While initially they may have had fairly positive relationships, they question how their parents could just let them stay in the [state-run] home. Some even escape, discouraged and resentful that they have been left alone so long. Some may be too young to understand what is happening, and if the staff do not explain it clearly, or worse, speak disparagingly of the parents, it can be very damaging for the children.'

Additionally, detention may cause children to miss the start of the school year.

In practice, police roundups are rare. Yet, because young people below the age of 14 do not have a legal right to work, they also cannot depend on police, social workers or other state actors for support. According to an adult coordinator of a dining hall for working children:

'Controls are not as strong in this [poorer] zone as in San Isidro, Miraflores [wealthy neighbourhoods] ... Here, [police operations] are not as frequent. There is not as much control. The children need to be careful. Police do not help. If they intervene, it is to take their supplies. But this is not the solution. They take away their manner to earn money and live. This type of intervention does not work.'

Young people reported feeling targeted, not only because of their age, but because they were from the highlands. An adolescent girl who came to Lima from Cusco in search of work opportunities explained that employers "discriminate against people from the jungle and the highlands.[7] Some people don't pay ... Police do not help minors. They say we need to go to some special centre. If the exploitation is very strong, they might listen, but probably not." Although it is well-established that experiences of migration are shaped by access to support, young migrants perceived police and social workers as either indifferent or abusive. In the absence of formal state support, they frequently turned to extended social networks.

Social networks in the face of limited support

Despite representations of children as migrating alone, the young people in this study instead came in groups from their villages or with the material and emotional support of relatives and friends. In the case of children and adolescents who come to Lima during school vacations, they frequently rent rooms together and may travel from the same village, often accompanied by a father or uncle of one of the boys. Every year, some of these young people shine shoes near a dining hall for working children. Through word-of-mouth and outreach by educators, they have learned that they can eat lunch at the dining hall with the other young people in the area. In 2014, at the time of this research, eight boys had arrived, although the exact number varies each year.[8] The coordinator of the dining hall explained, "There might be 10 boys in one room. The conditions are not very hygienic. They save money and share together. Many are from the same family – they are brothers, cousins, uncles." Despite formal laws that subject adults who assist in the transport of children to charges of human trafficking,[9] there is little indication that the laws are enforced or act as an impediment to migration. The coordinator added, "People who rent rooms take advantage of them [child migrants], but it is not human trafficking. They treat them differently, charge them more. Being in a group is a form of defence." Knowledge of potential social services and experience in negotiating rental rates and finding rooms become important factors in shaping young people's supposedly 'independent' migration.

In some situations, strengthening relationships between families in rural areas and families in urban areas is a specific goal of migration, with wealthier adults in cities taking on the role of godparent. Such practices make it difficult to assess and target exploitative labour relations. Seventeen-year old Rosita left Pucallpa in Peru's jungle region for Lima when she was 13. "I came to know Lima and to study. My godparents helped me … People came to my town and asked if we were looking for godparents to help us study. This happens a lot." In the case of Rosita, she continues to live with her godparents. She helps in the house during the day, and studies at a night school in the evening. She reported that she is paid 800 soles a month (about $250 US), more than half of which she sends to her parents.[10] "In this manner I can help. My siblings are younger. It was very difficult when I first arrived. I missed my parents. I didn't have friends. In school, I made friends." Although Rosita states that she likes "Lima more ... When I have my family, I want to go back to Pucallpa. Lima is dangerous. Pucallpa is less dangerous." Temporary migration to Lima, although linked with loneliness, also facilitates education for Rosita and her younger siblings and helps the family foster social relationships (see Leinaweaver, 2007).

In contrast, 16 year old Ana came to Lima when she was 13 to escape an abusive home. "I was studying and my dad wanted to take me out of school. I am the oldest. We are four children," Ana explained:

'My father said it cost a lot to study. We would fight about this. My mom wanted me to continue to study. I had told my mom at one point that I was thinking of leaving but the day I came, I didn't say anything. That day, my dad wanted to punish me. He said ugly things. I was scared. My aunt came. She saw me and suggested I go to Lima. She said I could work and study. She lent me the money for the bus ... When I arrived, I went to the house of my aunt's sister-in-law, by the airport. I told my mom. She told her sister to come get me and find me work. I work in a house ... My aunt knew of the job because she had worked with a relative of hers. They pay me 500 soles [about $150 US] and give me a room and food. I don't feel great there. Sometimes the woman gets bothered and speaks badly to me. She makes the rules. I work from 6 am until 5 pm. Then I have one hour for my homework. At 6 pm I go to school. I feel good at school. The woman took me to the school. I asked if I could study. I said, "I will work with you, but I want to study." I send money, food or sweets to my family.'

In contrast to depictions of migration hindering education, in Ana's case, her migration directly opened more schooling opportunities. While working and then studying arguably leads to a long day, Ana reported that she was better off as a result. She explained, 'I study to be somebody in life, to help my parents and be professional. You need to have at least completed secondary school to apply for most jobs.'

Young people's views on migration were often conflicted, and reflected the complexity involved in decisions to migrate. Seventeen-year old Rolando from Huancavelica explained,

> 'My brother brought me. We all talked about it and decided he should. I wanted to buy clothes. I have a little brother. I buy him shoes and send them with friends. A lot of people come and go during vacations … At 10 [when he first came to Lima], it did not feel good but I had to come. I would like to work to maintain the family. I want to work until I have something. I might want to study mechanics or engineering at a university. I do not know. I am afraid at night. People can rob you. I will stay in Lima because there is no work in Huancavelica. There is more poverty in the highlands. We work hard, we can eat, but we cannot get much.'

Although Rolando did not want to come to Lima at the age of 10 and seven years later still must manage fears related to the city, through his migration, he can help himself and his brothers.

Lack of opportunities

The lack of opportunities in rural highland regions of Peru has long shaped rural-to-urban migration. In addition to historical processes of exclusion and discrimination, however, in recent years, Andean communities face increasing instability in livelihoods due to changing environmental conditions and melting glaciers, as well as environmental degradation from mining (Hoffman and Grigera, 2013). According to a government report on children's migration to Lima, 'the land is tired, and with much effort, it only produces what a farm family can themselves consume' (Chavarray Vicente, 2015: 25). Further, extreme cold has led to increased mortality among alpaca herds, on which many family livelihoods depend. Even if young people want to stay in their provinces, they cannot engage in the same types of survival strategies as their parents.

The Peruvian government has taken some steps to invest more in rural parts of the country. By creating more development opportunities, they hope to stem the prevalence of people migrating to Lima and other coastal cities. Yet, such opportunities cannot counter the changes resulting from a shifting climate. Further, other studies argue that migration to Lima improves one's status (Chavarray Vicente, 2015).

One elementary school teacher explained, "The government gave each ministry resources so that people would stay in the provinces but it did not work because everyone wanted to be in Lima."

Traveling to Lima allows young people to improve their status and acquire material items that their parents cannot afford. Yet, life in Lima can be more difficult than young people imagined. According to the psychologist at a night school in Lima:

> 'They come to Lima, but it is a great mistake. Lima is polluted. They eat foods that decrease their life expectancy. People in the provinces live to be 100 years old. Here, it [life expectancy] goes down. It is more diverse here. Many girls do not finish because they become pregnant. Other girls abandon school because they are dedicated to their work. And then there is a group that finishes. The majority work in technical positions. A few study to have a profession. Some join the police force.'

This study found young migrants expressed a desire to stay in Lima primarily because of work opportunities and *not* because of the actual quality of life in Lima. Sixteen-year old Ana quoted earlier explained,

> 'Life here is hurried. There is a lot of pressure. In my village, there is more fruit on your land. You have vegetables from your own fields. Here, you need to buy them. Life is healthier there. Here there is more delinquency. But I came to Lima to move forward. There are only a few jobs [in Junin], and they are not stable. I suppose I will stay here [when I finish high school] for work. It depends.'

Similarly, 14-year old Edgar from Huancavelica explained, "Here, I work in what there is. There I sell cattle and work in our fields. The food is better there but life is better here because people do not suffer as much. I want to stay here because there is more work."

Some young people specifically migrate to escape abusive situations. Seventeen-year old Oscar, from Huancavelica, reported that his stepmother hit him and his brother "so much that my brother escaped to Lima. He stayed with an uncle and after two years, when he had established himself, he came for me. She hit us with sticks, threw rocks at us, and would not let us eat." In such situations, the importance of Lima extends beyond economic opportunities to encompass possibilities to access protective supports. In the case of Oscar, he and his brother were already familiar with Lima because they had been working during school vacations, selling candies and shining shoes. This familiarity, along with other family networks, facilitated Oscar and his brother's ability to move more permanently to Lima.

Governmental efforts to reduce the seasonal migration of young people from rural areas to Lima and other coastal cities are based on the premise that children plan on remaining (or returning) to their villages as adults. However, in the face of limited opportunities, exacerbated by climate change, more and more young people migrate permanently. In situations in which children perceive a need to migrate, efforts to limit migration to Lima may result in decisions to find work in more precarious places.

Schooling and opportunities

Nearly all the young people in this study migrated at least in part to improve their access to formal education. Margot came to Lima from Cajamarca, a province in the highlands, one year before I interviewed her, when she was 16:

> 'I came to work to keep studying. There was not money there to study ... I decided to come. I wanted to study. I saved money with the help of my mom and my grandmother and then took a bus to Lima with my cousin. I first lived with my aunt when I arrived. My aunt met a woman who needed help. I take care of her son, clean, cook and iron. I work Monday through Saturday, until 5 pm, and then I get ready for school. I feel happy in school. I love it.'

While education is a primary motivation behind much migration, young migrants' material necessities mean that they are likely to work and study at the same time, as in the case of Margot. As a result, those who do study in Lima usually enroll in evening schools or alternative education programmes. The psychologist for an evening school explained,

> 'At first there was discrimination for this type of education. Now, it's a little better. It's been about 10 years ... We get less money from the state than day programmes get. Also, the Parent Association will not let our students use computers or the library because they bought the materials

themselves. Labs too. The night school does not have a Parent Association because most of the students do not live with parents. The students [in the night school] say they get a better education than they do in the province. The majority of students here are migrants.'

Because of young people's competing work demands and frequent movement between Lima and their home towns, attendance is sporadic.

'They might come one month, leave, and then come back. It is a very open system. It gives them a lot of possibilities. It is really incredible and they appreciate the opportunity. Those that come feel very supported. They identify with other people from rural zones and it gives them a little distraction from their work.'

While the quality of education in evening schools may not be comparable to that of day schools, of those studying in Lima, all but one reported that they 'loved school', as was the case with Margot.

Narratives that present formal schooling as the primary way to get ahead do not consider the changing context faced by many young people, however. Within Lima, there is a level of secondary degree saturation, and more jobs require additional education. Poorer youth are rarely able to afford programmes to prepare for competitive university entrance examinations, nor do they have the resources to access technical programmes. Further, while secondary school qualifications are still less common in some of the more remote parts of Peru, job opportunities have not increased evenly, and many young people migrate again as young adults. Although not writing in the context of migration, scholars have raised questions about whether formal schooling necessarily provides young people with skills and knowledge that are useful for them (Katz, 2004; Jeffrey et al, 2008). Previous research in urban areas of Peru found that children valued education 'to become someone,' but also indicated that they had significant concerns about what jobs they would be able to access with only a secondary education (Aufseeser, 2014b). This mismatch between narratives about transitions to adulthood and the experiences reported by young people calls into question the focus of existing social policies and children's rights agendas.

Determining whether migration is a 'good' strategy to address inequality and improve wellbeing and opportunities is complex. In some situations, young people do not accomplish what they hoped to by migrating. When she was 13 years old, 21-year old Maribel came to Lima with the specific goal of studying:

> 'There are not any schools in my village. My parents did not have much to give me. I came to study to improve myself ... I did not study because I did not have stable work. I arrived home tired. I could not find work. I could not study since I had no money ... The problem is that I came to study but I do not have the support of anyone. Life in Lima is not very easy. You need to work to be able to live and to study. If you do not work, no one gives you anything. No one says, "Here. Take this." In Huanuco [a province], it is very different. We have the fields to plant. You have food to eat. If you work, it is for you yourself. But if you are sick, there is no hospital. There are not many schools. You cannot study ... I would like to go back because I miss my parents.'

Over the eight years that Maribel has been in Lima, she studied for two of them by going to school in the evening. While she continues to frame Lima as a place that potentially offers greater opportunities and has more resources, the reality of her day-to-day life as a teenager without her parents has been difficult. When Maribel first arrived, she stayed with her sister and then with her cousin. "The first days, I felt scared. I was not accepted. There was more heat. I could not sleep. There were so many cars. I was used to the countryside. I was scared. I cried a lot because I missed my parents." Maribel eventually reported that she 'got used to Lima' and with the help of her sister, connected with the Institute for the Promotion and Formation of Domestic Workers, which helped her find more stable work.

Yet, schools are more than just a site of learning or obtaining formal credentials. Especially in the case of girls who engage in domestic work, school may be one of the only sites in which they are able to meet friends and connect with other young people from the provinces. Schools play an important role in reducing their sense of isolation, providing them with a support network, and connecting them to other possible resources. Ana, mentioned earlier, takes free painting classes at an NGO for domestic workers, which she found out about through a friend at school. "I paint to de-stress" she explained.

Changing contexts of poverty

As mentioned earlier, Peru's economic growth has led to the overall decline of official poverty rates. However, it is less clear how that translates into young people's understandings of their own wellbeing and perceptions of poverty. According to official government poverty measures, poverty rates are much higher in rural areas. Yet, the young people in this study expressed more nuanced views. As 16-year old Ana explained,

> 'Poor people are people who have nothing. They do not own their own house. They have nothing to survive. In my village [in Junin], everyone has their own house. It's different. Here you need land to get a house and that costs a lot of money. There are not poor people in my village because everyone has a room.'

For Jeferson, poverty manifested itself differently in Lima than it did in the small jungle community from which he came:

> 'To be poor in Lima, you have a greater likelihood to get sick. You do not have resources to buy food, so you need to buy rotten food. In the province, you do not have resources but you have your field, you can eat. If there is a river, you can fish. It is not as polluted. It is better to be poor in the province. Here you are poor socially.'

Yet, despite a preference for life in his village, Jeferson planned to stay in Lima when he turned 18 to access higher quality universities. Aspirations to 'become someone' in life are still strongly linked with schooling and work in coastal cities such as Lima.

In contrast, 16-year old Margot planned to return to Cajamarca after she finished her studies.

> '[When I first arrived] I was afraid. They told me there were gangs. I was afraid at night. I do not leave alone. I sometimes go out with my cousin on Saturday afternoons. I like Lima, more or less. I like that I study and can go out to the park. But I do not like gangs, that they rob, that there is a lot of violence. In Cajamarca, it is not like that. I live in the countryside. It is pretty. Everyone helps. If you do not have

enough to eat, they help you. Here, if you have no money, you do not eat. Life is better in Cajamarca. I want to return when I finish studying.'

During a group discussion with adolescent female migrants who studied at a night school and had worked as domestic workers, they talked about the difficulties of balancing work and school, as well as challenges adjusting to life in Lima. "It is very different here. There are more opportunities for work. More opportunities to learn things. In the province, everyone is dedicated to agriculture," explained one girl. Yet, they also expressed a longing for various aspects of life in their provinces, which they still considered home. Comments included: "I miss the fresh air and the singing birds", "It is more connected to nature there", "Here, it's a big change", "I miss the environment", "There is not much delinquency there" and "I miss my family."

In addition to the quality of the environment, safety was a frequent topic of conversation:

Girl 1: In the province, there is more freedom. Nothing happens. Here, I am afraid of car accidents.
Girl 2: Or you can get attacked with a knife or raped. For this reason, we can't leave alone.
Girl 1: You have to go out with your uncle or your cousin.
Girl 3: The poverty here is different. If you are not able to find work or somewhere to live, you might have to live in the street.

The challenges of life in Lima can be exacerbated by discrimination against indigenous populations, based on beliefs that they are 'out of place' in the city, backwards and more ignorant (see Thorp and Paredes, 2010). During a group discussion with the adolescents mentioned earlier, one 15-year old explained, 'They treat you badly because you are from the highlands. They treat you like you are less,' to which her classmates chimed in in agreement (field notes, 2014). Seventeen-year old Rolando from Huancavelica similarly explained, "There is discrimination at night schools. They say, 'chato' or 'enano' [slang words to indicate 'short'].[11] It has been difficult to get used to being here. I came from a village in Huancavelica. I speak Quechua at home. I learned Spanish in school."

Language, clothing and other customs are used to differentiate between those people recently arrived from the provinces, and those who were born in Lima. An adult coordinator of the child workers' movement said they actively work on integrating migrants into their regular activities.

> 'The kids here also feel they are different. We work with them on this but Lima is a bit hostile. We tell them that they [the migrants] share the same background. The children from Lima have parents from the same provinces. They live in the same physical conditions. But they are the first to discriminate based on migrants' form of speaking.'

Greater levels of discrimination and social exclusion shape young people's perceptions of their own wellbeing, and their need to find alternative social supports.

When support is weaker, risks to young migrants increase. Many of the young people who migrate do not have expansive knowledge regarding the legal rights they have as children under the age of 18 or the rights they have as domestic workers. This lack of knowledge hinders their ability to protect themselves in potential situations of abuse. In some circumstances, employers capitalise on young people's fear and lack of familiarity with Lima to control them more. "They tell the girls how dangerous Lima is, that they will be attacked if they leave. They are so isolated from other people, and afraid of being on their own, that they commit all of their time to their employers," explained a programme director at an NGO providing supports for child and adolescent domestic workers. In other situations, youth may be recruited with the promise of work, and then when they get to Lima, they are forced to work in the periphery of Lima in bars or are brought to Madre de Dios, a province dominated by the mining industry.[12]

In some cases, young people rely on resources from social movements and NGOs, as well as schools as previously mentioned. The JOC [Christian Youth Workers] organisation provides a network of information and emotional and material support for some newly arrived migrants. "There is a substantial need for emotional support. How can you not feel alone? Many times they feel alone. They do not have parents here. We realise this and we try to give them this support. We speak to them. We know how they are feeling," explained one of the youth representatives of the JOC. In addition to emotional support and connections, newly arrived migrants may stay for two to three months at the JOC's base in Lima where they are asked to voluntarily support expenses of the house.

Similarly, the Institute for the Promotion and Formation of Domestic Workers (IPROFOTH) provides a place where youth can meet, which can be vital for young women who are living in the homes in which they are working. In one situation, some of the women organised a baby shower and held it at IPROFOTH. They said they often go to the office on weekends. At the time of this research, one young woman was living in IPROFOTH's office with her 2-year old daughter. She explained, "People do not want you as a domestic worker if you have a young child." The ability to organise around their identity as workers plays an essential role in reducing isolation by connecting young people with other migrants, and in some situations providing much needed material support.

Within Peru, there is a long history of young people from rural areas who utilise short-term migration as a strategy for social and economic advancement (Anderson, 2013). Networks that have been built up over time between rural communities and Lima facilitate youth movement and provide them with knowledge and social connections that can lead to more positive outcomes from migration. However, in the face of discrimination, campaigns against informal street work, and sometimes difficult transitions to life in a city of around 10 million people, some of the young people with whom I spoke reported feeling isolated and not having people of whom they felt they could ask for help if needed. In the situation of Pedro, for example, migration to Lima in the absence of any strong support network resulted in him having no savings at the end of the summer. The 14-year-old had migrated to Lima with a friend. Pedro reported that he had not known where to go when arriving to Lima. He met some local youth in the centre of the city, and they showed him and his friend where they could rent rooms. After a police officer took his shoe shining box, he began selling candy on buses. He 'felt ashamed' and eventually started sniffing glue with some local youth. At the time of this research, he told me that he had not earned any money to bring home and was not sure what he would do. He had already missed the first week of the start of the school year and was afraid to communicate with his mother.

It is clear that young migrants do face potential risks when migrating. However, analysing their migration primarily through a lens of vulnerability overlooks the active roles they play in deciding to migrate and the benefits that may accrue. Many of the people in this study plan to return to Lima more permanently, as is the case with Erwin. Seventeen-year old Erwin from Huancavelica started coming to Lima in 2007 during school vacations. He would return in time to study in Huancavelica.

'I came for work. I would sell candies on Aramburu [a street in Lima] … I came to earn money to buy my uniform and notebooks. Then I would return to Huancavelica. I was 10 when I first came. I came with my brother. He is 20 now. I was not afraid. I worked alone but I knew friends and my cousin. They shined shoes … This year I stayed to help my brother. I feel okay. Now I prepare sandwiches. When I was shining shoes I didn't earn much. The municipal police would kick me out. But a friend I knew from back home works for a restaurant by Kennedy Park and he called me. I feel good. I learned to make hamburgers and am learning to make juice. I work the cash register. I would like to be a chef.'

Through his seasonal work, Erwin acquired a comfort and familiarity with Lima that eased his transition and helped him not feel afraid. He also used social connections to find more stable work. Other studies indicate that temporary migration may improve one's Spanish, which can be important for native Quechua speakers (Barker, 2007). Child migrants also improve selling strategies, learning what locations are most lucrative and where they can buy the best products in Lima (Chavarray Vicente, 2015). Such experiences are likely to contribute to greater financial success during subsequent trips.

The benefits and risks of migration are complex and constantly changing. In some situations, while migration may present some short-term hardships, such as being away from family, it allows young people to build up relationships, gain experience in Lima, and earn much needed money for school fees, clothing and other material items. Yet, discrimination based on both indigeneity and age pushed young people to more vulnerable situations and decreased the likelihood that migrants seek out additional supports. Further, while Lima is frequently represented as a place of opportunity and low poverty, the experiences of young people in this study were more nuanced. On the one hand, nearly all of those interviewed migrated to Lima because of greater potential to earn money and better access to schooling. However, the villages from which they came were also described as less 'poor' in the sense of community and more consistent access to food. Such insights necessitate an expansion of understandings of wellbeing that move beyond economic poverty lines to consider other factors. By recognising young migrants' situations and listening to their aspirations and opinions, government and social services can better support migration as a path to equity.

Conclusion

The examples in this chapter complicate narratives about the relationship between labour, poverty and migration. Despite discourses and policies that frame young migrants as victims, the young people in this study use migration as an active strategy to create more opportunities for themselves and their families. Their actions and reflections challenge assumptions that children's work, especially in the context of informality, is detrimental to educational opportunities and future wellbeing. Elsewhere, I have argued that international discourse and policy specifically frame work in opposition to learning (Aufseeser, 2014b). Yet, the realities of young migrants' lives challenge this assumption. Education is one of the primary motivating factors behind young people's movement. In some situations, migration does limit young people's ability to regularly attend school. However, in other situations, they specifically use the money they earn through work to pay their own school fees or the school fees of their siblings. This necessitates that we rethink discourses about what childhood and adolescence should look like, and the policies that we enact to support young people.

Internationally-funded government programmes and NGOs send a strong message that childhood is a time for school, play and to be spent with the nuclear family, rather than working. Yet, models of global childhood not only fail to reflect young people's experiences but themselves may be detrimental to children's wellbeing. Young people's experiences are shaped by social networks and family support, even in situations in which young people are viewed as 'independent' migrants. And despite the assumptions on which policies are based, many young people work and study at the same time. The mismatch between legal policies about childhood and the realities of the lives of children in this study actively limits young working migrants' ability to access the support networks they need. Given the reality of geographically uneven economic and educational opportunities, along with changing climate, it is unrealistic to prevent young people's movement, both within Peru and on a global scale. Discourses that focus on the vulnerability of young people who migrate fail to consider the vulnerabilities to which young people are exposed in the places from which they migrate, and the complex tradeoffs that are involved in moving from one place to another. Further, ideas of wellbeing are not static but, rather, change as children grow and are exposed to new ideas and experiences. Young people can and do act to address inequalities and increase their opportunities, moving to Lima in search of employment and better access to education. By expanding conceptions of childhood and poverty, governments can better support young people to use migration as a strategy to address social inequalities.

Notes

1   Program Yachay, meaning 'learning' in Quechua, was created in 2012 by the new Ministry of Women and Vulnerable Populations. The programme aims to restore the rights of children and adolescents in street situations with the goal of promoting comprehensive development and preventing additional exposure to risk.

2   All translations are mine.

3   While public education (Grades 1–12) is supposed to be free, families are usually required to pay fees for the Association of Parents of Family in order to matriculate their children (around $20 US). They also need to buy uniforms and school supplies, which can vary significantly in price, but cost around $200 US.

4   The number of those young people engaging in both types of migration is likely to be higher. However, only three specifically discussed earlier short-term migration.

5   While differences in household characteristics can explain part of this performance gap, Castro and Rolleston (2015) found that the quality of schooling and teachers in rural areas was equally important.

6   For example, the Correo, a leading newspaper in Lima, wrote the headline, 'Child migrants suffer physical and sexual violence'. Government press releases discuss the number of children who have been 'rescued' by program Yachay, a government initiative working with street and working children.

7   Discrimination extends beyond lower pay to also encompass the attitudes with which young people are treated. Discourses of race and belonging in Peru position highlanders as 'out of place' in city streets, and frame them as backwards and ignorant (Weismental, 2001). This can manifest itself in verbal abuse, job discrimination, and worse working conditions.

8   In 2019, no children from the provinces arrived at the dining hall. While there are no official records, anecdotally, NGO workers and professors report that because of more police interventions and competition from migrants from Venezuela, fewer young people from the provinces are migrating to Lima.

9   For critical analyses of the regulation of young people's migration through human trafficking laws, see Boyden and Howard (2013) or Huijsman (2011).

10   Average household incomes in coastal areas, including Lima, are about 1.5 times average incomes in jungle and highland regions.

11   A number of young people who migrated discussed how Lima's population was 'whiter' and 'taller' compared to those who came from the highlands.

12   The methodology I used to get to know young migrants decreased the likelihood I would meet young people in situations of forced labour or migration, as they would need to have the ability to attend school or NGO activities.

References

Anderson, J. (2013) 'Movimiento, movilidad, y migracion: Una vision dinamica de la ninez andina', Bulletin de I'Institut francais d'etudes andines, 42(3): 453–471.

Aufseeser, D. (2014a) ' "Protecting" street children? Urban revitalization and regulation in Lima, Peru', *Urban Geography*, 35(6): 870–888.

Aufseeser, D. (2014b) 'The problems of child labor and education in Peru: A critical analysis of universal approaches to youth development', in: P. Kelly and A. Kamp (eds) *A Critical Youth Studies for the 21st Century*, Leiden: Brill, pp.181–195.

Barker, C. (2007) 'Migration and rural development: An assessment of the impact of migration on rural communities in Huancavelica, Peru', *LBJ Journal of Public Affairs*, 18(3): 42–51.

Boyden, J. and Howard, N. (2013) 'Why does child trafficking policy need to be reformed? The moral economy of children's movement in Benin and Ethiopia', *Children's Geographies*, 11(3): 354–368.

Castro, J. and Rolleston, C (2015) *Explaining the urban–rural gap in cognitive achievement in Peru: The role of early childhood environments and school influences*. Oxford: Young Lives Working Papers.

Chavarray Valiente, C. (2015) *Destino: Lima Crónica de una infancia en busca de oportunidades*, Lima: MIMP.

Crivello, G. (2011) ' "Becoming somebody": Youth transitions through education and migration in Peru', *Journal of Youth Studies*, 14(4): 395–411.

Crivello, G. (2015) ' "There's no future here": The time and place of children's migration aspirations in Peru', *Geoforum*, 62: 38–46.

Cueto, S. Escobal, J., Penny, M. and Ames, P. (2011) *Tracking disparities: Who gets left behind? Initial findings from Peru*. Oxford: Young Lives Working Papers.

Hashim, I. and Thorsen, D. (2011) *Child migration in Africa*, London: Zed Books.

Hoffman, M. and Grigera, A. (2013) *Climate change, migration and conflict in the Amazon and the Andes*, https://www.americanprogress.org/wp-content/uploads/2013/02/SouthAmericaClimateMigration.pdf

Huijsmans, R. (2011) 'Child migration and questions of agency', *Development and Change*, 42(5): 1307–1321.

INEI (Instituto Nacional de Estadística e Informática) (2020) *Informe técnico: Evolución de la pobreza monetaria 2008–2019*, Lima: INEI.

Jeffrey, C., Jeffrey, P. and Jeffrey, R. (2008) *Degrees without freedom? Education, masculinities and unemployment in North India*, Stanford, CA: Stanford University Press.

Katz, C. (2004) *Growing up global: Economic restructuring and children's everyday lives*, Minneapolis, MN: University of Minnesota Press.

Leinaweaver, J. (2007) 'On moving children: The social implications of Andean child circulation', *American Ethnologist*, 34(1): 163–180.

Thorp, R. and Paredes, M. (2010) *Ethnicity and the persistence of inequality: The case of Peru*, New York: Palgrave Macmillan.

Weismantel, M. (2001) *Cholas and pishtacos: Stories of race and sex in the Andes*, Chicago: University of Chicago Press.

4

Sleepless in Seoul: understanding sleepless youth and their practices at 24-hour cafés through neoliberal governmentality

Jonghee Lee-Caldararo

Introduction

Sleeping in public is understood as taboo in South Korea, as in many other societies. Yet, it is likely tolerated and even sympathised with, if the sleeping person is a Korean youth napping in a café, the field of discussion in this chapter. Chronic fatigue in many South Koreans' lives, and especially in youths' lives, is an institutionalised phenomenon (Seo, 2019; Lee, 2019), specifically in contemporary Seoul where a highly competitive education system and increasing commuting times pressures youths into a certain time-economy and deprives them of sleep. In extreme cases, a traditional saying '*4 dang 5 lak (四當五落)*' becomes doxa, which means that four hours of sleep will lead you to admission into a university (or any job that a person seeks) whereas five hours of sleep results in failing. The fallacious maxim has been authorised by different social and institutional apparatuses, mainly the media's and some educational service providers' representations of legendary stories about well-known figures who slept as little as possible to succeed in their fields (Seo, 2019). Youths that I met at night-time cafés persistently mentioned this maxim when it came to ideal number of sleep hours. This anecdote epitomises how sleep habits involve local morals, although where and when to sleep is inevitably a product of an individual's agency.

Night-time sleep deprivation could also represent an individual's emotional status. As discussed later, the South Korean economy has been restructured in a way that is disproportionately detrimental to the younger generation (Woo and Park, 2006; Johan et al, 2016). The South Korean government's implementation of neoliberal doctrine, characterised as free-market competition, job flexibility, public service reduction and privatisation (Harvey, 2005), as well as increasing unemployment and job insecurity after the economic recession in 2008 have resulted in high levels of anxiety, depression and job-related stress among young adults (Standing, 2011). In this chapter, then, I suggest that South Korean young adults' late-night dozing and working activities at cafés, in lieu of maintaining regular sleep schedules, embodies the entanglement between individuals and a certain milieu in which they negotiate their anxious lives. In so doing, I aim to demonstrate that 'neoliberalism' is not a given state that exists independently from the lives of young people; rather, it is mutually constituted and differentiated by the continuous agentic and corporeal reflection of individuals.

My discussion here derives from my doctoral dissertation project that problematises the spatial and temporal context of everyday practices of franchise/chain cafés that remain open 24/7. Compared to evening/night-time only businesses such as bars and clubs, these cafés are sites of seemingly constant mundane practices from working to chatting, taking a rest, and so on. Yet, such everyday practices could turn easily to outright sleeping as the night wears on into morning. To understand these deep-night practices, I conducted the majority of my field work in 2017 at 15 '24-hour cafés' of top ranked brands in the districts of Shinchon, Gangnam, and Sillim in Seoul (see Figure 4.1).

Since the mid-2000s, 24-hour cafés have emerged across the city and are concentrated in several neighbourhoods of Seoul including the three districts mentioned earlier, which are adjacent to major universities, other educational institutions, or commercial districts targeted at young people in their 20s and 30s (*The Chosunilbo*, 2012). I reached out to random patrons staying in cafés between midnight and five in the morning and conducted semi-structured interviews with 60 of them. In this chapter, I focus on the selective cases of 20 South Koreans in their early 20s, who currently attend or have taken a leave of absence from their universities to prepare for exams for future employment, and whose main practice at cafés is *gongbu* in Korean, or simply put, 'study' (see Figure 4.2).

By *study*, I refer to a wide range of activities associated with university coursework, self-improvement and exams required for future jobs. While *work* is used as a complement to the term 'study' in this chapter, I acknowledge that my research participants' articulation of the word 'study' represents how they perceive themselves and their practices at cafés despite differences between specific activities that they engaged

Figure 4.1: Examples of 24-hour cafés in Seoul

24-hour cafés are easily recognisable in the dark due to '24' signs and light emitted from a café housed in a multi-storey building (taken by author, in Sillim at 4:29 am (left) and Sinchon at 11:47 pm (right), 2017).

Figure 4.2: The night-time studying tribe

This photograph portrays research participants' individualised practice of study through the night (taken by author, in Gangnam at 12:46 am, 2017).

in. As elaborated later in the chapter, study in their context is highly associated with self-driven learning and persistent effort. Such connotation possibly embodies Confucian spirituality as well as East Asian countries' cultural morals in a broader sense. Indeed, study is a highly regarded ethic in traditional East Asian cultures as a means of empowerment and emancipation to 'fulfil the pre-established telos of any human being' (Ni, 2016: 60). Such cultural morals align themselves with (or complement) the effects of neoliberal governmentality. That is, the perspective of East Asian philosophy supports the main arguments of this chapter: that 1) youths' night-time work/study in my project could be interpreted not merely as representative of their precarious life, but also considered as an exercise of self-realisation, or 'practices of freedom' in Foucault's definition of ethics, and 2) that individual's ethical practices, however, are inevitably entangled with the milieu of a certain cultural and economic space in which one lives.

French philosopher Michel Foucault's conceptualisation of neoliberal governmentality is a useful term to frame how practices are configured by individuals who live in a certain milieu, which constitutes and is also constituted by these very individuals. In what follows, I first discuss ideas around neoliberal governmentality to frame the present research. Then, I will elucidate how South Korean young people's night-time practices are constituted in the specific context of their austere and precarious life, and what it means to youths that they work/study at cafés overnight.

Neoliberal governmentality

For Foucault, governmentality refers to how different 'powers' operate and are entangled. Thus, knowing the way in which Foucault defined power is necessary to understand the concept of governmentality. Throughout his academic life, Foucault sought to demonstrate that power is not a state of domination but the capability to affect the 'conduct of conduct' (Foucault, 1991; 1997). As he highlighted, power always exists in between relations that are 'not fixed once and for all' (Foucault, 1997: 292). In Foucault's (1991: 15) argument that governmentality consists of two technologies, 'technologies of self' and 'technologies of Power', he distinguished between a series of powers: one from inside and one from outside the (corporeal) subject (to distinguish this with 'powers' (as the capability to affect), I capitalise Power when it only refers to the powers from outside the (corporeal) subject). This does not mean that he understood that subject (self) and other effects (Power) are separable from each other nor that they are static (Heller, 1996; McWhorter, 1999). Instead, he noted that neither subjectivities nor milieu pre-exist and cannot be fully in control (McWhorter, 1999). In that sense, Foucault's milieu allows intervention (Anderson, 2014), in which different powers are entangled therein intra- and inter-actively.

Bearing this in mind, Foucault described how the emergence of 'neo-liberalism', which should be distinguished from liberalism insofar as the former rearranges society for the interests of markets (Foucault, 2008), contributed to developing new forms of governmentalities. He explains that the instillation of market principles in society consequently created a particular milieu where 'neoliberal subjects (*homo economicus*)' normalise the logics of individualism and entrepreneurialism, equate freedom with self-interested choices, and become responsible for their own wellbeing (Foucault, 2008). An incomplete understanding of his idea could reproduce a fallacy: that the more a subject exercises their freedom, the more their practices only contribute to conforming to the system. Yet, as elaborated later, neoliberal subjects in my project are neither duped nor simply manipulated by neoliberal policies and programmes. In Foucault's notion of relational and mobile powers, the neoliberal subject is not an end-product of a certain power (Koh, 2011). Furthermore, the way in which neoliberal governmentality operates keeps changing in relation to other powers as well as subjects' exercise of practices and embodied experience.

Again, as one type of governmentality, neoliberal governmentality should not be understood as a single technique of a particular neoliberal regime, policy, milieu, or subject since it exists relationally and in between differentiating powers. In contrast, the existing governmentality approach seems to overlook Foucault's emphasis on the mutual entanglement of different powers and their differentiation (Anderson, 2016). Accordingly, Anderson (2014; 2016) advocated for a new term, 'neoliberal affect', to capture how individuals' bodily experiences contribute to constituting and changing a particular neoliberalism. Yet, I believe that his emphasis on the mutual entanglement between milieu and individual was in fact what Foucault instills in his conceptualisation of governmentality as described earlier. In that sense, I stick to Foucault's term although my emphasis might not be so different from Anderson's. Indeed, I suggest that the limitations of previous research do not reflect the inherent deficiency of Foucault's concept itself, but the way scholars have applied the term. Regarding Foucault's original idea on power relations and governmentality, I will explore how individual young people could experience and differentiate their precarious lives through their night-time work/study at cafés. What follows is an account of the context of South Korean youths' bodily experiences and motives for their night-time practices at cafés under which a particular form of Korean neoliberal governmentality operates.

The economic challenges of South Korean young adults

A substantial literature has revealed that young adults in the 21st century are unevenly exposed to social and economic consequences from the implementation of neoliberal doctrines (Bessant et al, 2017). South Korean young adults are not likely to be an exception unless they have wealthy families who can cover increasing tuition, living costs and home mortgages. Since the International Monetary Fund (IMF) imposed neoliberal doctrines on the Korean government in 1998, non-regular jobs have increasingly become the norm in South Korea. In 2016, about half of all employees aged 20 to 30 are in non-regular jobs (Statistics Korea, 2017). This means that the majority of South Korean young people are on short-term contracts, freelancing, or working through temporary agencies. Moreover, the economic recession after 2008 resulted in an unemployment rate for those in their 20s that was double the national average (Statistics Korea, 2017). As only a limited number of jobs can provide a 'successful' life, South Korean young people are exposed to a higher degree of insecurity in terms of income and employment (Johan et al, 2016).

With their financial constraints, many young adults are now unable to follow what was considered a 'normal' life path by previous generations (Ock, 2015). The contemporary South Korean young adults are known as *Sampo-* or *Dapo-Seadea* (the generation of giving-up), meaning that they tend to give up or postpone many common elements of people's life-cycles including dating, relationships, marriage, and having children (Jeong, 2016). Additionally, they have increasing difficulties obtaining a job, owning a residence, maintaining personal relationships, having hobbies, and more generally 'hope' (Park, 2015). As it becomes harder to attain economic independence even after compulsory education and graduation from university, many South Koreans now remain as 'youth' even until their 30s. The term 'youth' (*Cheong-Nyeon* in Korean) traditionally referred to the most prosperous aged group, but it now implies economic dependency and instability of life first. Accordingly, in 2008, the South Korean government officially defined youth as those aged 15 to 29, and there has been a movement to extend the age range even further to 34. In that sense, although I limit the present study to those aged 20 to 24, youths as referred to in this chapter might still be an older cohort than those discussed in other chapters of this book.

South Korean young people's austere life and the anticipated precarity of their future has impelled them to position themselves as students. Indeed, the obsession with endless education has become ever more intense in South Korea (Kim, 2016; also see Bessant et al, 2017). Many South Korean youths have internalised competition and overachievement by dedicating themselves to entering the most prestigious universities (Sharif, 2018) and then to obtain more '*specs*', so as to be more competitive applicants for a position in a few major companies in South Korea. *Specs* originated from the English word 'specifications' with which people compare items before their purchase. It refers now to competitive elements that make individuals' CVs stand out, such as switching to a better university, attaining high scores on English tests, certificates and other social experiences. Yet, the inflation of higher education ironically has resulted in the removal of an 'educational premium' (Kim, 2016: 306). In the past, the current youths' parents' generation could certainly experience or witness social mobility as a result of their higher education (Bessant et al, 2017). Based on such successful experiences, educational aspirations can be bequeathed to the younger Korean generations too. In contrast, since the Asian financial crisis in 1998, the benefits of higher education have declined steadily in terms of differences in wage levels and job security across all educational attainment levels (Kim, 2016). For instance, due to the increased skill profile of the labour force, only 44% of those who graduate from tertiary education have found permanent, full-time employment (OECD, 2017). Thus, young people's effort to obtain better *specs* cannot necessarily guarantee a secure income and a secure job. As result, an increasing number of youths began to put their greatest effort into the most secure types of jobs by preparing for an admission test that is accepted by law schools, medical schools, or the civil service (Kim and Yoo, 2017).

Such a situation has set in motion scholarly and public discussion to challenge the idea that young people's unemployment and financial difficulties have resulted from their lack of effort. Woo and Park (2006) initially played a significant role in juxtaposing youths' issues with the structural limitations of the 'Korean economy' by their conceptualisation of *Pal-sib-pal-man won Seadea* (the ₩880,000 generation). This term describes the reality that the majority of youths relying on their part-time job live with an average monthly salary of 880,000 won (US$750). Given that Seoul's living cost is as high as New York City's, they can hardly escape their vulnerable economic position (Woo and Park, 2006). Since this issue was first addressed, there have been some political gestures made at the city and national government levels to aid a series of youth issues such as high university tuition fees, expensive rent, unemployment and job insecurity. Nevertheless, the legacies from the long history of South Korea's pro-business policies cannot be easily erased (Johan et al, 2016). The following discussion describes how South Korean youths have experienced and confronted such a reality, which youths begin to be disaffected by, but cannot simply abandon.

Sleepless youth and their practices

The relationship between youth's night-time practices of work/study at cafés and the socio-economic and political change mentioned earlier, is uncovered through three related questions: (1) why these youths engage in work/study at night instead of taking rest, (2) how their fatigue becomes endurable and rationalised, and (3) why they work late at cafés instead of their home, or in any other space.

Night-time work/study

When I first saw my research participants, they were each involved in their school-related assignments, reading, drawing, typing and preparing for an exam. I asked them if their assignment was due the day after, and if they needed to cram for the assignment. I was surprised to learn that many of them were not working under urgent deadlines, but rather used their night-time sessions as an opportunity to maintain steady progress with their work/study. They gave two explicit reasons for this.

First, utilising night-time is seen as familiar and preferable for working/studying. Youths in my project have normalised the practice of spending time for themselves after 10 pm, or even later since their middle/high school years. Back then, their 'me time' was only taken at night after they finally came back home from *hagwon* (private education institutions), or after their parents went to bed (see Chu, 2018; Sharif, 2018). The effect of disciplinary apparatuses, such as family and school, seem inscribed in their bodies even if they are now university students and no longer need to follow such discipline. Yet, I should highlight that their utilisation of night-time is not necessarily pitiful, but rather tactical in de Certeau's sense (1984). My research participants 'like' night-time since it allows them to 'concentrate on [their] inner voice and what [they] want' (Interviewee, Suah). Youths in my project believed that night-time is theirs alone, and that they can absorb themselves in any subject as much as they like without feeling rushed, anxious, or interrupted. As one participant remarked:

'Perhaps I should've worked more efficiently like others. I tend to study more than is assigned if the subject matters to me … Well, I know how to work fast and efficiently to complete an assignment to meet deadlines. I do sometimes. But there is something [that I'd call] *my own study subject* [emphasis added] … I know I will regret later [laughs]. Still I feel free to dig up more and more until I master it.' (Nain)

Like Nain, young people that I met highly valued studying time so that they could study in depth, and not just 'enough' to complete an assignment, as 'neoliberalized education' (Jeong, 2019) might expect them to do.

Nonetheless, these young people did not simply pursue what they desired. They acknowledged an unavoidable pressure that they could not and should not ignore 'in order to survive in Korean society'. Sociologist Hong-Jung Kim (2015) defined contemporary Korean youths as 'the survivalist generation' to whom not being excluded from society (in other words, survival) is more important than living well. I do not entirely agree that surviving is the sole or the most important concern of the youths in my study, but it is true that 'survival' attains moral importance to some extent. In an age of uncertainty, as Bauman (2007) describes, '[w]hat is left for [one's] concerns and efforts … is the fight against losing: try at least to stay among the *hunters*, since the only alternative is to find [oneself] among the *hunted*' (p.104). According to this division, youths in my study seemed to choose both, to be *hunters* (who follows the dominate rules in the 'hell' without questioning), yet, without thoroughly giving up being the *hunted* (who stops to think about ways to escape from hell) as well. They had devised ways to hide themselves or (temporarily) emancipate themselves from the position of the hunted by staying awake at night.

Second, studying at night helps them to spend time 'wisely'. Jihyeon was a senior student who patronised 24-hour cafés every weekend. She came to the café near her part-time workplace at 10 pm and left the café for the next shift at 5 pm on the day after. She was one of the participants who seemed to have the greatest time pressure in which she had no "room for losing any one second for sleep". To juggle her life with her academic passion, she tactically goes to bed during the day because, as she explained:

> 'You never get deep sleep if going to bed after sun rise, and … there are always daytime duties … which we can't avoid. Because of this, I am good at waking up after only a couple of hours' sleep whereas I likely sleep more than I should if I go to bed at night.' (Jihyeon)

Despite the extreme nature of her case, Jihyeon's understanding of sleep calls attention to the general tendency that I found among my research participants: they consider time as an important resource. As Melbin (1987) indicated, night-time is considered as a frontier to be extended further. One student who patronised a 24-hour café every day also vindicated this by noting:

> 'I don't think I am an innate genius, but I am passionate, and I like to accomplish my goals. For that, what I can do is only relying on my body, my time. To achieve the same outcome that such genius easily makes, I need more time. This is all I have. This is a bit sad [laughs], but I am proud of myself.' (Yunyoung)

Like Jihyeon, Yunyoung also used night-time as a means to 'accomplish her goals' and nurture her passion. Another senior student, Byeonghyeon, showed how such economic perception of time could be internalised even further. He and I met in another 24-hour café in Sillim where his girlfriend lived while he usually patronised a 24-hour café near his home. He explained about his visit that day:

Byeonghyeon:	I came here today since I have class tomorrow. After meeting her [his girlfriend], it was already late evening and I had things to read anyway. I like to lock myself up in the café for night. I can't sleep here anyway so I surely can get something done ... I often go to school directly from here; it saves me a lot of time because I may transfer only once ... [it is] a much better option than going home and then going to school from there ... It's not worth spending time that way
Interviewer:	Do you have time pressure? What is your purpose in saving time this way? Did you plan to study more, or give yourself a rest by saving time?
Byeonghyeon:	Well, there is no specific purpose for that. I didn't mean to do something with the saved time, or squeeze time for something else. I just begrudge spending time unwisely [laughs].
Interviewer:	Begrudge?
Byeonghyeon:	Yes ... I don't think I ever think like 'Oh, I now have one saved or remaining hour because I didn't spend one hour for the other.' I always ... just don't wanna waste time unnecessarily.

This long excerpt from the interview transcript with him articulates how my research participants valorise time, how these neoliberal subjects further internalise the importance of cherishing time. With such an economic perception of time, night-time work/study at cafés becomes an eminently practical and economic decision. Furthermore, the more time is emphasised as a resource, the more the boundary of night is possibly invaded.

Night-time sleep deprivation as ethical practices

Youths in my study tried to sleep less than five hours and, instead, sporadically have a day off to sleep for half a day or they take fragmented naps during a day. Such sleep habits partly reflect what they think is a standard amount of night-time sleep, which refers back to the myth of 4 dang 5 lak as introduced at the beginning. Compared to the majority of youths who do not think that they sleep enough, two participants explained to me that they sleep as much as needed during a day in order to study at night more efficiently. Still, I found that in this case, they see themselves as being 'inappropriate' because they think they sleep more than what is perceived as a 'socially acceptable amount of sleep'. Both cases indicate that night-time practices of those sleepless or guilt-ridden youths likely reproduce a specifically South Korean morality around sleep. Yet, youths in my study, at the same time, provided me with a new account of their exhausted body and tiredness as a sign of self-cultivation, as Byeonghyeon said:

> 'No matter how hard we work, what is given to us is so blurry and always out of our hand ... There is no hopeful or certain future, and we all are exhausted ... Because we live in such a society, (pause) it [studying at night] is *helpful* [emphasis added]. Perhaps I sound like a dreamer, but anyway ... I don't think I can get a nice job by minimising my sleep time, or after this life pattern ends. Although I can't confidently envision my future, I just want to do my best in this given situation. As neither our society nor companies reward individuals with better income, enough paid-off days, a secure future, and so on, I think people just work more and try to prove themselves that "I am not wrong, I do my best, I did all I can".' (Byeonghyeon)

His explanation parallels East Asian ethics with which discipline and effort have long been perceived and emphasised as highly respectable in South Korea (Koh, 2011). For instance, Confucian spirituality considers individual's devotion as sincerely practising one's own responsibility to nurture their potential. Buddhist tradition has also highlighted 'human capacity to be good under certain conditions of cultivation'(Varela 1992, cited in Gibson-Graham, 2006). Despite (or because of) this emphasis on personal effort, the effort is hardly recognised in the South Korean society unless it leads people to accomplish what they pursued. Otherwise, people could find other measures to quantify their intangible effort. As Byeongheyon describes earlier, since the milieu youths live in often makes them doubt their efforts and their decisions, they need such self-affirmation by prolonging their working hours, working when others take a rest, appreciating a sense of their tired body, and overcoming their sleepiness.

I believe this is an important example of the individual constitution of the self. At first glance, youths' night-time work might seem to only affirm how neoliberal subjectivities involve a naïve commitment to improving their 'human capital'. However, as I discussed earlier too, many Korean youths are no longer necessarily entrapped in a 'cruel optimism' (Berlant, 2011) about their future or an expectation of what they believe they should be given. My research participants demonstrated how they deal with the broken promise and rather 'optimise' given options through their hard work. Hyeonseok's case is an explicit example of this. He was one participant who took a one-year absence from his current university to enter a graduate school programme in a college of pharmacy. What he wanted was not to be a pharmacist, but he knew the certificate would ensure that he could open and own a pharmacy later on, and do something else that he likes for the rest of his life without actually working a day in his life at a pharmacy. *Hyeonseok* as well as many other youths who can no longer connect or associate their current university education with a future job seemed to expect the least from the society.

Given that chronic sleep deprivation normally results in negative emotional status (Rhie and Chae, 2018), it was surprising that youths in my study described the day we met as 'happy' although they simultaneously acknowledged the absence of any particular 'promise of happiness' (Ahmed, 2010) and were quite familiar with feelings of precarity. They claimed that happiness comes 'when one could possess freedom' and highlighted that they could come to a café when they needed and wanted. That is, their happiness was associated with the fact that at the very least, they are trying and doing their best with everything they do. As some participants noted, even if they could not study as much as they wished, they still likely felt proud of themselves since they did not 'give up their day' (Nain) by staying at home and resting. In that sense, youths' night-time work could be considered as the practice of self-respect, related to the practice of eliminating their guilt and anxiety or devoting oneself to their present moment.

In *The History of Sexuality*, Volume 3, Foucault (1986) described how the emphasis on sexual austerity among the Stoics takes the form of 'an intensification of the relation to oneself by which one constituted oneself as the subject of one's acts' (Foucault, 1986: 41). Arguably, sleep is an even more important source of human pleasure and wellbeing. Accordingly, working at night by overcoming the inherent desire and need for sleep could play a role as self-affirmation to prove their effort individually. In East Asian philosophy as encapsulated in the *I Ching (Book of Changes)*, it is highlighted that even though humans do not have full control of everything, how to order the given fate relies on human activities. The youths in my study seemed confident about themselves and their 'survival' not because they expect a secure

Figure 4.3: Contradictory images within a 24-hour café

Those who study in cafés usually seat themselves away from people who patronise them for the sole purpose of relaxation and fellowship. Despite such spatial division, the existence of the opposite sides plays an important role in enticing the other into the cafés (taken by author, in Gangnam, at 5 am, 2017).

future to exist, but because they believe that they have the capability to confront their reality without losing the way they are, and thus have the capacity to shape their own lives.

Working at cafés

Youths' choice of cafés for night-time work seems ironic in that highly priced coffee is a luxury regarding their economic constraints. Certainly, the top ranked brand cafés, *Holly's Coffee*, *TomNTom's*, *Angelinus* and *TowSomePlace*, that operate franchise/chain 24-hour cafés are not the most affordable working space in Seoul. If they simply seek out caffeine at night, youths in my study could have made coffee at home or buy a cheaper take-out coffee. The choice of cafés over other available spaces is rather associated with two contradictory images of cafés, as a represented space for breaktime and as an actually experienced space where other studying bodies are in fact ubiquitous (see Figure 3). For instance, as one of my research participants described, cafés are "fuel to help [their] passion to burn". At the same time, they still regarded cafés as a 'relaxing space' or 'refuge' where they can stop thinking about the reality that 'shakes their belief'. The juxtaposed images of cafés reveal the similar 'tactic' addressed earlier: playing *both* 'hunter' and 'the hunted'.

First, for those who 'live fully', cafés are a preferable space to home since staying in a café helps them to stay productive. One important attribute is the materiality of cafés including the existence of others. Taking other customers' invisible gaze into account, the youths voluntarily and willingly 'lock themselves up' in 24-hour cafés until sun rise, or until the city buses start to operate again. In other words, the initial payment for coffee becomes a motive with which those neoliberal subjects are driven to be productive in order to rationalise the expensive cost of coffee. In that sense, cafés play a role as a pseudo 'panopticon' (Foucault, 1995) to discipline the youths themselves.

On the contrary, the choice of cafés indicates how the youths want the effect of space to be in their control too. This is vindicated by their choice over other available 24-hour studying spaces in Seoul, such as *Dokseosil* (dedicated reading rooms). *Dokseosil* is a popular form of space-rental service for South Koreans who need to isolate themselves to prepare for an exam in which they have an assigned desk. The youths in my project have prior experiences with *Dokseosil*, but they considered it undesirable in their situation because, as one of the participants explained:

> '[For that service] I have to pay in advance. Once I pay, I might feel stressed out because I then must go. I don't want to be anxious about the situation when I can't make it. Studying at a café is simple. If I decide "I don't go today", then, it's okay not to go'. (Nain)

Compared to *Dokseosil* that normally requires a monthly-paid membership, cafés are spaces where youths feel less obligation emotionally and financially. Similarly, youths preferred cafés over libraries because the former implied fewer constraints. As might be expected, libraries have fundamental limitations in terms of access: they are either too far from home or not open all night. Jieun explained that under the austerity programme, some universities have even stopped operating 24-hour libraries except for midterm and final exam periods. Moreover, libraries in Korea are actualised spaces of Korean youths' intensive study and lingering hope for the future. In these most quiet and serious spaces, people are expected to be self-conscious about what they are doing and the sound that they make. As my research participants described, being around high-strung people all day at libraries (or any other space specifically designed for studying youth) becomes a 'source of anxiety about being appropriate or being left behind'. Therein, the youths easily fall into an endless comparison between themselves and those hard-working people. Finally, the youths go to cafés to be disaffected from their present reality and their perception of an uncertain future, the competitive milieu, and the perceived *hunters*. By being at cafés, youths in my project rather voluntarily become the *hunted* while remaining the *hunter* too. Although they would be working at cafés anyway, the existence of other non-studying bodies, the sounds of others chatting, the smell of coffee, music, warmer lighting, and the norm of cafés as a resting space all help them to take care of themselves and suggest to them other possibilities in life. This in turn makes their work thoroughly their own.

Conclusion

Sleep and sleepiness interegrate both individual and societal dimensions because possible available places for sleep, the optimal amount of sleep, and the ideal timing to go to bed are constituted differently in accordance with an individual's corporeal response and material conditions as well as local morals and norms in various societies (Kraftl and Horton, 2008; Galinier et al, 2010). South Korean youths' late-night dozing and working at cafés can be also understood, first, in the context of South Korean society where a long hour working culture has generated individuals' demand for night-time activities, either for extra work or for a break in lieu of normal sleep schedules. Furthermore, their night-time practices are inseparable from the current political economic situation to which youths' precarious lives are attributed. However, as this chapter has also highlighted, individuals' wills are inherently entangled within 'a social or institutional body' (Ahmed, 2014: 18). In other words, precarity is not merely sensed or tolerated as given, but it is transformable and generative. For instance, to transcend the neoliberal milieu and chase their own happiness, youths in my study find 24-hour cafés in which they can enact a new boundary of their day (and night) and the way that they study and conduct themselves. In so doing, they practice holding their freedom and power over their lives while they cope with what they insist on calling 'a hell'. That is, night-time work/study at cafés is a means to subjectify them as ethical beings and cultivate competence to remain conscious about what and why they are doing as they do.

The way that the youths in my study deal with their reality crystallises into an inspiration of hope in relation to their capability of, in the words of Gibson-Graham (2006), 'opening to what is novel rather than familiar in situations'. Indeed, neoliberalised youths simultaneously reference and transgress the existing spatio-temporal norms, meanings and morals of South Korean society. For instance, their night-time activities refer to how they were disciplined during teenage years. Yet, their practice appears unfamiliar in terms of their spatial choice of cafés since South Korean young adults' nights has been spatially linked to either alcohol-related consuming spaces or other working spaces such as school, private tutoring services (*hagwon*), 24-hour studying spaces (*Doseosil*), as well as their home. Likewise, youths' night-time work/study, on the one hand, perpetuates the myth of '4 *dang* 5 *lak*' and embodies an emphasis on the effort in East Asian culture. On the other hand, those who feel disaffected by 'the broken promise' negotiate their anxious life by practising proactively and differently, which both reflects and cultivates their 'technologies of the self'. In that sense, the sleepless youths are not simply fooled by the *Spec* society. Their sleep deprivation is rather the fate that befalls those who "want to live more fully than everyone else" (Seulgi). In sum, the South Korean youths' night life, embodied experiences, and ethical practices are intra- and inter-actively entangled within South Korean culture and political economy. To theorise such ongoing entanglement and mutual constitution of individuals and other effects of apparatuses, things, materials and meanings, I advocate for a holistic understanding of neoliberal governmentality. Indeed, Foucault's notion of relational and mobile powers implies that youths' hard work and passion should not be simply reduced to a pitiful example of the ways in which neoliberalism programmes young people to commit to self-improvement and take responsibility for their lives. Instead, it opens the possibility that South Korean neoliberal governmentality has been differentiated and differently experienced in relation to the given milieu as well as individual youths' agentic and embodied response.

Overall, this chapter contributes to exploring the different international context of neoliberalism. Furthermore, the case study demonstrates that individually-experienced neoliberalism can infinitely deform and transform even in the same society. Certainly, it is unlikely that all South Korean youths choose to willingly minimise their sleep or come to cafés as the youths in my study do. In that sense, it is relevant to understand neoliberalism as neoliberal governmentality, so as not to overlook the potentiality and mobility of subjects and the indeterminate effect of other elements of the lived milieu. The present case of sleepless youths cannot be a sustainable way or ideal solution of current neoliberalism because a healthier future is likely possible when these youths can still appreciate their happy life without sacrificing their sleep hours. Nevertheless, the case contributes to reconstructing a 'politics of possibility and hope'. Given that emotions are not individual, but are socially mediated (Ahmed, 2004), many youth-related studies have discussed how the current political economic experience has configured youth's precarity and structured feelings. Embracing those invaluable discussions, I would call further attention to individual youths' freedom to act and think in response to the ongoing entanglement of these embodied experiences of neoliberalism, which might not necessarily appear revolutionary, but are still influential and resilient in a politically meaningful way. Indeed, the embodied dimension of neoliberalism is constantly differentiated according to what individual youths are doing, how they interpret it, and what affects them. As suggested in Foucault's conceptualisation of governmentality, youths live in, and with, a certain milieu that is experienced bodily while they simultaneously reinforce and transform the same milieu. In that sense, youths cannot be completely disaffected by society even if the current economic circumstance has challenged their happiness. Still, youths would not relinquish control of their life in despair either because they have the capability of 'conducting their conduct' both as the *hunter* and the *hunted*.

References

Ahmed, S. (2004) *The cultural politics of emotion*, New York: Routledge.

Ahmed, S. (2010) *The promise of happiness*, Durham, NC: Duke University Press.

Ahmed, S. (2014) *Willful subjects*, Durham, NC: Duke University Press.

Anderson, B. (2014) *Encountering affect: Capacities, apparatuses, conditions*, New York: Routledge.

Anderson, B. (2016) 'Neoliberal affects', *Progress in Human Geography*, 40(6): 734–753.

Bauman, Z. (2007) *Liquid times: Living in an age of uncertainty*, Malden, MA: Polity Press.

Berlant L. (2011) *Cruel optimism*, Durham NC: Duke University Press.

Bessant, J., Farthing, R. and Watts, R. (eds) (2017) *The precarious generation: A political economy of young people*, London: Routledge.

Chu, H. (2018) What is life like for South Korean kids? Busy, *The Washington Post*, https://www.washingtonpost.com/lifestyle/kidspost/what-is-life-like-for-south-korean-kids/2018/01/23/0424f570-fc90-11e7-ad8c-ecbb62019393_story.html

de Certeau, M. (1984) *The practice of everyday life*, Berkeley, CA: University of California Press.

Foucault, M. (1986) *The history of sexuality Vol. 3: The care of the self*, New York: Pantheon.

Foucault, M. (1988) 'Technologies of the self', in: L. Martin, H. Gutman and P. Hutton (eds) *Technologies of the self: A seminar with Michel Foucault*, Amherst, MA: University of Masschusetts Press.

Foucault, M. (1991) 'Governmentality', in: G. Burchell, C. Gordon and P. Miller (eds) *The Foucault effect: Studies in governmentality*, Chicago, IL: University of Chicago Press.

Foucault, M. (1995) 'Panopticism,' *Discipline and punish: The birth of the prison*, New York: Vitage, pp.195–228.

Foucault, M. (1997) *Ethics, subjectivity, and truth: Essential works of Foucault, 1954–1986*, Paul Rabinow (ed), New York: The New Press.

Foucault, M. (2007) *Security, territory, population: Lectures at the College de France 1977–1978*, New York: Picador.

Foucault, M. (2008) *The birth of biopolitics: Lectures at the College de France 1978–1979*, New York: Picador.

Galinier, J, Becquelin, A, Bordin, G., Fontaine, L., Fourmaux, F., Roullet Ponce, J., Salzarulo P., Simonnot, P., Therrien, M., and Zilli, I. (2010) 'Anthropology of the night: Cross-disciplinary investigations', *Current Anthropology*, 51(6): 819–36.

Gibson-Graham, J. K. (2006) *Postcapitalist politics*, Minneapolis, MN: University of Minnesota Press.

Haas, B. (2018) 'Life without evenings: The people left behind by South Korea's war on overwork', *The Guardian*, https://www.theguardian.com/world/2018/aug/14/life-without-evenings-the-people-left-behind-by-south-koreas-war-on-overwork

Harvey, D. (2005) *A brief history of neoliberalism*, Oxford: Oxford University Press.

Heller, K. J. (1996) 'Power, subjectification and resistance in Foucault', *SubStance*, 25: 78–110.

Jeong, J. (2016) 'Hell joseoneui n-po seadaewa noryeokeui jeongeuiron (The giving-up generation and morals of effort in hell Joseon)', *Culture/Science*, 86: 132–154.

Jeong, M. (2019) 'Myeonmilhan geuireona miwaneui (Precise but incomplete),' *Economy and Society*, 121: 323–330.

Johan, H., Um, G. and Chun, J. (2016) *Noohryeokeui baesin (Betrayal of effort)*, Paju, South Korea: Changbi.

Kim, D. (2016) 'Paradox of education fever in Korea: Forming highly educated youth and shifting education paradigm', *Saheosasanggwa Munhwa*, 19: 297–335.

Kim, H. (2009) 'The ethical deconstruction of the incarnated neo-liberalism', *Society and Theory* 14: 173–212.

Kim, H. (2015) 'Survival, survivalism, young generation from the viewpoint of the sociology of the heart', *Korean Journal of Sociology*, 49: 179–212.

Kim, S. and Yoo, S. (2017) 'Jobseekers trapped in civil service exams', *The Korean Times*, https://www.koreatimes.co.kr/www/nation/2017/06/371_230941.html

Koh, E. (2011) 'Rethinking risk society and "self-improvement" in Korea: With a special focus on Foucault's ethics and early East Asian ethics', *Korean Studies Quarterly*, 34: 99–119.

Kraftl, P. and Horton, J. (2008) 'Spaces of every-night life: For geographies of sleep, sleeping and sleepiness', *Progress in Human Geography*, 32(4): 509–524.

Lee, S. (2019) 'The price of a good night's sleep', *The Korean Herald*, http://www.koreaherald.com/view.php?ud=20190628000147

McWhorter, L. (1999) *Bodies and pleasures: Foucault and the politics of sexual normalization*, Bloomington, IN: Indiana University Press.

Melbin, M. (1987) *Night as frontier: Colonizing the world after dark*, New York: The Free Press.

Ni, P. (2016) *Confucius: The man and the way of gongfu*, London: Rowman & Littlefield.

Ock, H. (2015) 'Koreans' changing perceptions on marriage', *The Korean Herald*, http://www.koreaherald.com/view.php?ud=20150327001036%20

OECD (2017) *OECD Employment Outlook*, https://www.oecd-ilibrary.org

Park, N. (2015) '"Hell Joseon": A country where sleepless toil brings no mobility', *Hankyoreh*, http://english.hani.co.kr/arti/english_edition/e_national/711631.html

Rhie, S. and Chae, K. Y. (2018) 'Effects of school time on sleep duration and sleepiness in adolescents', *PLoS One*, 13(9): e0203318, https://doi.org/10.1371/journal.pone.0203318

Seo, J. (2019) *Good sleep, good life*, Seoul: Booksan.

Sharif, H. (2018) 'Suneung: The day silence falls over South Korea', https://www.bbc.com/news/world-asia-46181240

Standing, G. (2011) *The precariat: The new dangerous class*, New York: Bloomsbury.

Statistics Korea. (2017) *Statistics on the youth*, http://www.kostat.go.kr

The Chosunilbo (2012) 'More coffee shops open all night', http://english.chosun.com/site/data/html_dir/2012/09/26/2012092601281.html

Woo, S. and Park, G. (2006) *Pal-sib-pal-man won Seadea*, Seoul: Redian.

5

'Live like a college student': student loan debt and the college experience

Denise Goerisch

Introduction

I sat with Robin State University's director of financial aid the week before final exams in the autumn of 2014.[1] When I asked her what she thought students used their loans for she said, 'You don't want your financial aid recipients to be driving Cadillacs' then mentioned that students use their loans on 'frivolous and excessive' items not related to their education like pizza, alcohol and drugs. This was not the reality I observed at Robin State University (RSU), a small public liberal arts university, in Wisconsin. For two years, I conducted ethnographic fieldwork on the affordability of college with 11 low-to-middle income first year college students; each one of them had student loan debt and not one of them purchased a car, let alone a Cadillac. While many young people experience debt and indebtedness throughout their childhood and adolescence, the university is often seen as a gateway to Americans' experiences with debt, which makes it an imperative site to understanding how Americans feel about and understand debt and indebtedness. However, we cannot limit our understanding of this relationship to the space of the university. Rather, students' relationships with debt are often produced, governed and lived through other key spaces and actors such as federal and state governments, local economies, and the students' families and homes. Through student narratives, I argue that universities are not simply containers for indebted individuals but rather key spaces in which debt becomes embedded in the totality of students' lives in ways that both perpetuate and deviate from neoliberal conceptions of the college experience.

Debt is not seen as occupying one singular space but rather intertwined and embedded in a complex network of spaces and actors (Deville, 2015; Harker and Kirwan, 2019). In the case of student debt, students are both aware and unconscious of these networks and their extent. In this chapter, I explore how assumptions about students' spatial-temporal relationships with debt lead to complexities and complications within these networks, not just for the students but for other actors and spaces as well.

During my time in Wisconsin, I became familiar with a campaign associated with borrowing called, 'Live Like a College Student'. The campaign was to educate students on loans, borrowing and debt. However, the campaign became less about educating students and more about regulating students' spending decisions based upon decades-old assumptions of student life such as subsisting on ramen and living in overcrowded, run-down apartments. This campaign, and those perpetuating it, often lack a complete or accurate perception of student spending. Furthermore, this campaign and other actors, such as college administrators and policymakers, emphasise student loan debt as it relates to the university and do not account for how federal and state governments, local economies and families influence that relationship. In this chapter, I illustrate how inaccurate assumptions regarding students' relationships with debt, not only grossly misaligns with students' lived experiences, but has both short- and long-term consequences for students' academic, economic, and personal realities and futures.

Methods

From 2014 to 2016, I and three other ethnographers conducted research at four public universities in Wisconsin. We each followed the lives of between 11 and 15 low-to-middle income (LMI) first year college students for over a year. At RSU, the 11 students I worked with were largely first-generation college students and Pell grant recipients, a federal needs-based grant, which signifies that most of these students came from low income families. Of those 11 students, seven identified as students of colour, most of which were Hmong, a Southeast Asian ethnic group and seven identified as women (the other four identified as men). Their majors were housed in STEM, Business, Education, Humanities, Social Sciences and Nursing programmes with several students being undeclared their first year.

I conducted numerous in-depth semi-structured interviews, which delved into the students' personal histories, finances and academics. I also spent several days walking alongside students during a typical day (that is, attending class, eating meals, studying and hanging out together) and spent a day with them over the summer to check in and visit with their families. I analysed pertinent documents such as academic transcripts and financial aid award summaries, as well as photographs students took capturing their college experience. These data are presented here as narratives based upon three students' experiences: Brenda, Lily and Kyle. These students were selected to highlight the inequalities and obstacles that many young people face when encountering debt. Other students at RSU and across the larger ethnographic study had similar experiences, which demonstrates how commonplace and normalised indebtedness and these complexities have become in American society. While there are similarities across the narratives, each narrative does demonstrate varying spatial-temporal networks of debt and indebtedness and how these configurations impact their academics, personal wellbeing and futures.

Additionally, I, along with my co-researchers, interviewed other students, faculty, staff and administrators across the universities. These interviews were to contextualise the histories and present realities at each university. These interviews also helped us identify key perceived issues at each university surrounding college affordability and socio-economic inequalities such as racial and gender violence. I also spent time observing 'public spaces' at RSU, which included eating at the student union, hanging out in the library, and attending events, lectures and town halls. I took photographs as a recall mechanism as well as to visualise college affordability.

Geographies of student debt

As of 2019, Americans owe nearly $1.56 trillion in student loan debt spread out among approximately 45 million borrowers, with the average accumulated student loan debt from both public (federal government-sponsored) and private (bank-sponsored) loans being $33,460 ('U.S. Student Loan Debt Statistics for 2019,' n.d.). Over the last 15 years, student debt has grown larger as the cost of tuition and fees, cost of living, and other educational expenses continue to rise with yearly increases ranging from 40% to 56% (Baum, 2016). While the response by federal and state governments and universities and colleges is to provide more student aid, students are still being forced and encouraged to take out loans, not only due to the mounting costs but also because household incomes have not increased at the same rates (Baum, 2016). Rather, rates of poverty have increased, making borrowing the only option for students if they want to get by in college (Goldrick-Rab, 2016). Due to the neoliberalisation of education, there has been a national de-investment of public higher education, which has resulted in massive budget cuts and lay-offs, which have profoundly impacted the ways in which students receive aid and support (Goldrick-Rab, 2016).

To receive aid, students must apply for the Free Application for Federal Student Aid, most commonly known as the FAFSA. Through the FAFSA, students can receive grants, scholarships, work-study (wherein a student is paid a stipend to work on campus) and federal loans. The amount of needs-based aid awarded is determined largely by their family's income, also referred to as the Estimated Family Contribution (EFC) (Goldrick-Rab, 2016). The EFC is an estimate of how much a family can afford to pay for their child's college education. Most of the students in the study had incredibly low EFCs, with many of those having an EFC of $0. While the FAFSA is able to assess a family's financial strengths, it does not account for their financial liabilities such as mortgages, auto loans, credit cards and medical debt (Goldrick-Rab, 2016). This information could permit a much more accurate representation of a family's ability and capacity to contribute towards their child's college education. Thus, it is important when spatialising student loan debt to understand the relationality of it through a variety of spaces, including the home and local economies.

Much of the scholarship surrounding debt focuses on two key perspectives: social and economic phenomena and the temporality of debt. These approaches emphasise the socio-economic inequalities that permeate debt structures and present consumption bought with future labour (Harker, 2017). Harker and Kirwan (2019) argue that a geographic approach to debt is needed to better understand the effects of debt on or in space(s), in terms of mobilities, boundaries, places or distributions. By conceiving debt as a topological bind, it exposes the multifaceted, nuanced, and troubling ways in which debt is entangled in our everyday lives (Harker, 2017). As such, there is currently little discussion on the ways in which space constructs, modifies, maintains, and/or undermines debt and indebtedness (Harker and Kirwan, 2019). Indeed, there are a variety of spaces in which student debt can be resisted or undercut, but due to overwhelming assumptions about students' relationship with debt, this is often not the case, leaving it to the debtor and not others to challenge the systems in which debt occupies and transcends.

Spatialising student debt is essential for two key reasons. First, student debt is often discussed within the context of large-scale quantitative research (Hillman, 2015), which excludes the everydayness of debt and indebtedness of students (Horton, 2017). Second, policymakers and university administrators make inaccurate assumptions based upon neoliberal ideals regarding the spatialisation of student loan debt, which deeply impacts students in astounding, unforeseen ways. Many policymakers and universities see student loan debt as a temporal issue rather than as a spatial issue, most illustrated through the 'Live like a College Student' campaign, which fixes student loan debt to particular spaces and times within the university and in the future economy. This campaign has extended though to beyond the space and time of college to reflect, perhaps, a more pessimistic perspective of students' relationship with debt. During my first semester at RSU, I attended an alumni event, which featured alumni from the financial sector. Each gave advice on how to find internships and employment, set goals, and to think about their futures. An older alumnus, who worked for a student loan managing company, offered this piece of advice, 'Live like a college student now and later.' He elaborated that with the increases in student loan debt it will take more time to pay off loans and that students should live frugally. While well-intentioned, this advice is loaded in assumptions of students' agency in how they should and can live, as well as should and can spend their financial aid awards, including loans, which is often rooted in racialised, gendered and classed discourses surrounding debt.

These assumptions, which are not based upon students' realities, influence institutional policy and the university's relationship to students (as well as with faculty and staff), which is particularly damaging to LMI students. Through three student narratives, I demonstrate the complexities of student loan debt networks and that student loan debt does not exist solely within the time and place of the university.

Brenda

Before coming to college, Brenda grew up in an industrial city in Wisconsin. Her parents, who identify as Hmong, immigrated from Southeast Asia in the 1980s due to the poor living conditions at the refugee camps and to provide more opportunities for their children. Being the middle child of seven, Brenda shared everything with her siblings, which frustrated her as she craved more independence and privacy. Brenda was an average high school student. In addition to her traditional high school classes, she took several Advanced Placement courses where she earned college credit. She picked RSU, not because it was a good school, but because her sister and boyfriend would be there. As she knew she would be taking out loans, Brenda worked at a local fast food restaurant for two years to save money for college. She did not particularly like working there but it was the only place in her hometown that would hire teenagers.

While Brenda passed all her classes in her first year at RSU, she was not interested in the course content and often found herself procrastinating. Her boyfriend would often encourage her to do her homework but that was not enough. While she was active in the Hmong Student Association, she did not socialise much with others beyond her boyfriend and his friends. In Spring 2015, Brenda discovered that her parents were victims of identity theft. This negatively impacted her financial aid status as she was selected for verification. Since the verification process can take months to resolve, she was unsure if she would have enough money for the following year to attend school. She worked at two jobs: one at a local fast food restaurant and another as a campus custodian in order to save up enough money to afford tuition. Working both these jobs negatively impacted her academics as she was often too tired to complete her homework or study for exams.

During the summer, Brenda stayed in Robin City in order to make more money. She could not afford to live off-campus with friends, so she moved in with her boyfriend, which she kept secret from her parents. Brenda decided to quit her job at the fast food restaurant and find other work. She continued to work as a custodian, but due to state-wide budget cuts, Brenda was laid off. As her parents spoke and read limited English, Brenda spent the summer trying to resolve her issues with financial aid, which involved countless phone calls with the Internal Revenue Service and Department of Education, both federal agencies.

When autumn came, Brenda was left without financial aid. She found herself often stressed out by not being able to pay for college, which had a negative impact on her studies. She found work as a night attendant at a convalescent home to cover basic living expenses and make small payments toward tuition. The long hours and lack of sleep prevented her from doing well in her classes. During this time, Brenda reached out to the Office of Financial Aid for emergency aid and for strategies to prevent this from happening in the future, including possibly filing as an independent. Filing as an independent would mean that she would no longer need her parents' financial information to be awarded financial aid. Her sister was able to file as an independent but Brenda was denied because she did not meet the criteria, despite RSU's ability to be discretionary in how it defines that criteria. She was too scared to ask about emergency aid, which the office staff failed to mention. In December, she was finally awarded financial aid, mostly in the form of loans as all the grants and scholarships had been awarded to others by that point. She decided to quit her job and finally pay her tuition with her loans. She hoped that she could recover from her poor academic performance by doing well on her final exams. By the end of her second year, Brenda took out over $15,000 in federal loans. She began to seriously question whether college was worth it.

Brenda's experience highlights the power and social inequalities that emerge across spaces of debt, which are often not recognised in public discourses surrounding student loan debt. Student debt, like other forms of debt, is often conceived as an exclusive relationship between the debtor (the student) and the creditor (the US government) or their representatives (the university). Like Brenda, many debtors feel that their relationship to their debt is manipulated, fuelled and mitigated by the creditor or representatives of the creditor, which makes them feel disempowered and at the mercy of others (Harker and Kirwan, 2019). While the amount of aid is determined by the federal and state governments, the university, particularly financial aid offices, have the power to decide who should receive aid and how it is disseminated, which makes Brenda's case acutely frustrating.

As we see with Brenda and with the other students featured in this chapter, the financial aid office takes a significant role in facilitating and dictating students' debt. In his research on debt advisors, Kirwan (2019) argues that while debt advisors are there to provide assistance and support, they do to a certain extent have the ability to control and contain debtors or keep them 'still'. In a similar vein, financial aid offices keep students 'still' and in place. By not allowing Brenda the opportunity to apply for independent status, which would relieve her dependency on her parents' tax information, they are ensuring that Brenda will be 'stuck', which would not only mean that she would more than likely be going through this process next year but also increasing the likelihood of being dependent on loans.

Financial aid processes are purposely developed to make it incredibly difficult for low-income, first generation college students, like Brenda, to receive aid. Two other students in the study went through the verification process. Verification is an auditing process to confirm the data presented in the FAFSA is accurate (FinAid, n.d.). Participants are randomly selected; however, Pell grant recipients with an EFC of $0 are 70% more likely to be selected for verification as are women and students of colour (Cochrane, 2010). As demonstrated through Brenda's experience, verification slows down the process towards receiving federal, state and institutional aid, which often results in dire consequences for economically precarious students such as dropping classes, working multiple jobs, or jeopardising future eligibility for financial aid (Ahlman et al, 2016; Cochrane, 2010). Brenda spent an absurd amount of time trying to receive her aid; time and energy that could have been dedicated towards her academics or earning income. The verification process is incredibly convoluted and difficult to navigate and more often than not, forms often get misplaced or lost (Ahlman et al, 2016).

Much of the current geographic literature emphasises the ways in which space controls, regulates and exacerbates debt and indebtedness. However, there is a need to recognise and acknowledge the power in which spaces can engender, enable, destabilise and challenge debt and indebtedness (Harker and Kirwan, 2019). With the amount of individual authority financial offices have, they have the ability to empower and advocate for vulnerable students like Brenda. Yet, many financial aid offices, including RSU, have a narrow perception of what it means to 'live like a college student' and who is deserving of support and guidance. In doing so, financial aid offices potentially do more to perpetuate cycles of indebtedness, which counters their overarching mission to support students as they finance their college education.

Lily

Lily, a white first-generation college student, was always interested in the medical field. Growing up on a dairy farm in rural Wisconsin, she wanted to become a veterinarian. Lily was responsible for taking care of the animals and would show her animals at local competitions. As she knew her family had a significant amount of debt due to declines in the agricultural industry in the Midwest, Lily sold off her pigs to earn money for college (see Figure 5.1). As she grew older, she realised that she would rather work with people than animals and sought to become a nurse. She selected RSU because it was relatively close to home and enabled her to go home at the weekends to work as an emergency medical technician, homecare provider for a young man with cerebral palsy, and group home attendant. She put most of her earnings in a safety deposit box so that she would not be tempted to spend it. Her father would occasionally take some of her money to help pay bills but replaced the money as soon as he could. Despite all her savings, Lily still had to take out a significant amount in federal loans to attend RSU.

To accomplish her goal of getting into the nursing programme, Lily had to maintain a high grade point average (GPA), take course pre-requisites, and demonstrate in an essay why she would be a good fit for the programme. She had a high GPA and had done well in many of her difficult classes such as Chemistry and Biology. The RSU nursing programme is incredibly competitive. Every year, the programme has

Figure 5.1: Lily auctioned her pigs at the county fair to help pay for college and reduce her loan debt (photographed by the author)

nearly 200 applicants with a 25% acceptance rate. RSU also offered an offsite programme in a small town three hours away, where Lily's older sister lives, providing her with a way to save on living expenses. Due to being offsite and far from any major city, this programme had a higher acceptance rate of 40%, which gave Lily more hope.

During the summer, Lily received her acceptance letter to the offsite nursing programme. She was beyond ecstatic! She then received her financial aid award letter for the coming academic year. She was only going to receive $7,000 in federal loans, which would cover less than half of expected costs (including tuition, fees, housing and so on). She was devastated, but being the resourceful young person she was, Lily got on the phone to RSU's financial aid office to figure out why she received so little. Lily's EFC had increased over the past year because her father sold off the majority of his cattle in order to pay down a $600,000 debt to the local farm bureau. While his income from the sale of the cattle was reported on the FAFSA, his debts and immediate use of the new 'income' were not. Lily petitioned for RSU's financial aid office to review her case and her father drove out to the campus to provide the necessary documentation to prove his indebtedness. Lily's financial aid award was revised and she was able to pay for most of her expenses that year. She still had to take out loans but it was significantly less than initially awarded. Upon returning to RSU in the autumn, Lily felt more secure and was able to focus on her academics. Given the demands for nurses in Wisconsin, Lily was confident that she would be able to pay her debts off quickly so that she could buy a farm and start a family.

While the federal government and university both played equally similar roles in terms of Lily's relationship to debt, rurality and national economic policies held greater significance. Poverty and debt remain largely invisible within the physical, political and sociocultural rural landscape (Milbourne, 2016). Rurality and student indebtedness is widely underrepresented (for an exception see Goldrick-Rab, 2016) with much of the existing literature on student debt and rural spaces focusing on student migrations to rural spaces and the subsequent impacts (Royston et al, 2012). Rural students often have economic and educational barriers that differ from their non-rural peers. These barriers include lower family income and parental education, fewer educational resources, less academically rigorous courses, lower academic achievement and post-secondary aspirations and lower college attendance and completion rates (Means et al, 2016).

Given the rapidly changing size of American farms, alongside the utilisation of new agricultural technologies and practices and an increasing dependency on government subsidies, farmers have become reliant on debt (Brewer and Featherstone, 2017). After years of growth in the agricultural sector, farmers' incomes dropped dramatically beginning in 2014 due to declines in commodity revenue (Patrick et al, 2016). In the case of dairy farmers, there have been increasing trends to have fewer, larger herds resulting in only a few dairies providing the nation's milk supply (Christopher et al, 2016), essentially pushing out the small farmer. It is no surprise then that farmers like Lily's father go into debt and also no surprise how they begin to pay off that debt. The FAFSA does not account for a family's debt, which results in overestimating the EFC, less aid overall, and more reliance on loans for rural students, thus creating new indebted rural landscapes in the US.

Students' futures and indebtedness is tied to economic spaces such as employment and further education. Many of the students discussed in this chapter, excluding Lily, wanted to go into careers that Wisconsin no longer valued given recent economic and political shifts. Students, who wanted to become educators, especially were keen to move out of Wisconsin due to then Governor Scott Walker's anti-union policies and lack of support for public education in general (Timeline, 2011). While the cost of living is higher in neighbouring states, such as Minnesota, many students believed that they would be paid a higher wage there due to their perception of the state having a more stable economy and job growth. With more young people leaving Wisconsin and other Midwest states, students, like Lily, see this as an opportunity. Even though she will probably receive lower pay, she knows that there is a nursing shortage in the state and that she will be able to find a job to begin paying off her debt. However, it should be noted that Lily's aspirations actually perpetuate neoliberal and gendered assumptions of how students live and plan for their futures: get a job, pay off loans, and start a family.

Lily's experiences highlight the intertwined connection between not only the debtor and creditor but how national and local policy and economies deeply impact that relationship in ways that are often unaccounted for. Her experience also demonstrates perhaps one of the most egregious flaws with the FAFSA, as the FAFSA does not account for the wider family context, especially in regards to debt and family expenses. Furthermore, her experiences emphasise the influence rurality has on that relationship. While Lily is unique in some regards, her relationship with debt speaks to how commonplace her experiences are and how those experiences can potentially impact the futures of local and national policy and economies often rooted in neoliberalism.

Kyle

Kyle's life before coming to RSU was unstable. Kyle's parents were alcoholics and had a violent relationship. When his parents separated, Kyle, his mother and his younger brother moved into a domestic violence shelter. For Kyle and his family, this was a very stressful time filled with anxiety and depression. Despite all the hardships in his life, Kyle was a good student and great musician. He learned to play several instruments on his own including drums, guitar, bass, piano, ukulele and banjo. Music had always come naturally to him, which led him to aspire to a career in music. He decided to go to RSU because the institution had one of the best music programmes in the state. He auditioned to be in the music programme but fell short as he was never classically trained. Not being accepted into the programme derailed Kyle. He had trouble sleeping, he didn't make many friends, and he procrastinated on much of his schoolwork, which led him to receiving a low GPA during his first year. He believed his sleeplessness was also caused by worrying about his finances, including his loans, which only exacerbated his anxiety and depression.

About halfway through his second semester of college, Kyle stopped attending classes. He decided that since he was still having issues with his mental health and wanted to pursue a career in the music industry that it would be best for him to drop out. He stayed at RSU during the spring semester because he enjoyed his work as a technician for campus events. Kyle's attendance caught the attention of the Dean's Office. He spoke to them about what he wanted to do and the representative from the Dean's Office was very understanding, genuine and supportive; Kyle felt that he was not the first student to leave RSU. The Dean did caution Kyle about his financial aid status and encouraged him to go to one class so that he wouldn't have to return his financial aid money. He knew he would have to start paying back his loans once the semester ended and that it would be difficult especially if he didn't have a decent paying job.

During the summer, Kyle pieced together an income through some paid music gigs between his hometown and Robin City doing audio/visual work for local bars and clubs. Kyle worked for several bands and rappers throughout the state. Sometimes he did stage work, at other times he performed as a drummer. Additionally, Kyle created music, which he uploaded to YouTube, earning him a few hundred dollars every couple of months. Kyle received a bill for $2,500 from RSU because he failed all his classes. Kyle was frustrated as he didn't expect to pay back that much. Since he did not have a stable income during the summer, he was worried about paying back that amount of money in such a short amount of time. Following the summer, Kyle moved back home and his depression returned. The music gigs dried up and the only income he received was from his YouTube channel. Kyle felt that being in a regular 9–5 job would only exacerbate his depression due to the monotony. Kyle wished that he had never attended college as the only thing he got out of college was 'over $6,500 of debt and a mental illness'.

As relationships with debt change and evolve within different spatial-temporal contexts, our emotional and affective responses to debt evolve and change as well. Emotional and affective responses have become a space for much needed discussion around the relationship between debt and the body as they highlight the everydayness and the visceralities of indebtedness (Deville and Seigworth, 2015). In his work on young people and debt, Horton (2017) argues that young people feel the emotional and physical weight of debt and those emotions impact their experiences in the present. Most of the work surrounding young people and debt emphasises the potential future outcomes rather than present realities, which speaks to how debt is often conceived of and justified as a means to an aspirational future of upward mobility (Horton, 2017). For many young people, debt has become normalised as an expectation that one must 'get on with' (Horton, 2017). Many college students envision their futures as tied to their indebtedness and they generally fear being able to hit significant life milestones (Xu et al, 2015).

Kyle's narrative highlights the precariousness of the gig economy and its potential impact on student loan debt as well as student wellbeing. Since most student employment is characterised by low wages, students have become more creative when it comes to financing their college degree and potentially reducing their loan debt. Over the past decade, more Americans are participating in the informal, creative and gig economies to make ends meet (Carter, 2018). While this may mean a way to lessen the burden of loan debt, this type of work and revenue streams are often precarious, especially for young people (MacDonald and Giazitzoglu, 2019). Kyle acknowledged this precariousness but for him, it was the only space that allowed him to gain the work experience needed to pursue a career in music, as he felt that RSU had failed him. The gig economy can enable students to pursue pathways that are obstructed within the space of the university. Despite the benefits for his emotional and mental wellbeing and gaining valuable work experience, the precariousness of gig economy labour can deeply negatively impact students' relationships with debt.

Unlike Lily, Kyle (and to some extent, Brenda) very much lives in the present with regards to his debt, which offers a counternarrative to dominant discourse on students' futures and aspirations and how that relates to debt and indebtedness. Debt is very much a part of his present rather than his future, that he is constantly worrying and stressing over. Due to this, Kyle is unable to keep a job, which would potentially help him get out of debt. For Kyle, given his mental health status, he does not have the luxury of thinking about a future life of indebtedness, which is counter to the dominant narrative of student debt being a future issue but rather than a lived experience in the present.

Conclusion

Before stepping foot in the space of the college campus, Kyle, Brenda and Lily were already 'living like college students' as they were already indebted subjects, a reality often ignored by institutions allocating aid, including federal loans. For many students, their indebtedness was not a choice but an outcome due to their families' relationships with debt and indebtedness and how that debt is managed and regulated by institutional forces. As much of the public discourse on student debt and time focuses on students' futures, emphasising their roles as future workers and consumers (Ross, 2013), this ignores students' present realities and histories as indebted subjects as well as them currently being workers and consumers.

Students, like Lily, may be resourceful and find ways to alleviate some of their debt burden, however, many students are at the mercy of universities and government agencies as they cannot turn to their families for support. This dependency on universities and government agencies forces students into a relationship that often takes time and energy away from their studies or earning an income as they have to plead and negotiate for aid, which negatively impacts their physical, emotional, mental and intellectual wellbeing. In doing so, students often do not have the capacity to recover when they experience crisis.

There is a need to (re)conceptualise the spaces of student debt beyond college campuses. Universities do not exist in vacuums, rather they are a part of an elaborate network of actors and spaces that operate both in relation and opposition to one another as demonstrated through these three student narratives. If there is to be significant change, particularly policy change, made to student loan structures and schemes, it will most likely happen at the institutional level. Universities, particularly financial aid offices, while undeniably tied to other spaces, have autonomy when it comes to not only how they allocate aid but how they provide support for precarious students.

Note

[1]   Pseudonyms have been used for people and institutions to protect confidentiality.

References

Ahlman, L., Cochrane, D. and Thompson, J. (2016) *On the sidelines of simplification: Stories of navigating the FAFSA verification process*, https://ticas.org/sites/default/files/pub_files/on_the_sidelines_of_simplification.pdf

Baum, S. (2016) *Student debt: Rhetoric and realities of higher education*, New York: Palgrave Macmillan.

Brewer, B. and Featherstone, A. M. (2017) 'Agency cost of debt: evidence from Kansas farm operations', *Agricultural Finance Review*, 77(1): 111–124.

Carter, C. M. (2018) 'How new college students are earning money in the gig economy', https://www.forbes.com/sites/christinecarter/2018/09/06/how-new-college-students-are-earning-money-in-the-gig-economy/

Christopher, A. W., Stephenson, M. W., Knoblauch, W. A. and Novakovic, A. M. (2016) 'Dairy farm financial performance: Firm, year, and size effects', *Agricultural Finance Review*, 76(4), 532–543.

Cochrane, D. F. (2010) 'After the FAFSA: How red tape can prevent eligible students from receiving financial aid', https://ticas.org/sites/default/files/pub_files/AfterFAFSA.pdf

Deville, J. (2015) *Lived economies of default: Consumer credit, debt collection and the capture of affect*, London: Routledge.

Deville, J. and Seigworth, G. J. (2015) 'Everyday debt and credit', *Cultural Studies*, 29(5–6): 615–629.

FinAid (n.d.) *FAFSA – Verification*, http://www.finaid.org/fafsa/verification.phtml

Goldrick-Rab, S. (2016) *Paying the price: College costs, financial aid, and the betrayal of the American Dream*, Chicago, IL: University of Chicago Press.

Harker, C. (2017) 'Debt space: Topologies, ecologies and Ramallah, Palestine', Environment and Planning D, 35(4): 600–619.

Harker, C. and Kirwan, S. (2019) 'Introduction: Geographies of debt and indebtedness', *Geoforum*, 100: 236–238.

Hillman, N. W. (2015) 'Borrowing and repaying student loans', *Journal of Student Financial Aid*, 45(3): 35–48.

Horton, J. (2017) 'Young people and debt: Getting on with austerities', *Area*, 49(3): 280–287.

Kirwan, S. (2019) 'On "those who shout the loudest": Debt advice and the work of disrupting attachments', *Geoforum*, 98: 318–326.

MacDonald, R. and Giazitzoglu, A. (2019) 'Youth, enterprise and precarity: Or, what is, and what is wrong with, the "gig economy"?', *Journal of Sociology,* 55(4): 724-740. .

Means, D. R., Clayton, A. B., Conzelmann, J. G., Baynes, P. and Umbach, P. D. (2016) 'Bounded aspirations: Rural, African-American high school students and college access', *Review of Higher Education*, 39(4): 543–569.

Milbourne, P. (2016) 'Poverty and welfare in rural places', in: M. Shucksmith and D. L. Brown (eds) *Routledge international handbook of rural studies*, London: Routledge, pp.450–461.

Patrick, K., Kuhns, R. and Borchers, A. (2016) 'Recent trends in U.S. farm income, wealth, and financial health', *Choices*, 31(1): 1–8.

Ross, A. (2013) 'Mortgaging the future: Student debt in the age of austerity', *New Labor Forum*, 22(1): 23–28.

Royston, P., Mathieson, K., Leafman, J. and Ojan-Sheehan, O. (2012) 'Medical student characteristics predictive of intent for rural practice', *Rural and Remote Health*, 12. 1–11.

Timeline (2011) 'Scott Walker's 2011 battle over union rights', https://madison.com/wsj/news/local/govt-and-politics/timeline-scott-walker-s-battle-over-union-rights/html_ad5218a0-17ed-5d5e-8937-ed2fca459f54.html

U.S. Student Loan Debt Statistics for 2019 (n.d.) https://studentloanhero.com/student-loan-debt-statistics/

Xu, Y., Johnson, C., Bartholomae, S., O'Neill, B. and Gutter, M. S. (2015) 'Home-ownership among millennials: The deferred American dream?', *Family and Consumer Sciences Research Journal*, 44(2): 201–212.

6

'Everywhere feels like home': transnational neoliberal subjects negotiating the future

Michael Boampong

Introduction

The neoliberal household

In the last four decades, globalised capitalism and the drive towards neoliberalism which was associated with the Thatcher and Reagan governments of the UK and US respectively has become a major research area for understanding households and the political economy. The gradual demise of social welfare in the face of neoliberalism has reconfigured the household to take on the burden of caring for itself, thereby increasing insecurity, reducing leisure time, and constituting greater reliance on global capitalism's commodified and privatised services for care work and childhood.

The 'neoliberal household' that has to bear the cost of household reproduction therefore encouraged all household members to work outside domestic settings and bring back wages in order to reduce the burden or cost of social reproduction on a few people. Working outside the home could imply migration. In most cases, movements have intensified middle-class lifestyles in developing countries, including dependence on other people, especially the poor and working class, for care work. Similarly, such burdens also often fall on women or are redistributed among younger people, especially girls. The relationship between globalised capitalist production and migration has also been an important area of inquiry in transnational migration studies. Geographers and sociologists examining labour migration effects of globalised capitalist production have emphasised unpaid domestic labour and exploitation as its hallmarks (Katz, 2001; Parreñas, 2001). Moreover, neoliberal reforms impact on childhoods and social reproduction processes across geographic scales are analysed in the work of Katz (2004) and Waters (2012). Scholars who focus on migrant parent and child relationships, including notions of 'mothering from a distance' have focused extensively on how relationships are maintained across borders to avoid family breakdown. In essence there is a representation of an adult migrant worker and the child who expresses emotional affective connection with the parent abroad (Hondagneu-Sotelo and Avila, 1997; Parreñas, 2005) and how it was mostly mothers who maintained contact with their children through letters and phone calls.

Work on how neoliberalism has shaped migration at global scales and intensified inequalities for migrant workers has been important, but it also effectively shifts attention away from children of migrants in advanced countries who have come of age and may draw on the cultural capital of the neoliberal household for economic capital accumulation.

In this chapter, I address this gap by focusing on the working lives of British-Ghanaian young adults to explore their transitions into work amid both economic opportunities and constraints. The chapter shows that in addition to local factors, migration trajectories for work are influenced by neoliberal globalisation and economic processes. Neoliberal globalisation is linked to 'deregulation, the growth of transnational corporations, the competition for skilled labour, growing income inequality and the opening of emerging economies [that] are introducing new risks, opportunities and networks' (Goldin and Reinert, 2012: 160). Notably, a sub-sample of my research respondents in the UK were young people whose working lives are characterised by experiences of being a global risk-bearing subject, that leverages social networks and uneven development (economic opportunities and constraints) from different places and with diverse people for capital accumulation (Katz, 2004). Thus, in pursuing their life goals, the young people live 'more as a citizen of a non-bounded society (one shaped by extraterritorial social, economic and cultural forces) than as a citizen of a bounded territorial state' (Nevins, 2002: 180).

I trace the conceptual linkages between young people's social reproduction and their neoliberal subjectivities to their parent's historical youth migration experiences (including paid and unpaid work) and present working conditions to offer an understanding of contemporary neoliberalism. Scholars have indicated the need to 'look at the nuances of global migrations, the breaks and disruptions but also the continuities of daily life' (Boehm et al, 2011: 6). Thus, this chapter briefly explores the employment trajectories of the parents of the British-Ghanaian youth in this study, many of whom moved to the UK between the late 1980s and 1990s. It then turns to explore the working experiences of the children of these migrant parents who have come of age in the UK.

Methods

This chapter is based on a sub-sample of a multi-sited ethnographic study carried out with 95 people (33 children, 22 young people and 40 adults) between March 2016 to April 2017. Qualitative methods, including repeated semi-structured interviews, observations and group discussions, as well as visual methods, were used in data gathering. To understand the working lives of young people as they transition from childhood into adulthood, in-depth interviews and observations were conducted with one child (10–13 years,) three young people (20–24 years), five young adults (25–35 years) and three adults (aged 50+) in London. Participants were recruited through snowball sampling and, by this, friends and acquaintances in London were useful introductions to potential interviewees.

Additionally, Simultaneous Matched Sample method (SMS) was utilised to link London-based respondents with people with whom they maintained some form of transnational practices who were living in Ghana (Mazzucato, 2016). Consequently, in Ghana, one young woman (aged 20–24) consented to be interviewed after her cousin in London referred her to me. While all 13 people's experiences will be used in my analysis, I will draw on the situation of four people (three of them based in south-east London in the UK and one in Accra, Ghana) to exemplify the neoliberal subject's social space. Analysis will also be done in relation to parents' or adults' historical accounts. Primarily, the sample of young adults' childhoods were bi-transnational (between Ghana and UK) shaped by family return visits to Ghana; I will argue that their youth and young adulthood is characterised by 'going global', involving circular migration practices and embeddedness in multinational social spaces (Castles, 2010: 1566).

Research interviews were conducted in either Twi or English depending on each participant's preference and language competence. Interestingly, patterns of language competence differences appeared during my conversations: all second-generation immigrant youth interacted with me in English. However, those who had stayed in Ghana for more than six months often responded with Twi and English. Pseudonyms have been used to anonymise and protect the identity of interviewees.

Historical context: migration for a better life?

Kwesi, who is now in his 50s, came to the UK in his late 20s after graduating with an Information and Communication Technology (ICT) degree from Kwame Nkrumah University of Science and Technology (KNUST). His goal of moving to the UK to find 'office work' or work that does not require lots of energy or force, 'with good pay, save some and send some money home' is very typical of how most young Ghanaians perceive the purpose or benefit of labour migration. To his dismay, he could only secure a cleaning offer working 48 hours weekly after a referral by a friend who was also working for the shop. In fact prior to leaving Ghana he informed his friend about the need for a job. As noted by Kelly and Lusis (2006: 841–842), most migrants' social capital is often activated from the origin country rather than on arrival. However, his weekly salary was insufficient to cater for accommodation and food costs. Thus, an extra job with 20 hours of work was taken at a location that was 2 hours on a bus from his first job. The second job enabled him to save some money to send back to Ghana, as noted here: "It was my eldest sister who supported me through a connection to come to the UK. She paid for my flight, visa and gave me some pocket money as well so I needed to work hard to pay her back and move on."

At certain times, however, the long working hours (at least 10 hours a day) meant that he regretted leaving Ghana as he felt that he would not have done a "cleaning job as a graduate in Ghana". Moreover, there were instances of unpaid 'overtime' or working additional hours as well as delayed payments: "The first cleaning job was … cash-in-hand pay … This Jamaican guy who was my supervisor and I had worked for three weeks and the guy did not want to pay me. However, I had to force him to pay me."

While he has not been a victim of racial discrimination, after 30 years of living in the UK, he perceives that barriers to securing jobs or career progression affects certain black people:

> 'Some people here are racist. Some English people if they do not like you, then they do not like you. Even though you could have an opportunity here, there is a limit you can go if you are an immigrant. With the recent flow of immigrants from other Eastern European countries, the amount of opportunities for blacks has reduced. Most employers or whites prefer their people.'

One day, Kwesi invited me to a hometown association meeting in South London, where he introduced me to one of his friends, Clara from Kumasi. Clara is also in her early 50s. She first came to the UK in her teenage years to visit her father, who was studying in London. Later her family relocated to Ghana, but she moved to the UK in her 20s. Before coming to the UK, she had broken up her relationship with her fiancé who promised to marry her after his graduation from medical school. Clara now regrets deciding to break up with him because of her migration intention. However, she feels her decision was also informed by poor communication options before the year 2000 (Manuh, 2001):

> 'You know those days; the internet was not easily accessible on the phone as we have today ... I remember my relatives abroad by then will record messages on cassette tape and post it. It will take weeks for you to receive and you reply in the same way, and it takes another time ... all the suspense if there is an emergency. Same with letters ... and calls you have to go and wait at the communication centre hours for a call. Today is different; with WhatsApp which is cheaper and instant.'

Her first job in the UK was for 30 hours per week as a security guard. She also did a second job in a famous food service company in London to be able to "survive the cost of living in London":

> 'I remember those days; I will finish my first job and then quickly rush home and change into the working uniform for the second job. One day I was working over there and my friends whom I knew in Ghana came there and they were like, Clara is that you? They were shocked because my Dad is a lawyer in Ghana, and we were well to do. I could have stayed with my sister and avoided all that hustle, but at the same time, I wanted to be independent – have my own house and money to spend.'

Her friends being 'shocked', reflects the perhaps unexpected displacement in migrants' economic and social status as they move to places with uncertainty (Punch, 2012). Later on, she decided to take on a caregiving job outside London which involved much logistical and emotional effort:

> 'Always I was going for work I had to get some Ghanaian food, like Yam and Kenkey and other things like Shea

butter, Maggi and Milo. I will also fry some fish and chicken to take along. It was a long commute. Sometimes when I get there, even to get a taxi is exhausting. I was often scared when I was going [or] coming back alone at night. Sometimes the person who will come and replace me will not come early and I had to spend extra time that was not paid for.'

Both Clara and Kwesi are now UK citizens. Kwesi is currently an ICT consultant after completing a master's degree in the UK. He owns a house and is married to Louisa, an Ashanti woman in her 40s and they have two children. Clara also has a bachelor's degree in social policy and works for a council and takes care of her two children as a single parent.

Clara and Kwesi illustrate the social reproduction experiences of young people as they move with the hope of getting a job that matches their skills. For most young migrants, despite their existing social network of relations that may offer insights for job searches, only low-skilled jobs may be available. This contributes to their deskilling as they were unable to utilise their skills in another country. Interviews revealed that while most Ghanaian migrants were working as skilled personnel in the health sector, ICT and teaching in Ghana, they ended up in cleaning, customer assistant, personal homecare assistant and security guard jobs in the UK. Moreover, some jobs were irregular and sub-contracted with salary uncertainties and delays from agencies or agents (Manuh, 2001). As many of these jobs are socio-spatially isolated, non-unionised and outside contemporary labour laws, workers are often left powerless or with insufficient income to meet their reproductive needs. However, as recent migrants and transnational youth returning to Ghana immediately or declining job offers was not an option because of existing social contracts to send remittances or repay the money to relations who supported travel arrangements or fulfil family obligations of helping younger siblings in Ghana.

Moreover, migration for work or education is considered beneficial in the Ghanaian cultural context. Thus left-behind relations do not easily concur with return decisions. Accordingly, working extra hours (overtime) or multiple jobs at different locations to earn an income or sharing accommodation to reduce the cost of living were some of the coping strategies that enabled young migrants to 'survive' in the UK.

The inaccessibility of skilled work with better pay also resulted in delays in remittances with consequential effects on social reproduction arrangements. For some respondents family tensions were experienced with left-behind family relations who are often unaware of the challenges of integration in the UK job market or "the high cost of remittances which often eats into the amount sent to Ghana", as Kwesi noted. Thus, from a transnational perspective, inadequate income, unpaid work or delayed pay has effects on social reproduction translocally or across geographic scales or borders and also indicates a spatial and temporal relation between productive and reproductive spheres of life. Concerns regarding rising remittance costs have resulted in informal channels of sending money to relations. When I was going to Ghana for my fieldwork, some respondents, mostly working-class families, gave me money to take to their relations in Ghana. Furthermore, for certain respondents, the lack of recognition and devaluation of their academic qualification and the skills mismatch 'forced' them to acquire similarly or higher qualifications in the UK. This delayed young people's capital accumulation goals thereby affecting their social status or a transition into adulthood as money has become a key marker of other symbols of adulthood. The poor labour market integration experiences challenge the easily held assumption in most migration-development migration discourse by international development organisations/agencies which suggest social and economic upward mobility when people have the opportunity to migrate. Moreover, the fact that institutional cultural capital (for example, an academic degree certificate) is devalued upon arrival suggests a contradiction between it being a visa requirement and yet being less useful than migrants' expectations. That being said, institutional capital can have the 'use value' based on alumni networks with the potential of sharing employment information as noted in Kwesi's experience.

Although in the 1990s labour market integration challenges existed, it is also clear that within the past decade Britain's gig economy has become one of the leading employment avenues for immigrants who are employed in low skilled poorly-paid, long working hours, insecure jobs including zero-hour contract jobs. Reports of the implications of contemporary working models were noted. For instance, Ivan (36+ adult, London), a father of four girls, noted: "With this job, sometimes I go to work not even knowing whether I will get the hours I want in a day … it is such that you do not even know what you will earn in a week or month … meanwhile, you have bills and children to take care of."

Instead of having policies that promote comparability of qualifications, the devaluing of the qualifications of migrants has enabled a supply and demand environment for low-paid work and further perpetuates master–servant relations (Parreñas, 2001; Hochschild and Machung, 2012; Bhattacharya and Vogel, 2017: 370).

Shifts in social status also characterised the experiences of younger first-generation Ghanaian immigrants who have been in the UK for the past ten to 15 years. A famous phrase among younger first-generation migrants was, 'London the leveller'. The word leveller could not be taken literally as it had social and economic connotations. A 35-year-old respondent's comment captured its meaning by comparing life in Ghana to the UK:

> 'In Ghana, with my degree and work experience, I had a car, house and a driver for my work. Since I came here I have done all sort of jobs like cleaning ... here you work long hours. The funny thing is here, a doctor or professor will be using a bicycle to work. Often before we travel, we feel we are coming here to work, get money, buy a house, a car and enjoy but there is no enjoyment over here. You spend your time working, working and all of it goes into paying bills, and you come back to square one. The other thing is, like, in Ghana there are men's job and women's job. In Ghana, men will rarely do cleaning or homecare work for money, but here you do what you get.'

The term 'London the leveller', to my respondents, represents how migration removes any form of class-based privilege among most Ghanaians living in London. Among Ghanaian's specific social and economic indicators are critical markers of a 'good life'. For instance, higher education qualification, a big housing or a flashy car are pointers of a good life. On the one hand, while levelling shows the constraints faced by Ghanaian immigrants, it also suggests discontinuities in certain gendered practices such as what men or women's work is (Manuh, 1999).

Young people who had no legal documents or what most Ghanaians refer to as 'nkrataa' (papers) were also trapped in exploitative jobs. For instance, Kwabena, who is 33 years old, had overstayed his visit visa because he felt he would "never have a visa in the future". Having become undocumented and working as a cleaner and at a bakery, sometimes he was unpaid by the employer. He noted that he does "not complain due to fear of losing his job". Moreover, as an effect of long working hours, health problems were expressed by some respondents in London. In a group discussion, one leader of a church noted the death of a church member due to poor working conditions.

Similarly, Portia, 25-year-old woman living in Ghana whose father works in London noted, "I wish I can ask my father to come back home because each time I call ... he is working." Until 2018, the UK Home Office collected data from the National Health Service (NHS) on immigration. In response undocumented Ghanaians chose to avoid healthcare from the hospitals due to fear of arrest (Kilner, 2014). Moreover, in addition to asking for prayers from relatives and their churches in the UK, the transnational practice of requesting for prayers from individual pastors or relations and requesting for herbs was common. Medicinal herbs were often brought by other Ghanaians returning from family visits to London.

The constraints illustrated are similar to the account presented Manuh's (1998; 2005) research regarding Ghanaian immigrants in Canada who had to settle for jobs that were lower than their expectations or what they previously did in Ghana as a means of surviving on a daily basis, in the absence of specific social support (for example, extended family or community support) on arrival. Likewise, the vicissitude of Ghanaian immigrants' working experiences is captured in the song 'Sansa Akroma' (which means Ghanaians moving from one place to the other like a migratory bird (from the *Dabi Dabi Ɛbɛ Yɛ Yie* (which suggests the hope of circumstances abroad getting better in the near future) Album by Amakye Dede in the 1990s (Dede, 1990). This Ghanaian song is often the 'go-to' Youtube video used to express or channel their emotional response to the social reproduction needs of most Ghanaians during challenging working conditions and in the absence of close relations who could offer encouragement or solidarity. As noted by Baily and Collyer (2006), the cultural production of music and its consumption is important in the migration process. Amid feelings of loneliness and acute exploitation, exported music can be therapeutic and empowering, especially for poor and working-class individual migrants and immigrant communities.

It is also worth mentioning that apart from virtual sites, for most Ghanaian transnational households, social capital was also built through networks of friends and old school mates. One such group often met as a community fortnightly around Lambeth to discuss the social and economic needs of their members. Sometimes, they collected donations for bereaved members or attended the graduation or naming ceremony of a member while local Ghanaian music was being played to reaffirm their identities, where they came from, everyday challenges of being a migrant and a sense of solidarity. They made a WhatsApp community group chat which played an important role in connecting members virtually while reminding people of meetings or social events (for example, weddings or funerals) similar to those they would attend in Ghana. Essentially, social capital was an important 'use value' in translocal connections in London while reducing the emotional and psychological affects of being away from Ghana.

Parental experiences: extended time and reproduction spaces

The working experiences of most first-generation migrant parents in the UK were often shared during conversations with relations and at various social spaces, including churches or hometown meetings. These immigration conversations were known in Twi language as *Akwantuo mu nsɛm* (Immigration matters). While one would imagine that such experiences shared with relations in Ghana would discourage left-behind relations from migrating, it did not. As noted earlier, the culture of migration is rooted in the notion that people can make it elsewhere, especially outside of Ghana. Moreover, most young people believe that the gains associated with migration are higher than any risks or challenges (Nevins, 2002). Similarly, left-behind relations felt that they needed to 'experience things for themselves'. As a 23-year-old male noted, "If things are that bad there [overseas] why is it that they always come and go back again?" Consequently, most Ghanaians feel that every aspiring migrant should have the opportunity to travel *Aburokyire* (abroad) in order to inform their future migration intentions or decide where the so-called 'better life' can be found, that is whether in Ghana or overseas.

Amid experiences of rising costs of living and declining social services support for families, the homes of most respondents became a primary (re)production site for extra work. Most Ghanaian migrant parents are of the view that "depending on government for social support will not allow one to accomplish certain migration goals, including owning a house in Ghana", as an informant noted. Therefore, almost all adults were involved in local and transnational entrepreneurial activities in addition to their regular jobs outside the house. For instance, Adjoa's mother, Clara and Alberta's mother, Louisa, are friends. They attend the same church in South East London. Similar to historical accounts of Ashanti women who travelled by commercial buses to Togo, Ivory Coast and other places to purchase commodities including food or clothing for sale in Ghana, these two women also embark on bus trips to Paris to purchase bags and shoes for sale in London (Clark, 2010). These trips were often undertaken during weekends or holidays from their regular work. During such business travel, Alberta is cared for by her older sister, a school headteacher, whom she refers to as 'super nanny' owing to her disciplinary attitude.

Similarly, commercial material resources are sent from Ghana during return family visits or through other people. British-Ghanaian transnational children living in the UK and Ghana are equally involved in this work practice by running errands or marketing products. For example, during fieldwork in Ghana, Maaboa a 'sister' (that is, social kinship) to Alberta brought me Kente to be given to Louisa. Later on, I discovered that the items are sold in London to 'make ends meet'. Besides, women's fabric popularly known as Holland and also other second-hand items such as iron, clothing, cooking utensils and shoes were shipped to Ghana and sold and the money from the sales sent back by the left behind young people. Principally, youth left behind were involved in the form of reverse remittance through sending sales revenue to their parents in London. Likewise, British-Ghanaian transnational children in London helped their mothers in marketing products. For instance, before bedtime Adjoa (10–13 years old years, high school student, London) photographs and posts pictures of various Kente cloth designs for display on the WhatsApp status or her mother's Facebook profile and adds phrases like 'Quality kente available … call (Number)' and sends responses to online queries from potential buyers based on her mother's advice. Adjoa's work is unpaid, but she feels her role is to 'help' her mother. Interestingly, children involved in home-based enterprise London or Ghana through selling, market or negotiations were all girls and older girls controlled remittances. The role of women in the clothing industry is well documented in the work of Sylvanus (2016).

Home-based enterprises illustrate the potentially blurred line between production and reproduction spheres of everyday life. Due to economic needs or constraints, the house or home, a site which is assumed to be a resting place after regular work becomes an extended place for commercialised work in addition to other domestic work that may be taken for granted. While it can be argued that transnational children may undertake unwaged work for their parents, I argue that in a culture of reciprocity, children may support or 'help' their parent's work with the expectation that their parents will provide for their needs when requested. Additionally, it can be argued that parental attitudes of self-making, independence, capital accumulation as well as local and transnational practices of importing goods from other places or marketing goods on social media are essential in socialising children on aspects of how to be an enterprising individual.

For some middle-class families confronted with the choice of keeping their regular jobs and getting childcare from institutions, or sending their child to Ghana, mothers decided to provide childcare personally. For instance, Amanpene's mother resigned from her regular office work to start an enterprise, "because of the rising cost of childcare and also there was no time for the children when I was working for the company. It's [a] low-paid job with no room for better conditions or negotiations … I could not do drop off and pick up the children from school." Parents' decision to provide personal care is often motivated by an emotional and moral 'sense of responsibility' to care for children (Ansell, 2008: 808). Sometimes parents negotiated with neighbours, including friends or housemates for unpaid childcare; resigning regular jobs and taking on personal enterprise was a way of orientating children about work being a regular part of adult (for both women and men) life (Hochschild, 2000; Hochschild and Machung, 2012).

When care was defined as 'being there', [it perpetuated a norm of selfless motherhood] which assumes that women should place "children's interest first" until "they have matured teeth". Children are expected to reciprocate by taking care of parents till the "parents lose their teeth" in old age as Amanpene noted. Hence there is a link between a good childhood provided by parents and a good old age as children were being socialised to appreciate family-based care – which ultimately most parents will require in old age and a critical dimension of the inter-generational reciprocal network of care and connection (Coe, 2017).

Children can be orientated towards possibilities of an individual neoliberal subject independent of government support through their parent's decision to resign from capitalist firms into entrepreneurship or self-employment. First, resigning from a regular job in a capitalist firm could mean taking a 'risk' into the unknown or uncertainty about the profit prospects of a new business. However, as mentioned earlier, this action is taken by certain households to increase household income while having more time to take care of domestic duties including childcare.

Parents perceive education as an essential cultural capital that British-Ghanaian children need to negotiate various constraints including barriers in career progression as a racialised category of people who are likely to experience specific employment barriers including racism. When the parents of children in London, recalled their own school-to-work transition experiences as discussed earlier, they felt that their children were 'privileged' to benefit from a UK education. Thus, British-Ghanaian transnational children's education was often prioritised with UK–Ghana opportunities compared:

'I have always encouraged them to take their education seriously as in this country if only you study, you will get something to do … For the past five to ten years, the situation is bad in Ghana. Here [London] if only you study, you will get somewhere.' (Kwesi, Rosemary's father)

'It is about building a certain class system that we wanted to maintain. While other people are thinking about building houses in Ghana or going to live in Ghana we were thinking about here and maintaining a level over here … to make sure our children get a good school, private tutoring after school.' (Amanpene's mother)

This account of Amanpene's mother clearly indicated that cultural capital is considered to be 'convertible into money' (Bourdieu, 1986: 243). In other words, cultural capital is considered a more meaningful or effective approach towards building economic capital than building a house in Ghana.

Three case studies of young people growing up, leveraging capital and going global

Unlike their parents, young people who have come of age demonstrated networks and ties that went beyond Ghanaian communities into more extensive networks through their working lives which can be associated with extending transnationalism from below. To illustrate this within the transnational social space, I draw on fieldwork data to explain the working lives of three British-Ghanaian young working adults in the UK aged between 23 and 35 years.

Rosemary and Hilda

Rosemary is 23 years old and Alberta's older sister. She has a bachelor's degree in International Relations and has a regular job as a retail associate with a large company in London. She started a master's degree in 2016 but dropped out of it due to financial constraints and does not intend to continue her education as she perceives that: "When you are in school, they do not show you where you can get jobs that will help you progress … they just advise to apply for a job in retail or go to job centre, but they do not show you anything else."

Rosemary feels that her income is inadequate and notes that "at the end of the day when transport, food and other expenses are calculated I run at a loss, but because I wanted to get the experience I had to sacrifice." Her long-term aspiration is to become a "business tycoon as that will allow her flexibility of time". She stressed that she wants to avoid the nature of work her parents do as " they are never home together … one comes, and the other is leaving. If I have my own business that will allow me to make money, control my time." Since 2015, she has been collecting donations from her friends at work in London for an orphanage in Ghana. She feels Ghana is a difficult place to live and she mentioned that her cousin, Hilda, is unemployed, but she has started a beads business with her. In 2016, I met Hilda during my data collection in Ghana, who mentioned:

> 'I was looking for a job whiles in school and after completing its more challenging. But even when you find a job here in Ghana, the take-home pay does not even take you home. You have to find other things doing; you have to take on other businesses so that you can get money from both sides and make a better living. For the beads business, I usually make them ready for shipment, or we give it to someone to take it along as sometimes the shipment can be expensive.'

When the items arrive in London, they are advertised on social media platforms like WhatsApp, Instagram and Facebook. Stephane also learned about the qualities of each Kente design, including meanings behind each cloth pattern and various designs for different events. She explained, "I have learned a lot of these from my mum because she had most of these." Interestingly, her customers are not just Ghanaians but Africans and Europeans living in Europe interested in "African or colourful prints" as she puts it.

Jerry

Jerry's ideas are very much in line with the typical migration for development agenda that is being advanced by most neoliberal institutions like the United Nations' agency International Organisation for Migration where migrants are seen as agents of development. During my interview with Jerry in London, he noted that he "struggled with his identity as a child of a Ghanaian migrant" and therefore he established an organisation called 'Mfri-Ghana' (literally, I come from Ghana). The organisation currently undertakes programmes including award ceremonies for young Ghanaians living abroad and a weekend professional social networking and skills training for young British-Ghanaians. At the 2018 award ceremony, the Ghana Embassy in London's representative applauded Jerry's organisation and encouraged them to continue to 'mobilise British-Ghanaians to contribute to the development of Ghana'.

Moreover, since 2012, his organisation organised a business mentoring initiative with one of Ghana's private universities. While Jerry is based in London, he has established chapters of his organisation in five other European countries and the USA and often moves to these countries for activities including planning and fundraising with funds from donors including the European Commission. After his master's graduation, Jerry worked for his university but resigned to focus on his organisation while providing childcare at home. Jerry exemplifies the neoliberal global subject: those who take risks act as agents of development for developing countries through capital accumulation and moving between places and connecting young people through ideas and activities. Jerry's father built a house in Ghana, but he does not think he will acquire any property in Ghana though he feels "there are a lot of business opportunities in Ghana and Africa in general". Though, as a researcher I am not related to Jerry, he would often refer to me as 'brother' and sometimes referred to other Africans as "my brother or sister from another mother". To him, schoolmates and church members "are scattered across the world" and anybody he can "trust whether Nigerian or Polish is a brother and sister". He emphasised that trust is a more critical element of kin and non-kin relationships and he illustrated this by a previous experience:

> 'some time ago in 2015, I felt I could count on family relations in Ghana for a project I was doing, but they misused the money and were telling me stories. Meanwhile, I have not experienced this same level of dishonesty from my business partners ... that is why I refer to others as brothers.'

In terms of capital, Jerry's social network and therefore, the inclusion of non-kin relations in the family, contributes to social capital formation, an essential aspect of contemporary businesses.

Abena

Abena is Adjoa's eldest sister. She is married with four children and is the founding director of a private enterprise that focuses on promoting Africans in the UK. She is fluent in English, Twi and French. In an interview session, she showed me a picture of her receiving an MBE medal at Buckingham Palace and a Forbes recognition. She noted that after her university graduation, it was difficult finding a flexible job that would allow her to take care of her children and thus she was unemployed for a while until she had a business idea. She has an office for her enterprise in Ghana and feels that there are "many opportunities to tap into in Ghana". She involved in various activities, including being a Brand Ambassador for two hotels in Ghana and also sitting on the Board of government agencies. In 2018, she was involved in planning Ghana's 'Year of Return' annual celebration of the return of Africans in the diaspora and noted that through that work she has been able to meet famous people including African-American actors from Hollywood. She also confirmed plans for an event she is hosting in the USA for Africans living in the USA. Her view is that the USA has a wide variety of women's products including cosmetics and clothing which are much cheaper, so she does "big shopping from the US and sometimes sells some of the purchased items on the return to the UK". She attends a multicultural church that was founded by a Nigerian pastor. Through her church, she met a Senegalese member in New York who was introduced to her by her pastor in the UK, and they have been planning the US event together. She regularly posts updates about her movements and activities 'here and there' and sometimes advertises third-party events for a fee on her social media and noted in a conversation that "the job I am doing now has a future … you move, and you can monetise other things you are doing to get an extra income". Similarly, she has opened an Instagram account for her three children where she posts about her children's everyday life including their African dresses, dancing and Twi speaking skills. She said, "I created it for them. Maybe by the time they grow, it will have more followers from everywhere, and they can get money from these platforms." As a frequent traveller with her UK passport which most Ghanaians refer to as 'Red book', she noted that "everywhere feels like home" and that she believes that she "can make an impact around the world and not just to Ghana". Abena feels that her husband has been very supportive of her ambitions as she is often not at home. Her mother has an African market in London, and she used to work there at weekends during her teen years into her 20s. Her father also had a dry-cleaning business, but that was closed down due to poor returns. Abena also exemplifies young adults who have accumulated cultural capital, and her social capital has allowed her to take advantage of further possibilities for capital accumulation in Ghana and the UK.

Conclusion

Young people stretching the transnational social field and the role of capital

The movement of people and the flow of entrepreneurial ideas and material resources for sale in London places their transnational ties in the context of global capitalism. While Kente is a native Ghanaian cloth, the consumption of this product by non-Ghanaians illustrates how young people are stretching the British-Ghanaian transnationals' social field (Castells, 1996). Of course, the export of African prints has a much longer history than this suggests (Kriger, 2006; Boateng, 2011).

The experiences of the young people described in this chapter can be situated within the intersection of globalisation, mobilities, capital accumulation and life transitions from childhood to adulthood as they come of age as children of transnational migrant parents in the world of work.

The forms of movement that emerge among these young adults as children of migrant parents must be seen as an expression of their agential competence in responding to global economic constraints and opportunity structures at the local level and across transnational geographical spaces. For instance, as noted in the case of Abena, her unemployment situation – as a constraint – in the UK and then, later on, her developed business idea enabled her to take advantage of opportunities in multiple countries including the UK, Ghana and the UK. However, it is also clear that transnational social capital and therefore the networks and contacts with diverse people including kin-relations in Ghana and network of new 'brothers or sisters' from various social fields such as churches located in the UK or across other countries are critical to facilitating mobilities as well as ideas and material resources flows. Moreover, it is often assumed that transnational ties with kin relations are very strong or preferred within the family set-up. However, with trust being an essential element of transnational arrangements as seen in the case of Jerry, it is clear that certain moral values in transnational practices guide young people in 'doing family' in a different way. Here the transnational social space can be extended to incorporate diverse people from 'other' cultural backgrounds to facilitate transnational work arrangements amid changing global opportunities (Castells, 1996). Thus, new network formation of non-kin relations or fictive relationships that are based on how economic capital is utilised and how social capital is valued as well as its potential use is emphasised in transnational work arrangements.

In their transnational work engagement with developing countries, British-Ghanaian transnational youth and adults are seen as 'agents of development' who are expected to use their status as a person in an advanced country to support development interventions elsewhere. This reflects neoliberal migration and development interventions aimed at addressing uneven topographies of development between developing and developed countries (Katz, 2004). The contemporary neoliberal agenda to liberalise the migration of some economic subjects while increasing the constraints and barriers for others can be understood in two principal ways: first, adult migrants and children of migrant parents (often referred to as second-generation in migration policies as well as in some transnational and diaspora studies) who have come of age are positioned as developmental agents. Their developmental contribution is often linked to the establishment of business in developing countries and diaspora philanthropy or remittances. Second, investor visas and citizenship often obtainable in most advanced nation-states like the USA and UK enable wealthy owners of capital to move as part of the capitalist production system. While the young people whom I interviewed did not possess an investor visa, they believed their British passport to be powerful.[1] Consequently, this symbolic cultural capital enables them to enter developing and developed countries without restrictions. Moreover, all the British-Ghanaian young adults had dual nationality and as such, had a Ghanaian passport that allowed them to move to Ghana and some African countries without visa restrictions as per the provisions in Ghana's migration policy (Ministry of Interior, 2016). British-Ghanaian transnational youth who have dual citizenship are involved in fluid physical movements between places which is a crucial characteristic of neoliberal globalisation that often benefits people in certain developed countries, thereby creating inequalities. The fact that their movements are also enabled by the advantages of citizenship provisions attached to their passport(s) also suggest the role of the state in their transnational – and transglobal practices (Collyer and King, 2015).

In growing up, young people are expected to work and earn an income that enables an individual to acquire or engage in specific markers of adulthood (for example, housing or getting married). Thus, money has become a key currency in achieving the status of adulthood. Unfortunately, there are not many job options in the labour market for young people to choose from and some may be unemployed after university graduation. When they get a job, there is often the challenge of combining productive work under one employer to other reproductive demands at home. As noted in the account of Hilda, even for those who are employed within capitalist production relations, something like an extra job is required to make a living in the city or the margins of society. Furthermore, as they engage in 'buying and selling' locally and transnationally via various social networks and spaces such as on social media or at church, they are contributing to (re)producing or globalising Ghanaian culture as well as stretching the boundaries of Ghanaian culture from a local to a transnational status. Also, given that Ghanaian culture encourages migration, for British-Ghanaian transnational youth, the ability to work transnationally by moving from one place to the other is important, as is sharing images about their movement and activities on social media, in order to construct a sense of a hardworking, independent and self-sufficient adult.

Note

1 In fact, the Global Passport Index (https://www.passportindex.org/byRank.php) ranks passports. Comparatively, holders of British passports have greater visa-free access to more countries than holders of only Ghanaian passports.

References

Ansell, N. (2008) 'Substituting for families? Schools and social reproduction in AIDS-affected Lesotho', *Antipode*, 40(5): 802–824.

Baily, J. and Collyer, M. (2006) 'Introduction: Music and migration', *Journal of Ethnic and Migration Studies*, 32(2): 167–182.

Bhattacharya, T. (ed) (2017) *Social reproduction theory: Remapping class, recentering oppression*, London: Pluto Press.

Boateng, B. (2011) *The copyright thing doesn't work here : Adinkra and Kente cloth and intellectual property in Ghana*, Minneapolis, MN: University of Minnesota Press.

Boehm, D., Meredith Hess, J., Coe, C., Rae-Espinoza, H. and Reynolds, R. (2011) 'Introduction: Children, youth and the everyday ruptures of migration', in: C. Coe, R. Reynolds, D. Boehm, J. Meredith Hess, and H. Rae-Espinoza (eds) *Everyday ruptures: Children, youth, and migration in global perspective*, Nashville, TN: Vanderbilt University Press, pp.1–19.

Bourdieu, P. (1986) 'The forms of capital', in: J. Richardson (ed) *Handbook of theory and research for the sociology of education*, Westport, CT: Greenwood, pp.241–58.

Castells, M. (1996) *The rise of the network society*, Chichester: Wiley.

Castles, S. (2010) 'Understanding global migration: A social transformation perspective', *Journal of Ethnic and Migration Studies*, 36(10): 1565–1586.

Clark, G. (2010) *Onions are my husband: Survival and accumulation by west African market women*, Chicago, IL: University of Chicago Press.

Coe, C. (2017) 'Transnational migration and the commodification of eldercare in urban Ghana', *Identities*, 24(5): 542–556.

Collyer, M. and King, R. (2015) 'Producing transnational space: International migration and the extra-territorial reach of state power', *Progress in Human Geography*, 39(2): 185–204.

Dede, A. (1990) *Sansa Akroma*, *YouTube*, https://www.youtube.com/watch?v=smzvaztEX0o

Goldin, I. and Reinert, K. A. (2012) *Globalization for development: Meeting new challenges*, Oxford: Oxford University Press.

Hochschild, A. (2000) 'Global care chains and emotional surplus value' in: A. Giddens and W. Hutton (eds) *On the edge: Living with global capitalism*, London: Jonathan Cape, pp.130–146.

Hochschild, A. R. and Machung, A. (2012) *The second shift: Working parents and the revolution at home*, New York: Viking.

Hondagneu-Sotelo, P. and Avila, E. (1997) ' "I'm here, but I'm there": The meanings of Latina transnational motherhood', *Gender & Society*, 11(5): 548–571.

Howard, E. K., Sarpong, G. D. and Amankwah, A. M. (2012) 'Symbolic significance of African prints: A dying phenomenon in contemporary print designs in Ghana', *Innovative Research and Development*, 1(11): 609–624.

Katz, C. (2001) 'Vagabond capitalism and the necessity of social reproduction', *Antipode*: 709–728.

Katz, C. (2004) *Growing up global: Economic restructuring and children's everyday lives*, Minneapolis, MN: University of Minnesota Press.

Kelly, P. and Lusis, T. (2006) 'Migration and the transnational habitus: Evidence from Canada and the Philippines', *Environment and Planning A*, 38(5): 831–847.

Kilner, H. (2014) 'Hostile health care: Why charging migrants will harm the most vulnerable', *British Journal of General Practice*, 64(626): 590–592.

Kriger, C. E. (2006) *Cloth in west African history*, Lanham, MD: AltaMira Press.

Manuh, T. (1998) 'Ghanaians, Ghanaian Canadians, and Asantes: Citizenship and identity among migrants in Toronto', *Africa Today*, 45(3): 481–493.

Manuh, T. (1999) '"This place is not Ghana": Gender and rights discourse among Ghanaian men and women in Toronto', *Ghana Studies*, 2: 77–95.

Manuh, T. (2001) 'Ghanaian migrants in Toronto, Canada – care of kin and gender', *Research Review*, 17(2): 17–26.

Manuh, T. (ed) (2005) *At home in the world? International migration and development in contemporary Ghana and West Africa*, Accra: Sub-Saharan Publishers.

Mazzucato, V. (2016) Bridging boundaries with a transnational research approach: A simultaneous matched sample methodology. In Falzon, M (ed) *Multi-sited ethnography. Theory, praxis and locality in contemporary research*, Farnham: Ashgate, 215-232.

Ministry of Interior (2016) 'National migration policy for Ghana', Accra: Ministry of Interior.

Nevins, J. (2002a) *Operation Gatekeeper: The rise of the 'illegal alien' and the making of the U.S.–Mexico boundary*, New York: Routledge.

Parreñas, R. S. (2001) *Servants of globalization: Women, migration and domestic work*, Stanford, CA: Stanford University Press.

Parreñas, R. (2005) 'Long distance intimacy: Gender and intergenerational relations in transnational families', *Global Networks*, 5(4): 317–336.

Punch, S. (2012) 'Studying transnational children: A multi-sited, longitudinal, ethnographic approach', *Journal of Ethnic and Migration Studies*, 38(6): 1007–1023.

Sylvanus, N. (2016) *Patterns in circulation: Cloth, gender, and materiality in West Africa*, Chicago, IL: University of Chicago Press.

Waters, J. L. (2012) 'Geographies of international education: Mobilities and the reproduction of social (dis)advantage', *Geography Compass*, 6(3): 123–136.

PART II

Intersections/inequalities

7

Negotiating social and familial norms: women's labour market participation in rural Bangladesh and North India

Heather Piggott

Introduction

This chapter argues that traditional representations of women's labour in rural regions of Bangladesh and India have largely been homogenised. Taking a new perspective, informed by both survey and interview data from the same sample, this chapter briefly demonstrates how survey methodologies are limited in their capacity to truly capture the labour of women by contrasting data from semi-structured interviews and a wider survey. Following this, it describes how many women negotiate their traditional role as a housewife, mother and caregiver with income generating labour in various ways. The chapter shows how this is often experienced through caring intra-households relations that are encouraging both men and women to stretch social norms to fit personal circumstances and needs. Overall it is argued that the issue of women's participation in the labour market is far more dynamic and diverse than wider statistical analyses have been able to capture.

Within both India and Bangladesh, women have the right to work. Both the Indian and Bangladeshi government legally guarantee women equality through their respective constitutions. However, over the past 30 years, both Bangladesh and India have experienced interesting labour market participation patterns, particularly regarding rural women. In 1995 the total number of Bangladeshi women in the labour market was 5.4 million, yet by 2005–2006, this had more than doubled to 12.1 million (Mahmud and Tasneem, 2011; BBS, 2010). Within India a different pattern has occurred, unlike other countries, during India's period of steady and persistent economic growth that began in 2002, women's participation in the labour market declined (Lahoti and Swaminathan, 2015). There was a very sharp decline between 2004–2005 and 2009–2010, where approximately 20 million women withdrew from the labour market (Rangarajan et al, 2011), with this decline being most notable in rural areas (Himanshu, 2011; Chaudhary and Verick, 2014).

Within geographical research and beyond, knowledge of what has caused these labour market patterns to occur remains poorly understood (Silvey, 2003; Neff et al, 2012; Kabeer, 2012), and a number of 'unanswered puzzles' remain (Neff et al, 2012; Chaudhary and Verick, 2014). Indeed, within the South Asian labour literature Lahoti and Swaminathan (2015) have explicitly stated that although attention has been given to women's labour market participation in these regions, 'the causal mechanisms that affect women's economic activity are not well understood' (p.5). In response to this, the PhD research upon which this chapter is based explored the labour market participation of rural Bangladeshi and Indian women and the lived reality of this labour for women. This research moved away from only quantifying labour market participation, and considered how social norms and social attitudes shaped the lived experiences of women and their families when women participate in the labour market. To facilitate this, a very specific research approach was needed. The author was a member of a wider international project team with three partners: the University of Manchester (Manchester, UK), the Banaras Hindu University (Varanasi, India) and the BRAC Development Institute (Dhaka, Bangladesh) who worked collaboratively on an Economic and Social Research Council (ESRC) and Department for International Development (DFID) funded project. This research was conducted within three central neighbouring northern states of India and within three districts of Bangladesh – a mixed methods approach was adopted (please see Table 7.1 for a description of all the data collected). Both the survey and interviews took place with husband and wife pairs so that the family dynamics related to women's labour market participation could explored.

Masked employment

It has previously been suggested that surveys in these regions may misrepresent the labour of rural women (Sudarshan, 1998; Mahmud and Tasneem, 2011). A key finding from this research enhances this argument – by comparing and contrasting the survey and interview data the issue of 'masked employment' emerged. Many rural Bangladeshi and rural North Indian women within this study who partook in income

Table 7.1: Research methods used in Bangladesh and India

	Quantitative		Qualitative	
Country	Bangladesh	India	Bangladesh	India
Method	Survey	Survey	Semi-structured interview	Semi-structured interview
N	444 household surveys	477 household surveys	40 interviews in total	45 interviews in total
Sample	3 districts Satkhira, Gaibandha and Lalmonirhat	3 states Utter Pradesh, Bihar and Jharkhand	3 districts Satkhira, Gaibandha and Lalmonirhat	3 states Utter Pradesh, Bihar and Jharkhand

Table 7.2: Primary and subsidiary occupations for Bangladeshi and Indian men and women surveyed in this project

Primary occupation	Bangladesh women n (%)	Bangladesh men n (%)	India women n (%)	India men n (%)
Professional	0 (0)	10 (2.77)	1 (0.21)	7 (1.83)
Self-employed (with employees)	0 (0)	58 (16.07)	1 (0.21)	9 (2.36)
Employed	2 (0.45)	13 (3.60)	12 (2.52)	83 (21.23)
Self-employed (without employees)	4 (0.90)	130 (36.01)	16 (3.35)	148 (38.74)
Manual labourer	3 (0.68)	101 (27.98)	12 (0.42)	119 (31.15)
Family worker	0 (0)	0 (0)	6 (2.52)	6 (1.57)
Unemployed	0 (0)	1 (0.28)	0 (0)	3 (0.79)
Housewife	**413 (93.02)**	0 (0)	**424 (88.88)**	4 (1.05)
Student	0 (0)	2 (0.55)	2 (0.42)	1 (0.26)
Beggar	0 (0)	1 (0.28)	1 (0.21)	0 (0)
Retired	0 (0)	0 (0)	0 (0.42)	0 (0)
Occupation not given	22 (4.95)	45 (12.47)	2 (0.42)	2 (0.52)

generating labour did not define their occupation within the survey in a way that truly reflected their labour. Instead, a large proportion of these women stated that they were solely a housewife regardless of their actual occupation. An investigation into the occupation women gave in their survey response versus the occupation they explained within their interview highlighted the extent of this issue. As Table 7.2 shows, the majority of women within the rural Indian and Bangladeshi survey sample defined themselves as a housewife (93.02% of the Bangladeshi women surveyed, and 88.88% of the Indian women surveyed). The project collected 28 interviews from Bangladeshi women and 35 from Indian women; therefore cross checking whether the occupation these women gave in their survey response was reflective of their daily labour described in their interview was possible. Of 35 women interviewed in India, 17 revealed a different occupation during their interview to the occupation given in the survey. Within Bangladesh the same issue occurred, of the 28 women interviewed the project had survey information for 27 women (as one of the interviewed women did not give her occupation in the survey). In Bangladesh 11 out these 27 women did not define their labour in the survey in the way it was described within their interview. The consistent trend among all of these women was that they stated their primary occupation as a housewife in the survey, yet in their interview they described how they were partaking in income-generating labour. Interestingly, the type of labour women were 'masking' in their survey is varied from educated women in professional roles to waged agricultural workers.

The desire to be a 'housewife' in these rural communities is argued to be due to the expectation of traditional family dynamics linked to the patriarchal system. 'Patriarchy' is a confusing term that is difficult to define (Gregson et al, 1997; Reeves and Baden, 2000), and is also widely criticised (Butler, 2010). However, Sultana (2010) states that patriarchy is generally considered as the 'manifestation and institutionalisation of male dominance over women and children in the family, and the extension of male dominance over women in society in general' (p.3). Patriarchy is multi-scalar, and through this male dominance it organises the household in a hierarchy, with the male head being the most powerful and primary authority figure, followed by any adult male family members, then adult female family members and finally children (Mahmud and Tasneem, 2011; Kabeer et al, 2011). Due to patriarchy, a woman's relationship with the men in her household (particularly her husband if she is married) can have pivotal influences upon her desire and/or ability to partake in labour aside of her role as a traditional housewife, mother and carer.

Kabeer (2000b) and Ludvig (2006) have argued that in Bangladesh, intra-household relations between a woman and her husband can act as a further 'control point' of a women's ability to access an income generating opportunity. Male resistance to women's employment has also been noted by Kabeer (2000b) in Bangladesh. This resistance varies according to the family relationships involved, and the individual circumstances, however it can lead to husbands not wanting their wives to work, and sons not wanting their mothers to work. This control echoes ideas raised by Holdsworth et al (2013) that 'family lives continue to be influenced by gendered social relations, which influence patterns of employment both within and outside the home' (p.145). Much of this resistance regarding women's labour is grounded within issues of male identity and masculinities – the inherent and dominant power relations that are associated with the social construction of being male (Little, 2002; McDowell and Sharp, 1999). It was apparent within this PhD research that there was a desire for women to portray their occupation as the traditional role of a being a housewife which encompassed her role as a mother and carer irrespective of whether she was partaking in income generating labour.

The interview data provided a range of examples of women clearly masking their income generating labour, for example Pooja, a 27-year-old Indian woman describes in her interview that she partakes in "household work, farming work on own family [land], all these things … repairing and general domestic work for wages". However in her survey she stated her primary occupation was a 'housewife'. Similarly, Sumitra a 29-year-old Indian woman, describes the work of her and her family: "we do cultivation work, we all are labourers". Sumitra explains that she works on others' farmland, and rhetorically asked the interviewer "could I feed my stomach by staying at home?" demonstrating that she knowingly works outside of her home, yet she too stated in the survey that her occupation was a 'housewife'. Similarly, in the Bangladeshi interviews, Koli (a 56-year-old woman) and Shafia (a 30-year-old woman) both carry out domestic work in other people's houses, they also work as day labourers when they need to, and yet in the survey they gave 'housewife' as their occupation.

The interview data revealed that many women appear to mask their income generating labour within their survey responses somewhat unconsciously as they view their housewife duties as their primary occupation, irrespective of their labour outside of the home. Only when probed during an interview and when given the opportunity to discuss their labour does the reality of many women's lived labour experiences become exposed. South Asian Labour literature has previously critiqued that Bangladeshi and Indian labour market statistics are incapable of capturing the labour of women, particularly rural women (Mahmud and Tasneem, 2011). It is often argued that this leads to unreliable estimates of women's labour (Srinivasan, 2010). The findings described here add further weight to this issue, as survey responses are shown to mask some individuals' true lived labour experiences, particularly if the labour they undertake goes against dominant social and gendered familial norms of labour.

Inspired by Holdsworth et al (2013) the author wanted to 'consider the extent to which women are increasingly "free" to negotiate their own biographies, particularly relating to combining work and motherhood' (p.145). This is particularly so, as it has been argued by development geographers such as Rigg (2007) and Nightingale (2011) that investigations into the ways people 'get by' and their household strategies are often left unexplored within global South literature. Furthermore, Agarwal (1997) has argued that the lack of intra-household analyses in the global South 'certainly indicates blindness' (p.37) of qualitative stories regarding wider social and cultural norms, processes and structures, including the institution of the family. Responding to this gap in existing knowledge, the author explored intra-household labour relations and negotiations that took place within the family. This approach enabled the lived reality of the unusual labour market trends in these rural regions to be explored further.

Intra-household labour relations and negotiations

The ways in which labour relations are discussed, experienced and negotiated within a household are argued by Tufour et al (2016) to be a reflection of wider social norms and moral codes by which the family live. Given that in rural India 'the decision *of* and ability *for* women to participate in the labour market is the outcome of various economic and social factors that interact in a complex fashion at both the household and macro level' (Verick, 2014: 2), exploring labour negotiations at a household level is essential. The intra-household relations between spouses in this study were overwhelmingly described in a highly positive way. Notions of support, care, kindness, sharing and openness were demonstrated among most interviewees.

Both women *and* men appear to negotiate traditional gendered norms of labour within the home *together*. One way in which married men and women negotiate stereotypical gendered norms of labour is to work together on tasks that are typically considered masculine or feminine. Rather than gendered divisions of labour being fixed, these roles are discussed and negotiated at a household level, depending upon individual circumstances. Evans (2006; 2011) encourages researchers to consider how norms can be negotiated in her analysis of young people negotiating their 'street careers' in Tanzania. In adopting this approach here, I find that many women negotiate their role as a housewife, mother and carer with income generating labour by working with their husbands. This finding is in contrast to Kabeer (2000a) who found many rural Bangladeshi women did not want to work as they 'tactically understood, and often empathised with male anxieties and fears' (p.133) regarding women's participation in paid labour.

For many rural Bangladeshi and Indian women, the everyday lived reality of their labour is working with their husbands and earning an income together, as the following narratives show:

> 'Say for example, if my husband went to work and there was something he could not do alone, he could call me, and we would do that together.' (Shewly Bala, 55-year-old Bangladeshi woman)

> 'We work together ... we see the benefits that help us make a living.' (Bachani, 35-year-old Indian woman)

> 'If a husband and wife work together then it helps the family earn, if both earn, then the pressure becomes less on one.' (Hosna, 55-year-old Bangladeshi woman)

> 'We have to go to the field, we work there for the whole day, after coming from there, we cook eat and sleep ... we go together, he says "let us go for the harvesting of the chilies and watering the field. You pick chilies and I will water the field".' (Rabita, 25-year-old Indian woman)

These extracts highlight the informal intra-household labour relations for these participants. They show the subtle ways in which negotiations of labour roles takes place within many rural Bangladeshi and Indian homes, highlighting diverse forms and discourses of men and women working 'together' in different contexts.

Interestingly, this notion that both men and women work together within a household occurred among Bangladeshi and Indian men in the interview sample too, as described by Kartik (a 42-year-old Bangladeshi man) and Ram Prasad (a 37-year-old Indian man):

> 'I think women should be able to work outside and this is a good thing. It is good if two people, husband and wife work together ... it is better, if two people consult each other and work together.' (Kartik, 42-year-old Bangladeshi man)

> 'See wife and husband make for a four wheeled vehicle, if two go away, the vehicle of life can't run, if it can't run

properly, it will stand still, never go anywhere.' (Ram Prasad, 37-year-old Indian man)

Kartik and Ram Prasad also stress how it is a 'good thing' if a man and wife work together. For Kartik who partakes in a range of work including cultivating land and working in a shop selling bicycles, he describes how "it is better if two people consult each other and work together". Similarly, Ram Prasad who works at home with his wife on their land growing crops stresses the importance of both people in a relationship working together. He describes an analogy of how he perceives his relationship with his wife to be a "four wheeled vehicle" that requires two people. These findings contradict a notion argued by Kabeer (2000a) and Ludvig (2006) in a Bangladeshi context whereby if a woman partakes in labour beyond a 'housewife' role then masculine gender identity can be at stake. Instead, these findings suggest that these rural Bangladeshi men encourage their wives to work with them, opposing notions that a women's husband can act as a further 'control point' of a women's ability to access labour (Kabeer, 2000a; Ludvig, 2006). Arguably, the relationships described here reflect the power relations of a household (Valentine, 2008). Such power relations appear far less hierarchical, patriarchal and based upon stereotypical definitions of rural South Asian gender norms, when compared to earlier research (Dhawan, 2005; Bridges et al, 2011; Banks, 2013). This is important, as it suggests that structural processes are perhaps less controlling than previously understood.

Negotiating social and gendered norms

There have been numerous calls for researchers to explore if, how and why men and women can negotiate socially normative behaviours in the rural south (Olsen and Metha, 2006; Kabeer, 2000b; Williams et al, 2014). In a wider global South context, Rigg (2007) has argued that intra-household relations can soften or strengthen the impact of these norms. This research found many Bangladeshi and women and men negotiate these norms subtly, through an everyday resistance of masculine and feminine roles. For example, Afjal a 45-year-old Bangladeshi man explained in his interview that his wife Jahanara (a 35-year-old Bangladeshi woman) helps him with work outside the home: "For example, when water collects at the base of the corn stalks, I ask her to come with me, she helps me with my work for a few hours." He later explains how he, in turn, helps his wife with work typically assigned to her: "I'll fetch firewood, or if she is cooking and needs water, I'd fetch it for her, if she asks for help, I always help her."

Jahanara also explained in her interview how she and her husband work together, describing how, "He helps me a lot, we do work together, I can't do all the work on my own." These subtle negotiations indicate how households 'get by', they show how through a process of informal discussion and decision-making, traditional understandings of gendered norms of labour are being broken down.

This theme was echoed throughout several other interviews, with stories of supportive of intra-household labour relations being frequent. Both Rubina (an 18 year old Bangladeshi woman) and Aminul (a 28-year-old Bangladeshi man) describe how for them, their intra-household labour relations with their partners are built upon a notion of sharing and working together. As the following narratives exemplify:

> 'He looks after the baby, for example, if I am cooking and the baby cries, he sits by the stove with the baby, if he cannot look after the baby, I take the child and he cooks, he cooks he does all the chores, he helps me in a lot of chores.' (Rubina, 18-year-old Bangladeshi woman)

> 'I take our baby to the store. This morning for example, my wife was praying and my son was crying, so I took him out for a bit, I later gave him back to my wife. I do what I can, when I have time … I enjoy this, I enjoy doing things together.' (Aminul, 28-year-old Bangladeshi man)

In addition to women helping men with work traditionally considered a 'man's job' such as labouring in fields, many Bangladeshi and Indian men describe how they also help their wives, with work traditionally associated with women. Rubina describes how her husband helps her with her chores, and Aminul describes how he helps his wife with the childcare of their 3-year-old son, that he does what he can, when he has time, he explicitly states that "I enjoy doing these things together".

Korima, a Bangladeshi woman described how during times of hardship she has worked outside the home while carrying her son:

> 'We needed the money to pay the debts, we had to work back then, he disagreed at first, I strongly insisted, it's no use I sit at home … on the one hand he didn't let me work

outside, and on the other hand we have no money ... but together, we have to do the work together ... I started at dawn, I cooked and fed my family, and then I went to work carrying my son. He stayed roadside while I worked, then in the later afternoon I worked at home, my fellow women workers covered for me while I breast-fed my son. It was a difficult time.' (Korima, 50-year-old Bangladeshi woman)

In this abstract Korima describes how when her son was a baby, she worked alongside her husband with their son placed 'roadside' while they worked. This story displays how Korima was persistent in her desire to partake in income generating labour, and that she negotiated her role as a housewife and mother to ensure her family had enough income to get by. Furthermore, Korima shows her husband's ability to be flexible in his social attitudes towards her participation in labour.

These findings indicate that rather than these traditionally patriarchal rural regions producing social barriers to women's employment (Asadullah and Wahhaj, 2016; Bridges et al, 2011), which reinforce stereotypical gender behaviours (Balk, 1997), the lived reality reveals how many women and men negotiate and reconfigure socially normative behaviours in their everyday life, both inside and outside of the home. The supportive caring and sharing intra-household labour relations demonstrated here show how traditional norms of labour are being stretched in these regions. This happens not only by men allowing and encouraging their wives to work outside the home, but by men bending typical gendered norms of labour and partaking in housework and childcare – tasks that are normatively argued to be the responsibility of women in these regions (Beneria, 2003; Sahoo and Rath, 2003; Sudarshan, 2014). This contrasts with previous literature that has argued that the division of gender roles is so extreme in South Asia that 'most the activities, especially in the household, are defined as either male or female' (Rao and Rao,1985: 608). In these rural communities, many women and men appear to be 'eroding the patriarchal contract' – a term coined by Kabeer (2000a) by sharing their work and communicating with one another more openly about their labour. This research found many women and men bending the traditional norms where 'men contribute [to] productive labour while women contribute reproductive labour and care labour' (Mahmud and Tasneem, 2011: 6) by partaking in labour to provide for their children and families, *together*.

A shift in social attitudes?

It could be argued that the interview data from this research indicates a shift in social attitudes towards women's labour within this sample of rural Bangladeshi and Indian communities – as both the social attitudes towards women's labour and lived experiences of labour within the household largely appear less fixed and traditional than within previous literature (Bridges et al, 2011; Takeuchi and Tsutsui, 2015). Interestingly, there was an explicit acknowledgement of this 'shift' or 'change' within the Bangladeshi interview data. In rural India, although the wider project data indicates a positive change in social attitudes, norms and lived experiences of women's labour when compared to previous literature, no explicit narrative among the interviewees corroborates this claim.

Within the Bangladeshi data, very specific references to this shift in social attitudes were made. For example, Proshun, a 33-year-old Bangladeshi man clearly articulated how for him "things have changed" regarding intra-household labour relations and social attitudes towards women's labour:

> 'In the past, if the wife worked and the husband stayed at home, people in the village looked down upon it, but things have changed, the thing is, in the current age, everything is so expensive and it is better if two people are earning an income. For example there are lots of families where the man works in the field cultivating and it is better when the woman helps out, whether that's financial assistance or in terms of the work itself, it's better if two people work together … people do not think these things anymore, people are no longer concerned with these things, a lot has changed now.' (Proshun, 33-year-old Bangladeshi man)

For Proshun, "a lot has changed" regarding labour in rural Bangladesh. He describes how both men and women contributing to household income is "better", and women are now able to partake in labour outside the home more freely. Proshun notes a shift in what other people think too, suggesting that his view is not in isolation and this shift in social attitudes towards women's labour is a wider community level change. Jahanara (a 35 year old Bangladeshi woman) also describes how for her, changes in social attitudes towards women's labour have occurred:

'Changes took place, now women work with their husbands, other times, people didn't understand it. They thought why would women go out to work? They will stay with respect in the house, now everyone goes out, one's self-respect stays, if someone has good behaviour, then everything is ok. Wherever you go, manner and behaviour is important.' (Jahanara, 35-year-old Bangladeshi woman)

For Jahanara, like Afjal, she highlights how not only has her social attitude towards women's labour changed, but she suggests that so have the opinions of others in her wider community. She describes that women's participation in labour outside of the home is common, and "now everyone goes out". Kabeer et al (2011) have argued that in Bangladesh access to paid work "does make a difference to women's lives, but its impact is strongest and most consistent in the case of women whose employment is characterised by some degree of regularity, visibility and social benefits" (p.38). As the labour described by many rural Bangladeshi women in their interviews is visible 'outside labour' on their own 'inside' land, it could be argued that, in line with Kabeer et al (2011), this shift in social attitudes has occurred as more women are being seen outside and that their neighbours and local communities are responding well to this.

This shift in social attitudes described here within rural Bangladesh is important. Kabeer (2012) has expressed concerns over the durability and persistence of gendered norms and their effects upon women in South Asia. These findings demonstrate that the durability of these social norms may not be as strong as previous literature has argued, with many women and men working together and breaking down these norms. This is important, especially given that 'over the past few decades there has been tremendous change in laws, attitudes and norms affecting women's status, roles and development ... however not much empirical knowledge is available about these changes and the impact they have upon a women's behaviour, values or attitudes and identities' (Dhawan, 2005: 81).

It appears that this shift in social attitudes towards women partaking in labour, may have the potential to lead to further positive change. It appears that educating the younger generations is becoming more of a priority, and educating all children, including girls, is perhaps becoming a new norm. Several urban and western studies from around the world reveal that higher levels of education correlate with less traditional and more progressive social attitudes towards women's labour and this can lead towards women entering the labour market (Fortin, 2005; Elamin and Omair, 2010; Barker et al, 2011). Previous analysis of education within Bangladesh and India found that within households, expenditure on boy's education was often prioritised if money was an issue (Shonchoy and Rabbani, 2015; Craigie and Dasgupta, 2017), however the findings from this research suggests otherwise, as demonstrated by the excerpts which follow:

'The boy and girl are both getting an education. They have a future ahead of them.' (Sufia, 55-year-old Bangladeshi woman)

'It is regarding making the children of some worth not about making them worthless.' (Bindu, 25-year-old Indian woman)

'For me, boys and girls are the same. If I have money, I will extend education to both.' (Saraswati, 35-year-old Indian woman)

Sufia articulates how her grandchildren, one boy and one girl, are both being educated. Furthermore, Sufia adds that due to this education, in her opinion, the children will have a future ahead of them. Similarly, Saraswati, a widowed 35-year-old Hindu Indian woman, who has two daughters and two sons echoes this optimistic social attitude towards the education of both girls and boys. Bindu demonstrates that she believes education leads to improved prospects. For Bindu, a child having an education gives them worth. For Saraswati, education of sons and daughters are the same, however she suggests that access to financial resources may limit her ability to educate girls. Previous analysis of education within Bangladesh by Shonchoy and Rabbani (2015) also found that within households, expenditure on boy's education was often prioritised if money was an issue. Although this issue is raised here, the majority of narratives surrounding education are highly positive. For example, Sumaiya, a 39-year-old Bangladeshi Muslim woman who has five children (three sons and two daughters) makes a direct link between the education of girls and their access to the labour market. It appears that she views education as a pathway to a professional occupation. "I feel so good when I hear that someone's daughter is receiving an education ... she may be[come] a teacher, teaching other children. I like this" (Sumaiya, 39-year-old Bangladeshi woman).

I argue that this apparent shift in social attitudes towards the education of girls could be indicative of a subtle wider change in social attitudes towards women's prospects and their role in society. These changes arguably indicate a subconscious awareness of social reproduction. Through parents placing such value and concern upon their children's education (especially the education of daughters), they demonstrate awareness that education is central to an improved social standing (Butler and Hamnett, 2007). By parents expressing a desire to remove structures that obstruct them from reaching their full potential, they are contesting the education system that previously produced the social norms that education was for wealthier families and that education was for boys (Collins and Coleman, 2008). If this shift in social attitudes continues, and actions and behaviours that support these views persist, more rural girls will be encouraged and supported through their education, and a wider shift in gendered norms of labour may occur.

Conclusion

Using evidence from a wider project, this chapter has argued that traditional representations of women's labour in rural regions of Bangladesh and India are largely homogenised as they are too often heavily based upon quantitative measures and traditional understandings of patriarchy and social norms. Taking a new perspective, utilising both survey and interview data from the same sample, this chapter has described how these normative assumptions of women's labour in these regions have been limited in their scope. Survey methodologies alone have been unable to truly capture the complexities, lived realities and negotiations that take place within families and communities regarding the labour market participation of many rural Bangladeshi and Indian women.

In contrast to much South Asian labour literature, this research found that labour related household relations between a husband and wife, in most cases, appeared optimistic indicating progression from previous literature regarding labour norms in these regions This research found that many of the rural women in this study negotiated their traditional role as a housewife, mother and caregiver with income generating labour in various ways. Rather than labour being fixed, traditional, based on social norms or homogenous it appears that gendered and labour-related norms are being stretched to fit family circumstances and needs.

A notion that 'things have changed' regarding social norms and social attitudes towards women's labour in rural Bangladesh and India was not only inherent within the findings, but was made explicit within Bangladeshi interview data. This shows many Bangladeshi individuals themselves acknowledging that a 'change' has occurred regarding women's labour. Optimistically, the education of young people, and particularly the education of girls was discussed favourably, further indicating that a 'change' may be occurring. If this way of thinking continues, and behaviours that support these views persist, more rural girls may be encouraged and supported through their education, and a wider shift in gendered norms of women partaking in the labour market may occur.

Overall this chapter has highlighted the need for macro level analyses of complex issues such as this, and for normative assumptions of inequalities related to women's labour and women's roles within the family in the global South to be unpicked. While these findings are encouraging, and the narratives reveal a more positive story than previously indicated – these stories are of course not reflective of all women's experiences of the labour market. Further research that explores the everyday and lived realities of labour of families within rural Bangladesh and India is required to enhance this area of work. Researchers and policymakers must remain cautious that within rural India and Bangladesh there are many intersecting factors that can strongly affect people's public and private behaviours, and societal issues related to religion, class and caste norms are important factors to consider.

References

Agarwal, B. (1997) 'Bargaining with gender relations: Within and beyond the household', *Feminist Economics*, 3(1): 1–51.

Asadullah, N. and Wahhaj, Z. (2016) 'Missing from the market: Purdah norm and women's paid participation in Bangladesh', *IZA Institute of Labour Economics Discussion Papers* 10463.

Balk, D. (1997) 'Defying gender norms in rural Bangladesh: A social demographic analysis', *Population Studies*, 15(2): 153–172.

Barker, G., Contreras, J.M., Heilman, B., Singh, A.K., Verma, R.K., and Nascimento, M. (2011) *Evolving men: Initial results from the International Men and Gender Equality Survey (IMAGES)*, Washington, DC: International Centre for Research on Women.

Banks, N. (2013) 'Female employment in Dhaka, Bangladesh: Participation, perceptions and pressures', *Environment and Urbanisation*, 25(1): 95–109.

BBS (Bangladesh Bureau of Statistics) (2010) *Report on Labour Force Survey 2010*, https://www.ilo.org/surveyLib/index.php/catalog/1125/download/9433

Beneria, L. (2003) *Gender, development and globalisation: Economics as if people mattered*, London: Routledge.

Bridges, S., Lawson, D. and Begum, S. (2011) 'Labour market outcomes in Bangladesh: The role of poverty and gender norms', *European Journal of Development Research*, 21(3): 459–487.

Butler, J. (2010) *Gender trouble*, London: Routledge.

Butler, T. and Hamnett, C. (2007) 'The geography of education: Introduction', *Urban Studies*, 44(7): 1161–1174.

Chaudhary, R. and Verick, S. (2014) *Female labour force participation in India and beyond*, Geneva: International Labour Organisation Asia-Pacific Working Paper Series.

Collins, D. and Coleman, T. (2008) 'Social geographies of education: Looking within, and beyond, school boundaries', *Geography Compass*, 2(1): 281–299.

Craige, T. and Dasgupta, S. (2017) 'The gender pay gap and son preference: Evidence from India', *Oxford Development Studies*, 45(1): 1–20.

Dhawan, N. (2005) 'Women's role expectations and identity development in India', *Psychology Developing Societies*, 17(1): 81–92.

Elamin, A., M. and Omair, K. (2010) 'Male attitudes towards working females in Saudi Arabia', *Personnel Review*, 31(6): 746–766.

Evans, R. (2006) 'Negotiating social identities, the influence of gender, age and ethnicity on young peoples "street careers" in Tanzania', *Children's Geographies*, 4(1): 109–128.

Evans, R. (2011) '"We are managing our own lives"…: Life transitions and care in sibling headed households effected by AIDS in Tanzania and Uganda', *Area*, 43(3): 384–396.

Fortin, N. (2005) 'Gender role attitudes and the labour market outcomes of women across OECD countries', *Oxford Review of Economic Policy*, 21(3): 416–438.

Gregson, N., Kothari, U., Cream, J., Dwyer, C., Holloway, S., Maddrell, A. and Rose, G. (1997) 'Gender in feminist geography', in: Women and Geography Study Group [WGSG] (ed) *Feminist geographies: Explorations in diversity and difference*, London: Longman, pp.49–85.

Himanshu (2011) 'Employment trends in India: A re-examination', *Economic and Political Weekly*, 46(37): 43–59.

Holdsworth, C. (2013) *Family and intimate mobilities*, London: Palgrave.

Kabeer, N. (2000a) *A field of one's own: Bangladeshi women and labour market decisions in London and Dhaka*, London: Verso.

Kabeer, N. (2000b) *The power to choose: Bangladeshi women and labour market decisions in London and Dhaka*, London: Verso.

Kabeer, N. (2012) *Women's economic empowerment and inclusive growth: Labour markets and enterprise development*, London: Centre for Development Policy and Research Working Papers.

Kabeer, N., Mahmud, S. and Tasneem, S. (2011) *Does paid work provide a pathway to women's empowerment? Empirical findings from Bangladesh*, Brighton: Institute of Development Studies.

Lahoti, R. and Swaminathan, H. (2015) 'Economic development and women's labour force participation in India', *Feminist Economics*, 22(2): 168–195.

Little, J. (2002) 'Rural geography: Rural gender identity and the performance of masculinity and femininity', *Progress in Human Geography*, 26(5): 665–670.

Ludvig, A. (2006) 'Differences between women? Intersecting voices in a female narrative', *European Journal of Women's Studies*, 13(3): 245–258.

Mahmud, S. and Tasneem, S. (2011) *The under reporting of women's economic activity in Bangladesh: An examination of official statistics*, Bangladesh: BRAC Development Institute Working Papers.

McDowell, L. and Sharp, J. (1999) *A feminist glossary of human geography*, London: Arnold.

Neff, D., Sen, K. and Kling, V. (2012) *The puzzling decline in rural women's labour force participation in India: A re-examination*, Hamburg: German Institute of Global and Area Studies.

Nightingale, A. (2011) 'Bounding difference: Intersectionality and the material production of gender, caste, class and environment in Nepal', *Geoforum*, 42: 153–162.

Olsen, W. and Mehta, S. (2006) *A pluralist account of labour participation in India*, Oxford: Global Poverty Research Group.

Rangarajan, C., Kaul, P. and Seema (2011) 'Where is the missing labour force?', *Economic and Political Weekly*, 46(39): 68–72.

Rao, P. and Rao, N. (1985) 'Sex-role attitudes across two cultures: United States and India', *Sex Roles*, 13(11–12): 607–624.

Reeves, H. and Baden, S. (2000) *Gender and development: Concepts and definitions*, Brighton: Institute of Development Studies.

Rigg, J. (2007) *An everyday geography of the global South*, London: Routledge.

Sahoo, F. M. and Rath, S. (2003) 'Self efficacy and well-being in working and nonworking women; Moderating the role of involvement', *Psychology and Developing Societies*, 15(2): 187–200.

Shonchoy, A. and Rabbani, M. (2015) 'The Bangladesh gender gap in education: Biased intra-household educational expenditures', Institute of Developing Economies, IDE Paper No. 522.

Silvery, R. (2003) 'Gender geographies of activism: Motherhood, migration and labour protest in west Java, Indonesia', *Gender Geographies of Activism*, 31(2): 340–363.

Srivastava, N. and Srivastava, R. (2010) 'Women, work and employment outcomes in rural India', *Economic and Political Weekly*, 45(28): 49–63.

Sudarshan, M. (1998) 'Employment of women, trends and characteristics', New Delhi: Directorate General of Employment and Training Women's Vocational Training Programme.

Sudarshan, R. (2014) *Enabling women's work*, Geneva: International Labour Organisation Asia-Pacific Working Paper Series.

Sultana, A. (2010) 'Patriarchy and women's subordination: A theoretical analysis', *The Arts Faculty Journal*, 4: 1–18.

Takeuchi, M. and Tsutsui, J. (2015) 'Combining egalitarian working lives with traditional attitudes: Gender role attitudes in Taiwan, Japan, and Korea', *International Journal of Japanese Sociology*, 25(1): 100–116.

Tufuor, T., Sato, C. and Niehof, A. (2016) 'Gender, households and reintegration: Everyday lives of returned migrant women in rural northern India', *Gender, Place and Culture*, 23(10): 1480–1495.

Valentine, G. (2008) 'Living with difference: Reflections on geographies of encounter', *Progress in Human Geography*, 32(3): 232–337.

Verick, S. (2014) 'Women's labour force participation in India: Why is it so low?', http://www.ilo.org/wcmsp5/groups/public/---asia/---ro-bangkok/---sro-new_delhi/documents/genericdocument/wcms_342357.pdf

Williams, G., Meth, P. and Willis, K. (2014) *Geographies of developing areas*, London: Routledge.

8

Marginalised youth perspectives and positive uncertainty in Addis Ababa and Kathmandu

Vicky Johnson and Andy West

Introduction

The analysis presented in this chapter starts from the perspective of marginalised and street-connected young people in the capital cities of Ethiopia and Nepal. Many had lived in fragile and conflict-affected rural areas and migrated to small towns and then larger cities in search of work to meet expectations in communities to support their families. Some stayed living and working on the streets independently and with peers, some moved to informal settlements with family members. Although many attempted to navigate different institutional support, including residential, offered by government and non-governmental agencies, others prefer the freedom they find working on the street in small businesses as part of the informal sector. Many of the young people from case studies in the two capital cities find that they cannot survive on the income from their own independent strategies or from employment by others in the informal sector.

This chapter is based on evidence from youth-centred research conducted for the Youth Uncertainty Rights (YOUR) World Research project in Ethiopia and Nepal. YOUR World Research places youth perspectives as central to understanding how uncertainty features in their complex and precarious lives. Uncertainty is the defining concept in this comparative research that examines the lives of young women, men and youth who are gender fluid or of the third gender, as they grow up in insecure and changing cultural and political contexts. This project does not see uncertainty as necessarily negative, as further explained in this chapter. The youth-centred research approach, modelled on rights-based research and Johnson's (2011, 2017) youth-centred 'change-scape' framework, is first outlined in the next section, followed by an outline of the research locations in Ethiopia and Nepal, before discussing young people's perspectives and experiences of marginalisation, and strategies involving positive uncertainty to respond to social norms and their circumstances.

The chapter focuses on young people living in the two capital cities, but the interaction and movement between rural and urban life, often involving towns and smaller cities, means that there is a need to take account of the norms in rural areas that young people take with them and often adapt or change in the transition to urban life. The research teams in Ethiopia and Nepal worked with marginalised and street-connected young people to explore how they negotiate and navigate uncertainty in attempting pathways out of poverty as they shape their rights. The sometimes fearful feelings of not knowing what would be the outcome of pressures from family and peers to migrate both internally and abroad, were countered with a sense of expectation and excitement, because many young people, including rural residents and those connected to the streets of Addis and Kathmandu, otherwise face a situation of almost certain poverty.

Youth-centred research, changescapes and uncertainty

The youth-centred nature of the research took account of children's rights to participate, principles of rights-based research that respect young people as experts in their own lives (Beazley and Ennew 2006), as well as a recent re-conceptualisation of children's rights in international development as including living rights, social justice and translations (Hanson and Nieuwenhuys, 2013). 'Living rights' acknowledges the need to translate rights agreed internationally into the complex realities and contexts of young people's lives on the ground. The youth-centred research aimed to ultimately achieve impact in the form of lasting and transformational, institutional and societal/policy change (Beazley and Ennew, 2006; Johnson, 2017). The research design and co-production with partners, national researchers and marginalised youth applied Johnson's 'change-scape' so that youth agency was central and mechanisms for youth participation with adults and decision-makers were built into the process. In this large-scale qualitative research engaging with 1,000 young people, a combination of themed interviews were used alongside creative, visual and moving methods that were developed to understand young lives (Johnson et al, 2019). Flexibility of methods ensured the complexity of the lives of youth living in uncertainty is captured and that research addresses the difficulties of working with 'youth as a shifting social position and fluid process' (Langevang, 2008: 2046).

The 'change-scape' (after Johnson, 2011) links child and youth agency to their relationships with others, the places and spaces they interact in and inhabit, their contexts and local power dynamics. It suggests ensuring the development of mechanisms for making youth participation more meaningful where their perspectives are listened to, for example in co-construction of research and the creation of spaces for dialogue with service providers and policymakers. The change-scape takes into account time, such as to incorporate analysis of how children transition to adulthood as they grow up and how contexts rapidly change.

In this research the change-scape was modified to take into account the mobility in the lives of many young people in Ethiopia and Nepal, and also the theories of Bauman (particularly 2001; 2004; 2007). Bauman's ideas on wasted lives suggest that people living in precarity, insecurity and 'liquid modernity' are labelled as outcasts and seen as disposable in communities. These concepts provided a starting point for understanding how young people may regard marginalisation and uncertainty. Their creative strategies in constantly changing contexts has helped to layer an analysis of uncertainty as potentially positive, particularly paying attention to young people's feelings about traditional bonds in families and communities and forming new bonds.

The qualitative nature of the research helped form an understanding of local constructions of and definitions of 'youth' within the context of their social relations and position in society and how these are problematised in society (Mizen, 2004). The research built on previous work in Nepal (for example Johnson et al, 1995, and case studies in Johnson and West, 2018) and Ethiopia (Johnson et al, 2013; Johnson et al, 2016a). Over 1,000 marginalised and street-connected youth were engaged across eight sites in the two countries (see Johnson et al, forthcoming 2020). This chapter draws on research with over 100 youth from the capital city sites in both Addis Ababa and Kathmandu. Youth in this research are those aged 15–24 years (following the main UN definition of youth), although national policies vary, to include youth up to 30 years of age in Ethiopia and up to 40 years of age in Nepal.

Ethiopia and Nepal

Nepal and Ethiopia are among the poorest low-income countries (LICs) in the world: they were 157th and 173rd respectively, of 187 countries in the 2013 Human Development Index (UNDP, 2013), and remain in the UK Government's Department for International

Development (DFID) listing of LICs (IZA/DFID, 2019). Each has high internal and international migration that is often viewed as a key source of uncertainty. DFID funded research showed that, in Ethiopia, extreme poverty in rural areas, early marriage, violence and sexual abuse are all drivers for migration. In these contexts, young people migrate into seemingly uncertain situations where they are subjected to poor working conditions and low wages; but despite insecure employment many view their living conditions after migration as better and feel a greater sense of autonomy (Atnafu et al, 2014). Both countries are conflict-affected and prone to natural disasters. In Nepal violence linked to former and ongoing political conflict is said to be a source of uncertainty facing migrants (Magar, 2009). Recent (2015) earthquakes in Nepal are an additional cause of instability and as a result a Youth Alliance for Reconstruction has developed nationally.

The economies of the countries are enmeshed with global neoliberalism, but the government in both changed during the course of the research, and currently express a concern for marginalised, poor, disabled and vulnerable groups, in contrast to, for example, the neoliberal UK government's attacks on poor and disabled people and reductions in welfare (Ryan, 2019). This concern was evident in the instigation of national meetings with the involvement of senior personnel on the research findings, as outlined later.

YOUR World Research was conducted in four locations in each country, two rural and two urban. Although this chapter focuses on young people in the capital cities, many of these migrated from rural and smaller urban areas, and might move on to international destinations. Rural research sites were conflict affected, environmentally fragile or prone to natural disasters. All selected locations are particularly impoverished, include a range of ethnicities/castes, religion, and involve youth living and working in different family and street situations, experiencing various vulnerabilities that affect the way they navigate and negotiate uncertainty.

Sites within the capital cities were Addis Ketema, a sub-city of Addis Ababa in Ethiopia and central Kathmandu in Nepal. In these sites over 20 youth participated in co-construction early in the research; 40 in the in-depth qualitative and comparative interviews; 30–40 in focus group discussions on issues arising from analysis; and over 100 others in verification and youth seminars to engage with peers, practitioners and policymakers on future strategies. Adults and stakeholders were interviewed to understand intergenerational power dynamics in communities and services that may support youth strategies.

Processes of marginalisation and changing social norms

Young people's perspectives on marginalisation surprised the non-governmental organisations working with the research project locally. Based on young people's views and research evidence, these NGOs subsequently extended their work to reach more marginalised youth. In the research process, community-based partner organisations initially identified young people whom they regarded as the most marginalised. When groups of these young people, in poor areas, met for the co-construction phase of the project, they identified other youth as being more marginalised than themselves and so a snowball approach (a participant driven selection process in this hard to reach population) was applied. Young people therefore identified more and more marginalised youth in the research sites. Invariably, this included youth who had dropped out of school or failed their national exams, and those who did not already interact with services.

Youth perceptions of marginalisation

Young people's definitions of marginalisation went further than government definitions in both Ethiopia and Nepal. These official, more formal national definitions include notions of marginalisation relating to gender, ethnicity or caste, poverty and also, in Ethiopia, living on the peripheries of the country. In contrast, although they recognised these aspects of marginalisation as important, youth understandings showed that marginalisation and precarity were central to all communities. Marginalisation was explained by young people in forms that align with what Philo and colleagues (2019) discussing precarious urbanisms refer to as 'living on edge'. For example, Young people in YOUR World research described experiences of insecurity that encompass and embody precarity, anxiety and fear.

Young people's understandings of marginalisation in the community extended beyond issues of gender, ethnicity/caste, poverty to include family situations, experiences of abuse, involvement in exploitative work and living with disabilities. It is evident from this research that notions of youth marginalisation need rethinking to encompass young people's perspectives, experiences and the consequences of marginalisation in their lives, including their engagement with education and work (see Kelly et al, 2019). For example, in Addis

Ketema, a young woman spoke about her marginalisation due to being a pregnant teenager:

> 'Teenage pregnancy is socially and religiously unacceptable in my community. I was identified as a careless and deviant person. People started blaming and back-biting me. My social relationships in the community became very weak. People started pointing at me as a deviant person. They prevented their children from becoming a friend of mine ... I wished it didn't happen in my life. It is the support I received from my friends and family that gave me the strength to continue to live in this community.' (Nardos, young woman aged 19 years, Addis Ketema)

In both countries, particular aspects of identity were identified by young people as leading to marginalisation, including in Nepal being genderfluid (locally known as 'third gender') and especially in Ethiopia (although also in Nepal) living with disability. In Kathmandu, a young third gender youth, Pinky (aged 24 years) talked about their difficulties and problems. The researchers heard that many third gender young people are engaged in sex work, with many realising that they have contracted HIV. Although social perceptions are changing gradually, it seems that much more support is required to enable youth to express their changing feelings about personal sexual identities, to gain help from peers and within communities, and to benefit from services. Over ten detailed case studies conducted with genderfluid young people in Kathmandu consistently suggested that services for sexual rights and reproductive health need to be both youth-friendly and aware of the specific needs of third gender youth. This corresponds with previous research in Nepal (Johnson et al, 2013), implying a lack of change. Third gender youth felt that they were at best misunderstood and at worst discriminated against by health professionals. In Ethiopia it was not even possible to carry out the planned work with genderfluid youth as any form of homosexuality or expression of non-binary sexuality was not legal during the research period.

In both countries, young people described being disabled as limiting their education, economic, social and migration activities, and an indicator of marginalisation in communities. An example is Beyene, a 24-year-old young man paralysed in one leg in the rural area of Amhara. He dropped out of school and migrated to Addis Ababa where he tries to access services. As a requirement of many government and non-governmental services, he and other street connected youth living with disability have to produce identity cards to demonstrate they are city residents. Beyene appealed to the Ministry of Labour and Social Affairs when he was refused services but did not find any support. Having lost all contact with relatives in his rural home town he was then isolated on the streets. Requirements for certificates from his school also restricted his entry into any form of education. He then found work as a shoe-shiner and lived with four other youth in a shared rented bedroom. He finds solace in chewing Khat and drinking alcohol as he finds it helps him with depression.

This case study touches on some of the issues that marginalised young people face in their precarious street situations. They described the discrimination experienced when they start to become street connected, living and working on the streets often in the informal sector, and frequently being pushed into more and more exploitative areas of work, such as commercial sex work, cleaning and providing temporary toilets, shoe-shining, and selling sweets, second-hand clothes and shoes or drugs, often as part of survival strategies once their attempts at education or small businesses had failed. Some managed to continue making a living but recounted violence from other young people, adults and the police. They also invariably faced issues of access to and discrimination within services, especially when they could not process identity cards, as was the case for many of the marginalised youth interviewed.

Changing policy norms

In Ethiopia, in March 2019, at the end of the research process, the Ministry for Women, Children and Youth of the new government held a joint seminar with research partners and other Ethiopian agencies focused on three thematic and policy areas: street connected children and youth, disability and youth justice. This provided a forum for academics and practitioners, along with policymakers and service providers from government and non-governmental organisations, in parallel with workshops involving marginalised young people who are disabled, with street connections or involved in justice systems. Recommendations from the research were provided to the new government line ministries that are working with young people. Recommendations included more efficient provision of identity cards wherein the most marginalised who have migrated are given assistance, inclusive education and policymaking, and development of health and criminal justice systems that are more child and youth friendly, and involve more training for health professionals and police.

In Nepal, a National Youth Seminar was held with ActionAid Nepal and national partners including Youth Advocacy Nepal, with representatives from government ministries. The Ministry of Youth and Sports was given a remit by the parliamentary Leader of the House to implement youth demands to support inclusive education and employment critically including support for those working in the informal sector. At a local level in Nepal, youth declarations to provincial and national government, compiled by young people at seminars in each of the research locations were received by key members of rural municipalities and local mayors. Apart from any future changes arising from these national events, in both countries the research had impact on the policy and practice of local and national NGOs in their planning and work with young people (see Johnson et al, 2019b).

Changing social norms

In both countries, the young people interviewed echoed the perspectives of previous Nepalese youth researchers who talked about respecting traditional and religious beliefs but wanting to 'edit' cultural norms so that young people could access their rights (Johnson et al, 2013). In the rural research sites across Ethiopia and Nepal, young people felt a heavy expectation from families to follow in their parents' footsteps and to provide financially for their families, but which would now likely involve urban migration. Yet they were strongly invested in agency that was bound by the intergenerational power dynamics of their families and communities. Some who stayed in rural areas wanted to change small aspects of convention, such as dress and hairstyle. Lidet, a young woman aged 18 years, from one of the rural kebeles in Ethiopia discussed how she felt concerned about changing social norms and that youth should be thoughtful about what changes they would make: "The traditions are changing through time. People are not respecting each other as they used to do previously. The dressing style has also changed. The traditional norms and cultures are disappearing in the name of modernisation. People need to be selective and reasonable while accepting new norms."

In some case studies young people spoke of discussions with parents, that they wanted to choose their own partners for marriage and to wait rather than be married early. In Ethiopia, many of the young women who participated in co-construction workshops described how they were left with even heavier burdens when young men had to migrate to find work and how some of the young women also wanted to leave behind the prospect of early marriage. They discussed the marriage

Figure 8.1: On the move: travelling for work in drought-prone Hetosa, Ethiopia

season as being a time they did not look forward to. Some also told their own histories, of having been abducted for marriage and that parents became complicit. This meant that some young women chose to migrate to cities, for example from the rural site of Hetosa in Oromia to local towns and then often to the capital (Figure 8.1).

Reta, a young man living in Addis, aged 17, discussed his feelings that there were very cruel and risky acts of harmful traditional practices in the community. He suggested some degrees of progress as many people in the community feel that rape and female genital mutilation no longer represent their culture. But although he also suggested that abduction is decreasing significantly, he feels that there should be more interventions to raise community awareness to end such practices. He also described young people's agency in terms of adopting identities. Sometimes dressing in a different way was seen as belonging with a group of peers and rejecting some of the traditional practices that they felt they could not support:

> 'We call those who follow new styles in our area dopes. When you follow new styles, people get attracted to you. Clothes are way of showing your belongingness. When I say to a young guy in our area who dresses well "hey dope"

and if he replies "hey real dope" it means he thinks I also belong to the group.' (Reta, young man aged 17 years)

Youth agency links young people to peers and to adults in the community, and is strongly situated in the places and spaces that youth interact in and inhabit, and the cultural, socio-economic and environmental contexts, as used in change-scape theory. In the research, while young people were keen to understand how to form new social bonds and 'belong' with their peers, they did not want to totally change all of the traditional or religious practices or social norms but to 'edit them' (as in Johnson et al, 2013). Some young people suggested changing traditional practices that were harmful to them, but they still wanted to please their families and be accepted back into communities when they returned after migrating to towns and cities for work. If they stayed in the city, young people interviewed often wanted to have some links to their families even if they had become estranged or had previously experienced an abusive situation.

Young people wanted to satisfy adult expectations and were aware of intergenerational power dynamics in decision making. They suggested awareness change is needed among adults in communities in addition to young people's actions in building on their own often creative strategies in order to both access their rights and find a way of being accepted as part of their communities. This questions Bauman's ideas of breaking traditional social bonds in order to form new ones (Bauman, 2001), and instead implies that youth do this on a temporary basis while finding strategies to navigate precarious and uncertain landscapes in processes of change. What the research reconfirmed is that while recognising youth agency and their creative strategies, it is productive to analyse how agency is relational and situated in place and power, and attempts to respond to precarity (as in Johnson et al, 2016; and Philo et al, 2019).

Positive uncertainty

Uncertainty is a major trope of the times (see, for example, Scoones, 2019). The core concept of positive uncertainty in this research contrasts with widespread popular perceptions of uncertainty as negative. Instead, in particular circumstances young people can envision the uncertainty they expect to face, such as in terms of migration, as having potentially positive outcomes (see Johnson et al, 2020).
Young people experienced precarity and uncertainty in both rural and urban areas, as evidenced in the research. Although this chapter

Figure 8.2: Migrants at work in the urban construction sector in Nepal

focuses on the capital cities in Ethiopia and Nepal, it is important to recognise the experience of transition and movement, and the shifts and continuities in young people's lives. Many young people in the city, particularly those who are street connected, in informal sector occupations, and living highly precarious and uncertain lives, have come from rural areas and smaller urban locations (see Figure 8.2).

Young migrants thus carry their experiences, aspirations and precarities of being on the edge (as in Philo et al, 2019) in their movements and migrations. For example, many marginalised youth interviewed in Ethiopian rural sites portrayed feelings of hopelessness, and the following case study of Nehil shows the situation from which youth make decisions to migrate to towns and then cities in search of new futures. This migration is often an escape they seek in order to fulfil expectations in their communities. Young people also described their decisions to subsequently migrate internationally to the Gulf states in search of work to support their families. Many noted that their role models were successful migrants rather than educated professionals:

'I was born and grown up in a rural area. The primary school was a bit far from my home. I used to walk for long distances. As I used to go to Eteya [the nearby town], I was accustomed to life in the town from my childhood.

Though there is no means of transportation from Danisa Kebele to Eteya, I took the courage to walk for long distances to get to know the lifestyle in town. People in urban areas believe in communication and discussion while people in rural areas are stubborn. People fight for silly reasons in rural areas. Moreover, parents in rural areas do not care for their children. The fact they have many children made them to feel careless about their children. They don't care whether their child disappears or not whereas people in urban areas care for their children. There is a saying ... "if a brave man dies another one will come". Besides there is no employment opportunity in rural areas. My parents didn't have land, and rent on contractual bases to cultivate crops. I didn't see any change to the lives of my parents though they cultivated for more than thirty years. I lost hope in agriculture. These all made me to feel uncomfortable staying in a rural area. It didn't give me happiness to stay in that situation. Hence, I decided to move out and work in towns.' (Nehil, young man aged 22 years, from Hetosa rural site)

Across the research young people described precarious lives due to poverty and processes of marginalisation that related to their feelings about their identities, for example in relation to gender, sexuality and disability, and whether they felt that they could meet the expectations of adults in families and communities. In the contexts of environmental fragility, local conflict due to ethnicity and religion, widespread unemployment, marginalised youth feel that education is irrelevant and unachievable or simply not possible because of the paid and unpaid work necessary to provide for their families, and so many young people migrate to towns and cities. Since the smaller towns do not always have services or opportunities they could access, many continued travelling to capital cities and often on to international destinations.

The following case study demonstrates the way in which youth who are street connected can feel that their certainty is poverty and that they need to embrace uncertainty to migrate even if illegal and risky. Abdi, a young man in Addis Ketema talked of how he and peers live under a railway bridge and set up and rented out temporary toilets with plastic bottles. Even with the little they earnt, police still tried to move them on and take a cut of the money. Abdi therefore kept his passport in his pocket and, even though his previous migration experiences were unsuccessful, he waits for an opportunity to leave again with an attitude that is positive in the face of uncertainty:

> 'My parents have given me nothing, apart from advice. I am living in the street under the bridge with a community of street connected young people. I have migrated several times to the Gulf but unfortunately deported due to my illegal entry. I am always ready to migrate again, if you check my pocket now, I have kept my passport with me. Whenever I get money, I will send it for my journey. Living here poverty is certain, I feel happy when I migrate, it is uncertain but it offers hope.' (Abdi, young man aged 19 years, Addis Ketema)

In all research sites in Ethiopia and Nepal there are examples of young people forming creative strategies based on positive uncertainly and then using the results to support their families. For example, in Nepal, in the earthquake-affected rural area of Sindhupalchowk, there is the story of two Dalit young men (Dalit being regarded as a low status caste and marginalised). They told of their family house being destroyed in the 2015 earthquake. They travelled together to Kathmandu to seek opportunity. There they learnt skills as silversmiths, making candlesticks in a local factory (metalworking is also traditionally regarded as low status). When the research team were in Kathmandu, they were taken on a series of youth-led walks and interviews and learned how these young men melted, carved, washed and polished first on the streets and later in the factory. Having made enough money, they returned to their Sindhupalchowk village to rebuild their family house in the hills, but also continued to work in the city. This example also shows how young people tended to want to maintain their links with family and contribute to regeneration in the community.

Analysis across the research sites indicates that youth of all genders feel that social norms need to shift through awareness-changing of adults, but that ultimately they have to work together to overcome the processes of marginalisation with which they broadly identify and perceive to encompass discrimination and abuse. Yet, they do not want to change all traditions or to break all family or community bonds. The strategies they provided in case studies suggest that social norms need to change to some extent, but young people generally support each other in peer groups. In-depth interviews show youth were desperate for approval from their families. They want to feel that they belong when they return from migration to their communities of origin, even if they have to hide the exploitative or sometimes illegal work in which they had to engage for survival.

The research found that positive uncertainty is temporal and young people seek a sense of belonging and an agency that is relational. At first their agency may be bounded by adults and social norms in their communities, and youth do seek to break these bonds and find support mainly from peers and some small community-based organisations, but in time they also want to think, work and gain approval with and from adults. Services and authorities can be discriminatory to the most marginalised and those young people suggest that they are willing to interact positively when invited to participate. Uncertainty is a constant state in transitions to adulthoods. Older people could learn to navigate uncertainty from younger people, but experience through the research suggests that as people grow older a shift occurs and there is a general seeking of some form of certainty. These processes reinforce a need for mechanisms in research to be developed to ensure dialogue between generations and to remind decision-makers that youth have different and creative strategies in rapidly changing times.

Conclusion

Similarities were found across Ethiopia and Nepal, some unexpected. In both counties, young people were experiencing transition to adulthood in situations that were environmentally and politically fragile, but without education and in the face of widespread unemployment while expectations for them to provide economically for their families remained. Despite living in a liquid modernity, with changing political and environmental contexts, the certainty young people felt that they faced, if they followed traditional paths and practices, is persistent poverty and exposure to some harmful practices, such as early marriage. They see that a possible solution is to embrace uncertainty with creativity, and to learn new skills, try to make their way in the informal sector and to migrate.

In both countries there were unexpected changes in political systems and government during the course of the research. In some senses these appeared to be working against neoliberalism, for example where government services were devolved to provincial level in Nepal, and line ministries made positive moves to create forums to hear youth perspectives, look to the marginalised, and consider openly how the responsibilities of the state and services should take on board their concerns. On the other hand, neoliberalism has permeated and structured inappropriate and inaccessible education systems, so that the most marginalised who drop out of school and fail exams can no longer aspire to formal employment but need to be creative and enter the informal sector or migrate. Youth centred research applying a change-scape is valuable in understanding their circumstances by starting from their own perspectives on their precarious lives and intergenerational and peer relationships. This change-scape approach taken in YOUR World Research mirrors youth-scapes suggested by anthropologists and human geographers working in Africa on youth transitions (Christiansen et al, 2006).

The research has also shown that while treating children and young people as active participants and agents of change (Boyden and Ennew, 1997; Johnson et al, 1998), it is necessary to understand the vulnerabilities and stresses facing young people (Mizen and Ofosu-kusi, 2013). It is also necessary to recognise that marginalisation and vulnerability may be linked to political agency and resistance (Butler 2014), rather than being stuck in a fixed position where individuals suffer abuse and cope with uncertainty, and power lies only in the state or aid organisations. But where young people support each other in creative responses to positive uncertainty, they also need support from adults as part of a fight for material and political conditions. Paying attention to youth perspectives and their relational agency is therefore at the centre of a supported struggle for the voices, views and actions of marginalised children and young people to be heard, included and addressed.

Young people's experiences of precarity because of the poverty and other effects of changing, fragile environments, political and communal conflict, and economic lives increasingly affected through globalised consumption and shifting expectations, were compounded by marginalisation. The neoliberalist impact on local economies is evident in marginalised young people being drawn into often exploitative work in the informal sector in the capital cities. In both countries young people's perceptions of marginalisation, being at the margins or on the edge (following Philo et al, 2019) show how that edge and those margins are often hidden or simply ignored even at the heart of the city. They respond to this inherent uncertainty with strategies that embrace at least some uncertain opportunities and aspects of action as positive, perceiving the potentially beneficial outcome as an only solution to a certainty of poverty. Their experiences show the need for working and living in peer groups to achieve rights and improve chances of strategic success. But they also reveal the depths of precarity and marginalisation that remain much hidden from public perception and require significant shifts in government paradigms and action to change.

Acknowledgements

The formal title of the research is: *Insecurity and uncertainty: Marginalised young people's living rights in fragile and conflict affected situations in Nepal and Ethiopia.* The project was funded by ESRC/DFID Joint Fund for Poverty Alleviation Research, grant numbers ES/N014391/1 and ES/N014391/2.

The national team in Ethiopia, were Dr Melese Getu, Amid Ahmed, Milki Getachew and in Nepal, Dr Sumon Kamal Tuladhar, Sabitra Neupane and Shubhendra Man Shrestha. In Ethiopia principal partners were CHADET, Childhope, and the School of Social Work at Addis Abbaba University; in Nepal principal partners were ActionAid Nepal, CERID (Research Centre for Educational Innovation and Development) at Tribhuvan University as well as local partners in Kathmandu: Youth Advocacy Nepal, HomeNet Nepal, Nepal Mahila Ekata Samaj, CWIN Nepal, CWCN, Blue Diamond Society, SOBER Recovery; in Kapilvastu: Sahaj Nepal; in Sindhupalchowk: Community Self Reliance Centre.

References

Atnafu, A., Oucho, L. and Zeitlyn, B. (2014) *Poverty, youth and rural–urban migration in Ethiopia: Migrating out of poverty*, Falmer: University of Sussex Working Paper 17

Bauman, Z. (2001) *Community: Seeking safety in an insecure world*, Cambridge: Polity Press.

Bauman, Z. (2004) *Wasted lives: Modernity and its outcasts*, Cambridge: Polity Press

Bauman, Z. (2007) *Liquid times: Living in an age of uncertainty*, Cambridge: Polity Press

Beazley, H. and Ennew, J. (2006) 'Participatory methods and approaches: Tackling the two tyrannies', in: V. Desai and R. Potter (2006) *Doing development research*, London: Sage, pp.189–199.

Boyden, J. and Ennew, J. (eds) (1997) *Children in focus: A manual for participatory research with children*, Stockholm: Save the Children.

Butler, J. (2014) 'Rethinking vulnerability and resistance', http://www.bibacc.org/wp-content/uploads/2016/07/Rethinking-Vulnerability-and-Resistance-Judith-Butler.pdf

Christiansen, C., Utas, M. and Vigh, H. E. (2006) *Navigating youth, generating adulthood: Social becoming in an African context*, Stockholm: Elanders Gotab AB.

Hanson, K. and Nieuwenhuys, O. (eds) (2013) *Reconceptualizing children's rights in international development: Living rights, social justice and translations*, Cambridge: Cambridge University Press.

Johnson, V. (2010) 'Revisiting children and researchers in Nepal: What facilitates and hinders change in a context of conflict and the changing political economy?', *Journal for International Development,* 22(8): 1076–1089.

Johnson, V. (2011) 'Conditions for change for children and young people's participation in evaluation: 'Change-scape', *Child Indicators Research,* 4(4): 577–596.

Johnson, V. (2017) 'Moving beyond voice in children and young people's participation', *Action Research,* 15 (1): 104–124.

Johnson, V. and West, A. (2018) *Children's participation in global contexts. Beyond voice,* London: Routledge.

Johnson, V., Hill, J., Rana, S., Bharadwaj, M., Sapkota, P., Lamichanne, R., Basnet, B., Ghimimire, S., Sapkota, D., Lamichanne, R. and Ghimire, S. (1995) *Listening to smaller voices: Children in an environment of change (Nepal case study),* Kathmandu: ActionAid Nepal.

Johnson, V., Ivan-Smith, E., Gordon, G., Pridmore, P. and Scott, P. (eds) (1998) *Stepping forward: Children and young people's participation in the development process,* London: IT Publications.

Johnson, V., Leach, B., Beardon, H., Covey, M. and Miskelly, C. (2013) *Love, sexual rights and young people: Learning from our peer educators in how to be a youth-centred organisation,* London: International Planned Parenthood Federation.

Johnson V., Hart R. and Colwell, J. (2016a) 'International innovative methods for engaging young children in research', in: R. Evans, L. Holt and T. Skelton (eds) *Methodological approaches,* Singapore: Springer, pp.335–356.

Johnson, V., Johnson, L., Magati, B. O. and Walker, D. (2016b) 'Breaking intergenerational transmissions of poverty: perspectives of street connected girls in Nairobi', in: L. Murray and S. Robertson (eds) *Intergenerational mobilities: Relationality, age and lifecourse,* London: Routledge, pp.34–53.

Johnson, V., West, A., Tuladhar, S., Shrestha, S. and Neupane, S. (forthcoming) 'Marginalised youth navigating uncertainty: Reflections on co-construction and methodology in Nepal' in: C. Walker, A. Zoli and S. Zlotowitz (eds) *New ideas for new times: a handbook of innovative community and clinical psychologies,* London: Palgrave.

Johnson, V., Admassu, A., Church, A., Healey, J. and Mathema, S. (2019) 'Layered and linking research partnerships: Learning from YOUR World research in Ethiopia and Nepal', *Institute of Development Studies Bulletin,* 50(1): 79–98.

Johnson, V., West, A. and Gosmann, S. (eds) (forthcoming 2020) *Youth and positive uncertainty: Negotiating life in post conflict and fragile environments*, Warwickshire: Practical Action Publishing.

IZA/DFID (2019) *Growth and labour markets in low income countries programme: 2019 call for proposals list of low income countries*, https://glm-lic.iza.org/call-phase-iv/list-of-lic/

Kelly, P. Campbell, P. and Howie, L. (2019) *Rethinking young people's marginalisation: Beyond neo-liberal futures?*, London: Routledge.

Langevang, T. (2008) ' "We are managing!" Uncertain paths to respectable adulthoods in Accra, Ghana', *Geoforum*, 39(6): 2039–2047.

Magar, J. B. R. (2009) 'Implication of rural to urban migration in Nepal: A social inclusion perspective', https://www.researchgate.net/publication/256068787_Migration_from_Rural_Nepal_A_Social_Exclusion_Framework

Mizen, P. (2004) *The changing state of youth*, London: Palgrave.

Mizen, P. and Ofosu-kusi, Y. (2013) 'Agency as vulnerability: Accounting for children's movement to the streets of Accra', *Sociological Review*, 61(2): 363–382.

Philo, C., Parr, H. and Soderstrom, O. (2019) ' "On edge?": Studies in precarious urbanisms', *Geoforum*, 101: 150–155.

Ryan, F. (2019) *Crippled: Austerity and the demonisation of disabled people*, London: Verso.

Scoones, I. (2019) *What is uncertainty and why does it matter?*, Brighton: STEPS Centre.

UNDP (United Nations Development Programme) (2013) *Human development report 2013. The rise of the south: human progress in a diverse world*, New York: UNDP.

9

Infantilised parents and criminalised children: the frame of childhood in UK poverty discourse

Aura Lehtonen and Jacob Breslow

Introduction

Over the last decade, UK governments appear to have utilised various discursive frames of childhood to claim that they are tackling child poverty (despite putting in place no real measures to do so), and to shift the blame for poverty from their own decimation of structures for economic advancement and protection, to the so-called 'troubled' cultures of poor families. This chapter interrogates this policy climate and argues that part of what has allowed governments to justify and obfuscate their abandoning of poverty as a key policy focus was, and is, deployments of discourses of 'childhood'. The Coalition (2010–15) and Conservative (2015–) governments, we argue, have mobilised two distinct discourses of childhood, simultaneously infantilising poor parents and adultifying poor children. Together, these somewhat contradictory processes suggest that the frame of childhood is central not only to the discourses that continue to blame the poor family for their own poverty, but also to the processes that have seen children and young people bear the brunt of a decade of austerity and anti-welfare politics in the UK. Evoking childhood to substantiate their spurious frames of 'worklessness' and 'troubled families', the austerity-era governments have worked to move poverty discourse away from material and towards cultural and criminalised understandings of poverty. Our chapter thus investigates these shifts with reference to the frame of childhood, focusing specifically on how 'childhood' is deployed as part of the individualisation, culturalisation and criminalisation of disadvantage or poverty.

To make this argument we must first explain what we mean by childhood as a framing device. Here, childhood is understood as both a lived stage of life, and a figuration. As has been argued elsewhere, 'childhood' must be understood as a motivated term whose uneven distribution to individuals and populations facilitates various claims in and as the political (Berlant, 1997; Castañeda, 2002; Edelman, 2004; Levander, 2006; Bernstein, 2011; Breslow, 2019). In this conceptualisation, childhood is not just a description of a particular stage of life, nor an age group, but rather an expansive *and* constricting location within particular relationships of power. 'Childhood' often excludes many subjects within the early years of life, while simultaneously expanding outwards to 'stick' to older subjects. To be located within the frame of childhood, in other words, is less to be understood as within a particular age bracket, and more to be positioned as child-like, as contained by particular notions of ignorance, defencelessness and sociality, as well as to be dependent on parental figures, state institutions and the social world more generally. In this chapter, then, we address both 'real' and figurative children. Our concern is with the ways in which child poverty has been intentionally obfuscated by the austerity-era governments as part of their anti-welfare politics, but also with the use of childhood as a frame to justify the policy and discursive mechanisms that facilitate this obfuscation.

Almost a decade after the beginning of austerity politics in the UK in 2010, the *impacts* of the raft of welfare and other policies implemented initially to reduce public spending by the coalition government are well known. The consequences of austerity policies have tended to fall disproportionately on the poorest and most disadvantaged in society, with black households, lone parents and people with disabilities among the most severely affected (Portes and Reed, 2017). Children have also been hit harder than other groups, as the poorest families with children have suffered the biggest losses in income, and families with children endured the largest cuts in services (Bradshaw, 2016a). No doubt at least in part as a consequence of the reduced policy emphasis on child poverty discussed later, child poverty has been rising in the UK since 2011–12, with 4.1 million children living in poverty in 2017–18, 70% of whom are in working families (CPAG, 2019). The increases follow a period of significant reductions between the mid-1990s and 2010 (Bradshaw and Main, 2016), and the UK continues to underperform in international league tables on child wellbeing, particularly in regards to material wellbeing, education and health (Bradshaw, 2016b). For example, Taylor-Robinson et al find that a third of 'the sustained and unprecedented rise in infant mortality in England from 2014 to 2017' can be attributed to rising child poverty, with the poorest areas of the country affected disproportionately while affluent areas remain largely unaffected (2019: 1).

Concomitant to these trends in the distribution of poverty and disadvantage, the austerity era has also seen considerable shifts and changes in how – and whether – poverty and child poverty are talked about within policy arenas. In this chapter we identify three key shifts in poverty discourse: the individualisation and culturalisation of poverty; the dropping of 'poverty' off the policy agenda altogether; and finally the convergence of poverty and criminality in both policy discourse and agendas. We suggest that the first two of these shifts are justified through infantilising discourses of poor parents, and that the latter shift is enabled through an adultification of poor children. Our chapter then concludes by suggesting that these shifts are indicative and telling of the wider decimation of state-provided universal support services over the austerity period, in favour of conditional programmes designed to offer limited and limiting support to those deemed 'troubled'.

From material to cultural poverty

As many (Gillies, 2012; MacDonald et al, 2014; Main and Bradshaw, 2016; Pemberton et al, 2016; Lehtonen, 2018) have argued, discourses that position poor people as the architects of their own poverty have certainly intensified in the last decade. At the same time, the notion of 'cultural poverty', whereby the origins and causes of poverty are located in the *cultures* of poor people rather than in the economic and financial conditions that they face, has a long history in the UK. Conventionally, such discursive positionings cast poor and disadvantaged people as both culturally deficient and individually irresponsible, while social welfare is designated one of the causes of such dysfunction (Wiggan, 2012). Given this longer history, it is no surprise that one of the central tactics deployed by recent UK governments to avoid accountability for reducing child poverty has been to re-define what child poverty means. As we outline later, this re-definition has sought to shift the discursive and policy terrain from material and economic indicators to cultural and familial dynamics.

In their first attempt to distance themselves from the previous Labour government's flagship policy and commitment to eradicate child poverty in the UK by 2020,[1] the coalition government consulted on 'better measures of child poverty' in 2012 (CPU, 2012). The aim of the consultation was to replace child poverty targets introduced in the Child Poverty Act – related to relative, absolute and 'persistent' poverty with measures focusing on the 'root causes' of poverty instead (CPU, 2012: 1). The process culminated in the passing of the Welfare Reform and Work Act 2016, which commands the government to monitor and report on the number of children living in 'workless households' and 'long-term workless households', as well as on the educational attainment of all children and 'disadvantaged children' at the end of Key Stage 4. While the income-based measures are still published annually, the legal requirement for the government to meet specific child poverty reduction targets was removed in the 2016 act. In other words, the act effectively abolished the government's responsibility to report on and subsequently end child poverty by locating the source of economic disadvantage within cultural practices and behaviours in the family, rather than within material inequalities.

The replacement of the income-based measures with the 'worklessness' measures is not just a troubling rhetorical manoeuvre, but the measures are also misleading and inattentive to the realities of 'worklessness' as it relates to poverty. Specifically, they disregard the fact that out of the 14 million people who live in poverty in the UK, eight million live in families where at least one person is in work (JRF, 2018), assuming instead that poverty can be successfully tackled simply by moving more people into employment. The claim that work is 'the best route out of poverty', repeated throughout the relevant policy papers (CPU, 2012: 3; DWP, 2017: 8), has been refuted by many (Bailey, 2016; Main and Bradshaw, 2016). Further, in regards to worklessness the policy focus has tended to be explicitly on the reproduction of the *norm* of worklessness from one generation to the next, rather than on the reproduction of the material conditions engendered by prolonged unemployment (Lehtonen, 2018) – a notion at least partially disproven by Robert MacDonald et al's (2014) study that found no evidence of intergenerational cultures of worklessness in the UK. The focus on the normative nature of worklessness bolsters the idea that poverty and disadvantage are an issue for specific groups of people, who are trapped in a 'cycle of disadvantage' (DWP, 2017: 8) or 'intergenerational cycles of poverty' (DfE, 2011: 24) – thereby also ignoring the high levels of movement between categories (Bailey, 2016). Thus, rather than something that can touch the lives of many individuals and families at various points in their lives, poverty is here transformed into an affliction of the few – and specifically, a few whose own values and norms are to blame for their deprivation.

Furthermore, the measures consulted on in 2012 and introduced in 2016 emphasise *behavioural* outcomes over material conditions, reproducing an individualised framing of poverty that views poor individuals as responsible for their own circumstances – as well as for lifting themselves out of them (Main and Bradshaw, 2016; Pemberton et al, 2016). The emphasis on the cultural transmission of poverty also positions parents – rather than material or income poverty – as centrally responsible for their children's development and outcomes, suggesting that parents can ensure better futures for their children by simply passing on the right kind of cultural values, norms and behaviours. The shift away from measuring, tracking and basing policy on the income-based child poverty measures, thus, overall, signals a move away from material and structural, and towards cultural and individual understandings of poverty, as well as reflecting the notion that deprivation is both distinct and self-perpetuating (Gillies, 2012).

From poverty to troubled families

Besides the culturalisation and individualisation of poverty, in recent times (child) poverty has, at least discursively, dropped off of the policy agenda of the Conservative government(s) entirely. Following the passing of the Welfare Reform and Work Act in 2016, the Department for Work and Pensions (DWP) published a policy paper that sets out the government's vision for 'tackling poverty and engrained disadvantage' (DWP, 2017: 3). This paper constitutes the only one published by the DWP specifically on poverty or disadvantage since the 2016 Act, and overall the paper serves both to intensify the discursive trends towards individualisation and culturalisation of poverty, and to move policy discourse away from poverty altogether.

In moving the emphasis away from poverty and towards, first, worklessness, and second, the ephemeral 'disadvantage' – which is, additionally, framed mostly as disadvantage in the labour market – the latest paper succeeds in presenting poverty and disadvantage as akin to by-products of the real problem, worklessness, rather than as warranting attention in their own right (Lehtonen, 2018). The policy solutions offered as part of the 2017 paper's discussion reflect the prominent emphasis on workless families (rather than on all poor families) in governmental efforts to tackle poverty and disadvantage. Central to the policy interventions offered in the paper is the Troubled Families Programme (TFP), led by the then Secretary of State for Communities and Local Government Eric Pickles and launched in 2012 with the aim to 'turn around' the lives of 120,000 families with multiple problems across England by May 2015 (DCLG, 2016a: 5), increasing to 400,000 families in the second iteration of the programme running from 2015 to 2020 (DCLG, 2016a). This programme, and the policy guidance that accompanies it, is the most recent incarnation of the policy and discursive landscape that blames poor families – now identified as both 'workless' and 'troubled' – for their own circumstances.

The second TFP was touted as having a 'renewed focus on worklessness' (DWP, 2017: 18; see DCLG, 2016a), with one of the programme's key goals being 'to make work an ambition for all troubled families' (MHCLG, 2019: 7). As previously, the focus here is squarely on *attitudes* towards work, rather than on the income generated by work. Further, this focus on worklessness, specifically framed here as normative and cultural, as one of the key criteria for the programme raises the broader question of what and who is excluded when the government's flagship programme to tackle disadvantage aims to only or primarily deal with *workless* families with multiple problems. Since a significant proportion of those living in poverty in the UK are actually in work, large numbers of poor people are excluded from the programme, and indeed from much intervention at all.[2] The limited reach of the programme thus belies the government's disproportionate emphasis on the programme and its 'success' in 'turning around' troubled families. Indeed, the rhetoric around the programme claimed that 'significant progress' had been made, by the very fact that one or more adults in the families helped by the programme have 'succeeded in moving into continuous employment' (MHCLG, 2018a: 7). Here, again, success is *not* defined by no longer being poor, but rather by being in work.

Like the category of 'worklessness', the framing of 'troubled families' produces gaps in meaning between what it allegedly speaks to and its rhetorical force. The ways in which the figures of 120,000 and 400,000 troubled families were arrived at, and subsequently used as the basis for policy, have faced significant criticism (Levitas, 2012; 2014; Shildrick et al, 2016), not the least for the misrepresentation of the original piece of research that generated this figure, as is discussed in more detail later. In 2015 the Department for Communities and Local Government (DCLG) claimed that an astonishing '99% of the actual number of families targeted', or '116,654 of the most troubled families', had been 'turned around' by the first TFP (DCLG, 2015). However, research suggests that this figure was arrived at through some rather questionable manoeuvres.

Because the programme operates on a 'payment by results' principle, Levitas (2014) suggests that local authorities had an incentive to find and work with exactly the number of families given by the DCLG as an estimate of 'troubled families' in their area. A 2016 Channel 4 *Dispatches* documentary (Dispatches, 2016) focusing on the programme suggests, further, that some councils were engaging in data matching – selecting families who had already had positive outcomes prior to the start of the programme as part of their target figure; replacing families that were unlikely to be 'turned around' with ones that allowed for 'quick wins'; and using such a wide definition of 'anti-social behaviour' (one of the key criteria of the programme) that families were being included as successes on rather flimsy grounds. Indeed, despite the early claim that 99% of families on the programme had been turned around, the DCLG's own impact assessment of the first TFP stated: 'we were unable to find consistent evidence that the Troubled Families Programme had any significant or systematic impact' (DCLG, 2016b: 49). In concentrating its efforts to tackle 'poverty and engrained disadvantage' (DWP, 2017: 3) on a small number of 'troubled' families, rather than on poverty as such, the policy discourse around poverty has significantly shifted – to the extent that it is questionable whether such a thing as 'poverty discourse', or indeed '*child* poverty discourse', still exists in mainstream policy arenas in the UK. As we show in the following section, the shifts discussed in this chapter so far both rely on and produce a discursive framing of 'workless' parents as infantile subjects.

Infantilising 'troubled' families

Viewing poor families as distinct – and usually culturally so – from the rest of the population typically leads to an assumption that these groups also warrant specific policy attention, often in the form of policies that aim at behavioural change rather than at direct improvement in the financial circumstances of poor families. As we have now argued, and as Lehtonen has established elsewhere (2018), it is specifically in the family – and in specific families – that governmental interventions to tackle the 'entrenched problems' (DWP, 2017: 21) and 'intergenerational cycle[s] of disadvantage' (DWP, 2017: 8) faced by disadvantaged families and children are centred. More specifically, the relevant policy papers (CPU, 2012; DWP, 2017) have tended to focus their interventions on parental values, norms and behaviours, thus contributing to the increasing 'parental determinism' (Gillies, 2012; see De Benedictis, 2012; Jensen, 2012; Jensen and Tyler, 2012) in policymaking in the austerity period. The Troubled Families Programme continues this trend, and here we want to highlight and interrogate some of the discursive framings of the notion of cultural poverty, arguing that it carries particular meanings that position families on the programme as infantile subjects.

The infantilisation of parents on the programme takes place at the level of both service delivery and rhetoric. The programme's mode of delivery has focused heavily on matching families with key workers, whose job it is to 'increase resilience by supporting with parenting, mental health issues, household budgeting, interparental relationships and any other significant issues that should be addressed' (MHCLG, 2019: 9). The one-on-one support also includes more specialist services such as work coaches. While the funding of work coaches and key workers is not in and of itself a problem, what is of concern to us is the limited reach of these resources – only particular families, designated as 'troubled', are assigned them – as well as the discursive – and, as we argue in the conclusion, institutional – landscape that envelops this support. Speaking in the Commons Chamber in 2015, for example, Mr Eric Pickles, the communities secretary in charge of the TFP, described the need for and the 'success' of the programme. He begins by conjuring up an image of inherited cultural poverty that we have critiqued earlier, and uses it to paint a picture of the need for the TFP:

> How many of us know families in our constituencies who have been failed by services but have at the same time placed a huge and disproportionate burden on those services through successive generations? Young men follow in their fathers' footsteps into trouble; young women fall victim to abusive relationships; and families push through the revolving doors of hard-pressed services with recurring problems of addiction, violence and mental and physical ill-health. I believed that there was a better way for those hard-pressed services to operate and through the troubled families programme we have found it. (HC Deb, 2015: c157).

Having set up cultural poverty as the central issue for 'troubled families', Pickles' rhetoric then mobilises an infantilising and paternalistic frame:

> Families in the programme have signed up to a plan that gets to the root cause of their problems and makes a real difference to their lives. It involves tough love and practical help from people who take a no-nonsense, persistent approach, who will not go away and will not give up, and who will not be put off by missed appointments or unanswered doors. (HC Deb, 2015: c157)

As should be clear by now, Pickles is completely avoiding the language of poverty and material inequality, framing the issue instead as the intergenerational cultural transmission of 'bad' behaviour. What is needed, he suggests, is the paternalistic state intervention of 'tough love' – replacing 'absent' and 'troubled' fathers with the paternal state's supposed care and support (see De Benedictis, 2012).[3]

In this rhetorical framing, then, infantilised parents *require* the state, and the state justifies its own authority as the arbiter of good and bad family behaviour. As Ruth Levitas argues, ' "troubled families" discursively collapses "families with troubles" and "troublesome families", while simultaneously implying that they are dysfunctional as families. This discursive strategy is successful in feeding vindictive attitudes to the poor' (2012: 5). The language of troubled, troubling and troublesome, we argue, relies on positioning these families as child-like, as infantile subjects whose unchecked libidinal desires are the cause of their poverty. Locating these families within the frame of childhood thus legitimates both a cultural blame and a paternalistic state. It also enables a complete bypassing of the material poverty faced by a significant proportion of TFP participants: an estimated 'two-thirds (66%) [of programme participants] had a net household income below £12,500 a year' (MCHLG, 2019: 17). Thus, while work coaching or the support of a keyworker to 'increase resilience' may be useful interventions, they are not, we argue, the most appropriate or successful strategies to 'turn around' families whose main issue is, in fact, poverty.

Troubled adults, criminal children

The argument that there is something culturally distinct about poor and disadvantaged populations, whose deprivation is the result of their allegedly lacking the norms and cultural resources to see the value in work, has been linked to the long-standing 'underclass' discourse that frames poverty as intrinsically linked to dysfunctional and criminal cultures (Pemberton et al, 2016; Shildrick et al, 2016). With this analysis in mind, the third and final discursive shift we discuss in this chapter is that of the convergence of poverty and criminalising discourses in recent policy agendas (Bond-Taylor, 2014), including but not exclusive to the Troubled Families Programme.

The original figure, cited earlier, of 120,000 'troubled families', was based on research conducted by the Social Exclusion Task Force (SETF). This research suggested that more policy attention should be focused on 'the complex needs of a small minority of families who face multiple and entrenched problems' (SETF, 2007: 4; see Levitas, 2012). However, while there is some overlap in the indicators identified in the original research and the ones chosen as key criteria for the TFP, two key differences should be highlighted. First, poverty (represented in the SETF research by a relative income measure) was one of the key indicators included in the original research, but not in the TFP. Second, crime or anti-social behaviour was not included in the original research, but was in the TFP. Thus, that there is a correlation between being poor or disadvantaged and causing crime was not among the original findings – and in fact, only 10% of the children in multiply disadvantaged families had had any contact with the police at all (Levitas, 2012: 10).

Nonetheless, 'crime and anti-social behaviour' became one of the 'headline problems' of the TFP (MCHLG, 2019: 8), and in 2014 the DCLG argued explicitly that 'troubled families are families who both have problems and often cause problems – where children are truanting or excluded, where there is youth crime or anti-social behaviour and where parents are not working' (2014: 7). That one of the key catalysts for the programme was the 2011 England 'riots' also suggests that the criminalisation of poor and multiply disadvantaged families and children was at the centre of the programme from the very beginning. In his speech following the 'riots' in August 2011, then Prime Minister David Cameron stated 'we need more urgent action, too, on the families that some people call "problem", others call "troubled"' (2011a). Naming the 'riots' as a 'wake-up call' (2011b), Cameron announced the TFP shortly after, in December 2011. Apart from, as previously discussed, raising questions about the original figure of 120,000 'troubled families' and the selection of participants, these moves also suggest a convergence between poverty and criminality in both policy discourse and measures. Overall, then, the discursive framing of the TFP makes a series of discursive jumps from poverty, via cultural dysfunction, to criminality.

In 2018 the Ministry of Housing, Communities and Local Government (MHCLG) announced 'a new £5 million fund to address [the issue of youth crime] through the existing Troubled Families Programme' (MHCLG, 2018b: 4), specifying that bids 'that will support families to build resilience and confidence in recognising and resisting the dangers of crime and violence and to make positive choices' (MHCLG, 2018b: 5) would be supported. This suggests that a further convergence between policy agendas addressing poverty and disadvantage on the one hand, and criminality on the other, is taking place. Further, the fund was specifically seeking proposals that aim to 'develop resilience', 'raise awareness', and increase understanding of 'the dangers and risks surrounding gang crime' (MHCLG, 2018b: 8) – rather than, again, addressing the material conditions in which disadvantaged children grow up – indicating a further individualisation and culturalisation of the discourses surrounding poverty and disadvantage, as well as, in this case, youth crime.

What we are identifying here, then, is that the government's attempts to obfuscate their own responsibility for economic inequality functioned not only through an infantilising discourse of poor parents, but also through placing poor children into a tenuous relationship to childhood. Across the discursive landscape of these policy shifts, there is a tacit refusal to speak about poor children *as children*. The qualifiers used – 'truanting', 'anti-social', 'cautioned and convicted' (MHCLG, 2018a) – work to remove the normative contours of innocence and purity from these children. Doing so avoids, at all costs, naming the issue as the poverty that children experience (a framing of the child as victim or object *of* the violence of poverty) and instead blames the child as an *agent* of their own misfortune. This is not a new manoeuvre: childhood has historically been a privileged subject space, one whose limited confines work to render marginalised populations less deserving. The normative frame of childhood that renders its subjects innocent and deserving of support is, thus, actively being worked against within the language of the TFP, as it relates to poor children.

This framing, however, is ambivalent. The TFP both relies on the sympathy that normative childhood evokes in order to render these policies – which it claims are 'helping' poor and disadvantaged children – as justifiably intervening in the 'bad behaviour' of poor families. But, at the same time, it uses criminality, deviance and adult-like agency as frames for discussing poor children themselves, removing them from the very frame of childhood that has just been mobilised to blame and stigmatise their parents. Consider the following contrast in discursive framings of childhood. At the start of his discussion of the TFP in the Commons Chambers, Pickles congratulates poor families for 'grasp[ing] the opportunity that this programme has offered to them to end a dysfunctional and negative way of life and offer their children a better future' (HC Deb, 2015: c157). Here, childhood as futurity is mobilised to justify the TFP's framing of individual and familial responsibility for economic disparity. Childhood, in this frame, is cast through the lens of what Lee Edelman designates as 'the Child': 'the perpetual horizon of every acknowledged politics, the fantasmatic beneficiary of every political intervention' (2004: 3). And yet, the stigmatising and hostile rhetoric of the TFP's individualising blame is palpable and indicative of a wider disdain of poor and disadvantaged children themselves. Qualifying the success of the programme, Pickles, in the same session, makes an extraordinary claim: 'We need to be absolutely clear that we are almost certainly not turning out model citizens ... Turning [children's] lives around mean[s]: drastically reducing the antisocial behaviour and crime for which they were responsible; [and] ensuring that truanting children were back attending school' (HC Deb, 2015: c162).

While childhood as futurity is being mobilised, then, to bolster the claim of the TFP's successes, the actual children who are supposedly being supported by this very programme are clearly not understood to have a hold on this futurity. Their location within childhood, within innocence and 'a better future', is discursively cast as tenuous at best. Growing up under the UK's regime of austerity, a regime that criminalises and stigmatises the conditions of poverty that austerity itself reproduces and entrenches, means, in other words, growing up with a partial hold on childhood.

Conclusion

What might be required, then, to ensure that poor children and their families could have a tangible hold on 'a better future'? While we are remiss to suggest a particular policy agenda that speaks on behalf of poor children, we want to conclude by suggesting that our method of using childhood as a frame of analysis might be useful in revealing the broader discursive manoeuvres that have enabled a governmental shirking of responsibility in addressing child poverty. Our discussion in this chapter has focused on the discursive framings that position poor children and poor parents as not-quite-children and child-like, respectively, but it is not just the poor families themselves who incur these rhetorical positionings. Tellingly, and importantly, local authorities have also been positioned in a paternalistic relationship vis- à-vis the government through the TFP. Here, we conclude by interrogating this framing and discussing briefly what it suggests about the decimation of universal care and services more generally.

The TFP's funding structure has, until recently, operated entirely on a 'payment by results' basis, requiring local authorities to achieve success in 'turning around' troubled families before receiving any central government funding. This funding model, as well as the new model discussed later that has partially supplanted it, must be understood within the wider political economy of austerity and the associated cuts to universally accessible state support and services. The austerity period has seen local authority funding cut considerably, with significant consequences for councils' ability to offer both statutory and discretionary services (Morse, 2014). Martin Smith and Rhonda Jones (2015), for example, document average cuts of 10.4% per local authority between 2010 and 2012, with some of the most deprived areas facing cuts of up to 25% by 2016. At the same time, the last ten years have also seen a gradual shift whereby the responsibility for service provision has increasingly been placed at the doorsteps of various public and private bodies, including local authorities, instead of the central government. The TFP funding model – which places the onus of ending 'worklessness' and tackling child poverty on local authorities – is thus indicative of the wider move away from universally accessible, state-provided, funding and services, and towards a model whereby local authorities are increasingly seen as akin to private sector enterprises, competing for central government funding that, when gained, comes attached to significant conditions as to how the money can be spent.

This context also places the local authority actions to match the estimated numbers of 'troubled families' in their area, discussed earlier, in a starkly different light, particularly given the significant financial benefits attached to 'turning around' the highest possible number of families. To be clear, then, our argument here is not that local authorities are to blame for the TFP's shortcomings. On the contrary, we are suggesting that blaming local authorities is part and parcel of the government's decentralising and obfuscating of its own responsibility for universal service provision. As a tactic, this blaming demands that individuals – here: local authorities – somehow compensate for the structural issues that they are mired in.

This becomes all the more clear in relation to the more recent shift in the TFP's funding structure, which has moved from operating solely through a 'payment by results' model (discussed previously) to what has been called an 'earned autonomy' model (MHCLG, 2018a). Following a review of the original funding structure in 2017, the new model was introduced to allow particular local authorities to access investment upfront for specific projects. This framing of 'earned autonomy', particularly in contrast to the decimation of local authority funding that has occurred concurrently to the discursive and policy shifts discussed in this chapter, all too clearly demarcates local authorities as child-like (dis)obedient citizens whose 'earned' capacity for agency and selfhood is dependent on 'good behaviour', as defined by the paternal government.

This recent move indicates two final points. First, it suggests that deployments of the frame of childhood are not limited to young people, nor individuals. Local authorities, akin to the parents they are desperately seeking to care for, are designated child-like as well, in as much as this designation places them in a relation of dependency to the paternalistic government. This relation of dependency, we have argued, seeks to reify the government's position of power in the face of its abandonment of its role in caring for those who face circumstances of poverty and disadvantage. Second, the expansion of the frame of childhood to local authorities as a means of furthering the government's refusal to take ownership of the effects of austerity suggests that, while the support made possible by an expanded TFP might be beneficial for some, we cannot envision a 'successful' version of this programme within the current political context.

In recognising that both families and local authorities are positioned in such a way, it becomes clear that the discursive shifts we have discussed in this chapter are telling of the broader, systemic decimation of state-provided universal support services over the last ten years. And yet, in acknowledging this, we are not suggesting that all hope is lost. On the contrary, while we cannot feign to predict what the next few years will look like in the UK (as we write this conclusion, the UK is preparing for yet another general election after three years of seeking to negotiate a withdrawal from the EU), we are suggesting that the frame of analysis we have offered here might support the articulation of critical future engagements with the state. Using childhood as a frame, we have argued, means becoming aware of the ways in which individuals and populations are being insidiously positioned across scales in relationship to power. It is a form of analysis that exposes the multiple layers of political will that are invested in denying governmental accountability for the circumstances that poor children face growing up under austerity. Our hope is that in directing scholars' attention to this frame we might collectively be enabled to push back against future moments in which governments again seek to shirk their responsibilities, leaving poor families and children in the wake.

Notes

[1] This aim was enshrined in legislation in the Child Poverty Act 2010, passed with cross-party support just a few months before the formation of the coalition government in 2010. The act established four income-based child poverty targets, as well as required the government to publish a regular child poverty strategy and annual progress reports, and initiated the setting up of the Child Poverty Commission to independently monitor governmental progress in eradicating child poverty.

[2] Apart from the TFP, the 2017 paper offers few solutions to tackling poverty and disadvantage. Universal Credit is touted as 'reforming the welfare system to make work pay' (DWP, 2017: 15), and paid employment is also positioned centrally within almost all of the other solutions presented in the paper, including the solutions offered to people with disabilities or with drug and alcohol dependency (Lehtonen, 2018).

3   While here we have focused specifically on comments made by Eric Pickles, similar
    rhetorical moves have been made by various others – see for instance Labour MP
    Fiona O'Donnell (HC Deb, 2014: cols 341WH–342WH) and then Prime Minister
    David Cameron (HC Deb, 2011: c1054).

References

Bailey, N. (2016) 'Exclusionary employment in Britain's broken labour market', *Critical Social Policy*, 36(1): 82–103.

Berlant, L. (1997) *The queen of American goes to Washington City: Essays on sex and citizenship*, Durham, NC: Duke University Press.

Bernstein, R. (2011) *Racial innocence: Performing American childhood from slavery to civil rights*, New York: New York University Press.

Bond-Taylor, S. (2014) 'The politics of "anti-social" behaviour within the 'Troubled Families' Programme', in: S. Pickard (ed) *Anti-social behaviour in Britain: Victorian and contemporary perspectives*, Basingstoke: Palgrave MacMillan, pp.141–54.

Bradshaw, J. (2016a) 'Introduction', in: J. Bradshaw (ed) *The well-being of children in the UK* (4th edn), Bristol: Policy Press, pp.1–12.

Bradshaw, J. (2016b) 'Conclusion', in: J. Bradshaw (ed) *The well-being of children in the UK* (4th edn), Bristol: Policy Press, pp.347–58.

Bradshaw, J. and Main, G. (2016) 'Child poverty and deprivation', in: J. Bradshaw (ed) *The well-being of children in the UK* (4th edn), Bristol: Policy Press, pp.31–70.

Breslow, J. (2019) 'Adolescent citizenship, or temporality and the negation of black childhood in two eras', *American Quarterly*, 71(2): 473–494.

Cameron, D. (2011a) *PM's speech on the fightback after the riots*, Speech, 15 August, https://www.gov.uk/government/speeches/pms-speech-on-the-fightback-after-the-riots

Cameron, D. (2011b) *Troubled families speech*, Speech, 15 December, https://www.gov.uk/government/speeches/troubled-families-speech

Castañeda, C. (2002) *Figurations: Child, bodies, worlds*, Durham, NC: Duke University Press.

CPAG (Child Poverty Action Group) (2019). *Child poverty facts and figures*, https://cpag.org.uk/child-poverty/child-poverty-facts-and-figures

CPU (Child Poverty Unit) (2012) *Measuring child poverty: A consultation on better measures for child poverty*, London: The Stationery Office, https://assets.publishing.service.gov.uk/government/uploads/system/uploads/attachment_data/file/228829/8483.pdf

DCLG (Department for Communities and Local Government) (2014) *Understanding troubled families*, London: DCLG, https://assets. publishing.service.gov.uk/government/uploads/system/uploads/ attachment_data/file/336430/Understanding_Troubled_Families_ web_format.pdf

DCLG (Department for Communities and Local Government) (2015) 'PM praises Troubled Families Programme success', Press Release, 22 June, https://www.gov.uk/government/news/ pm-praises-troubled-families-programme-success

DCLG (Department for Communities and Local Government) (2016a) *The first Troubled Families Programme 2012 to 2015*, London: DCLG, https://assets.publishing.service.gov.uk/government/uploads/ system/uploads/attachment_data/file/560776/The_first_Troubled_ Families_Programme_an_overview.pdf

DCLG (Department for Communities and Local Government) (2016b) *National evaluation of the Troubled Families Programme: Final synthesis report*, London: DCLG, https://assets.publishing.service.gov.uk/ government/uploads/system/uploads/attachment_data/file/560499/ Troubled_Families_Evaluation_Synthesis_Report.pdf

De Benedictis, S. (2012) '"Feral" parents: Austerity parenting under neoliberalism', *Studies in the Maternal*, 4(2): 1–21.

DfE (Department for Education) (2011) *A new approach to child poverty: Tackling the causes of disadvantage and transforming families' lives*, London: The Stationery Office, https://www.gov.uk/government/ uploads/system/uploads/attachment_data/file/177031/CM-8061. pdf

Dispatches (2016) *Dispatches*, Channel 4, TV series, 17 October.

DWP (Department for Work and Pensions) (2017) *Improving lives: Helping workless families*, London: DWP, https://assets.publishing. service.gov.uk/government/uploads/system/uploads/attachment_ data/file/621364/improving-lives-helping-workless-families-web- version.pdf

Gillies, V. (2012) 'Personalising poverty: Parental determinism and the Big Society agenda', in: W. Atkinson, S. Roberts and M. Savage (eds) *Class inequality in austerity Britain: Power, difference and suffering*, Basingstoke: Palgrave Macmillan, pp.90–110.

HC Deb (House of Commons) (2011) *11 August Debate*, vol 531, cols 1053–1054, https://hansard.parliament.uk/commons/2011-08-11/ debates/1108117000001/PublicDisorder

HC Deb (House of Commons) (2014) *30 January Debate*, vol 574, cols 341WH–2WH, https://hansard.parliament.uk/Commons/2014-01- 30/debates/14013068000001/EarlyChildhoodDevelopment

HC Deb (House of Commons) (2015) *10 March Debate*, vol 594, cols 157–162, https://hansard.parliament.uk/Commons/2015-03-10/debates/15031024000002/TroubledFamiliesProgramme

Jensen, T. (2012) 'Tough love in tough times', *Studies in the Maternal*, 4(2): 1–26.

Jensen, T. and Tyler, I. (2012) 'Editorial. Austerity parenting: New economies of parent-citizenship', *Studies in the Maternal*, 4(2): 1.

JRF (Joseph Rowntree Foundation) (2018) *UK Poverty 2018: A comprehensive analysis of poverty trends and figures*, York: JRF.

Lehtonen, A. (2018) '"Helping workless families": Cultural poverty and the family in austerity and anti welfare discourse', *Sociological Research Online*, 23(1): 84–99.

Levander, C. (2006) *Cradle of liberty: Race, the child, and national belonging from Thomas Jefferson to W.E.B. Du Bois*, Durham, NC: Duke University Press.

Levitas, R. (2012) 'There may be "trouble" ahead: What we know about those 120,000 "troubled" families', Bristol/Glasgow: Poverty and Social Exclusion.

Levitas, R. (2014) 'Troubled families' in a spin, Bristol/Glasgow: Poverty and Social Exclusion, http://www.poverty.ac.uk/sites/default/files/attachments/Troubled%20Families%20in%20a%20Spin.pdf

MacDonald, R., Shildrick, T. and Furlong, A. (2014) 'In search of "intergenerational cultures of worklessness": Hunting the yeti and shooting zombies,' *Critical Social Policy*, 34(2): 199–220.

Main, G. and Bradshaw, J. (2016) 'Child poverty in the UK: Measures, prevalence and intra-household sharing', *Critical Social Policy*, 36(1): 38–61.

MHCLG (Ministry of Housing, Communities and Local Government) (2018a) *Supporting disadvantaged families: Annual report of the Troubled Families Programme 2017–18*, London: MHCLG, https://assets.publishing.service.gov.uk/government/uploads/system/uploads/attachment_data/file/694362/CCS207_CCS0318142796-1_Un_Act_Troubled_Families_AR_2017-18_Accessible__2_.pdf

MHCLG (Ministry of Housing, Communities and Local Government) (2018b) *Troubled Families Programme: Supporting families against youth crime*, London: MHCLG, https://assets.publishing.service.gov.uk/government/uploads/system/uploads/attachment_data/file/749843/Supporting_Families_Against_Youth_Crime_Prospectus.pdf

MHCLG (Ministry of Housing, Communities and Local Government) (2019) *National evaluation of the Troubled Families Programme 2015–2020: Findings*, London: MHCLG, https://assets.publishing. service.gov.uk/government/uploads/system/uploads/attachment_ data/file/786889/National_evaluation_of_the_Troubled_Families_ Programme_2015_to_2020_evaluation_overview_policy_report.pdf

Morse, A. (2014) *The impact of funding reductions on local authorities*, London: National Audit Office (NAO), https://www.nao.org.uk/ wp-content/uploads/2014/11/Impact-of-funding-reductions-on-local-authorities.pdf

Pemberton, S., Fahmy, E., Sutton, E. and Bell, K. (2016) 'Navigating the stigmatised identities of poverty in austere times: Resisting and responding to narratives of personal failure', *Critical Social Policy*, 36(1): 21–37.

Portes, J. and Reed, H. (2017) *Distributional results for the impact of tax and welfare reforms between 2010–17, modelled in the 2021/22 tax year: Interim findings, November 2017*, Manchester: Equality and Human Rights Commission (EHRC), https://www.equalityhumanrights. com/sites/default/files/impact-of-tax-and-welfare-reforms-2010-2017-interim-report_0.pdf

Shildrick, T., MacDonald, R. and Furlong, A. (2016) 'Not single spies but in battalions: A critical, sociological engagement with the idea of so-called "Troubled Families"', *The Sociological Review*, 64(4): 821–836.

SETF (Social Exclusion Task Force) (2007) *Families at risk: Background on families with multiple disadvantages*, London: Cabinet Office, https:// webarchive.nationalarchives.gov.uk/20100407191619/http://www. cabinetoffice.gov.uk/media/cabinetoffice/social_exclusion_task_ force/assets/families_at%20_risk/risk_data.pdf

Smith, M. and Jones, R. (2015) 'From big society to small state: Conservatism and the privatisation of government', *British Politics*, 10(2): 226–248.

Taylor-Robinson, D., Lai, E.T.C., Wickham, S., Rose, T., Norman, P., Bambra, C., Whitehead, M. and Barr, B. (2019) 'Assessing the impact of rising child poverty on the unprecedented rise in infant mortality in England, 2000–2017: Time trend analysis', *BMJ Open*, 9(10): 1–6.

Wiggan, J. (2012) 'Telling stories of 21st century welfare: The UK coalition government and the neo-liberal discourse of worklessness and dependency', *Critical Social Policy*, 32(3): 383–405.

10

Learning to pay: the financialisation of childhood

Carl Walker, Peter Squires and Carlie Goldsmith

Introduction

In the UK in 2020, there appears to be a broad consensus in academic, media and policy discourses on the value of financial education. Youth financial education in particular, remains a strong focus of policymakers, scholars and researchers, with the general agreement being that financial education for youth is of vital importance to the long-term fiscal wellbeing of individuals, families and indeed the UK as a whole (Fox et al, 2005; Sherraden et al, 2011). As Totenhagen at al (2015) state, 'Reaching youth before poor financial habits are established is essential for long-term financial well-being' (p.180). As evidenced by the work of the OECD over the last 20 years, the importance of financial education for financial stability and inclusive development is globally acknowledged (Atkinson and Messy, 2013; Maman and Rosenhek, 2020).

How best to deliver financial education, what materials to include and who should be charged with this responsibility are all areas for debate in the ethical drive to optimally influence young people's financial capability. However, the real fly in the ointment of the international financial education movement is the growing body of research which suggest that it doesn't actually work. Gudmunson and Dames (2011) note that the uncomfortable conundrum in this field was how often financial knowledge actually proved ineffective as a predictor of financial behaviour or indeed change in behaviour.

This chapter draws on an analysis of recent UK financial education tools and practices produced by for-profit financial institutions. We seek to reflect on what we consider to be some of the more questionable practices involved in youth financial education in the UK. We locate these practices in broader debates about the financialisation of childhood and suggest that, while financial education is a seductive imaginary for the neoliberal age, a range of fundamental misunderstandings about financial strain and its precursors, potentially toxic constructions of childhood and an increasingly questionable commercial shaping of youth fatally wound the promise of financial education.

Financialising childhood: shaping children's subjectivities

The OECD recently stated that financial education is 'the process by which financial consumers/investors improve their understanding of financial products, concepts and risks and, through information, instruction and/or objective advice, develop skills and confidence to become more aware of financial risks and opportunities, to make informed choices, to know where to go for help, and to take other effective actions to improve their financial wellbeing' (Arrondel, 2018: 246). In contemporary OECD policy contexts, such a take on the financial world is the dominant frame of reference in making sense of the need to equip citizens with financial knowledge. However, there is an increasing body of work that recognises and critiques financial education as a public pedagogy of financialisation that wholly fails to cultivate the skills and competencies to allow people to plug into an increasingly volatile and unforgiving globalised market (Haiven, 2014).

For Haiven (2014), financialisation is the way in which financial measurements, ideas, tropes, and metaphors migrate beyond the finance sector into other areas of society. Financialisation has encroached on many areas of public life – health, personal debt, decreased welfare, the prison system and school – and increasingly guides people to act in the world on the basis of economic imperatives. Moreover, for Haiven (2014), this financialisation is in the form taken by a neoliberal capitalism that is increasingly predicated on crafting subjectivities: that is, transforming the way we understand ourselves as citizens. Of relevance to this chapter is the way that these forces of cultural production, through which subjectivities are crafted, are able to monopolise meaning and broadcast knowledge through school curricula.

The economies of the west have been kept afloat by a willingness of people to go further into debt and where young adults and teens are encouraged to apply for credit cards to cultivate a credit rating and teach themselves 'financial literacy' (Haiven, 2014). For Marron (2014), the financial education paradigm ignores these realities and ignores the structural disadvantage facing certain young people, instead reframing the problem as one of insufficient or maladjusted behaviour. Here, the project of financial education concerns itself with formatting the ways in which individuals think about themselves such that political concerns about financial strain are refracted into the uncontested attributes of individuals.

Maman and Rosenhek (2018) position the creation of financialised subjectivities as part of a broader neoliberal responsibilisation that assumes, and purports to create, a world of knowable, calculable and manageable future risk. Through these financial education technologies, actors are encouraged to overcome uncertainty by developing imaginaries of possible futures and causal explanations that confer an economic world of order and predictability. The possibility that economic futures and their determinants may be essentially unforeseeable is not part of the discourse.

The fundamentally political character of these practices is evident in the way that they shape imaginaries of the future. Pinto and Coulson (2011) warn against the tremendous power held by the creators of financial education materials that infiltrate the classroom with their financial literacy resources. This is especially relevant when we consider that profit-making organisations have been providing teachers with their versions of financial literacy for decades (Pinto and Coulson, 2011).

Why financial education doesn't work

One key issue that undermines the promise of financial education concerns the potential options available to people who engage in financial transactions: that is, the capacity that people may or may not have to make what might be considered to be 'good' financial decisions. Research suggests that the prevalence of debt is substantial among young people in the UK: on average 49% were reported to have at least some debt, with 22% having financial problems (Hoeve et al, 2014). Ben-Galim and Lanning (2010) suggest that it was unlikely that financial planning could change things for a significant number of low income families in problem debt and that the literature suggests that low income families tend to do better than wealthier families when budgeting. In this frame, problem debt is an issue not of budgeting but of income inadequacy, where people lack the capacity to put into practice the fruits of their financial education learning (Williams, 2007).

A recent report by the Financial Conduct Authority (2014) suggests that 25% of the UK population feel burdened by debt and almost 30% of households with income lower than £13,500 spend more than 30% of their income servicing debts; 1.1m people on low incomes need credit access but are unable to borrow. Moreover, nearly one in five people with a household income of less than £20,000 are permanently overdrawn. An estimated 790,000 low income credit card holders habitually make minimum payments with 121,000 doing it for more than three years. The Equality and Human Rights Commission (EHRC) report, *Is Britain fairer?* (EHRC, 2015), showed that during the recession and up to 2013, people aged under 34 were hit by the steepest drops in pay and employment, had less access to decent housing and better paid jobs, and were experiencing deepening levels of poverty.

Thus any discussion of financial education and context needs to consider that these are played out across a continua of social class that enables and restricts certain ways to behave with money. Young adults from the highest income brackets and college-educated families are relatively protected from student loan debt compared to the less advantaged (Houle, 2013). Majamaa (2011) notes the invisible parental compensatory mechanism that offsets the economic vulnerability of many young adults. Atkinson (2005) found that poor children know far less about banks and banking services than their better off peers, but on the other hand if the family is poor, children tend to have a greater awareness of the budgeting techniques used by their parents and are acutely aware of parents regularly paying bills.

Kaiser and Menkoff (2017) suggests that there is a lack of compelling evidence that providing financial education is an effective policy for targeting financial behaviour, with impacts on debt-related behaviours among low income individuals being short-lived. It has been suggested that the effect of financial knowledge on the persistence and level of debt is equivocal (Kamleitner, 2012). Eturk et al (2007) argue that, although boosting financial literacy may be a worthwhile objective, improved literacy does not, in its own right, secure positive economic outcomes for people from indebted households. Mandell and Klein (2009) found that those who took a financial literacy course were no more financially literate than those who had not and did not appear to have better financial behaviour than those who took the course.

McCormick (2009) suggests that several studies show no relationship between financial education and knowledge and behaviour and rails against the 'blame the victim' subtext in much of the material. The authors suggest that, while the certainties of the financial education paradigm are seductive, they are empirically unsupported and implausible given the velocity of change in financial markets. Moreover, they don't take into consideration predatory lending, mortgage foreclosures, joblessness, and other key contextual forces. Indeed McCormick suggests that any realistic education should involve pawn shops and their costs and benefits.

Williams counselled on the need to face the sheer ungovernability of consumer decision making (Williams, 2007: 244). Studies repeatedly show that individuals select differently from among the same options depending on context of their choice and how it is framed, with departures from the assumptions of rational decision making common, persistent, and difficult for education to correct. Indeed even if it were possible to overcome through education the human contextual biases and heuristics that guide financial decision making in the age of mass consumerism, the sheer advantage in resources of the advertising and financial firms puts them in position to take advantage of biases and beat the educators who try to train biases out of them (McCormick, 2009).

There thus appears to be sufficient scope for reservations about the role of financial education in the broader financialisation of children's lives. We are unconvinced that most citizens behave in accordance with the rationalist precepts promulgated through financial guidance and believe that the sets of tools articulated in financial education do not speak well to the complexity of contextual disadvantage and the everyday debt ambience that characterises many people's lived experiences of money. It is with these considerations in mind that we analysed the children's financial education materials of several for-profit providers.

UK financial education resources

What follows is a series of analytic observations from an in-depth analysis of nine financial education websites, materials and teaching resources aimed at young people, parents and teachers in the UK. These were drawn from for-profit financial institutions, most of whom were high street banks. These include over 50 documents drawn from money and life skills programme with a particular focus on the financial educations resources. The key focus of this analysis was to understand how young people's economic citizenship is constructed through studying the pedagogic imaginaries, technologies and practices of these financial education materials. The focus was on the subjectivities, relationships and the orientations they seek to produce: how they position young people, debt, money and the economic sphere. A key limitation of the work within is that there is no data available currently about the degree to which these financial literacy resources are used (Pinto and Coulson, 2011). The analysis draws on multimodal critical discourse analysis through using Pauwels' (2011) multimodal model for analysing websites as social and cultural expressions. This multimodal framework for analysing websites is an overarching framework to guide data collection and interpretation. Pauwels (2012) suggests a systematic approach based on six phases: (1) Preservation of first impressions and reactions: this phase involves the ability for the researcher to pre-record initial interpretations; (2) Inventory of salient features and topics: here the collation and formation of an inventory of salient modalities present (and absent) is made. Once elements have been initially selected they are assembled so that semiotic resources can be assigned or as Pauwels (2012) suggests, clustered; (3) In-depth analysis of content and formal choices; (4) Embedded points of view or 'voice' and implied audience(s) and purposes; (5) Analysis of information organisation and spatial priming strategies; and (6) Contextual analysis, provenance and inference. Note that financial institutions are anonymised in the following analysis.

Brand promotion and rehabilitation

The 2008 financial crash did much to sharpen the conflict between banks and customers with considerable poor-feeling toward the banking sector as a whole (Ross, 2013). Bailouts from public funds accompanied by the ramping up of austerity and associated cuts in spending damaged the reputation of the banking sector as a whole (Dear et al, 2013). Indeed many billions of UK taxpayers' money has been used to support the banks although reform in bonuses and salaries was not publicly evidenced (Lewis, 2010). Banks have also been criticised for pursuing greater profits in the short term to the potential detriment of increasingly leveraged consumer borrowers in the longer term (Griffiths, 2007: 234; Mellor, 2010) with debt cast as big business for banks seeking to deliver ever more elusive record profits.

This was context in which these institutions appeared to produce materials which oriented them to a broader social justice portfolio. The programmes that we reviewed broadened the portfolio from simple money management to offering holistic life skills coaching embedded in a broader social context. The company branding was very much evident when these materials presented their new social justice remit.

Numerous programmes specifically used the same branding and colour schemes as their mainstream high street banking service. Familiar logos and palettes framed forays in social justice, with the organisations positioning themselves as uniquely able to challenge the big injustices facing society: 'Y programme is one of several flagship programmes which contribute X Banking group's ambition to help Britain prosper, focussing on the social and economic issues which the group is best placed to address.'

It was not uncommon for these programmes to make claims to a broader social purpose. These resources often positioned the banks as being 'more than a bank' — that is, an ethical social justice institution intent on addressing housing, skills and social disadvantage: 'We want to go beyond business as usual and help address systemic social and economic challenges such as Britain's housing shortage, the skills gap in key industries and social disadvantage.'

The education products were sometimes linked to clear offers of support from the financial organisations to come into schools and deliver the material (which is currently happening). That the products and training are free likely contributes to their uptake: 'Our X volunteers are ready and willing to run lifeskills lessons in local schools. Why not invite a volunteer into the classroom? We take requests with a minimum of 5–6 weeks' notice due to the phenomenal demand for volunteer-led workshops across the UK.'

For one high street bank, a budgeting tool included three clear steps of financial guidance after which a link said, 'Wait, *can someone else do the maths for me?*' whereupon the young person could call the high street bank for support, even without being a customer. Here, budget tools could also be read as an ingratiation device which pulls young people into a relationship with the bank. In conjunction with the social justice remit, some high street banks clearly position themselves as a financial services broker for young people. It takes around 20 minutes for a young person to complete one bank budgeting tool during which point the bank are, in essence banking for them, albeit without an account.

In one 'student finance myths' section, a series of myths chosen by the bank allows the institution to position itself as a lifestyle guru offering solutions in response to their own myths. What appears to be a notable disclaimer (with logo) is visible at the bottom of the webpage also appears conspicuously like a reminder to the reader of who it was who just offered them free advice on their money in their time of need: 'X programme is funded by the Y banking group'.

The money skills session overview for 11–14 year olds of one bank confidently states that they will *Help you to understand the skills you will need*. Here young people not only lack skills but lack the ability to understand the skills that they don't have. This bank then position themselves as the institution that is able to remediate these gaps, all written in, and framed by the same brand colouring of the main high street bank.

One programme positions itself as addressing the skills gap in the UK. However there was a disjunct between the skills being offered by these courses and the skills gap that is generally acknowledged in UK industry. The *actual* skills gap concerns a dwindling pool of skilled workers, software engineers, building trades, engineer, linguists, midwives, programmers and electricians (The Edge Foundation, 2018).

What one high street bank actually offers, however, is a curious mixture of guidance and self-help platitudes on networking, writing a CV, time and money management. We would argue that the labour achieved here is not a meaningful foray into industrial skills building, rather the skills gap rhetoric reveals a carefully branded exercise in constructing commercialised citizenship while warming a future cohort of banking customers to a trusted company.

These resources can be read at face value as an attempt to reach out and support young people facing life challenges. However, considering the toxic background context of high street banks, the emphasis on social justice work and the preponderance of branded life skills tools suggests that these resources also function as a brand detoxification exercise for the next generation of eager potential customers.

Financialising the self

Beyond the redemption and promotion of the company's banking services, there is the issue of the commercial construction of young citizenship which emerges from some of these programmes. A number of these money skills programmes are embedded in broader life skills programmes that purport to support young people with a range of life skills, with financial education sometimes playing a relatively small part.

Through their focus on enterprise, entrepreneurialism, teamwork, networking, writing a CV, interview skills, listening, identifying strengths, time and money management, these organisations are invoking a commercialised training in how young people should present themselves to the world. The imagining of young people as 'brands' suggests the creation of commercial notions of citizenship and the skills gap imaginaries on which they are premised: 'Supports young people to develop their self-awareness and self-confidence to support them in building a professional personal brand.'

This evidences a marketing approach to citizenship, where young people are asked to *develop an enterprising mindset* to sell their personal brand in the marketplace. Financial skills for a number of these programmes are embedded within this enterprise discourse, with financial education programmes explicitly oriented toward producing imaginaries of young entrepreneurs. Moreover, they are often specifically focused on '*Vulnerable young people*' to disseminate their enterprise programmes. Indeed for some of the websites, entrepreneurialism and an enterprising mindset are positioned as the solutions through which vulnerable young people can shed their vulnerability.

One bank's experts 'deliver practical enterprise experiences by giving young people access to interest-free loans and market places to set up their own initiatives. We also provide financial literacy and social enterprise education with the National Citizens Service'. Here citizenship is equated with taking part in the market in order to make profit. Banks' offers of interest-free loans allows them to fulfil 'their mission to empower young people to take charge of their future by bringing money and enterprise to life'.

The futures invoked here, are made possible by financially tying young people to a profit-driven financial entity via an interest-free loan such that young people can engage in practices that 'bring money to life'. Notably absent in the realisations of this enterprising brand guidance are why such citizenship work might resonate with an organisation that is beholden to the creation of profit for its shareholder. Indeed, one bank's 'mission' constructs it through a colonial religious discourse which moves the stake of the financial institutions closer to practices of morality and away from practices of providing shareholder value: '#laugh as you learn under our values ~straight up @Bank telling it how it really is'. We argue that such discourses entice vulnerable young people to relate to the institution as one that is value-based. These practices of commercial citizenship funnel all manner of activities through an enterprise mission with one bank reminding the user to 'see how our experts helped young single mothers and care leavers get on top of their finances and become digitally literate'.

Likewise 'For young people on zero-hour contracts, the unpredictability of incomes means their margins are much thinner than those in full time employment. See how we helped Matt take control.' These materials create imaginaries of young people, replete with cognitive and financial deficits, struggling with a world over which they have little control. Here these banks, and their associated financial materials, offer more than an ability to manage a budget or think through spending plans. They offer no less than a route by which to take control of the world around them through financialising it.

Depictions of poverty in these materials are rife with language that suggests that young people just need to control their spending and have 'confidence' in managing money. Multiple deficits of character are clearly articulated, often under case studies suggesting poor and profligate young people who, with the remediating help of the financial institution, were able to be reformed: 'I get why it's now important to be conservative with how I spend my money.'

The increasing gap between prices and incomes in most parts of the country, the growth of inequality and in-work poverty, and the stratification of financial strain through race and social class are solved by entrepreneurial directives to adapt to and thrive in this economic and social landscape. Young people's deficits are aligned with their minimal capacity to develop financial virtuosity and sophistication.

In these financial education materials we see the establishment of a financial relationship between the young person and the bank and between the young person and the world around them. It is clear from the materials that they function to enable the uptake of white, liberal, middle-class, male, norms around the entrepreneurial worker citizen. And while these materials are liberally spattered with brown faces, the financial imaginaries of adulthood invoked in their content rarely speaks to the lived realities and challenges facing young people of colour and those from low income backgrounds.

The contradictory, ill-fitting nature of the materials

In the year 2020 as we go to press, 15% of UK citizens have no savings at all, 33% have less than £1,500 in savings, and 53% of 22–29 year olds have no savings (Finder, 2020). Following the 2008 crash, household debt increased rapidly from £600 billion in 1999 up to £1,400 billion in 2008, according to Bank of England data (The Money Charity, 2020). With the Office for Budget Responsibility's March 2019 forecast projecting that, by 2023–24, household debt will reach £2.425 trillion, an average household debt of £86,388. According to the Bank of England there appears to be no immediate likelihood of this upward trend stopping.

A recent FCA (2014) survey showed that many people had issues with additional charges for missed payments or failed direct debits, and raising cash or making extended minimum payments on credit cards. Of people with a household income of less than £20,000, 18% are permanently overdrawn. Research by the Money Advice Service suggests that more than half of UK adults are worried their mental health is being affected by worries over money and two thirds of us are worried about a friend suffering because of money worries (Money Advice Service, 2018).

In short, personal debt has become normalised and ambient in Britain and is by most accounts on the increase. Andrew Ross (2013) describes a creditocracy where normal living costs require to be debt financed and where the moral injunction to pay back is the disciplinary backbone of today's finance capitalism. The websites and teaching materials made available through these organisations did not reflect well the day to day challenges of many people which were outlined earlier.

The financial coaching materials produced citizen imaginaries that were notable for the absence of the scale of many people's financial challenges and the reasons why people become indebted. Moreover, the banking institutions in the field of finance were largely constructed as benign, avuncular presences somewhat at odds with the reality (Walker et al, 2015).

The financial education materials reviewed provide a very 'slim' take on financial products and processes that appear to prepare mythical young people replete with agency and rational thought for a financial world that largely doesn't exist. The content is driven by narrow, outdated and problematic versions of financial products, young people, institutions and pressures that young people tend to encounter.

It was common for the materials to provide examples of young people's accounts routinely in credit. They uncritically introduce finance practices which could be read as problematic (banks rewarding young people with free gifts) and contain absences on the realities of debt collection practices, sales practices and problematic sales incentivisation structures (Walker et al, 2015), proportionality of bank charges, compound charges and rollovers and credit rating calculations, among others. Finally, there was almost nothing that recognised the links between low income and high cost of credit or indeed the high cost of credit generally.

These resources could be summarised as imagining an agentic young person who can perpetually maintain a positive bank balance through making the right choices. For instance, on a module on exploring bank accounts and credit cards:

A free overdraft facility can be helpful in certain situations (for example, budgeting on a student loan that comes termly) provided you manage it well and make sure you know when the free period ends. If you have a big overdraft you need to ensure you can clear it before you start being charged for it.

Here is a version of the student that is curiously antiquated, where such possibilities as 'clearing an overdraft' are routinely within the student's control. We would suggest that for many, the vision of the agentic saving young person is obsolete or at the very least hamstrung by class blindness: 'An instant access account is essential if you are likely to need savings quickly in an emergency, but it will pay less interest than an account for which you need to give a period of notice for withdrawals.' Or, on banking apps on their phone: 'Most providers now offer this facility and it's worth using ... You can set up a text alert system so you get a regular update on the balance of your account or a message when you are in danger of becoming overdrawn on your account.'

This appears to be premised on the idea that being overdrawn is due to lack of knowledge or financial mindfulness rather than an increasing number of young people who need to manage multiple credit cards, loans and overdrawn accounts. However, a survey of 2,042 18–24 year olds, conducted for the Money Advice Trust by YouGov, found that 37% are already in debt, owing an average of £2,989 (excluding student loans and mortgages) – with 51% of adults under 25 reporting that they regularly worry about money and 21% losing sleep as a result (Money Advice Trust, 2016). The report found that credit cards, overdrafts and loans from family and friends all feature strongly in 18–24 year olds' borrowing habits. More than two thirds (67%) of 18–24 year olds have some form of borrowing, with the average student loan balance standing at £25,505 (Money Advice Trust, 2016), and around a third (32%) feel that their debts are a 'heavy burden'.

Overwhelmingly, banks' charging practices are positioned as inevitable and unquestioned and banks once again as benign, avuncular presences rather than ferocious sales machines (Walker et al, 2015):

> explain to students that debits are taken from the account as they are made but a credit won't appear until the close of banking that day. It is important to monitor balances to make sure that your account doesn't go overdrawn to

avoid charges. If you need to overdraw or your overdraft isn't sufficient then always talk to your bank.

Good financial education appears to be the protector against the credit card industry: 'Remind students that while credit cards can be useful for providing a period of interest-free credit, they are an expensive method of borrowing unless you pay back the full balance every month.'

One set of teaching materials showed examples of four accounts with various financial and gift incentives to take on. Once such example is: '£5 out into your account for each month that you are in credit.' There was no conversation about how realistic this offer is for the many who become overdrawn, why a bank would offer such gifts, and what the implication of accepting such arrangements might be.

On fees and charges 'You may have to pay fees/charges when you borrow money, buy on credit or overdraw at the bank without an overdraft arrangement.' There was nothing provided on some of the more problematic consequences of being in debt that many experience, like proportionality of charges, compound charges, rollover or continual charges, or indeed the amount that industries make from fees. Absent also from all definitions are the often problematic and brutal debt collection practices that outsourced collection companies routinely engage in, the selling on of debt and the implications of this for the customer (Walker et al, 2012).

Conclusion

Millions of children now live in families with persistent and problem debt. Almost 1.4 million UK families with dependent children are currently in problem debt. An additional 2.9 million families with dependent children have struggled to pay their bills and credit commitments over the previous 12 months, putting them on the edge of falling into problem debt (The Children's Society, 2014). It is in this context that we must make sense of the financial resources produced and the institutions that produce them.

Clarke (2015) argues that, in the wake of a financial crisis as devastating in its impacts, even in the rich Anglo-American world, as anything witnessed since the Great Depression, it might sound slightly bizarre to speak of finance 'working' in the first place, let alone endorsing economic governance agendas that only a few years post-crisis seek to 'teach' a mass audience about 'how it works'.

In this context, financial education is an empty promise. The idea that FE programmes can, or indeed should, bridge the colossal gap between the average citizen's level of understanding and capability to act on the one hand, and the advanced technical and specialist skills that would be required to successfully and autonomously negotiate contemporary financial market transactions, products and innovations, on the other, is not credible (Clarke, 2015).

We will continue to labour under antiquated enlightenment logic if we choose to make sense of the financial education paradigm as a rationalist ship that has run aground on the rocky shores of human subjectivity where only better and earlier and more education resources will bring us better financial decision making. We would suggest that the financial education of young people is not necessarily to protect them but to enable institutions to more effectively relate to them and hence, ultimately, to profit from them. Spotton and Udofia (2016) noted that if financial education is to exist then it needs to be more socially and culturally relevant and to engage with participative and critical pedagogies for disengaged and marginalised youth for whom budgeting and money management is of little interest.

References

Arrondel, L. (2018) 'Financial literature and asset behaviour: Poor education and zero for conduct', *Comparative Economic Studies*, 60(1): 144–160.

Atkinson, A. (2005) *Introducing financial capability skills: A pilot study with Fairbridge West, Bristol*, Bristol: Personal Finance Research Centre.

Atkinson, A. and Messy, F. (2013) 'Promoting financial inclusion through financial education', *OECD Working Papers on Finance, Insurance and Private Pensions*, 34: 1–55.

Ben-Galim, D. and Lanning, T. (2010) *Strength against the shocks: Low income families and debt*, London: Institute for Public Policy Research.

Clarke, C. (2015) 'Learning to fail: Resilience and the empty promise of financial literacy education', *Consumption Markets & Culture*, 18(3): 257–276.

The Children's Society (2014) *The debt trap: Exposing the impact of problem debt on children*, London: The Children's Society.

Dear, J., Dear, P. and Jones, T. (2013) *Life and debt: Global studies of debt and resistance*, London: Jubilee Debt Campaign.

Edge Foundation (2018) *Skills shortages in the UK Economy*, London: Edge Foundation.

EHRC (Equality and Human Rights Commission) (2015) *Is Britain fairer?*, London: EHRC.

Erturk, I., Froud, J., Johal, S., Leaver, A., and Williams, K. (2007) 'The democratization of finance? Promises, outcomes and conditions', *Review of International Political Economy*, 14(4): 553–575.

FCA (Financial Conduct Authority) (2014) *Consumer credit and consumers in vulnerable circumstances*, London: FCA.

Finder (2020) Saving statistics, https://www.finder.com/uk/saving-statistics

Fox J., Bartholomae, S. and Lee, J. (2005) 'Building the case for financial education', *Journal of Consumer Affairs*, 39(1): 195–214.

Griffiths, M. (2007) 'Consumer debt in Australia: Why banks will not turn their backs on profit', *International Journal of Consumer Studies*, 31: 230–236.

Gudmunson, C. and Danes, S. (2011) 'Family financial socialisation: Theory and critical review', *Journal of Family and Economic Issues*, 32: 644–667.

Haiven, M. (2014) *Cultures of financialisation*, London: Palgrave.

Hoeve, M., Stams, G., Zouwen, M., Vergeer, M., Jurrius, K. and Asscher, J. (2014) 'A systematic review of financial debt in adolescents and young adults: Prevalence, correlates and associations with crime', *PLOS ONE*, 9(8): 1–16.

Houle, J. (2013) 'Disparities in debt: Parents' socioeconomic resources and young adult student loan debt', *Sociology of Education*, 87(1): 53–69.

Kaiser, T. and Menkoff, L. (2017) 'Does financial education impact financial literacy and financial behaviour, if so, when?', *The World Bank Economic Review*, 31(3): 611–630.

Kamleitner, B., Hoelzl, E. and Kirchler, E. (2012) 'Credit use: Psychological perspectives on a multifaceted phenomenon', *International Journal of Psychology*, 47(1): 1–27.

Lewis, A. (2010) 'The credit crunch: Ideological, psychological and epistemological perspectives', *The Journal of Socio-Economics*, 39: 127–131.

Majamaa, K. (2011) 'Dismissed intergenerational support? New social risks and the economic welfare of young adults', *Journal of Youth Studies*, 14(6): 729–743.

Maman, D. and Rosenhek, Z. (2020) 'Facing future uncertainties and risks through personal finance: Conventions in financial education', *Journal of Cultural Economy*, 13(3): 303–317.

Mandell, L. and Klein, L. (2009) 'The impact of financial literacy education on subsequent financial behaviour', *Journal of Financial Counselling and Planning*, 20(1): 15–24.

Marron, D. (2014) '"Informed, educated and more confident": Financial capability and the problematization of personal finance consumption', *Consumption Markets & Culture*, 17(5): 491–511.

McCormick, M. (2009) 'The effectiveness of youth financial education: A review of the literature', *Journal of Financial Counselling and Planning*, 20(1): 70–83.

Mellor, M. (2010) *The future of money: From financial crisis to public resource*, London: Pluto Press.

Money Advice Service (2018) *Money worries have left two in three Brits worried about loved one's mental health*, https://www.moneyadviceservice. org.uk/en/corporate/press-release--money-worries-have-left-two-in-three-brits-worried-about-loved-ones-mental-health

Money Advice Trust (2016) *The borrowed years*, http://www. moneyadvicetrust.org/SiteCollectionDocuments/Research%20 and%20reports/Borrowed%20Years%2c%20Young%20people%20 credit%20and%20debt%2c%20Aug%202016.pdf

The Money Charity (2020) *The money stats – January 2020*, https:// themoneycharity.org.uk/money-stats-january-2020-uk-2019-household-debt-closely-parallels-governments/

Pauwels, L. (2012) 'A multimodal framework for analyzing websites as cultural expressions', *Journal of Computer-Mediated Communication*, 17(3): 247–265.

Pinto, L. and Coulson Oise, E. (2011) 'Social justice and the gender politics of financial literacy education', *Journal of the Canadian Association for Curriculum Studies*, 9(2): 54–85.

Ross, A. (2013) *Creditocracy*, London: OR Books.

Sherraden, M., Johnson, L., Guo, B. and Elliott III, W. (2011) 'Financial capability in children: Effects of participation in a school-based financial education and savings program', *Journal of Family and Economic Issues*, 32(3): 385–399.

Spotton, B. and Udofia, I. (2016) 'Inclusive financial literacy education for inspiring a critical financial consciousness: An experiment in partnership with marginalised youth', *International Journal of Inclusive Education*, 21(7): 763–774.

Totenhagen, C., Casper, D., Faber, K., Bosch, L., Bracamonte Wiggs, C. and Borden, L. (2015) 'Youth financial literacy: A review of key considerations and promising delivery methods', *Journal of Family and Economic Issues*, 36: 167–191.

Walker, C., Hanna, P., Cunningham, L. and Ambrose, P. (2012) *Responsible individuals, irresponsible institutions? A report into mental health and the UK credit industry*, Brighton: University of Brighton.

Walker, C., Hanna, P., Cunningham, L. and Ambrose, P. (2015) 'Parasitic encounters in debt: The UK mainstream credit industry', *Theory & Psychology*, 25(2): 239–256.

Williams, T. (2007) 'Empowerment of whom and for what? Financial literacy education and the new regulation of consumer financial services', *Law and Policy*, 29(2): 226–256.

11

Immigration, employment precarity and masculinity in Filipino-Canadian families

Philip Kelly

Introduction

This chapter explores gender disparity and masculinity among Filipino-Canadian youth and the role this plays in shaping their aspirations. In particular, it highlights a concerning and anomalous pattern of intergenerational social (im)mobility for young Filipino-Canadian men. Taking post-secondary educational pathways as an indicator of social mobility, I first show how youth in the Filipino-Canadian community have anomalously low levels of university graduation relative to their peers in other major immigrant communities in Toronto. This is also anomalous in a second sense, because Filipino parents arrive in Canada with unusually high levels of education compared to first generation immigrants from other source countries. Nevertheless, expected patterns of intergenerational social reproduction (in which university-educated parents cultivate degree-gaining children) do not seem to hold, and this has been especially true for male Filipino youth who arrived in Canada as children. In fact by certain measures, and at certain times, male childhood immigrants from the Philippines have had the lowest levels of university graduation of any racialised immigrant community.

The reasons behind this pattern, at least among Filipino youth in general, have been explored elsewhere (Farrales, 2017; Kelly, 2014; 2015; Kelly and Maharaj, 2019). What has often been missed, however, are questions of gender disparity and masculinity (although see Waters, 2010). Conversely, while masculinity has been extensively addressed in relation to class reproduction in general (going back to the classic by Willis, 1980), the intersectional context of masculinity in racialised and immigrant families has been less explored (although there are some recent exceptions in the geographical literature, including

Hardgrove et al, 2015a; 2015b; and McDowell, 2014; 2020). In this chapter, I ask what are the particular circumstances that might produce marginalisation among young men in the Filipino community, with consequences for their educational, employment and economic outcomes. I suggest that there are two important sets of processes that have contributed to Filipino families' experiences of intergenerational mobility, both of which need to be viewed with regard to their gendered impacts and their effects on the performance of masculinity.

The first has been the specific migration streams through which Filipino immigrants have arrived in Canada. A temporary foreign worker programme for live-in domestic workers, known from 1993 until 2014 as the Live-In Caregiver Program (LCP), has been disproportionately used by Filipina women and has been an important channel through which they have eventually sponsored their family members to join them. The second process concerns the employment patterns of male Filipino immigrants, who have been heavily and disproportionately represented in the manufacturing sector. During the recession of 2007–08, manufacturing in major urban regions of Canada, such as Toronto, saw a precipitous decline in employment, which inevitably impacted Filipino immigrant men.

This chapter outlines both of these processes using both quantitative and qualitative data to examine the ways in which both immigration processes and the impacts of a recession contribute to a crisis of masculinity, thereby helping to explain the anomalous patterns of social immobility apparent among young Filipino men. I focus, in particular, on the ways in which aspirations may be set for boys and young men, and how 'possible selves' are rendered imaginable given the experiences of the wider Filipino community (Hardgrove et al, 2015b; Holloway et al, 2011; Pimlott-Wilson, 2011).

Youth outcomes

Youth outcomes can be defined in various ways, and 'success' should not be judged through the homogenising lens of stable, professional, well-paid employment. There are many pathways to a fulfilling life, including jobs that did not exist a generation ago and alternative definitions of success and happiness (Naafs and Skelton, 2018). Nevertheless, there remains a strong relationship between advancing through a degree programme and having access to jobs that include a more stable and less precarious employment relationship (Vuolo et al, 2016). In that sense, graduation from university is a reasonable proxy for social mobility between generations. Across Canada, for example, the average earnings premiums from a bachelor's degree relative to a high school diploma are 58% for women and 47.2% for men, while the differentials between a bachelor's degree and a college diploma are around 40% for women, and around 20% for men (Statistics Canada, 2017). University graduation is, therefore, still a reasonable proxy for social mobility.

Table 11.1 provides the rate of university degree holding for adults aged 25–29 in the Toronto census metropolitan area – an urban region of approximately 5.9 million (in 2016) and by far the largest settlement site for new immigrant families arriving in Canada. The table identifies several racialised groups according to the 'visible minority' categories used by the Canadian federal government. These are internally quite diverse categories and in most cases they do not reflect a single immigrant source country (Filipino being an exception). Nonetheless they are categories into which individuals self-declare in the census and they are intended to reflect the ways in which respondents understand themselves to be racialised in Canadian society. Table 11.1 then provides rates of degree holding by gender and according to immigration status. The latter is divided into those who are born in Canada (most, but not all, of whom are the children of immigrants), those who immigrated with their parent(s) at or before

Table 11.1: Characteristics of 25–29 year olds in Toronto census metropolitan area, by gender, visible minority category and immigration status, percentage with a university degree in 2016

		Filipino	Chinese	South Asian	Black	'White'/ Not a visible minority
Women (Ages 25–29)	Immigrated 0–13	41.2	81.7	67.1	35.4	63.0
	Immigrated 10–18	37.8	68.1	54.8	28.9	62.4
	Canadian-born	48.5	78.0	69.2	32.2	53.7
Men (Ages 25–29)	Immigrated 0–13	27.6	70.5	51.1	18.3	48.4
	Immigrated 10–18	25.3	56.0	49.0	24.1	43.3
	Canadian-born	31.7	64.4	50.4	16.7	30.5
'Parents' (Ages 55–64)	Immigrants	39.6	28.4	33.6	15	28.4

Source: Statistics Canada (2016a)

the age of 13, and those who arrived with their family aged 10–18 (the overlap in the age category is a product of how publicly available census data is reported).

Several points emerge from the data in Table 11.1. First, it is clear that women are more likely to hold degrees than men, and this applies across all racialised and non-racialised groups, and across all immigration circumstances. Second, non-immigrants and early childhood immigrants are more likely to graduate from university than those who arrive during the later years of childhood. This holds true for all racialised groups except for men who self-identify as black, where teenage immigrants are slightly more likely to hold a degree than early childhood immigrants or non-immigrants. Third, Filipino young adults are less likely to graduate with a degree than white youth, and they are significantly behind Chinese and South Asian youth. This comparison is particularly significant, because these three racialised groups include immigrants from Canada's most important source countries over the last few decades, notably China, India, Pakistan and the Philippines (IRCC, 2017). It is notable that Filipino men, in particular, are graduating with a degree at much lower rates, in some cases less than half the rate of Chinese or South Asian youth.

The last row of Table 11.1 provides the second part of the anomaly. Here we see the rate at which immigrants in the 55–64 year old age group hold degrees. These are not literally the parents of the younger cohorts in the table, but they represent an approximation of the parental generation as they are all immigrants who arrived as adults and are members of the same racialised groups. It is striking that every group, except Filipinos, sees upward mobility in terms of university graduation between generations. In particular, it is only Filipino men who are, on average, much less likely to hold a degree than their parents' generation. This pattern is not unique to this data set – other quantitative and qualitative studies have found similar patterns in the Filipino-Canadian community (Abada et al, 2009; Abada and Lin, 2011; Austria et al, 2017; Farrales and Pratt, 2012; Farrales, 2017; Kelly, 2014; Pratt et al, 2008).

To understand the specific circumstances that shaped the processes of intergenerational social mobility in the Filipino community in the 2010s, it is necessary to outline two contexts. The first relates to the immigration channels through which parents have arrived in Canada. The second concerns the patterns of industrial restructuring that intensified with the 2008–09 recession.

Immigration pathways

Like other racialised groups, Filipino immigrants to Canada started arriving in increasing numbers in the 1970s after Canadian immigration rules were changed to less explicitly favour the reproduction of a white European settler society. It was not until the 1990s, and especially in the 2000s, that the Philippines emerged as a top source country. The profile of Filipino arrivals is, however, quite distinctive because of the immigration categories used. The main categories, involving points-based skilled worker selection and family reunification, were certainly used by Filipino immigrants, but a category that involved conversion from temporary foreign worker to permanent resident status has been especially dominated by Filipina women.

The LCP was created by the Canadian federal government in 1993. The programme was significantly revised in 2014, and again in 2019, and by then the numbers arriving were much reduced. But, between 1993 and 2015, almost 100,000 applicants and dependents arrived through the LCP, nearly all of them women. Around 80% of the principal applicants were women from the Philippines (Kelly and de Leon, 2017). In the eight years from 2008 to 2015, approximately 280,000 immigrants arrived from the Philippines, which was the single largest source country for immigrants during that period. Around one third of that number arrived under the LCP as the principal applicant or spouse/dependent. Thus, while Filipinas have dominated the LCP, the LCP has also played an unusually large part in immigration from the Philippines.

The LCP required participants to complete at least 24 months or 3,900 hours of full-time work (within a four-year period) as caregivers for children, the disabled or the elderly before they could apply for permanent resident status (Pratt, 2012). Living in the employer's home was also mandatory until 2018. Although caregivers were eligible to apply for an open work permit and permanent residency after this live-in employment period, there were significant time lags between each of these stages. In many cases, the Canadian government took at least four years to process applications for permanent residency, leading to long periods of family separation (Pratt, 2012).

When caregivers eventually secured their open work permit and then permanent residency, their freedom to find a job in a different sector did not necessarily translate into the ability to do so (Tungohan et al, 2015). In fact, evidence suggests that caregiver immigrants have generally remained concentrated in a very narrow range of occupations, and incomes continue to lag well below those who have immigrated through other categories (Banerjee et al, 2018). Banerjee et al (2018) also find that ten years after settling as permanent residents, around 90% of caregiver immigrants continued working in just eight, mostly low-paid and feminised, occupations. These included in-home caregiving, healthcare aide, personal support worker, cleaner, hospitality, manufacturing and sales. The reasons for this kind of labour market segmentation included: the stigma and stereotyping associated with caregiving work, and the gendered and racialised bodies performing such work; the limited job search networks that caregivers had, given that their work was isolating and their social networks were mostly with other caregivers; and the financial obligation to support the immigration and settlement of their families, which precluded any training or skills upgrading. Thus, although caregivers are often the pioneer immigrants in their families, their own positioning in the labour market does not provide many advantages for their husbands or teenaged children when/if they eventually arrive.

The long-term family separation enforced by the LCP has often harmed spousal relationships. When husbands/fathers arrive to join their wives in Canada, reunification has often been difficult for both spouses and any accompanying children (Pratt, 2012). In addition, many fathers have faced unemployment or had to work in low-paid, insecure jobs that were below their qualifications and expertise. This too contributed to tension, anxiety and depression, and sometimes to marital breakdown. This chapter will turn later to the possible intergenerational effects of these difficulties, but first it is important to turn to some of the employment circumstances that Filipino men found themselves in, which provides a second context for understanding intergenerational outcomes.

Employment patterns

In 2008–09, while many of the 25–29 year olds in Table 11.1 were in high school or embarking on post-secondary education, an economic recession was unfolding. Although the impacts of the economic downturn were not as dramatic in Canada as they were in other contexts (such as the United States and the United Kingdom), it was nevertheless a period of contraction and retrenchment. Canadian GDP shrank by 3.3% and 400,000 jobs were lost across the country between October 2008 and October 2009 (LaRochelle-Côté and Gilmore, 2009).

While the 2008–09 recession came amid a longer-term trend toward precarious labour markets, it marked a sharp worsening of employment conditions. There was, however, a particular twist because the employment effects of the recession were differentiated according to the immigration circumstances of workers. The evidence shows that more recent immigrants took the brunt of the labour market impacts meaning that racialised minority groups were especially affected (Kelly et al, 2011). This may in part have been a reflection of a 'last in, first out' process going on in workplaces, and that racialised immigrants were over-represented in the kinds of precarious work that presented employers with 'numerical flexibility' during a downturn in demand. But it was also because the recession hit certain sectors harder than others, especially manufacturing. Furthermore, these jobs were predominantly male jobs (Ray et al, 2017). That said, there is evidence from the United States that gender-based wage differentials persisted and that male employment recovered after the so-called 'mancession', albeit with important geographical variations (Goodwin-White, 2018). There is thus no straightforward story to tell about the impacts of the recession, but it does clearly need to be analysed through the intersectional lenses of gender, race and immigration.

Figure 11.1 shows the pattern of unemployment based on a three-month moving average of monthly Labour Force Survey data from March 2006 to March 2011. Figure 11.1 differentiates Canadian-born workers, those who had achieved permanent residency within the last five years, and those who had gained permanent residency more than five years ago. Canadian-born workers saw an increase in peak unemployment rates from 5.8% to 8.8%, while established immigrants saw a larger increase, reaching rates just below 10%. It was, however, recent immigrants who bore the brunt of the recession, with nationwide unemployment rates reaching 14.3% in May 2009 and 15% a year later. The recession was, therefore, distinctively hard on recent immigrants. Furthermore, Figure 11.1 also shows that the recession provided more than a short-term 'blip' – unemployment levels remained elevated for all groups by 2011.

The recession was not, however, just an immigrant recession – as noted earlier, it also had sector-specific impacts. Table 11.2 shows the losses in employment in key sectors in the Toronto region based on census data between 2006 and 2011. What is striking is that the sectors with the largest job losses were male-dominated, with well over 50% male representation in manufacturing, waste management/remediation, wholesale trade and repair/maintenance. Meanwhile, most sectors with significant employment growth in the same five year period, including education and healthcare, were predominantly female or were relatively gender-balanced.

Figure 11.1: Unemployment rate of immigrants and Canadian-born, aged 25–54, Canada, 2006–11, 3-month moving average (3MMA)

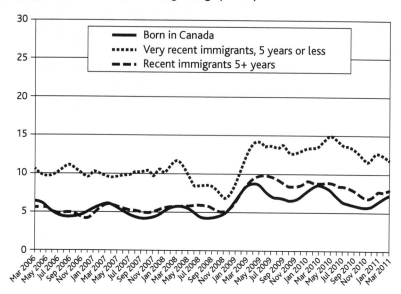

Source: Adapted from Statistics Canada (2011a), custom tabulations analysed by author

Table 11.2: Sectors with major employment changes, 2006–11,* Toronto census metropolitan area

Industry	Change in total employment 2006–11	% male in 2011
Manufacturing	-94900	66.5
Administrative/support, waste management, remediation services	-9405	54.5
Wholesale trade	-6755	60.7
Repair and maintenance	-4750	84.2
Professional, scientific and technical services	17725	55.8
Educational services	22030	32.7
Healthcare and social assistance	28245	19.5
Finance and insurance	29105	46.0
Public administration	32535	49.1

Source: Adapted from Statistics Canada (2006b, 2011b)

Note: *These two censuses used a different methodology to collect data and so comparisons need to be treated with caution.

Figure 11.2: Percentage of males, 25–54 years old, by visible minority group, employed in the manufacturing sector, Toronto, 2006

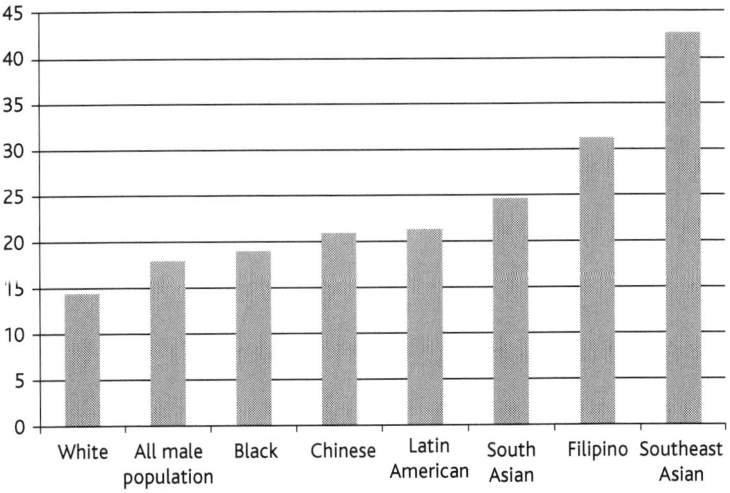

Source: Statistics Canada, Census of Population, 2006a

If the recession and its sectoral impacts appeared to be gendered and differentially impacting new immigrants, then a further intersectional source of vulnerability is found in specific racialised groups. Table 11.2 showed that Toronto's most impacted economic sector after the 2007–08 recession was a male-dominated manufacturing sector, with almost 100,000 jobs lost in the urban region over a five year period. But the profile of men in the manufacturing sector was also quite distinctive. Figure 11.2 shows the percentage of working-age males from various non-white racialised groups who were employed in manufacturing. What is striking here is that over 30% of Filipino males in the 25–54 age bracket were working in Toronto's manufacturing sector in 2006 – more than double the rate for white males. It is clear, then, that job losses in the recession were not just disproportionately felt by recent immigrants and men, but also by men in certain racialised groups. The impact of the recession therefore needs to be viewed through an intersectional lens – the effects on employment were differentially accentuated in specific vulnerable groups and especially recent male immigrants from certain racialised communities.

For Filipino men and women in particular, the effects of the recession are evident in more specific labour market data. Table 11.3 shows participation rates, unemployment rates, and employment insurance claim rates for Filipino men and women in the Toronto labour market for 2006 and 2011. For Filipino men, withdrawal from the labour

Table 11.3: Labour market indicators, Filipino (ethnic origin), Toronto, 2006–11

	2006	2011
Male participation rate	77.4	74.6
Female participation rate	74.8	75.1
Male unemployment rate	5.6	7.4
Female unemployment rate	5.5	6.2
% Male with income from EI benefits	0.9	1.6
% Female with income from EI benefits	1.9	2.1

Source: Adapted from Statistics Canada (2006c, 2011c)

market brought participation rates down from 77.4% to 74.6%, while participation among women actually increased slightly (albeit from a lower base) – perhaps reflecting the changing, and gendered, structure of employment opportunities noted earlier. Among those who have remained in the labour market we see the unemployment rate increasing slightly for women, from 5.5% to 6.2%, but for Filipino men the increase is much more pronounced, going from 5.6% to 7.4%. Linked to those figures, we also see a much larger jump in unemployment insurance claims among Filipino men (from 0.9% to 1.6%) than among women, whose rate of claim was already higher (from 1.9% to 2.1%).

The 2008–09 recession in Canada was, then, in certain ways, an episode that had differential impacts shaped by intersectional vulnerabilities defined through gender, racialised identity and length of immigrant residency. While these data do not contradict the male advantage that exists overall in the labour market, it is clear that recent male immigrants, and especially those from the Philippines, were especially exposed to job losses in areas such as manufacturing. Placing that phenomenon alongside gendered immigration processes provides a basis for understanding some of the processes that underpin intergenerational social mobility.

Filipino masculinities

We have seen two distinctive features of Filipino immigration and economic integration in Canada, both of which have implications for the performance of masculinity. The LCP involved an immigration process that was largely led by Filipina women who would arrive first and then sponsor their husbands and children. Meanwhile, the decline of manufacturing employment, especially during and after the 2008–09 recession, had a particular impact on Filipino men who were heavily overrepresented in that sector. In this section, through the lens of masculinity, the discussion will turn to consider the impacts of these circumstances on Filipino boys and young men.

This section draws upon qualitative data gathered by the Filipino Youth Transitions in Canada project, a research programme funded by Canada's Social Sciences and Humanities Research Council. The project ran from 2010 to 2015 and was therefore contemporaneous with both the peak of the caregiver programme and the aftermath of the economic recession in the lives of young Filipino men and women in Canada. The project involved a survey conducted across the country in 2011–13 that focused on young adults aged 18–40 who had at least one parent born in the Philippines and who were themselves either second generation (born in Canada) or 1.5 generation (immigrated during childhood). Over 600 surveys were completed and these were supplemented with 12 focus group discussions and over 70 key informant interviews in four cities (Toronto, Hamilton, Winnipeg and Vancouver).

The kinds of employment experiences faced by Filipino parents create limitations for the post-secondary ambitions of their children. As we have seen, the post-settlement employment options for caregivers are extremely circumscribed and are almost exclusively in low-paid service sector employment. The same would apply to Filipino men in the shrinking manufacturing sector. Among our survey respondents, 43% said that their fathers had been laid off at some point during their childhood, while 21% had mothers who had been made redundant. Among those who had not attended any post-secondary education, the incidence of retrenched fathers increased to 58%.

Family financial resources are therefore a key factor in the accessibility and affordability of a university degree as a post-secondary pathway. Parents' employment circumstances also have other effects. In a separate research project, which involved surveying Filipino-Canadian high school students in a suburban Catholic school board west of Toronto, we found that the school-aged children of parents who arrived under the caregiver programme were far more likely to work in part-time jobs, and to work much longer hours, than those whose parents came to Canada under other immigration programmes (Austria et al, 2017). Students' academic achievement often suffers because of these paid work commitments (which were in excess of 20 hours per week in some cases) and this too limited their post-secondary educational options. One key informant in our 2011–13 interviews noted that low incomes and cramped housing were similarly implicated in truncating the academic achievements of Filipino young people:

'Most of their problems were poverty, like their parents have three jobs, one regular job, nighttime, weekend jobs; and also they're cramped in a small apartment so they don't really have a space to learn, to study, and some of them they have to work as well so they drop out from school. They cannot cope with working and studying. So because of poverty, they choose working rather than studying.' (Female Filipino Community Centre Director, aged 50–55, Toronto, 2011)

Another key informant, with extensive experience supporting newcomer Filipino youth in the school system, also pointed to the impact that parental work schedules have on their ability to oversee their kids:

'And a lot of them, their parents aren't home, no one is there to enforce them to do their homework or to come to school on time. The school calls the parents and the parents say, oh I'm too busy to deal with this. I have 3 jobs, I got him to Canada, it's up to him now. You know? And that's also I think a lot of the reason they're not going to make it to university.' (Female Filipina School Settlement Worker, aged 25–30, Toronto, 2011)

While these are important factors in shaping Filipino youth outcomes, I want to focus on the question of male achievement in particular. There are, I suggest, two aspects of intergenerational mobility that are especially pertinent in understanding the outcomes of Filipino young men. The first is the undermining of a conventional Filipino male role as provider and head of household. The second is the way in which precarious employment, and unemployment, among fathers creates truncated aspirations and 'possible selves' among their sons.

In the Filipino community, the significance of the LCP has meant that women are often the migrant pioneers in the family as well as being the main provider and breadwinner (Stasiulis and Bakan, 2003). Fathers, on the other hand, may face difficulties in adapting to the deprofessionalised work that often awaits them in the Canadian labour market. This disrupts what are seen as normalised gender relations in the Philippines and undermines a husband/father's role as 'provider' and 'head of household' (Lukasiewicz, 2011). Within the family, they may feel that their authority is undermined and their ability to act as role models for young boys is compromised.

'My mom worked 3 jobs when I was in junior high and high school. Not 3 jobs, but a full-time job, a part-time job, and another part-time job. And my dad, he went through so many spells of working here, getting laid off; working there, getting laid off, working here and getting laid off. He just took care of us. He was always home taking care of things. It's a reverse role ... There are some dads who will stay home and take care of their kids and the mom will work because they can get a job easier ... It's just that hard for them to get a job. I could tell that it just started to eat away at him in terms of not being able to bring home the money. But I could tell, like, you know, it's probably one of the things that contributed to his death. Just the stress of it all.' (Male Filipino, aged 30–35, customer service representative, Winnipeg, 2011)

In this poignant quote, our respondent notes the way in which his mother was over-stretched in the labour market, taking on multiple jobs. This is a common story. It is also clear that there is a process at work in the labour market whereby jobs – albeit low-paid and precarious jobs – are accessible to women, but much less so to men. The respondent also notes that his father's inability to be the main breadwinner was a situation that would 'eat away' at him, possibly to the point of causing his premature death.

Another respondent (this time, a mother) similarly described how her husband felt undermined by the degradation of his employment status upon settling in Canada, and the impact this had on their children:

'Like for example, my husband he worked with [municipality] recycling as a safety officer, so it's not that bad, but yet because he has been a manufacturer, he was a manager himself of his own business. It's like he's not used working as a subordinate with people telling you what to do. So it had a really huge impact to him that he said that he felt here in Canada he feels he is disintegrating. So that alone, maybe if your kids is like witnessing that, that feeling, because it also affect like your, the way you're supervising your kids. So it's like, I don't know, maybe because as a father you are – like you don't feel having the same power you had before, so it's also maybe affecting the way you are supervising them.' (Filipina counsellor and mother, aged 50–55, Toronto, 2011)

A second dimension of masculine deprofessionalisation among fathers is more direct and involves the ways in which children internalise what might constitute reasonable aspirations for their own future. We heard from respondents for whom, and for boys especially, when their own well-educated father is reduced to precarious and low-skilled work, it can have an effect on their own sense of possibility. One community worker noted this idea clearly:

> 'I would hear comments from kids who let's say has somebody whose father used to be a seafarer. If you're a seafarer in the Philippines you actually have a good life there because you're bringing in dollars to your family. And then when they came here his father worked in a factory. His mother was a pharmacist before, she had a small business in their home town and now she also works in a factory. And so the kid said, why am I gonna exert so much more effort? Even if I have a diploma I won't get it anyway. I won't get the profession that I really want. He's seeing that in his parents.' (Female Filipina community centre settlement counsellor, aged 30–35, Toronto, 2011)

In this quote, the respondent is suggesting that children see the lack of utility associated with their parents' educational and professional credentials and therefore doubt the value of pursuing such qualifications for themselves.

Beyond fathers, however, our respondents also pointed to a broader lack of professional role models for young Filipino boys/men. A Filipino teacher working in Toronto expressed this idea by referencing a retired Filipino member of parliament, Rey Pagtakhan, who represented a Winnipeg constituency from 1998 to 2004. Pagtakhan remains, however, the only Filipino-Canadian to have ever served in the federal parliament, and there are very few Filipino elected officials at subnational levels of government across the country:

> 'But sometimes I often wonder do boys have role models to look up to within the larger Canadian society that has been a success? Do you know who was put up in front of me when I was growing up? It was Rey Pagtakhan who was the Member of Parliament from Winnipeg, right? And he was the one put in front of me, just because he had the same speech mannerism as my grandfather when he was speaking English, always formal English, so to speak.

And so sometimes I wonder now who is? ... Within the
community there really isn't anybody who is looked up to
in terms of a role model type figure.' (Male Filipino teacher,
aged 30–35, Toronto, 2011)

The point, then, is that male Filipino role models in public life are
scarce – a point that would not apply less to the other racialised group
discussed earlier, including those who identify as Chinese, South Asian
and Black. Siemiatycki (2011), for example, notes that while all visible
minority groups are underrepresented in elected offices, the size of
the Filipino community make an absence of political representatives
especially anomalous. The impact of such role models is unquantifiable,
but our respondents suggested that this absence of highly visible high-
achievers from within the community is a part of the process through
which aspirations are truncated.

Conclusion

Despite their anomalously high levels of education, Filipino parents
have often been integrated into segments of the Canadian labour
market that have failed to fully recognise and utilise their skills and
credentials. For some, this has been a product of the conditions and
trajectories dictated by the LIC programme. For others, it has simply
been a process of deprofessionalisation and downgrading that is familiar
to many immigrant communities. Filipino men in particular have
often found it difficult to identify a niche within the labour market.
Over the last few decades, they have frequently found themselves in
a declining manufacturing sector that was especially hard hit in the
Toronto region by the recession of 2008–09.

These circumstances go some way towards explaining the particular
challenges faced by young Filipino men who either arrived in
Canada as children or were born to immigrant parents. Our research
respondents identified a strong sense of frustration and anomie
resulting among their fathers who felt that they could no longer play
the conventional gender role of provider and head of household.
Their fathers were, in many ways, emasculated by their experiences
of immigration, (un)employment and racialisation. The interviews
we conducted pointed to a link between these experiences of fathers
and the aspirations and outcomes of their sons. There is also a wider
point concerning the demonstration effect of deprofessionalised men
of the first immigrant generation. Role models, at least in terms
of secure professional employment, in whom boys could see their

own 'possible selves', were lacking, not just within their own family circles, but also in the community at large. That said, it would be wrong to suggest that success stories do not exist or that there is some kind of problem or pathology with the Filipino community in Canada. Rather, it is clear that an immigration programme that necessitates deprofessionalisation and family separation, and the decline of manufacturing employment, have both had distinctive consequences for the Filipino community – consequences which have been intergenerational in their impact.

More broadly, this chapter has suggested that the employment precarity associated with immigrant families needs to be viewed through an intersectional lens so that specifically gendered and racialised experiences become legible. Such labour market experiences then have consequences for the reproduction of education (and labour market) outcomes in the next generation. Sometimes this is through the material financial limitations experienced by immigrant families in precarious employment, which restrict the post-secondary options available to their children. But, I have also suggested that intergenerational class reproduction needs to be viewed through the lens of masculinity and family relations, so that it is not just the material limitations that are recognised, but also the ways in which aspirations are attenuated for possible futures and possible selves.

References

Abada, T. and Lin, S. (2011) *The educational attainments and labour market outcomes of the children of immigrants in Ontario*, Toronto, ON: Higher Education Quality Council of Ontario, https://crdcn. org/educational-attainments-and-labour-market-outcomes-children-immigrants-ontario

Abada, T., Hou, F. and Ram, B. (2009) 'Ethnic differences in educational attainment among the children of Canadian immigrants', *Canadian Journal of Sociology/Cahiers Canadiens De Sociologie*, 34(1): 1–28.

Austria, J., Kelly, P. F. and Wells, D. (2017) 'Precarious students and families in Halton, Ontario: Linking citizenship, employment and Filipino student success', in: S. Procyk, W. Lewchuk and J. Shields (eds) *Precarious employment: Causes, consequences and remedies*, Winnipeg: Fernwood, pp.57–73.

Banerjee, R., Kelly, P. F., Tungohan, E., Cleto, P., De Leon, C., Garcia, M., Luciano, M., Palmaria, C. and Sorio, C. (2018) 'From "migrant" to "citizen": labor market integration of former live-in caregivers in Canada', *ILR Review*, 71(4SI): 908–936.

Farrales, M. (2017) 'Delayed, deferred and dropped out: Geographies of Filipino-Canadian high school students', *Children's Geographies*, 15(2): 207–223.

Goodwin-White, J. (2018) ' "Go west, young woman?": The geography of the gender wage gap through the great recession', *Economic Geography*, 94(4): 331–354.

Hardgrove, A., McDowell, L. and Rootham, E. (2015a) 'Precarious lives, precarious labour: Family support and young men's transitions to work in the UK', *Journal of Youth Studies*, 18(8): 1057–1076.

Hardgrove, A., Rootham, E. and McDowell, L. (2015b) 'Possible selves in a precarious labour market: Youth, imagined futures, and transitions to work in the UK', *Geoforum*, 60: 163–171.

Holloway, S. L., Brown, G. and Pimlott Wilson, H. L. (2011) 'Geographies of education and aspiration', *Children's Geographies*, 9(1): 1–5.

IRCC (Immigration, Refugees and Citizenship Canada) (2017) *Facts and Figures 2017: Immigration overview – permanent residents*, https:// open.canada.ca/en/open-data

Kelly, P. F. (2014) 'Understanding intergenerational social mobility: Filipino youth in Canada', *IRPP Study 45*, https://irpp. org/wp-content/uploads/2014/02/kelly-feb-2014.pdf

Kelly, P. F. (2015) 'Transnationalism, emotion and second-generation social mobility in the Filipino-Canadian diaspora', *Singapore Journal of Tropical Geography*, 36(3): 280–299.

Kelly, P. F. and de Leon, C. (2017) 'Rescripting care work: Collaborative cultural production and caregiver advocacy in Toronto', in: S. Procyk, W. Lewchuk and J. Shields (eds) *Precarious employment: Causes, consequences and remedies*, Winnipeg: Fernwood Publishing, pp.91–108.

Kelly, P. F. and Maharaj, C. (2019) 'Geographies of the next generation: Outcomes for the children of immigrants through a spatial lens', in: K. Mitchell, R. Jones and J. L. Fluri (eds) *Handbook on critical geographies of migration*, Cheltenham: Edward Elgar, pp.315–326.

Kelly, P. F., Park, S. and Lepper, L. (2011) 'Economic recession and immigrant labour market outcomes in Canada, 2006–2011', *TIEDI Analytical Report*, 22: 1–16.

LaRochelle-Côté, S. and Gilmore, J. (2009) *Canada's employment downturn: Statistics Canada Perspective, December 2009*, Ottawa: Statistics Canada.

Lukasiewicz, A. (2011) 'Migration and gender identity in the rural Philippines', *Critical Asian Studies*, 43(4): 577–593.

McDowell, L. (2014) 'The sexual contract, youth, masculinity and the uncertain promise of waged work in austerity Britain', *Australian Feminist Studies*, 29(79): 31–49.

McDowell, L. (2020) 'Looking for work: Youth, masculine disadvantage and precarious employment in post-millennium England', *Journal of Youth Studies*, 23(8): 974–988.

Naafs, S. and Skelton, T. (2018) 'Youthful futures? Aspirations, education and employment in Asia', *Children's Geographies*, 16(1): 1–14.

Pimlott-Wilson, H. (2011) 'The role of familial habitus in shaping children's views of their future employment', *Children's Geographies*, 9(1): 111–118.

Pratt, G., in collaboration with the Philippine Women Centre of BC (2008) *Deskilling across the generations: Reunification among transnational Filipino families in Vancouver*, Metropolis BC Working Paper Series, No. 08-06.

Pratt, G. (2012) *Families apart: Migrant mothers and the conflicts of labor and love*, Minneapolis, MN: University of Minnesota Press.

Ray, D. M., MacLachlan, I., Lamarche, R. and Srinath, K. P. (2017) 'Economic shock and regional resilience: Continuity and change in Canada's regional employment structure, 1987–2012', *Environment and Planning A*, 49(4): 952–973.

Siemiatycki, M. (2011) *The diversity gap: The electoral under-representation of visible minorities*, Toronto: Diversity Institute in Management and Technology, Ryerson University.

Stasiulis, D. K. and Bakan, A. B. (2003) *Negotiating citizenship migrant women in Canada and the global system*, Basingstoke: Palgrave Macmillan.

Statistics Canada (2006a) 2006 Census of Population, Statistics Canada catalogue no. 97-564-XCB2006009. Ottawa, Statistics Canada.

Statistics Canada (2006b) 2006 Census of Population, Statistics Canada Catalogue no. 97-559-XCB2006023. Ottawa, Statistics Canada.

Statistics Canada (2006c) 2006 Census of Population, Statistics Canada Catalogue no. 97-564-XCB2006007. Ottawa, Statistics Canada.

Statistics Canada (2011a) Custom Tabulations from the Labour Force Survey 2006-2011. https://www150.statcan.gc.ca/t1/tbl1/en/tv.action?pid=1410001801

Statistics Canada (2011b) 2011 National Household Survey, Statistics Canada Catalogue no. 99-012-X2011030. Ottawa, Statistics Canada.

Statistics Canada (2011c) 2011 National Household Survey, Statistics Canada Catalogue no. 99-010-X2011036 . Ottawa, Statistics Canada.

Statistics Canada (2016) Census of Population, Statistics Canada Catalogue no. 98-400-X2016275. Ottawa, Statistics Canada.

Statistics Canada (2017) *Census brief: Does education pay? A comparison of earnings by level of education in Canada and its provinces and territories*, https://www12.statcan.gc.ca/census-recensement/2016/as-sa/98-200-x/2016024/98-200-x2016024-eng.cfm

Tungohan, E., Banerjee, R., Chu, W., Cleto, P., de Leon, C., Garcia, M., Kelly, P., Luciano, M., Palmaria, C. and Sorio, C. (2015) 'After the live-in caregiver program: Filipina caregivers' experiences of graduated and uneven citizenship', *Canadian Ethnic Studies/Etudes Ethniques Au Canada*, 47(1): 87–105.

Vuolo, M., Mortimer, J. T. and Staff, J. (2016) 'The value of educational degrees in turbulent economic times: Evidence from the Youth Development Study', *Social Science Research*, 57: 233–252.

Waters, J. L. (2010) 'Becoming a father, missing a wife: Chinese transnational families and the male experience of lone parenting in Canada', *Population, Space and Place*, 16(1). 63–74.

Willis, P. E. (1980) *Learning to labour: How working-class kids get working-class jobs*, Aldershot: Gower.

12

The undeserving poor and the happy poor: interrelations between the politics of global charity and austerity for young people in Britain

Ruth Cheung Judge

Introduction

This chapter explores how the politics of popular charity in the global South interact with the politics of austerity in young people's lives in the global North. The chapter draws out the parallels and *interrelations* between these two arenas through examining international volunteering trips to sub-Saharan Africa which engaged young people from low-income backgrounds in the UK. In such trips, idealised imaginaries of helping 'the grateful, happy poor' of the global South sit alongside anxieties about young people growing up in urban neighbourhoods in the UK as potential members of an 'ungrateful' and 'undeserving poor' who should become more responsible for themselves. Popular 'humanitarian' imaginaries which frame 'real poverty' as absolute material need, delegitimises relative poverty and inequality in Britain and mesh with the pressure on young people to adopt aspirational, responsible subjectivities under neoliberal austerity. Young people are also left with contradictory messages around material wealth as both something to be eschewed and something which defines their value. Many young people internalised the 'lessons' of the trips to become more grateful and motivated, though some resist narrow ideas around poverty and responsibility, and assert the challenges of classed stigma and poverty in their lives. Overall, the chapter raises critical questions about how the politics of neoliberal subjectification and the 'responsibilisation of poverty' occur and are normalised across diverse sites which stretch beyond the nation-state and 'the local'.

Barefoot kids and too-many-trainers kids

I talked about shoes – or the lack of shoes – surprisingly frequently during my research on young people's participation in international volunteering (see Cheung Judge, 2016). The research was specifically focused on short volunteering trips from the UK to sub-Saharan Africa which engaged young people from low-income urban neighbourhoods, rather than privileged participants. As young people talked about their experiences of volunteering, images of barefoot children in Kenya and Zimbabwe (the trip destinations), peppered the interviews. Anecdotes about children's lack of shoes were used to illustrate sadness and shock at witnessing deep material poverty, as well as admiration and amazement at the laughter and play which existed despite such poverty. But strikingly, in the UK volunteers' accounts, the barefoot children also had a mirror image – British young people with *too many* shoes – too many pairs of trainers, to be precise. The young people with too many trainers were *themselves*, and – according to their own narratives – their encounters in Africa had prompted them into greater gratitude, motivation and responsibility.

These problematic tropes – of the barefoot children, and the desperate-for-the-latest-Nike's 'urban youth' – signify that encasing these trips were strong normative imaginaries about 'the grateful, happy poor' (in Africa) and the 'ungrateful, undeserving poor' (in the UK), specifically, young people who should become more responsible. This chapter draws out under-explored links between classed politics in austerity Britain and international development politics through, as outlined, examining international volunteering trips which engaged young people from low-income backgrounds. Though these trips are by no means widespread, they take shape amid widespread and powerful contemporary social dynamics: the increasing prevalence of 'popular humanitarian' imaginaries and practices (Mathers, 2010; Mostafanezhad, 2013); and the pressure for young people to 'adjust themselves' away from stigmatised classed and racialised identities (Kulz, 2014; Archer et al, 2007) and undertake great labours to acquire 'experience' and perform individualised responsibility (Holdsworth, 2017; Pimlott-Wilson, 2017). Examining the trips is interesting because it allows for critical analysis of how these dynamics relate.

The chapter argues that the 'popular humanitarian imaginaries' evident in short volunteer tourism trips frame 'real poverty' as absolute, extreme embodied material need. In the cases of this research, this problematically reinforces the delegitimisation of relative poverty and inequality in Britain, and plays into the pressure for young people to become driven, enterprising, and self-improving individuals under neoliberal austerity (Pimlott-Wilson, 2017). Furthermore, it presents an ideal of doing good through charity in the global South which is reliant on material resources. Vivid first-hand experiences of encountering poverty in the global South can thus function as a benchmark for young British people to 'adjust' themselves into being more grateful for their relative wealth, and being more motivated, hard-working, responsible and productive. Many young people internalise such implicit 'lessons' of the trips, reflecting the pressure to position oneself on the 'right side' of the binary discourses of UK austerity politics of 'undeserving' versus 'deserving', 'risky' versus 'resourceful, 'striver' versus 'skiver' (Jupp, 2017). However, some young people resist or recast these politics, through presenting critiques of narrow ideas of poverty and the individualisation of responsibility, and asserting the challenges of classed stigma and austerity in their lives.

The chapter joins the dots between the politics of popular imaginaries and practices of global charity, with the politics of growing up under austerity in the UK. Scholarship on international volunteering has critiqued it as 'neoliberal' in terms of both the ideologies of poverty and the development it fuels (Mostafanezhad, 2013), and as a 'technology of the self' through which subjects constitute themselves as competitive, entrepreneurial, responsible and self-improving (Baillie Smith and Laurie, 2011). Similarly, scholarship on children, youth and families in contexts of austerity has critiqued the way that 'young people are increasingly tasked with looking toward the future, taking responsibility and "raising" their aspirations in order to contribute through economic production as active citizen-workers' (Pimlott-Wilson, 2017: 1). The chapter explores the parallels and *interrelations* between these 'global' and 'local' sites in which young people are exhorted to become good 'neoliberal subjects'.

In exploring these interrelations, the chapter contributes to two areas of scholarship. First, in the realm of development geographies, Baillie Smith (2013) points out a surprising lack of attention to how subjectivities in the global North, and 'established narratives of rich and poor are being both challenged and reinforced', are being constituted both 'in the context of austerity and recession in the Global North' and also 'the popularisation of development' (p.401). Second, in children's geographies, 'descaled' geographical analyses which situate young people's 'local' and everyday lives amid globe-spanning relations and forces (Ansell, 2009) have been underlined as having the capacity to both provide deeper insight into the everyday lived experiences of the political economy, and raise new theoretical questions (Pimlott-Wilson and Hall, 2017). Overall, drawing these links deepens our understandings of young people's experiences of 'neoliberal' politics, in particular the pressure or resistance to adopt aspirational, responsible subjectivities.

Methods and contexts

This chapter is based on ethnographic research undertaken in 2012–2014 around short international trips initiated by youth groups based in London council estates. These trips are somewhat unusual in the international volunteering landscape, whose elite and commercialised nature is illustrated by newspaper articles such as the Telegraph's 'Gap 100: an annual directory of the best gap year travel companies' or Guardian coverage such as 'Volunteer holidays: How to find an ethical project'.[1] However, at the same time, youth group trips reflect the increasing popularity of international volunteering initiated by community actors such as schools and religious organisations (Baillie Smith, 2013). The research project thus sought to explore *diverse* young people's engagements with popular practices of global charity beyond the established (and valid) critique that international volunteering reflects and reinforces the privilege of white, middle-class subjects. The project asked how volunteering is a site for subject formation in ways entangled *both* with global North–South relations *and* non-elite young people's social navigations (Vigh, 2009) in national and local contexts.

I engaged with two main case studies. Both were youth organisations primarily reliant on private philanthropy or community-based funding, thus themselves embedded in the austerity context of cuts to local government youth services (Jupp, 2017). The first was a relatively large youth charity, 'Springboard'[2] in Roehampton, south-west London. Overseas trips were a regular, high-profile strand of their work, which also included activity-based and 'drop in' youth clubs, mentoring programmes and youth enterprise schemes. I accompanied them on a ten-day trip to Kenya in February 2013, interviewing participants both before and after. I also undertook weekly participant observation with them for 14 months, and interviewed young people who had been on trips in past years, as well as youth workers and business funders. The second case study was a youth group associated with a church, 'Kingsfield' in Hackney, east London. The trip was a one-off initiated by the youth worker, a special addition to their work running various youth and community activities on the estate, most of which did not include overt religious content. With them, I accompanied a three-week trip to Zimbabwe in August 2013, again interviewing participants both before and after. Beyond the central case studies, I also interviewed key informants and young people who had been on similar trips. In total, 36 young people and 24 adults were interviewed, and 20 of the young people participated in multiple interviews. The young people who participated in the trips I accompanied were aged 14–20, and the young people I interviewed about their past experience of similar trips were aged 18–24.

Engaging with participants before, during, and after trips provided a rich understanding of both powerful hegemonic discourses, such as the trips as catalysts for 'transformation', and ambivalences around these. Ethnography revealed the intense embodied and affective dimensions to international encounters, and also the nuances of the everyday social contexts of young people's lives back in London. Out of the 36 young people interviewed, 27 were male and nine were female, in large part due to a masculine subculture in 'Springboard', as well as broader gendered norms around adventure and caring responsibility which shaped participation. The groups reflected the 'super-diverse' nature of London (Vertovec, 2012). Although identity categories often conceal as much as they illuminate, 11 were of Afro-Caribbean heritage, 13 'white', and 12 of 'mixed-race', South Asian, or Hispanic heritage. None of the young people had heritage links to the countries visited. In the Springboard case, almost all interviewees lived in social housing on the estate, and their parents were predominantly in low-wage or precarious employment in service or manual labour. Most of these young people were framed by youth workers, teachers and local authorities as 'marginalised', or 'at risk' (Turnbull and Spence, 2011) in relation to anxiety about their educational performance or involvement in criminalised behaviour. The Kingsfield group was more mixed, reflecting the cross-class community that had coalesced around the church. About half of the group lived in social housing, had parents in low-wage or precarious employment, and were framed as 'at risk'. The other half lived in a range of housing situations in the surrounding area, with parents mostly in skilled jobs with modest salaries such as nursing, with several of the group having parents in high-paid professions. All research participants bar one went to local state-funded schools.

The young people in this research were not growing up in wholly marginalised environments: they all attended schools designated 'good' or 'outstanding' by Ofsted, and could access a wide range of free extracurricular opportunities via a mix of local-government and philanthropic services, in part due to being surrounded by established wealth (in south-west London) and rapid gentrification (in east London). However, their experiences still speak of growing up in austerity. Participants' at the lower-income end of the spectrum talked in interviews about overcrowded housing situations, household economic stress (for example, paying basic bills), and anxiety around the peer violence and criminalised economies closely correlated with urban disinvestment and unemployment. Furthermore, being 'poor in a rich location' did not remove – and perhaps even exacerbated – the stigma associated with being a council estate resident, and/or having a denigrated classed habitus (Archer et al, 2007; McKenzie, 2013). Almost all of the participants, bar the most privileged, gave accounts of feeling 'labelled' in public spaces, and sometimes within education (Kulz, 2014).

In regard to the overseas trips in this research, young people's travel was funded by a mixture of private donations (especially in Springboard), local authority funding (predominantly 'youth opportunity fund' grants of ~£200 to individual young people) and community fundraising efforts (sponsored events). In the Springboard trip, volunteering in Kenya took place at a children's home on the outskirts of a regional city which the charity had visited several times. Work involved painting and refurbishment, helping lay a water pipe, and participating in activities and mealtimes with the children at the home, as well as visiting an extremely poor settlement on a rubbish dump. In Zimbabwe, volunteering occurred at several sites, facilitated through various local partners – running children's activities in an informal settlement in Harare, painting, refurbishment and children's activities in a school, and community gardening in a rural area. In both cases there were also days of leisure – such as going on a day safari, and market trips. In both cases youth workers brought agendas from their long-term work such as building soft skills (teamwork, communication), psycho-social capacities (self-esteem, anger management), or emotional and spiritual reflection. Overall, the trips closely reflected hybrid, popular ideas of doing good which emphasised 'hands-on' helping combined with self-development, fun and adventure, rather than being closely shaped by defined educational, religious, or development-sector visions. Having given this portrait of the everyday social contexts of young people's London lives, and the international volunteering trips, how did these two contexts relate?

Becoming 'rich': global comparisons and self-disciplining into responsibility

Ruth: How are you feeling about going to Kenya?
Payton: Excited. It's gonna be a good experience.
Kai: Excited, but to be honest I want it to be bad. If you know what I mean? – I want it to be a bad experience, but a good one at the end ...

Ruth: … tell me more about what you mean by that?

Kai: So, I do want it to change me, like, I want it to show me –

Payton: – When you see the worse stuff in Kenya, so – it changed your view on life here, so for example … a lot of guys … going to Kenya … they'll be like – 'what I got back home ain't that bad'. Like … compared to them, I'm kind of rich, like, I've got a lot of stuff. I'm wealthy.

(Payton and Kai,[3] both 16 years old,
pre-trip paired interview, Roehampton)

This exchange epitomises a taken-for-granted idea surrounding these short trips – that they are 'transformational' for the volunteers themselves. Ideas of *how* going abroad may catalyse change, and *what* sort of change will occur, rest in large part on powerful imaginaries around global wealth and poverty. Prior to the trips, young people recounted imaginings of sub-Saharan Africa as defined by "pure poverty" (Dylan, Roehampton). Encountering this, primarily through the gaze, as Payton says earlier, going to "see the worse stuff in Kenya" is imagined to prompt a shift towards being more grateful for one's relative material wealth. The idea that "hopefully when we get back, we will all be more grateful for what we have" (Nadia, Hackney), implies a degree of current 'ingratitude'. Payton and Kai (quoted earlier) discuss wanting to be shocked and challenged, and the slippage in Payton's language into the past tense to talk about a future experience, and from referring to others ("a lot of guys") to speaking in the first person ("I'm wealthy") illustrates that the narrative of becoming grateful through encountering material poverty frames and foreshadows the actual experience of the trips.

These expected lessons are situated in wider popular humanitarian imaginaries of sentimental charitable encounters (Mostafanezhad, 2013) which circulate in media and popular discussion. For instance, Benny's desire to be changed shows the pronounced way young people internalised the idea that 'the kids in Africa' would prompt a necessary transformation away from 'selfishness':

'Everyone from the church was telling me that I should go – it would be life changing … My cousin … went with a group to Ghana … and when he came back … saw life differently … wasn't selfish … 'Cos the kids in Africa didn't have a lot. So I thought, yeah, it's true. I should really go.' (Benny, 16 years old, Hackney)

The way that 'volunteering as a means to increase gratitude and motivation' is internalised by young people in a self-disciplinary manner was illustrated during a pre-trip 20-mile fundraising walk with the Roehampton-Kenya group. It was a freezing day in January, and we walked until well after dark. Part way through an arduous stretch I overhead one young man rallying another who was complaining of feeling tired, to think of how "they are walking that far to get water, it makes you feel selfish, try to put yourself in their shoes" (Dylan, Roehampton). An image of a generalised Kenyan subject, informed by charitable representations of rural poverty, was mobilised towards the labour of self-transformation into more motivated and less 'selfish' subjects, even before travel.

Adults involved with the trips also took for granted the idea that encounters with poverty would prompt a sense of gratitude. Some of Springboard's funders expressed with uncomfortable transparency their views that visits to abjectly poor settings, such as the community living on the rubbish dump, would prompt a visceral sense of comparative privilege:

> '[The Kenyan residents] all dancing and singing on the dump ... You can't help but have your thinking tested ... "So you think your life is shit. What about theirs?" You know, you don't even have to ask that question ... It's in your face. You're living, breathing it. Smelling it. ' (Martin, Springboard business supporter)

The implication here is that Martin feels that an encounter with the 'happy poor' in Africa, singing and dancing despite terrible conditions, should challenge a 'bad attitude' of young people from socio-economically marginal background in the UK. This view is clearly informed by long-standing moralised discourses which assume working-class young people are deviant or apathetic. Such views also enact a denial of poverty as anything other than material, and a delegitimisation of the way young people living under austerity in the UK may feel that 'life is shit' because of a poverty of equal opportunities in education or for meaningful work, and in their experiences of stress, conflict and violence produced by living in poor neighbourhoods and households, and in their experiences of classed (and often racialised) stigma (McKenzie, 2013; Shildrick and MacDonald, 2007).

One of the most striking aspects of the research was the way that young people internalised such ideas, as demonstrated in the field diary extract which follows. Here, there is a particular power to the embodied, emotional experiences of the 'happy poor' which are both interpreted through overdetermined imaginaries and works to put a stamp of authenticity on depoliticised ways of understanding poverty and inequality (Diprose, 2012):

> Zimbabwe[4] – We're sitting round the campfire just after dusk, the rapidly falling darkness adding to the feeling of togetherness and warmth inside the circle. Emma says we're going to reflect on how the trip is going. Richie talks about the 'joy' on faces in the boys' home, saying 'it brought so much strength for me ... I thought – the times when I'm suffering, and I'm not feeling joy ... these lot are feeling joy like, continuously ...' Peter talks, his voice saturated with emotion, about seeing a homeless young woman and her baby, and how 'it shows us that ... what we have is privileged. Like, we shouldn't take advantage of what we have, because like – some people will die for – just like, one minute in our lives ... I think – really, that opened all of our eyes up. That's it.' There's a long silence. Phillip speaks up, which is unusual. He says 'it made me ... think about times like, back at home, when sometimes our electricity would run out ... but some people over here don't even have a home to live in, so I have to be – grateful ...'

The power of this sense of comparative privilege prompted by embodied encounters with material poverty was expressed as being a sort of affective tool for betterment, as expressed by one youth worker:

> 'I don't want to take away from the fact that there is a sense of poverty still for them, relative to the UK ... but I think it is an important thing ... to almost slightly compare themselves against others who are less – even less – fortunate than them, in order for them to be grateful for what they do have. Because otherwise it's just some kind of negative cycle and ... it needs an injection of positivity.' (Emma, youth worker, Zimbabwe trip)

Emma espouses the narrative of comparative gratitude as about 'an injection of positivity' to jolt young people out of a sense of 'negativity'. Youth workers such as Emma undertook deeply admirable long-term work to support young people in myriad emotional and pragmatic ways through their experiences of growing up in precarious contexts. However, not only do such ideas of a comparative 'boost' still re-embed imaginaries of sub-Saharan Africa as defined by abject poverty, and imply that this poverty is *more* 'real', but they are informed by the idea that the (or one) solution to young people's difficulties lies in an affective adjustment of themselves. In this way, these volunteer tourism trips are complicit with pressures on young people to 'adjust' their 'habitus' (Kulz, 2014) and be 'more aspirational' (Brown, 2013) amid a politics in which 'accountability for inequalities shifts from social structures and institutions, to be managed affectively and emotionally by young people who internalise responsibility for their future success or failure in the neoliberal economy' (Pimlott-Wilson, 2017: 9).

This section has argued that neo-colonial imaginaries of Africa as defined by 'happy people' living in naturalised, abject poverty present in popular versions of global charity (Mathers, 2010) function as a backdrop to prompt comparative gratitude which in the case of *less privileged* volunteers neatly meshes with the drive towards the 'responsibilisation of poverty' in austerity Britain. 'Comparing oneself globally' via the practices (and imaginaries) of popular humanitarianism becomes mobilised as a benchmarking disciplinary tool for young people to self-regulate into having a 'better attitude' about the strictures of austerity Britain, and feeds into pressures to be responsible, motivated, and productive members of society. The next section turns to explore in greater detail the contradictory ideas about wealth and poverty that young people internalised and grappled with during their reflections after volunteering.

Stigmatised and celebrated materialistic subjects

In their post-trip reflections, in large part young people espoused ideas of comparative gratitude and individual responsibility. The way that their ideas took shape around the politics of popular humanitarianism *and* austerity is particularly clearly expressed by Jacob (Hackney) who condemns those who "choose unemployment", drawing in both domestic discourses around benefit cheats, and popular global inspirational tales:

> 'We've got to do things with our life ... here [in the UK] people choose to do nothing, and there [in Zimbabwe] it isn't necessarily a choice ... people who sit on benefits who don't need to ... like – you're taking the piss out of the other person who can't do that ... 'cos you have that choice, and

you're wasting it. It reminds me a bit of like – that little girl who got shot [Malala Yousafzai] ... she come on and say the English girls don't really respect their education.' (Jacob, 16 years old, Hackney)

Again, these lessons were given the visceral stamp of truth via the young people's embodied, emotional encounters with material poverty on the trips. As Jacob went on to say, referencing an LBC[5] radio segment he had heard on housing:

'they were talking about ... overcrowded houses in this country and ... honestly, I had a bad taste in my mouth because it was just like "how can you still be complaining?" I remember ... we went to this guy Charles' house ... he was sharing a shack with like four people ... I just kept thinking to myself "if he was here, what on earth would he think ...?"' (Jacob, 16 years old, Hackney)

Thus, many young people felt the trips underlined that there was no legitimacy to 'complain' unless you were at the bottom of a crude ladder of absolute material poverty, as expressed by Lisa, who at 20 was still living in her family's council flat and sharing a room with her two sisters due to her low-paid part-time job at a leisure centre and the unaffordability of housing:

'Sometimes you go back to your old ways, worrying ... "oh I can't go out this week, not enough money ..." – but people out there, they are worried about how they are going to be able to get their next meal and I'm complaining about ... a night out, or buying the latest pair of shoes!' (Lisa, 20 years old, Roehampton)

Here, in Lisa's self-exhortation not to complain about not having the latest shoes, we see the presence of discourses around young people as inappropriately invested in conspicuous consumption which are common tropes of classed stigma (Archer et al, 2007). However, young people didn't renounce material consumption, but gave accounts which suggested paradoxical feelings about it. For instance, Dave (in the next extract) talks of being inspired by happiness without material goods, but seems quickly compelled to list his consumer possessions: shoring up the boundaries of 'having something'. Furthermore, in the absence of more critical models of solidarity or development education, 'helping' is understood as donating more money to others so that they too can own things:

> 'They show you how happy you can be with nothing – like its amazing! They don't have my Xbox360, my racer bike, they don't have my 32-inch TV on my wall, they don't have my boots ... my phone. But they're more happy ... I'm now trying to sponsor a little girl in Kenya to make sure her life can be as good as mine.' (Dave, 16 years old, Roehampton)

Literature on international volunteering highlights that witnessing poverty can both feed into messages not to be 'ungratefully materialistic' *and* be a route to further 'appreciation' and veneration of consumer capitalism for western volunteers (Crossley, 2012). Quotes like Dave's suggests that this paradox may have been deepened for young people who are growing up in the 'double bind' of being stigmatised for being poor, and 'fixed' as denigrated working-class subjects when they respond to this stigmatisation through conspicuous consumption (Archer et al, 2007). Similarly, Richie (Hackney) made an initially confusing declaration that the trip to Zimbabwe had made him 'less materialistic' quickly followed by saying it had also made him want to 'dress to impress'. I realised that he was describing distancing himself from conspicuous consumption and trying to communicate a new, upwardly mobile identity through dress:

> 'Before the trip ... I'd think "ah I really NEED a new pair of trainers" but I realise that that's not really doing me anything 'Cos I don't wanna seem as – uh ... "gangster" ... I've never dressed like a gangster, but I'm just saying like – I wanna have a new look to me, I wanna look more smart, I wanna look more motivated.' (Richie, 16 years old, Hackney)

Richie's need to 'adjust himself' to create distance from a 'gangster' subject position as a young black man, highlights how experiences of global charity are made sense of through everyday social contexts of intersectional classed, racialised and gendered experience. Richie has linked his desire to perform a more 'smart', 'motivated' identity elsewhere in his interview to his dream for 'big money' entrepreneurial success. This fits well with critiques of 'aspiration nation' as a society in which narrow middle-class ideas of aspiration set out 'neoliberal ideas of fulfilment through material consumption: "the risk takers. The young people who dream of their first pay cheque, their first car, their first home" (Cameron, 2012)' (Pimlott-Wilson, 2017: 3). Within this, volunteering becomes a technology of the 'aspirational self' as well as an 'experience' acquired to gain an individual edge in an increasingly precarious labour market (Holdsworth, 2017).

This section has delved into the complex and contradictory messages around wealth and poverty for non-elite young people who participate in international volunteering. On the one hand there is a disciplinary edge to ideas that one has no right to complain in the face of poverty construed as absolute material need. This parallels and fortifies messages berating young working-class people for being 'too materialistic'. At the same time, young people cannot escape from the obligation to have material wealth in a UK society that stigmatises poverty and celebrates 'aspiration' as neoliberal consumption, *and* in popular humanitarian imaginaries which have been criticised as enmeshed with a wider 'celebrity-charity-corporate complex', in which seemingly apolitical (but often 'western-saviour') solutions to poverty are enacted through free-market capitalist logics (Brockington, 2014; Daley, 2013; Mostafanezhad, 2013). As such, young people are left grappling with confusing messages around whether wealth and consumption is something to be eschewed or celebrated. The final section turns to outline the limited, but significant, ways young people resisted and reworked the politics outlined so far in this chapter.

Reasons to complain and a desire for critical understandings of poverty

Young people did not take up wholesale these discourses about individual responsibility. Subtle reworkings of the lessons of the trip often occurred through painful articulations of disillusionment and frustration about the contrast between the valued and respected way they were treated as volunteers with classed stigma in the UK. Young people's positive feelings about the trips simply as 'adventures' were also often in friction with the dominant messages 'transformed' and 'improved' subjectivities through volunteering. Their investments in fun and friendship on the trips asserted a deservingness to leisure which was at odds with acquiescing to the pressure to become responsible, hardworking subjects.

Some young people explicitly problematised the politics of comparative gratitude, acknowledged the reality of poverty in the UK and legitimised economic hardships. For instance, Chris reflected that an unemployed friend of his has a "right to complain":

> 'He finds it really hard. I was sort of comparing it to the people in Zimbabwe ... sort of thinking – their lives are so much worse ... but then ... that doesn't mean you don't have a right to complain, as well ... there is a very good reason to complain.' (Chris, 17 years old, Hackney)

Some reflected from their own positionality. For instance, Peter – who in his pre-trip interview had told me of the financial precarity of his household, of extended family members from Nigeria staying in their flat, and his migrant parents' thwarted ambitions for meaningful work – expressed reflections that present a stark contrast to the idea of everyone in the UK 'having it easy':

> 'This country's very rich ... but it's not benefitting the homeless people, and the people that – are not exactly rich ... the council won't give them a house ... like – people from Africa, they go to England to get work, 'cos England's like, the way out for a better life ... but it's really like, not ... pfff ... (Peter, 15 years old, Hackney)

Therefore although at the headline level young people often reproduced the lessons reinforced through the trips about the 'ungrateful poor' in the UK, these statements were tempered and held paradoxically in tandem with their more personal and specific reflections, which asserted their and their communities' inherent worth and deservingness without needing to 'change'. For instance, Lisa's memories of the trips contained an affective sense of expanded confidence and worth, which she discusses as giving her a tangible feeling of counteracting visions of herself as defined by classed stigma. Though her 'feeling better' could be analysed as due to gaining a distinction through 'virtuous' (neo-colonial charity) work, I would argue it comes from less of a 'transformation' than as a stamp of 'proof' of her belief that she is a valuable member of society in the face on an onslaught of judgements of worth based on capital accumulation:

> 'It makes you look at yourself in a different light, like I'm – not a bad person ... I've done good as well. Yeah – makes you feel better in yourself ... older people especially, like, upper class people – can look down on you ... yeah, I don't

earn a lot of money, but I've been to Africa, and I've helped people.' (Lisa, 20 years old, Roehampton)

Reflections against the grain of sentimentalised ideas of charity and absolute poverty in the global South were rare, however. When young people articulated ideas around poverty in the global South as political rather than natural, most of them presented ideas of African corruption. The few explicitly critical politicised accounts young people gave in my research were self-developed. Anthony mentioned socially-conscious hip-hop, independent online research (youtube videos), conversations with friends from diverse backgrounds, and formal lessons at school as helping him develop a political consciousness through which he presented an articulate critique of the idea of the west as 'the saviour of the world', instead linking poverty and inequality to histories of imperialism, and actively perpetuated by corporate power:

> 'That really angered me and upset me ... that this [poverty] is allowed to continue by a lot of people who have actively taken steps to put people in that position ... and that ... really, really bugged me. The British government, and British businesses who've been doing business in these places for a long time ... they know exactly the situation over there, and they'd rather focus on making a healthy profit than investing in Africa – when ... it made and supported their empire, it was the lifeblood of their business. Now they're not getting so much, reaping so much out of it, they're not so interested in Africa.' (Anthony, 24 years old, Roehampton)

Although at the moment the trips 'succeed in keeping apart places with common problems and shared interests' (Katz, 2001: 722), Anthony's reflections highlight the potential for young working-class participation in international volunteering to be conducted in a different manner. Trips such as these could frame international action as solidarity, and provide critical consciousness raising around inequality and addressing the social dimensions of poverty.

Conclusion

This chapter has explored how popular imaginaries and practices of charity in the global South interact with the politics of austerity in young people's lives in the global North. Specifically, the chapter showed how in short international volunteering trips that engaged young people from low-income backgrounds, narrow ideas of poverty as absolute material need, and sentimental images of 'the happy poor' in sub-Saharan Africa became drawn into the stigmatisation of poverty in the UK, and the pressure on young people to 'adjust themselves' to become more grateful, motivated and responsible subjects. Thus, the chapter has contributed an examination of how seemingly disconnected global sites and dynamics become entangled and complicit in a wider politics that normalises the condemnation of 'wasting' oneself, despite one's structural position as 'excess' labour to capital accumulation (Katz, 2011), or long-term community disinvestment (McKenzie, 2013).

The chapter outlined that participating in short volunteer tourism trips and the powerful social imaginaries around them, paralleled and fortified pressure on young people to transform themselves into more grateful and motivated subjects. The chapter also explored how young people grapple with the contradictory messages present around material wealth in both 'popular humanitarian' and 'aspiration nation' politics. At times, eschewing wealth and consumption is a measure of virtue, yet money is also upheld as the means to development and the marker of hierarchies of fulfilment. Young people generally internalised such politics and took a self-disciplining stance to becoming more grateful and motivated, though they also asserted the difficulty of their lived experiences of poverty and inequality, and their own worth and deservingness.

The chapter highlights that it is fruitful to consider the politics of global charity in conversation with critiques of how local voluntarism can function as a counterpart to welfare reform and service cuts, even as volunteering has meanings which exceed that (Fyfe and Milligan, 2003). It also adds specificity, empirical texture, and nuance to ideological critiques around how volunteering can prepare young people for an insecure and flexible labour market (see Cremin, 2007; Holdsworth, 2017) by centring young people's own accounts. Finally, the chapter raises critical questions about how the stigmatisation and 'responsibilisation of poverty' occurs and is normalised across diverse sites, including those which reach beyond the nation-state and 'the local', and how contending with this may be enhanced by a space-crossing, multi-scalar view.

Notes

[1] https://www.telegraph.co.uk/travel/gap-year-travel/gap-year-100-companydirectoryvolunteering/; https://www.theguardian.com/travel/2014/feb/17/volunteer-holidays-how-to-find-right-project

2   All organisational names are pseudonyms.
3   All individual names are pseudonyms.
4   The quotes in this vignette are all verbatim, taken from a recording made at the time.
5   *Leading Britain's Conversation*, a London-based talk and call-in radio show.

References

Ansell, N. (2009) 'Childhood and the politics of scale: Descaling children's geographies?', *Progress in Human Geography*, 33(2): 190–209.

Archer, L., Hollingworth, S. and Halsall, A. (2007) ' "University's not for me – I'm a Nike person": Urban, working-class young people's negotiations of "style", identity and educational engagement', *Sociology*, 41(2): 219–237.

Baillie Smith, M. (2013) 'Public imaginaries of development and complex subjectivities: The challenge for development studies', *Canadian Journal of Development Studies/Revue Canadienne D'études Du Développement*, 34(3): 400–415.

Baillie Smith, M. and Laurie, N. (2011) 'International volunteering and development: Global citizenship and neoliberal professionalisation today', *Transactions of the Institute of British Geographers*, 36(4): 545–559.

Brockington, D. (2014) 'The production and construction of celebrity advocacy in international development', *Third World Quarterly*, 35(1): 88–108.

Brown, G. (2013) 'The revolt of aspirations: Contesting neoliberal social hope', *ACME*, 12(3): 419–430.

Cheung Judge, R. (2016) 'Volunteer tourism and non-elite young subjects: Local, global, and situated', in: C. Dwyer, N. Worth and T. Skelton (eds) *Geographies of children and young people*, Volume 4: *Geographies of identities and subjectivities*, Singapore: Springer, pp.249–268.

Cremin, C. (2007) 'Living and really living: The gap year and the commodification of the continent', *Ephemera*, 7(4): 526–542.

Crossley, É. (2012) 'Poor but happy: Volunteer tourists' encounters with poverty', *Tourism Geographies*, 14(2): 235–253.

Daley, P. (2013) 'Rescuing African bodies: Celebrities, consumerism and neoliberal humanitarianism', *Review of African Political Economy*, 40(137): 375–393.

Diprose, K. (2012) 'Critical distance: Doing development education through international volunteering', *Area*, 44(2): 186–192.

Fyfe, N. R. and Milligan, C. (2003) 'Out of the shadows: Exploring contemporary geographies of voluntarism', *Progress in Human Geography*, 27(4): 397–413.

Holdsworth, C. (2017) 'The cult of experience: Standing out from the crowd in an era of austerity', *Area*, 49(3): 296–302.

Jupp, E. (2017) 'Families, policy and place in times of austerity', *Area*, 49(3): 266–272.

Katz, C. (2001) 'Vagabond capitalism and the necessity of social reproduction', *Antipode*, 33(4): 709–728.

Katz, C. (2011) 'Accumulation, excess, childhood: Toward a countertopography of risk and waste', *Documents d'Anàlisi Geogràfica*, 57(1): 47–60.

Kulz, C. (2014) '"Structure liberates?": Mixing for mobility and the cultural transformation of "urban children" in a London academy', *Ethnic and Racial Studies*, 37(4): 685–701.

Mathers, K. (2010) *Travel, humanitarianism, and becoming American in Africa*, New York: Palgrave Macmillan.

Mckenzie, L. (2013) 'Fox-trotting the riot: Slow rioting in Britain's inner city', *Sociological Research Online*, 18(4): 68–99.

Mostafanezhad, M. (2013) '"Getting in touch with your inner Angelina": Celebrity humanitarianism and the cultural politics of gendered generosity in volunteer tourism', *Third World Quarterly*, 34(3): 485–499.

Pimlott-Wilson, H. (2017) 'Individualising the future: The emotional geographies of neoliberal governance in young people's aspirations', *Area*, 49(3): 288–295.

Pimlott-Wilson, H. and Hall, S. M. (2017) 'Everyday experiences of economic change: Repositioning geographies of children, youth and families', *Area*, 49(3): 258–265.

Shildrick, T. and MacDonald, R. (2007) 'Biographies of exclusion: Poor work and poor transitions', *International Journal of Lifelong Education*, 26(5): 589–604.

Turnbull, G. and Spence, J. (2011) 'What's at risk? The proliferation of risk across child and youth policy in England', *Journal of Youth Studies*, 14(8): 939–959.

Vigh, H. (2009) 'Motion squared: A second look at the concept of social navigation', *Anthropological Theory*, 9(4): 419–438.

Vertovec, S. (2007) 'Super-diversity and its implications', *Ethnic and Racial Studies*, 30(6): 1024–1054.

Vertovec, S. (2012) '"Diversity" and the social imaginary', *European Journal of Sociology*, 53(3): 287–312.

PART III

Futures

13

Looking towards the future: intersectionalities of race, class and place in young Colombians' lives

Sonja Marzi

Introduction

This chapter explores how the achievement of aspirations for young, urban Colombians (aged 15–22) in Cartagena is constrained by the inequalities reinforced through the intersection of different types of discrimination. In the example of the two annual beauty pageants, the elections of Miss Colombia and the popular queen, that take place during the Independence Day celebrations in Cartagena in November, this chapter shows how the intersection of social class, race, gender and place creates spaces of exclusion and restricts access to opportunities within Cartagena for young people. While raising aspirations are claimed as one of the main drivers of social mobility for young people in marginalised places (Brown, 2011; Hart, 2016), this chapter argues that unequal power relations and patterns of exclusion limit young Cartagenians' opportunities to pursue their aspirations. This is especially visible throughout the Independence Day celebrations in Cartagena where the events of the two beauty pageants reproduce patterns of discrimination and exclusion reminiscent of Cartagena's long history of slavery and colonialism. In particular, young people of the Afro-Colombian community living in high crime, lower social class neighbourhoods suffer from stigmatisation, discrimination and criminalisation. This chapter is based on data collected over nine months of ethnographic fieldwork, including interviews and participatory methods such as photography and filming, mapping activities and guided tours. By listening to the young Cartagenians' perceptions and experiences, and by analysing the interplay between aspirations and their relation to the inequalities reproduced through the intersection of race, social class, gender and place, the chapter provides a more complete picture of the boundaries to achieving their desired future selves faced by these young people. The author argues that, even though young people have high aspirations, this is not enough to overcome structural inequalities that constrain their social mobility.

Aspirations and social mobility

For over a decade, the concept of aspirations has been prominent in social science concerned with the wellbeing and future of young people worldwide. Aspirations and their conceptualisation describe future-oriented goals, wants or desires (Ibrahim, 2011; Brown, 2011; Prince, 2014). In contrast to dreams and wishes, aspirations take the investment of effort, time and capital into achieving them into consideration (Hart, 2016; Marzi, 2018). More importantly, social science has focused on the influence of aspirations on the upward social mobility of young people. Within this discussion, aspirations are the implicit drivers that can trigger change in people's social conditions towards upward social mobility (Appadurai, 2004). Following this idea, in cases where young people invest in achieving their desired futures, it would lead to some form of social mobility such as a change of status or class position within the hierarchy of their respective society (Marzi, 2015; Gough, 2008; Azevedo and Bouillon, 2010). This view of aspirations has been increasingly criticised as predominantly neoliberal, placing the responsibility of achieving upward social mobility on the young person alone (Brown, 2013; Holloway and Pimlott-Wilson, 2011; Pimlott-Wilson, 2017; Spohrer, 2011). Yet aspirations are formed 'in interaction and in the thick of social life' (Appadurai, 2004: 67), which means that important intersecting structural and contextual constraints, unequal power relations and aspects of discrimination affect the development and achievement of young people's aspirations. Social mobility opportunities can be limited by discriminative and oppressive structures based on the intersection of gender, class, race and place within a young person's social context (Kintrea et al, 2015; Marzi, 2015; Walker, 2018).

This chapter focuses on the influence of neo-colonial and structural inequalities that are reproduced through discrimination against young people aged 15–23 in Cartagena. The examples of two annual beauty pageants provide important insights into how these intersecting factors act as ordering and excluding mechanisms in the daily lives of the young people, reducing their ability to achieve their aspirations and realise upward social mobility. It argues that the relationship between young Cartagenians' aspirations and social mobility outcomes is significantly determined by the interplay between aspirations, opportunity structures and the reproduction of inequalities based on the intersection of race, class, gender and place. Therefore, this chapter speaks to other chapters in this book that showcase contemporary forms of inequality and precarity of young people and contributes to the book's aims with considering how young people cope with structural inequalities while at the same time striving for social justice and an alternative future.

Methods and context: Cartagena de Indias – a city of contrasts

This chapter draws on data from over nine months of ethnographic fieldwork in Cartagena, Colombia in 2013 and 2014 that was part of a research project to explore young Colombians' aspirations and social mobility opportunities. Interviews were conducted with young people of two disadvantaged neighbourhoods, so-called *barrios populares*, in Cartagena. Data was collected through spending most days accompanying the young people in their daily lives in order to understand what the challenges are for them to achieve their aspirations and social mobility. Additionally, group interviews and focus groups, data gathered through the use of participatory methods such as guided tours, mapping activities (of communities and characteristics of the city) and participatory photography and filming informed this study. The participatory methods in particular allowed for more agency and inclusion of the young peoples' views and perceptions (Cahill, 2007; Winton, 2007; Winton, 2016).

The author worked with two core groups of young people in two particular *barrios populares* in the city. One of these neighbourhoods is located next to the colonial centre and is here referred to as 'La Popa',[1] while the second neighbourhood, el Pozón, is located one hour by bus outside the colonial centre to the south-east. Both neighbourhoods consist of low socioeconomic status households and are labelled as very poor neighbourhoods within the city where young people have only limited quality education and work opportunities. People in these neighbourhoods are mostly of African descent or indigenous and white mixed ethnicity. Both neighbourhoods suffer from crime and some gang violence (Goyenche González et al, 2018), which often means that young people living in these places carry the label and reputation of their neighbourhood with them and become labelled as violent as well (Marzi, 2018).

The focus of this chapter is especially on the intersection of race, class and place, where place refers to the particular neighbourhood in which the young people live. While gender plays an important part in the chosen example of the annual beauty pageants, gender will be included to a lesser extent since the participant sample was disproportionately represented by males. However, the data allowed for a more detailed analysis of the intersecting categories of class, race and place. Cartagena and the annual beauty pageants provide an illustrative example to discuss the recurring patterns of discrimination and exclusion based on the intersection of race, class, gender and place that limit young people's ability to pursue their aspirations because each beauty pageant overtly caters to a starkly contrasting social class within the city.

In the past, Cartagena served as the major Spanish-speaking slavery port in Latin America and consequently a significant amount of the population in Cartagena is of African descent. However, many people in the city may have chosen not to self-identify as Afro-Colombian in the last census in 2005 and the official number of around 36.1% may not represent real numbers of Afro-Colombians in Cartagena (Rodríguez Garavito and Mosquera, 2010; DANE, 2010). Cartagena was also the first Colombian city to achieve independence from the Spanish crown in November 1811, an event that is celebrated every year and coincides with the national beauty pageants (Cunin, 2003). Cartagena is located on Colombia's Caribbean coast and today is one of the country's major tourist destinations. Despite this, the city struggles with poverty and faces challenges of racism and inequality (Moreno and González, 2011; Peréz V and Salazar Mejíra, 2007). Considering that a lot of economic capital enters the city through the tourism economy, one would think it should provide young people with diverse social mobility opportunities.

There is, however, a distinction between the Cartagena for tourists and higher social classes living in the city and the residential Cartagena of lower social classes, located outside the city centre and tourist areas. The former consists of the centre with beautiful colonial architecture and high apartment buildings and looks similar to the high-rise beachfront of Miami. This part of the city provides an impression of a modern and wealthy city, and reflects how higher social class and often lighter-skinned inhabitants live. The other side of the city, of marginalised neighbourhoods, poverty and inequality, consists of simple one-level houses with dirt floors and often only one or two rooms for a whole family of five people or more. In the poorest areas, these houses are built out of wood and waste material and streets are not paved but constitute dirt roads that become rivers of mud during the rainy season. This is where the lower social classes in Cartagena live, of which the majority is Afro-Colombian. The intersection of class, skin colour and race, and the neighbourhood one belongs to determines young people's ability to take advantage of opportunities towards upward social mobility to a great extent. Young people living in the poor and marginalised neighbourhoods are able to see wealthy neighbourhoods and living styles on their doorstep. They are able to visit them occasionally, but they are still excluded from the opportunities and material wealth they offer.

Contrary to the neoliberal discourse of aspirations, and despite the limiting and poor conditions in which they live, the research participants of this study demonstrated that they are indeed aspirational and have developed 'high' educational and occupational aspirations. Many of them aspire to study at university or are already studying to work in professional jobs. Some of the young people even study at private institutions financed through state credits (Marzi, 2016; Marzi, 2018). Yet, their social mobility has been rather low. Nonetheless, even though these young people are spatially segregated, discriminated against and labelled as criminals they are still ambitious with respect to their desired future selves (Marzi, 2016).

Patterns of exclusion: conceptualisation of class and race in Cartagena

'Intersectionality', a term coined by Crenshaw (1991), is a concept built on critical race and feminist theory that recognises the consequences of structural discrimination and oppression based on the intersection of forms of discrimination such as race, class and gender (Bastia, 2014; Moncrieffe, 2009; Nash, 2008). Thus intersectionality is a concept that explains how multiple forms of discrimination interrelate and 'are constructed by people reproducing inequality in different contexts and over time' (Gillborn, 2015: 278). Using an intersectionality lens to explore how race, social class, gender and place produce patterns of discrimination and inequalities for young people, limiting their aspiration attainment, allows one to capture the complexity of how discrimination works in Cartagena.

Social class distinctions in Colombia are identifiable through the system of estratos socioeconómicos (short form: estratos). Estratos are administrative categorisations on a scale from one to six and determine how much households have to pay for gas, water and electricity. Estrato six is assigned to the wealthiest households and requires them to pay more for utilities, while *estrato* one is assigned to the poorest households and requires them to pay less (Marzi, 2016; Marzi, 2018).

Even though the majority of Cartagenians associate discrimination with class, research has shown that discrimination on the basis of race is well intersected with class (Streicker, 1995). Yet, the concept of race in Cartagena does not follow a simple dualism, such as in the US, where blackness is defined by blood without any distinction of how mixed their blood may be. In Latin America, and in particular Colombia, there are different forms of the construction of race and ethnicity (Wade, 2010; Cunin, 2003; Mosquera Rosero-Labbé, 2010; Ng'weno, 2007; Restrepo, 2007). Due to its colonial history, Colombia has become a multi-ethnic country with a variety of terms that define various ethnic differences such as *mestizo* (indigenous and white mixed ethnicity), *mulatto* (black and white ethnicity), *zambo* (black and indigenous ethnicity), *blanco* (white) and *negro* (black) (Wade, 2010; Wade, 1993; Mosquera Rosero-Labbé, 2010).

More interestingly, according to Cunin (2003: 8) how black or white one is perceived is highly associated with one's identification to a social class. For example, a taxi driver may refer to himself as *más claro* (more white) because driving tourists around the city is associated with a higher social class status than the social class of a person selling fruit in the street who in turn would be defined as *más oscuro* (darker). Accordingly, the perception in Cartagenian society in relation to race and definition of skin colour does not describe the skin colour but rather the skin colour or their 'race' in intersection with their status in the social hierarchy of Cartagenian society.

Today, young Afro-Colombians suffer the consequences of historically-rooted structures connected to racism. These discriminatory structures are not discriminating against young people solely because of their skin colour, but on the basis of the broader social construction of being Afro-Colombian, an intersection of race, class and associated other characteristics such as the music they listen to and the way they dress. Therefore, being young, Afro-Colombian and dressed in a certain way that demonstrates that they are from poorer social classes may be enough for people to experience everyday discrimination such as being stopped and questioned by police on the street in richer neighbourhoods (see Marzi, 2018: 19). Other examples are that young people are excluded from entering shops and night clubs in tourist areas or are not employed because they are perceived as not trustworthy on the basis that they belong to dangerous neighbourhoods (Marzi, 2016).

Young people from poorer neighbourhoods mainly experience discrimination in the richer parts of the city. These parts are the locations of social mobility opportunities with the majority of universities and businesses. While young people may be able to access these places physically, it is still a struggle for them to realise their aspirations within them. I explained elsewhere (see Marzi, 2018) that belonging to poorer neighbourhoods disadvantages young people as their neighbourhoods are labelled as crime ridden and people from these neighbourhoods carry a bad reputation. Young people are labelled as gang members and as dangerous, even though they are not, because these neighbourhoods are home to gangs. This diminishes their social mobility opportunities through limited access to resources, such as cultural and economic capital, necessary to be successful at university and in future jobs as well as through being stigmatised and discriminated against, and thus not given the chance to realise their aspirations in the first place. While every form of discrimination creates its own barriers, it is the intersection of race, class, place and often gender that explains how discrimination is experienced for young people in Cartagena.

Independence day and beauty queens: intersectionalities of race, class, gender and place

> *Libertad, Libertad, a Fé con ardor gritó, y en un Once de Noviembre fue la Heroica Cartagena quien del yugo las cadenas cual fiera leona destrozó.*[2] [Freedom, freedom, the faithful with fervour shouted and on November eleventh it was the heroic Cartagena like a fierce lioness broke free from the yoke of chains.]

These are the lines of Cartagena's anthem that children learn in school.[3] Cartagena was the first Colombian city to declare independence from the Spanish crown in 1811 and this is celebrated annually with parades, events and two beauty pageants. The pageants provide interesting insights into how race, gender, class and place intersect and reinforce inequality and discrimination in young people's everyday lives.

The first of the two annual beauty pageants is the election of Miss Colombia. The winner of this beauty pageant will participate in the international Miss Universe competition. All Miss Colombia events in Cartagena start the week before 11 November, while the coronation is usually held one or two days after 11 November. At almost the same time, another beauty pageant takes place in Cartagena. The election of the 'Reina de la independencia' (Queen of independence), or the popular queen: a beauty queen elected by, and belonging to, one of the lower social class *barrios populares* in Cartagena.

Access to the prestigious Miss Colombia events is mostly denied to the lower social classes, as they cannot afford the high entry prices for tickets. The election of Miss Colombia is broadcasted on national TV, accompanying the women from the preparation for the contest until the final crowning. The majority of the events related to the Miss Colombia election take place in Cartagena's historical centre and in expensive high-rise hotels in Bocagrande. Participants of this beauty pageant represent their Colombian department (*departamento*) and belong to elite and wealthy families. However, while these women represent their respective Colombian department, they do not represent the average Colombian woman and her physical appearance. The appearance of Miss Colombia participants closely matches international beauty standards of 90–60–90 hourglass figures, 1.80m in height, light-skinned, straight long hair and they try to match Caucasian facial features, if necessary, even with the help of medical procedures. In contrast, the average Colombian woman is 1.65m tall, of mixed or black skin colour, and has rather curly, shorter hair (Rutter-Jensen et al, 2005). Consequently, Miss Colombia provides a picture of how a Colombian woman ought to be in order to satisfy western-oriented beauty standards; a surreal picture of female beauty that very few in Colombia embody. While this is not unusual for beauty pageants (Rasch, 2020), in Colombia, and especially in Cartagena, it discriminates against Afro-Colombian women.

Although the Miss Colombia beauty pageant committee asserts that no racism exists in the beauty pageants, all Miss Colombia queens are light skinned. In over 70 years, only one Afro-Colombian Miss Colombia has been elected, even though 25% of Colombia's population is Afro-Colombian (Refworld, 2019), which is one of the highest in Latin America. The tendency towards light-skinned beauty queens with long straight hair is further reinforced during the popular queen pageant. This shows how implicit racism and sexist gender roles are reinforced through these events.

Additionally, to conform to western-oriented beauty standards the Miss Colombia contestants are expected to follow behavioural rules that include staying at their residential address and not moving to other departments in the country. They have to remain unmarried before and during the contest (though they are allowed to have a *male* partner), which makes the beauty pageant experience more appealing to Colombia's heterosexual male population (by playing to their sexual fantasies) (Rutter-Jensen et al, 2005: 12). Plastic surgery is accepted and not unusual in order to perfectly conform to international beauty standards. Rhinoplasty, breast implants and fat removal surgeries are among the most common surgeries which Miss Colombia contestants are willing to undergo. Therefore, patriarchal and sexist gender ideals and norms are commonly reinforced through the Miss Colombia pageant. Young popular queen contestants also orientate themselves to these standards but without the economic means to realise them with the same success. Both beauty queen contestants are not expected to be intelligent, economically independent or politically involved (Rutter-Jensen et al, 2005), but to act according to sexist ideals of a machismo society (Quevedo-Gómez et al, 2011; Cunin, 2003; Cunin, 2006).

Participation in the Miss Colombia beauty pageant is only open to women if they have the necessary financial resources to pay for surgeries and related event costs that come with the preparation and participation of this beauty pageant. Costs to participate, covering preparation courses, clothes and travel costs, have been estimated to be at least 40 million pesos (£9,350) (Rutter-Jensen et al, 2005: 12). Miss Colombia contestants come from rich and elite families and they are frequently sponsored by national and international beauty product and fashion brands that cover their travel, food and hotel costs (Cunin, 2003: 194). Conversely, the popular queen contestants have to fundraise money for their personal expenses, such as clothes and make-up and only receive sponsorship from the council of Cartagena to cover the costs of events and their organisation, some of the clothes, preparation and travel costs.

The process to elect the popular queen, starts with so-called 'gozons', events that take place in the *barrios populares*. Similarly to other beauty pageants, the popular queen pageant of the *barrios populares* has specific meanings that are not necessarily related to sexist gender roles (Rasch, 2020). Here, it creates solidarity within the neighbourhoods and every *barrio* shows commitment and support for their popular queen. The popular queens are able to represent their *barrio* and discuss the social, economic and political problems that occur within it, such as the absence of good infrastructure and quality education in the local media.

Both beauty pageants apparently take place in the same Cartagena, but the reality is that Cartagena is a single, albeit very divided, city. A city that represent two different social classes of Cartagenian society (Cunin, 2003: 197) where one is of a lighter-skinned, wealthy people and one of disadvantaged Afro-Colombians. These reinforced, intersecting inequalities are also visible to the young people of this study as James and Andrea observed:

James: The two beauty queen pageants present the diet of the poor and the party of the rich! What has the beauty queen event to do with independence? Nothing it is just an event during the Independence Day parties.

Andrea: The contests do not represent the Cartagenian culture. What it does is reinforce economic and political inequality and racism.

Thus, the beauty pageants represent an illustrative example of contemporary discrimination and inequality in Colombia, and in particular in Cartagena. The election of Miss Colombia is a portrait of Cartagena how it wants to be perceived: white, rich and wealthy, glamorous and elite. The second beauty pageant, where Cartagenians elect their popular queen who belongs to the poor neighbourhoods of the city is a portrait of the 'real' Cartagena:[4] Afro-Colombian, mostly poor, and struggling for social mobility opportunities in a city that excludes them. These excluding and discriminating structures are clearly expressed during these events. Furthermore, as Yonas observes, electing a light-skinned Miss Colombia in Cartagena during Independence Day is a very paradoxical event reproducing neo-colonial structures, crowning a queen on the day the city became independent from the crown:

> 'The national queen [Miss Colombia] contest has been implemented into the Independence Day events to get more attention. So it was a strategic decision and reinforces the colonial culture in this city and its touristic context. The contest of the popular *barrios* has been implemented afterwards because we from the *barrios populares* do not have access to the national contest for economic, social status and racial reasons. Cartagena and their beauty queen contest are companies. And isn't it ironic that we celebrate Independence Day from the Spanish crown to vote for a queen?'

Hence, it is bizarre that the Miss Colombia pageant takes place in the colonial part of Cartagena instead of choosing a city such as Medellin or the capital Bogotá. The organisers decided to occupy one of the most historical places in Colombia during the Independence Day celebrations, excluding those Afro-Colombians who were supposed to have their Independence Day celebrations in exactly these parts of the city that play a historic role. At the heart of Cartagena's independence celebrations is a Miss Colombia contest that reflects and reproduces historical inequalities of which independence was meant to signal the end.

Boundaries to social mobility in Cartagena

The two beauty pageants reflect Cartagena's neo-colonial ordering structures and inequality dynamics that create the challenges young people face when trying to pursue their aspirations towards social mobility. Especially with respect to obtaining employment and generating income, exclusion based on the intersection of race, class, gender and place restricts young people's access to the resources that could lead to better living standards. According to the Colombian statistics department, DANE, youth unemployment rates in Cartagena decreased by 5.2% since 2018 to an overall of 12.4% in the period between January and March 2019 (DANE, 2019). However, the calculation of the unemployment rate excludes every person who works for just one hour per week, as well as part-time and informal employment. Furthermore, 50.6% of employment in Cartagena is informal (DANE, 2019), which suggests that official unemployment statistics may imply an improved employment situation, even though the realities of disadvantaged young people's social mobility did not necessarily change much, especially since the young people of this study expressed the desire to obtain formal employment in the future.

Some of the main perceived social mobility drivers to obtain formal work are education and social capital, but not all forms of education lead to this outcome. While there are various opportunities available to obtain some form of degree, from vocational colleges to private universities, many of the young people who do not enter a formal university are unable to obtain formal employment in the future. For example, Miguel, one of the participants of this study, completed a vocational course in which he learned to work with metal for construction sites. One would think this could be a useful skill with respect to the many construction sites in the city. However, he did not have the necessary social contacts to obtain a job, nor did he have the financial means to continue studying to obtain a formal university degree. Today, he tries to earn money selling various products on the street, while thinking about next steps to achieve some of his aspirations and obtain social mobility in the form of formal work in the construction sector. Thus, it is not only education but the right kind of education alongside having the necessary social capital, so called *palanca*, that opens social mobility opportunities for young people in

Cartagena. In fact, many Colombians use informal channels to obtain jobs (Viafara and Uribe, 2009; de la Hoz et al, 2013; Jiménez, 2011) as Hannes explains: "Being at university, that does not give you necessarily a good life. It does not give you a guarantee to have work, or let's say you study but you need the network, la rosca, la palanca as well or you won't enter in nothing."

Just as young women who wish to become the popular queen and orientate themselves to international beauty standards without the economic means to realise them, young Cartagenians orientate themselves to professional jobs for which they often need private university education, but do not have the financial means to actually access this kind of education. Additionally, young people from *barrios populares* are excluded from quality primary and secondary education, which in turn excludes them from accessing successful higher education. Good schools are only present in richer neighbourhoods, yet in order to access university everyone has to sit the same entry exam. In cases where they may obtain a professional degree at a public university, disadvantaged youth may still not have the necessary social capital to obtain a professional job, as professional networks again are restricted to people of higher social classes in the city. Cartagena is a city with invisible ceilings based on the intersection of race, class and place, which are difficult to get through if you are a poor young Afro-Colombian person from a *barrio popular*.

This resonates with the neo-colonial ordering structures of the beauty pageants. In the same way as the Miss Colombia election occupies the historic places in the city, higher social classes occupy the social mobility opportunities within Cartagena. Lower social class Cartagenians are excluded from profit making places in the city, many of them related to the increasing tourism industry, and young Cartagenians feel excluded from social mobility opportunities while at the same time being discriminated because of their class and race:

Alessandra: It is just people are working and live for work.
Hannes: Exactly and they work like slaves. Before [in terms of decades ago] they [the employers] did not pay money and now they pay money but this is the only difference in this slavery.

The annual beauty pageants during the Independence Day celebrations, and the fact that only a small fraction of the population of Cartagena benefits from the emerging tourist business, illustrate the reinforcement of neo-colonial structures of discrimination in Cartagena. While the historical centre has been renovated and big apartment buildings have been built along the coastline, the *barrios populares* have not changed much but continue to be violent and poor *barrios* in the city (see Goyenche González et al, 2018). The participants in this study had never been related to any gang or criminal activity, but experienced discrimination linked to their place of living nonetheless:

Andreas: If you say you come from Pozón or from Olaya or from one of the *barrios populares* they treat you like you are a thief … This is how we the weaker class have to endure this.

Although the popular queen is encouraged to represent her *barrio* proudly, this celebration of the *barrio* is limited to spaces and places outside the tourist areas and only appreciated during the November events. In everyday life, however, none of the young people are encouraged to represent their *barrio popular*. It is rather the converse, if they wish to obtain professional employment. Additionally, Miguel claims class exclusion and place discrimination are intentional in order for the powerful class to maintain their class privileges in the city: "The superior class doesn't want that the inferior class advances. The class with the money does not want that the lower class rises because they want to keep their things. So many times they do not let somebody climb up in the working life."

Social hierarchy follows neo-colonial structures and sets the opportunity structures that the young people must contend with as they try to pursue their aspirations. Alessandra observes how Cartagena's various industries produce income but young people from *barrios populares* do not have access to these social classes nor places. Alessandra reflects on these inequalities suggesting that young people struggle to achieve their aspirations and social mobility because of these neo-colonial patterns of exclusion:

'When one goes to the Perimentral, to Pozón, to Nelson Mandela [the most stigmatised and poor *barrios*] … all this money that the tourism industry produces is controlled by just a few people and one asks, there is so much money that enters (the city) so why is there so much poverty, why there are so many abused children, why are there so many women looking for different ways to escape and to survive (she means illegal prostitution here), why there are so many young people delinquent, so many young people without access to education and healthcare. So one asks where did all this money go with this complete inequality and bad distribution of money. I tell you, history is repeating itself. During the colonial times it has been the black people and the indigenous that they subordinated. The Spanish exploited them and now foreigners and people not from Cartagena are coming here and they manipulate us and exploit us. History is repeating itself.'

Conclusion

What do beauty pageants have to do with young Cartagenians' social mobility opportunities and aspirations achievement? Cartagena is in one of the most unequal departments in Colombia in terms of income inequality, having a Gini of 0.50 in 2013, rising to 0.51 in 2014 (DANE, 2015) (see Goyenche González et al, 2018)[5] reflecting the inequality that the young people experience in their everyday lives. Because aspirations are developed through interaction and are embedded in young people's social context, their achievement cannot be dependent on the young people's actions only. Access to resources such as quality education and social capital that enable young people to take advantage of social mobility opportunities are restricted through historical structures and reproduced discrimination. How these discriminatory and neo-colonial structures work in Cartagena is especially visible through the Independence Day celebrations and the two beauty pageants that illustrate well how neo-colonial ordering structures are reinforced in the city, something that is the reality of the young people in their everyday lives. Therefore, in contrast to arguments that young people lack aspirations, and that their social immobility is a consequence of this lack, this chapter argued that the achievement of their aspirations is restricted because of the inequalities and discrimination on the bases of the intersection of race, class, gender and place. These forms of discrimination and exclusion are important limiting factors for young people trying to pursue their aspirations when they belong to lower social classes with distinct historical roots, excluding them from taking advantage of what the city has to offer. In Cartagena, belonging to a certain group of people and neighbourhood influences how young people can negotiate their future trajectories. While it is necessary to have aspirations and to put effort into achieving them, this alone is not enough in Cartagena. Social mobility depends on life chances that are linked to intersections between race, class, gender and place and are embedded in neo-colonial structures of exclusion. In Cartagena, often only the elite actually have access to resources that allow them to achieve social mobility and overcome these restrictions while the lower social classes face neo-colonial ordering dynamics which, every November, openly repeat Cartagena's colonial history and in everyday life implicitly. Maybe Cartagena just switched from one crown to another and thus history actually never really changed.

Notes

1. The area called La Popa is an invented name for this *barrio popular* by the author as it actually consists of a variety of small *barrios populares* close to the hill La Popa in Cartagena. Instead of listing the names of all *barrios* included here, I invented the name La Popa for reasons of simplification.
2. Cartagena's anthem was composed by Rafael Nunez in 1887.
3. If the 11th falls on a Sunday or Monday Independence Day Celebrations are usually in the preceding week.
4. A short documentary by the New York Times presents the conflict of both beauty pageants here: http://www.nytimes.com/video/world/1248069392058/rival-pageants-divide-colombia.html
5. A Gini coefficient of zero states complete equality, while a coefficient of 1 expresses the opposite. The highest Gini according to the CIA World Factbook was 0.63, while the lowest was 0.24.

References

Appadurai, A. (2004) 'The capacity to aspire: Culture and the term of recognition', in: V. Rao and M. Walton (eds) *Culture and public action*, Washington, DC: World Bank, pp.59–84.

Azevedo, V. and Bouillon, C. (2010) 'Intergenerational social mobility in Latin America: A review of existing evidence', *Revista de Análisis Económico*, 25(2): 7–42.

Bastia, T. (2014) 'Intersectionality, migration and development', *Progress in Development Studies*, 14(3): 237–248.

Brown, G. (2011) 'Emotional geographies of young people's aspirations for adult life', *Children's Geographies*, 9(1): 7–22.

Brown, G. (2013) 'The revolt of aspirations: Contesting neoliberal social hope', *ACME*, 12(3): 419–430.

Cahill, C. (2007) 'Doing research with young people: Participatory research and the rituals of collective work', *Children's Geographies*, 5(3): 297–312.

Crenshaw, K. (1991) 'Mapping the margins: Intersectionality, identity politics, and violence against women of color', *Stanford Law Review*, 43(6): 1241–1299.

Cunin, E. (2003) *Identidades a flor de piel. Lo 'negro' entre apariencias y pertenencias: Mestizaje y categorìas raciale en Cartagena (Colombia)*, Bogotá: Instituto Colombiano de Antropologìa e Historia.

Cunin, E. (2006) 'El Caribe visto desde el interior del país: estereotipos raciales y sexuales', *Revista de estudios Colombianos*, 30: 6–14.

DANE (2010) *Boletín: Censo General 2005*, Bogotá: DANE.

DANE (2015) *Bolívar: Pobreza Monetaria 2014. Boletín Técnico*, Bogotá: DANE.

DANE (2019) *Mercado Laboral: Principales Resultados Marzo 2019*, Bogotá: DANE.

de la Hoz, F. J., Quejada, R. and Yánez, M. (2013) 'Desempleo juvenil en Cartagena de Indias: un análisis transversal de sus causas y consecuencias', *Papeles de Población*, 19: 1–27.

Gillborn, D. (2015) 'Intersectionality, critical race theory, and the primacy of racism: Race, class, gender, and disability in education', *Qualitative Inquiry*, 21(3): 277–287.

Gough, K. V. (2008) ' "Moving around": The social and spatial mobility of youth in Lusaka', *Geografiska Annaler: Series B, Human Geography*, 90(3): 243–255.

Goyenche González, F., Pardo Gómez, J. and Suarez B. E. (eds) (2018) *Diagnostico general de la violencia y la criminalidad en Cartagena de Indias, 2008–2017*, Cartagena: Alcadia Mayor de Cartagena de Indias.

Hart, C. S. (2016) 'How do aspirations matter?', *Journal of Human Development and Capabilities*, 17(3): 324–341.

Holloway, S. and Pimlott-Wilson, H. (2011) 'The politics of aspiration: Neo-liberal education policy, "low" parental aspirations, and primary school Extended Services in disadvantaged communities', *Children's Geographies*, 9(1): 79–94.

Ibrahim, S. (2011) *Poverty, aspirations and wellbeing: Afraid to aspire and unable to reach a better life – Voices from Egypt*, Manchester: Brooks World Poverty Institute.

Jiménez, D. (2011) '¿Cómo se busca y cómo se encuentra empleo en las principales áreas metropolitanas de Colombia? Un recuento para los segundos trimestres de 2009 y 2010', *Perfil de Coyuntura Económica*, 18, 127–143.

Kintrea, K., St Clair, R. and Houston, M. (2015) 'Shaped by place? Young people's aspirations in disadvantaged neighbourhoods', *Journal of Youth Studies*, 18(5): 666–684.

Marzi, S. (2015) 'Aspirations and social mobility: The role of social and spatial (im)mobilities in the development and achievement of young people's aspirations', in: C. ni Laoire, A. White and T. Skelton (eds) *Movement, mobilities and journeys*, Singapore: Springer, pp.1–20.

Marzi, S. (2016) *Social mobility and aspirations: Young Colombians in Cartagena navigating opportunities, spaces and futures*, Unpublished PhD Thesis, Norwich: University of East Anglia.

Marzi, S. (2018) ' "We are labeled as gang members, even though we are not": Belonging, aspirations and social mobility in Cartagena', *Development Studies Research*, 5(1): 15–25.

Moncrieffe, J. (2009) 'Introduction. Intergenerational transmissions: Cultivating children's agency?', *Institute of Development Studies Bulletin*, 40: 1–8.

Moreno, P. and González, E. (2011) *Juventud urbana en Cartagena: De los riesgos a las oportunidades*, Cartagena de Indias: Corporación Manos Visibles.

Mosquera Rosero-Labbé, C. (2010) *Introducción. La persistencia de los efectos de la 'raza' de los racismos y de la discriminación racial: obstácolus para la ciudadanía de personas y pueblos negros*, Bogotá: Universidad del Valle, Universidad Nacional.

Nash, J. C. (2008) 'Re-thinking intersectionality', *Feminist Review*, 89(1): 1–15.

Ng'weno, B. (2007) 'Can ethnicity replace race? Afro-Colombians, indigeneity and the Colombian multicultural state', *The Journal of Latin American and Caribbean Anthropology*, 12(2): 414–440.

Peréz, V. G. J. and Salazar Mejíra, I. (2007) *La pobreza en Cartagena: Un análisis por barrios*. Cartagena de Indias: Centro de Estudios Económicos Regionales [CEER].

Pimlott-Wilson, H. (2017) 'Individualising the future: The emotional geographies of neoliberal governance in young people's aspirations', *Area*, 49(3): 288–295.

Prince, D. (2014) 'What about place? Considering the role of physical environment on youth imagining of future possible selves', *Journal of Youth Studies*, 17(6): 697–716.

Quevedo-Gómez, M. C., Krumeich, A., Abadía-Barrero, C. E., Pastrana-Salcedo, E. and van den Borne, H. (2011) 'Machismo, public health and sexuality-related stigma in Cartagena', *Culture, Health and Sexuality*, 14(2): 223–235.

Rasch, E. (2020) 'Becoming a Maya woman: Beauty pageants at the intersection of indigeneity, gender and class in Quetzaltenango, Guatemala', *Journal of Latin American Studies*, 52(1): 133–156.

REFWORLD (2019) *Colombia: Situation of Afro-Colombians, particularly in Medellín; municipal efforts to address crime and poverty in Medellín*, https://www.refworld.org/docid/4f9e66382.html

Restrepo, E. (2007) 'Imágenes del "negro" y nociones de raza en Colombia en el siglo XX', *Revista de Estudios Sociales*, 27: 46–61.

Rodríguez Garavito, C. and Mosquera, J. P. (2010) *Las cifras de la discriminación racial y la situación de la población afrocolombiana*, Bogotá: Universidad del Valle, Universidad Nacional.

Rutter-Jensen, C., Bolivar, I., Cunin, E., Rosenberg, B., Morgan, N., Lobo, G. J., Khittel, S. and Guardiola-Rivera, O. (eds) (2005) *Pasarela paralela: escenarios de la estética y el poder en los reinados de belleza*, Bogotá: Pontificia Universidad Javeriana.

Spohrer, K. (2011) 'Deconstructing "aspiration": UK policy debates and European policy trends', *European Educational Research Journal*, 10(1): 53–63.

Streicker, J. (1995) 'Policing boundaries: Race, class, and gender in Cartagena, Colombia', *American Ethnologist*, 22(1): 54–74.

Viafara, C. and Uribe, J. (2009) 'Duración del desempleo y canales de busqueda de empleo en Colombia', *Revista de Economía Institucional*, 11(21): 139–160.

Wade, P. (1993) *Blackness and race mixture: The dynamics of racial identity in colombia*, Baltimore, MD: Johns Hopkins University Press.

Wade, P. (2010) *Race and ethnicity in Latin America*, London: Pluto Press.

Walker, M. (2018) 'Aspirations and equality in higher education: Gender in a South African university', *Cambridge Journal of Education*, 48(1): 123–139.

Winton, A. (2007) 'Using "participatory" methods with young people in contexts of violence: Reflections from Guatemala', *Bulletin of Latin American Research*, 26(4): 497–515.

Winton, A. (2016) 'Using photography as a creative, collaborative research tool', *The Qualitative Report*, 21(2): 428–449.

14

'My aim is to take over Zane Lowe': young people's imagined futures at a community radio station

Catherine Wilkinson

Introduction

Youth service provision, which is the responsibility of the local state, has seen significant reduction in available central funding since the UK financial crisis of 2007. Cuts to government spending in the UK have significantly affected young people. Figures released by the House of Commons show that 493,000 young people aged 16–24 were unemployed in March to May 2019 (Francis-Devine, 2019). This unemployment rate sits alongside cuts to state support for young people. For instance, under the 2010 to 2015 coalition government, Education Maintenance Allowance for 16–18-year-old pupils in education or training was cut. Correspondingly, there has been a significant increase in university fees in the UK. This combination has resulted in heightened uncertainty for young people who may feel both unsupported and 'priced out' of certain aspirations for their future.

Through the case study of a community youth-led radio station, KCC Live, this chapter explores the role of voluntary organisations in the aspirations of young people and the impact of budget cuts for the transitions of volunteers. KCC Live is a youth-led community radio station in Knowsley, neighbouring Liverpool, UK, to explore the imagined futures of young people not in education, employment or training (NEET) who volunteer at the station. This chapter proceeds as follows. First, I present a brief overview of literature on youth transitions and introduce the concept of young people's 'possible selves'. I then outline the methods used in this study, also introducing KCC Live and the Metropolitan Borough of Knowsley (referred to as Knowsley hereafter) where the radio station is based. Then I present the findings of this research around three themes: making it big; less defined possible selves; and the strength of weak ties. This chapter contributes to existing literature by providing an evidence-based consideration of contemporary ideas of youth as concerned about their futures, while critiquing existing understandings of young people and 'celebrity goals' (see Allen and Mendick, 2013 for further discussion of young people's uses of celebrity). The central argument of this chapter is that the achievement of possible selves often relies on social bonds rather than solely the actions/desires of the individual, and thus social capital matters. As such, this chapter critiques the emphasis on individualisation within neoliberalism (see also Pimlott-Wilson, 2017), and the stripping back of community support mechanisms.

Youth transitions

Being NEET is often positioned as an outcome of the 'fast-track' transition to adulthood (Macdonald, 2011: 430). The key markers of this transition have been considered to involve: completion of full-time education; entry into the labour market; leaving the parental home; establishing an independent household; entry into marriage or cohabitation, and parenthood (Evans and Furlong, 1997). This positions youth as a phase through which we pass in order to become adult, and adulthood is positioned as 'the age and stage of arrival, accomplishment and achievement' (Skelton, 2002: 107). Yet, for NEET young people who have not secured entry to the labour market, this model would imply that their transition to adulthood is incomplete. This idea of failed transitions is problematic as it reinforces negative representations of young people (Skelton, 2002).

Jeffrey (2010) identifies three problems with a transitions approach. First, a transitions approach implies that young people will achieve adulthood; in some parts of the world the scale of social crisis means that 'youth' is a permanent condition. Second, it is not clear how far transitions literatures have moved beyond some of the normative teleological assumptions of life stage models. Third, the concept of transitions is underpinned by the assumption that people move from dependence to autonomous selfhood. However, in many parts of the world, adulthood is imagined in terms of interdependence rather than autonomy (Punch, 2002), and people may become less, rather than more, independent as they mature. If the concept of transition is to have any real explanatory power, it must be broadened to include young people who do not fit with the conventional understandings of transition.

Other work critiquing the idea of a linear transition has advanced the theory of individualisation (for example, Beck, 1992; Beck and Beck-Gernsheim, 2002; Bryant and Ellard, 2015). Individualisation theories postulate that life is no longer clearly shaped by class divisions or traditions, and mapped out with defined stages, and that individuals now have greater agentic potential to choose between different lifestyles, subcultures and identities (Beck, 1992). While individualisation may be useful for explaining the complexity of young people's lived transitions, in arguing that each individual is free to choose their own life path it denies many structural factors which impede the opportunities of many young people (Tolonen, 2008). For instance, the social variables of class, gender and race have been positioned by other authors (for example, Morrow and Richards, 1996) as affecting transitions and the possible outcomes of different adulthoods. Skelton (2002: 103) critiques an individualised approach for not replacing, but 'tweaking', the idea of a normal transition, and thus placing the failure of transitions on the individual young person, as opposed to social and economic relations and structures.

Towards young people's possible selves

Markus and Nurius (1986) developed the term 'possible selves' to explore the link between imagined, possible outcomes and motivation in the present. Possible selves encompass 'visions of desired and undesired end states' (Markus and Nurius, 1986: 159). Possible selves are important because they function as incentives for future behaviour and provide an interpretive context to view the current self. Exploring narrative accounts of young men's transitions into the workforce in Luton and Swindon, UK, Hardgrove et al (2015) asked young men about their present circumstances, opportunities and future directions. They found that possible selves which possess a motivational capacity are usually accompanied by institutional and/or relational support, and by known routes to the young person's desired ends. This allows young people to direct their actions to achieve these goals. Some young men had 'viable pathways to imagined futures', others had 'vague or vacant possible selves' (Hardgrove et al 2015: 167, 168) and did not articulate specific fields in which they could see themselves working. Hardgrove et al (2015: 164) argue that, when young people are asked about aspirations, it is difficult to determine whether their responses are based on expectations, or 'hopes and dreams' that may or may not encourage them to pursue trajectories towards future possibilities. I join Hardgrove et al (2015) in promoting the usefulness of the concept of possible selves for a theorisation of the link between imagined possibilities in the future, the importance of institutional and social support, and the motivation to act in the present.

Methods

This chapter emerges from a larger research project which employed a range of methods, including 18 months of observant participation at KCC Live (see Wilkinson, 2017 for further discussion of this method), more than 95 semi-structured in-depth interviews with volunteers and staff, two focus groups; a listener survey which generated 460 responses; listener diaries with five listeners; and follow-up listener diary interviews. These methods enabled engagement with the different communities (listeners, staff and volunteers) involved in KCC Live. Herein, I focus on data arising from the interviews with volunteers and staff. In the presentation of findings that follows, the young people feature by their self-selected pseudonyms. Many of the young people chose pseudonyms after pop stars, DJs and presenters.

Tuning in to *KCC Live*

Founded in 2003, KCC Live was originally set up as a college-based enrichment and work experience radio station, based at Knowsley Community College. KCC Live acts as part of the college's retention strategy and intends to function as a bridge for NEET young people to re-enter education and training. When first set up, KCC Live had three full-time staff positions (Programme Controller, Station Coordinator and Community Liaison Coordinator). However, due to staffing cuts to reduce costs in the college, this dipped to one during the course of this research project. KCC Live positions itself as a youth-led radio station, with volunteers from the college and the wider community assuming the role of presenters, producers, newsreaders, segue-technicians, music programmers and web-editors. KCC Live hosts around 50–200 volunteers at any one time. The station typically has a 14–25-year-old volunteer base (KCC Live, 2007), although at the time of conducting this research all volunteers were aged over 16, and a number of volunteers were aged over 25.

KCC Live prides itself on a volunteer body that is representative of a variety of subgroups and cultures, in terms of hobbies, musical tastes and sexuality. Music aired on KCC Live predominantly falls into the following genres: Dance; Trance; Scouse House; Urban; Hip Hop; RnB; Chart; Classic Rock; Alternative; and Acoustic. The station also airs music by local unsigned artists. The station's target audience is 10–24-year-olds in the centre of Knowsley. KCC Live positions itself as an 'exciting, non-elitist, highly-varied radio' (KCC Live, 2007: 4), which values and explores young people's musical tastes, opinions and daily lives, in ways that are relevant to them. The station's ethos is to provide 'Community Radio with Attitude' and it aims to sound like a 'youth club in your bedroom' (KCC Live, 2007: 23, 56). This itself is interesting in the context of austerity; the closure of youth clubs have made young people retreat into private spaces, and thus are potentially more isolated.

KCC Live is based in Roby, a town within Knowsley, Merseyside, and forms part of the wider Liverpool City Region, in North West England. Knowsley is among the most deprived Boroughs in the country: 29.8% of children (under 16) in Knowsley live in relative poverty (Knowsley Council, 2015). Significantly, according to data published in the Knowsley Children and Young People's Plan 2017–2020, 7% of 16–18 year olds in Knowsley are NEET, compared to 4.2% nationally (The Knowsley Partnership, 2016). Though Knowsley has made progress in raising educational attainment, its performance lags behind the national level. Of the children educated in Knowsley, 35.7% achieve five A*–C GCSEs including English and Maths; significantly lower than the national average of 52.8% (The Knowsley Partnership, 2016). At the time of undertaking this research there was no A Level provision within schools and colleges in the borough.

Young people's imagined futures

Within the transitions literature, young people are characterised as thinking ahead and concerned with their futures (Hardgrove et al, 2015). This is important when considering that young people, particularly those from deprived areas such as Knowsley, can become 'locked in a revolving door of unemployment and low-paid insecure jobs' (Miller et al, 2015: 469). As Hywel, consultant to KCC Live, makes clear, for some young people, KCC Live is an important site for realising potential and possibility:

'Some young people have a lot of energy, and in a place like Knowsley that energy goes to destruction and they'll smash bus stops up. If you can give them something which they don't have much of in Knowsley ... if you can capture them, and if you give them a chance to do something, in my experience it really develops them … There was one kid who came in and he couldn't read very well at all, very very dyslexic, but also wasn't engaged with reading at all. He said 'I want to be a news reader', and we sort of went 'right?', and he taught himself to read. He started reading books constantly because he wanted so much to be on the radio as a news reader.' (Hywel, 34, consultant to KCC Live)

Hywel positions KCC Live as providing opportunities for young people to convert their energy into a positive resource. This can be understood through a resilience lens, whereby spare time activities can have resilience-enhancing potential (Gilligan, 2000). That is, for those young people who are experiencing adversity, it is important for them to have 'havens of respite or asylum in other spheres of their lives' (Gilligan, 2000: 38). Adding weight to this, KCC Live volunteers, Andy and Hendrix, speak of the transformative potential of KCC Live:

'I want a career in radio and this place has helped. It can open a lot of doors, it's just knowing how to take the opportunities kinda thing, so it's kinda just making contacts and biding your time, learning the trade.' (Andy, 24)

'I've never really known throughout the entirety of school, college, university, what I've wanted to do as a career … I think working in radio has helped me realise that I might want a career in radio yeah, but the creative media in general sort of, whether it be marketing, something along those lines. It's certainly helped me, err, look at different industries and decide what I want to do from there.' (Hendrix, 23)

Andy and Hendrix can be seen to be crafting 'agentive selves' (Hull and Katz, 2006). Andy acknowledges that KCC Live 'can open a lot of doors' for a broadcast career, while Hendrix has a more general aim of a career in the creative media. Such narratives are significant because, as Hull and Katz (2006) argue, for young people from marginalised or disadvantaged communities, it is especially important that they have confidence in their competences and imagined futures, as well as work experience and the ability to build bonds, capital and networks.

Making it big

For some young people, their imagined futures contain a vision of 'making it big' (Lange and Ito, 2010: 289), or as one participant described it, 'tunnel vision' for prominent commercial radio jobs:

> 'I'd love to do presenting for like a national radio. I have a bit of a tunnel vision for 1Xtra. Erm, so hopefully with all the experience and just, you know, the development of meself, it will hopefully lead to that goal … I'm just gunna keep on producing demos and building a KCC Live portfolio, which I can take with me and be like "well here's all, everything I've done so far." (Nikki, 22)

> 'My course [at university] is Television and Radio, but it's radio I wanna do and to graduate in that … I just wanna, my aim is to take over Zane Lowe[1] … I speak to Zane Lowe, he's a lovely man, and I'd just like, I'd feel horrible taking his show because it's his job, but I wanna be on Radio 1 … I just wanna get paid to present radio … preferably on the BBC, if not Capital or something like that.' (Calvin, 20)

The preceding quotation from Nikki is illustrative of how a young person's imagined future can affect their present (see Worth, 2009). Nikki is producing demos and building up a portfolio to assist her into her desired career. This relates to Hardgrove et al's (2015) point that possible selves are rooted in daily life and in personal experiences that help an individual to picture what his/her life could become. Nikki's 'possible self' took shape through her commitment to KCC Live. She believes the experience she has gained through KCC Live, including her placement at BBC Radio 1Xtra, puts her in good stead to secure her desired career. Calvin's more specific aspiration to 'take over Zane Lowe' stands apart from the socio-economic landscape within which his life is entrenched. As McInerney (2009: 28) says, 'young people who are subjugated by oppressive social, economic and cultural forces are denied any real sense of agency and lack a capacity to act on and change their world'. It is necessary to draw on the notion of habitus here, which Bourdieu (1984: 473) argues inculcates 'a sense of one's place', resulting in an individual's disinclination to seek employment and experiences outside of what is normalised for his/her particular habitus. Unlike in Bourdieu's (1984) thesis, Calvin has not become content with what he has, rather he is seeking opportunities to fulfil this goal, including forming a social tie with Zane Lowe himself.

Although other research (for example, King et al, 2008) finds that celebrity goals stated by participants masked a troubling reality of no career planning in their lives, Calvin's imagining of a high-profile career is supported by his active involvement in activities which help shape his biography, most principally his university course in Television and Radio. Calvin told me in a later interview: 'I'll be like that annoying kid who always walks in with stuff, constantly giving them CDs and demos.' As such, Calvin's narrative also opposes Prince's (2014) finding that young people's imaginings of their possible selves are interrelated to the physical and affective qualities of their localities. While Reay (2004) argues that social circumstances can impact dispositions towards possible futures, that is, habitus can be transformed through process to raise individual's aspirations, I attribute this potential to KCC Live.

Less defined possible selves

Although most young people at KCC Live are full of hope and optimism for the future, those with complicated biographical circumstances had 'far less defined possible selves' (Hardgrove et al, 2015: 168). Take the following illustrative quotations:

> 'I'm someone who's struggled to find a career or a job that kind of fits me. So erm, I think I've struggled a lot more over the last year or two, because I am reaching 30 and I think that I should have some sort of career. And I like radio and I like doing it, but at the same time it's difficult to get a career in radio, and I'm not the most motivated person when it comes to sending demos or networking ... I'm now looking for employment within the world of radio but I don't know quite what it is that I'm after, because there's so many jobs in the world of radio.' (Modest Mouse, 28)

> 'Me aims for the future is to get even more experience in radio and to pass me qualification, maybe even study Level 2 [BTEC award, certificate and diploma] next year. I also started thinking about uni lately, maybe that's a possibility, I'm not too sure yet, but I'm just taking each step at a time really.' (Chris, 17)

Modest Mouse and Chris struggle to imagine a concrete future beyond their current circumstances. Modest Mouse reveals that his future is characterised by uncertainty, owing to the difficulty in securing a job in radio, and that he lacks motivation in seeking out opportunities. Chris' career trajectory is less certain still. This resonates with Woodman's (2011: 113) finding that some young people are 'present-centred', owing to the overwhelming insecurity and scepticism they possess about their futures.

One volunteer, Fearne, discussed her fluid and varied senses of self. She is divided between her desire to be a solicitor and a DJ, although noting: 'at the minute I'm set on becoming a solicitor':

> 'I haven't really planned my future out, because like the way things are going now, it's changed a lot since I like started on KCC Live ... I do still wanna become a solicitor, but I think, like only if I was to get some sort of good way in the DJing and stuff, like have a proper job, like working in the night clubs and things, and you know residencies and stuff because you'd be getting paid good money for that ... Like, for example, Fearne Cotton,[2] she's doing well and stuff and obviously she's on Radio 1 and I wouldn't mind being her. But like at the minute I'm set on becoming a solicitor, that's why I'm at university doing Law and Criminal Justice, I've kept me options open because that was the safest thing to do.' (Fearne, 21)

A few weeks later, in a follow-up interview, Fearne told me that she now wishes to become a DJ:

> 'Since I last spoke to you, I won a competition for me DJing. And I get to warm up for a DJ ... if you're into the DJ scene and clubbing then you'll know who he is, and he's really big. So I'm getting to warm up for him, that was the prize you win in the competition. But erm, there was eight of us in the competition and I was the only girl, so it sounds boss, it sounds well good. It felt great like, my head just blew up from that. I definitely want to be a DJ now, I'm set on that.' (Fearne, 21)

Fearne's conflicting narratives illustrate how young people's 'storied selves' (Hull and Katz, 2006: 45) are numerous and shifting within the context of everyday actions and relations. Fearne, alongside Modest

Mouse and Chris, is experiencing confusion over 'who and what' (Halpernet al, 2000: 470) she may become. I thus argue that KCC Live's practice of training young people yet not providing them with direction for 'next steps' is reminiscent of 'sending youth on a journey without a map' (Brendtro et al, 2002: 107).

The strength of weak ties

Many young people used KCC Live as a platform to progress onto a career in the media or further education. To provide two examples during my fieldwork, one volunteer secured a place at Oxford University and another gained full-time paid employment at the Liverpool commercial station, Radio City. Many young people maintain/intend to maintain ties with KCC Live when they move on from the station. Take the following quotation:

> 'I'd always like to have some involvement at KCC Live, 'cos I'd like to think this is where it started. So, you know, whether it be in ten years or twenty years, when hopefully I'm getting a paid presenting job, you know, I'd come back here and teach the next generation ... and radio as well, it's such a hard area ... if you have a job and then all of a sudden you get dropped and one day you could have a job, one day you couldn't.' (Andy, 24)

Andy's discussion of KCC Live as 'this is where it started' evokes a sense of KCC Live as 'a simultaneity of stories-so-far' (Massey, 2005: 130), characterised by meaningful interactions attached to this place. Andy emphasises that he would 'always like to have some involvement at KCC Live' owing to the precarious nature of the radio industry. I therefore argue that some young people maintain/intend to maintain ties with KCC Live owing to the ambivalence in transitions to adulthood and the lengthening processes of these transitions (see also Jeffrey and McDowell, 2004).

A further explanation for maintaining ties with KCC Live can be attributed to the sense of home, family and belonging that young people feel in relation to the station:

Chrissie: The retention rate of KCC Live is really good, but it's not supposed to be. It's supposed to be a stepping stone into the world of radio, or employment or education or whatever it is, but it's not. We tend to retain people while

> they're on their journey of whatever it is they're going for. So whether it be going to uni, they'll still come back here, whether it will be going and getting a job, they'll still come back here.

CW: For what reason do you think you retain people?

Chrissie: I think the bonds that they have with people at the station, that sense of community and sense of family brings them back. So when you're in a world where life can become stressful ... I think we all need that escape from those norms of life, and I think the station has accidently found itself being that escape. (Chrissie, 30, station manager)

As Chrissie illustrates, KCC Live is intended as a 'stepping stone' (a step on a road towards future stability); in other words, young people should use the space to reengage with employability skills, but it should not be an 'end point' (Podkalicka and Staley, 2009: 5).

The young people Chrissie is speaking of have moved on from KCC Live (that is, secured employment or further education), but maintain ties. However, my research found that such ties and bonding social capital can be 'disabling and constraining' (White and Green, 2011: 51) in accessing additional training or work opportunities for some young people who remain at the station. Modest Mouse, who describes himself as a KCC Live 'veteran', explores this:

> 'With me being here for five years now, I do think it may be time for me to move on in the next year or so ... That's not a knock on KCC Live, that's more me feeling like I have to move on to progress ... I might get settled and get too comfortable in an environment and I almost get a little bit lazy and I sometimes feel like I need to push myself out of that and find a new challenge. Erm, and my ultimate goal is to get a job or career that pays and that's something that I haven't got at the moment, and that could very well mean moving away from KCC Live to achieve that.' (Modest Mouse, 28)

In an interview almost 18 months later, Modest Mouse subsequently told me:

> 'I feel like I've learnt everything that I possibly can ... The only way I'm going to learn to do new things is through

other places … obviously, I would prefer to not stay here for the next five years, because if that's the case I still won't have a proper full-time job, erm which isn't the be-all and end-all in life, but you know. Erm, so it does feel tough sometimes when it feels, it kind of feels to me like I'm treading water now. I've gained all the experience I need to gain.' (Modest Mouse, 29)

Modest Mouse is self-confessedly 'treading water'. He says that he remains at KCC Live despite having the experience that he needs to progress beyond the station. Within the first excerpt, Modest Mouse states that 'in the next year or so' he intends to move on from KCC Live yet 18 months later, Modest Mouse remains at the station. Unlike Modest Mouse, Bruce expresses no immediate desire to leave KCC Live:

'I need some more consistent work … I need to get out of that fucking house, argh, families! I've not got a job that is consistent enough to warrant paying for my own accommodation, electric, bills, water and so on. Personally, that's a massive goal for me because, well, independence. I think I'm reaching a period of stability, I am on the road to that period of stability. Right now I am just happy doing what I am doing for a bit. I don't have plans to leave any time soon. I'm happy as long as I have a little slot where I can do what I want. Obviously I'm quite, erm, spontaneous … I'm quite like "I'm done with that, what's the next thing?" But I'm unlikely to do that at KCC Live where people are relying on me.' (Bruce, 24)

For Bruce, 'independence' is seen as a key part of the transition, and to bring desire for stability. It is clear that Bruce has place attachment to KCC Live; despite his spontaneous character, he feels compelled to stay at the station because of the dependency people have on him; in other words, the strength of community ties. As Manzo and Perkins (2006: 347) explain, 'people are motivated to seek, stay in, protect, and improve places that are meaningful to them'. This is significant, as place attachment may limit social and geographical horizons (White and Green, 2011), and may impede social and spatial mobility and individual progress (Fried, 2000). As such, Bruce's emotional and affective bonds made at KCC Live, may limit his awareness of/ motivation for employment and training opportunities outside of the station. This links to broader debates concerning bonding capital helping people 'get by' in their communities, but not enabling people to move on (see Lowndes, 2004).

Thus, I argue that a regrettable consequence of KCC Live's homely environment, and the strong ties built, is that, for a small number of young people, the sense of belonging is so powerful that they do not wish to leave. The following quotations from MJ and Beard add credence to this point:

> 'I did five weeks [work experience] here and I fell in love with the studio and the people here and I decided to stay on for the summer, and that's why I'm still here.' (MJ, 22)

> 'It's a bit like the home is where the heart is, it's that saying where how you live your life is where you feel most comfortable. That's what I'm like at the station, that's why I've been here for donkey's [that is, many years].' (Beard, 28)

MJ says that, due to friendships she has made with volunteers at KCC Live, she has stayed at the radio station beyond the time allocated for her work experience. Further, Beard, who has volunteered at KCC Live for ten years, says that 'home is where the heart is', explaining that he has remained at the station as it is the place where he feels 'most comfortable'. This is perhaps an upshot of the fact that, through community radio, young people are producing new communities and founding new ways of belonging (Bloustien, 2007). Just as in White and Green's (2011: 51) study, 'the insular nature of strong ties' may result in 'bounded horizons' for some young people at KCC Live. Even if these young people are a minority, they indicate a need for support and encouragement to achieve imagined futures.

I presented the finding that some young people lack direction for moving on from KCC Live to station management. Hywel demonstrates acknowledgement of this trend:

> 'I hold my hands up, and this is all to do with staff reducing, and the amount of time that I would much rather be putting towards direction, rather than constantly trying to be the politician for the business ... I feel that we've sent them down a mineshaft with a pickaxe and a helmet and then we've not seen them again for six months and I totally totally agree. I'd certainly like to do that [supporting young people to move into paid work] more.' (Hywel, 34, consultant to KCC Live)

Hywel acknowledges KCC Live's role of training volunteers and equipping them with skills, yet not providing direction for life outside of the station, giving them tools yet few instructions to achieve their hopes. This implies that there must be a next step; the radio station cannot be an end in itself. Hywel attributes the limited support provided to volunteers to staffing cuts, yet affirms that he would like to devote more time towards working through future directions with volunteers. Thus, as Evans (2011) writes in relation to 'Big Society' in the UK, although volunteer time is unpaid, the training, coordination and support of volunteers' work requires accountable management, and requires clarity about the purpose to which their time and skills can contribute most meaningfully.

Conclusion

This chapter used the case study of youth-led community radio station KCC Live to explore the imagined futures of NEET young people. I have argued that the achievement of possible selves often relies on social bonds (and thus social capital matters), rather than solely the actions/desires of the individual. Some young people at KCC Live had 'celebrity aspirations' – to 'become the next Fearne Cotton' or 'take over Zane Lowe'. For those young people with complicated biographical circumstances, they had far less defined possible selves, characterised by an insecurity about their futures, and the competitiveness of the 'radio world'. For a small number of young people, the sense of belonging to KCC Live was so powerful that they did not wish to leave. Thus an unanticipated finding of this research was that bonding capital (communicated as the sense of 'home' and 'family') generated at community youth organisations can be disabling and constraining in accessing additional training or work opportunities. This chapter argues that even if these young people are a minority, they need support and encouragement to achieve imagined futures.

The key contribution to knowledge of this chapter is the critique it has offered for the emphasis on individualisation within neoliberalism, and the stripping back of community support mechanisms. Cuts under austerity have reduced the support available to young people to achieve the futures set out under neoliberal government agendas (that is, get a job and be less reliant on the state). These programmes offer valuable help, but with limited staff, moving on is difficult, and ignores ties young people have to community organisations such as KCC Live. While KCC Live provides an outlet and valuable work experience for its volunteers, cuts mean that staff cannot always support young people with the 'next step'. However, we must still celebrate the role of the radio station in providing a service to a broader community of young people who are spending more time in their bedrooms after cuts to youth clubs and other services.

Notes

[1] Zane Lowe is a UK radio DJ presenting on BBC Radio 1.
[2] An English television and radio presenter.

References

Allen, K. and Mendick, H. (2013) 'Young people's uses of celebrity: Class, gender and "improper" celebrity', *Discourse: Studies in the Cultural Politics of Education*, 34(1): 77–93.

Beck, U. (1992) *Risk society: Towards a new modernity*, London: Sage.

Beck, U. and Beck-Gernsheim, E. (2002) *Individualization: Institutionalised individualism and its social and political consequences*, London: Sage.

Bloustien, G. (2007) '"Wigging people out": Youth music practice and mediated communities', *Journal of Community & Applied Social Psychology*, 17(6): 446–462.

Bourdieu, P. (1984) *Distinction: A social critique of the judgment of taste*, Cambridge, MA: Harvard University Press.

Brendtro, L. K., Brokenleg, M. and Van Bockern, S. (2002) *Reclaiming youth and risk: Our hope for the future*, Bloomington, IN: Solution Tree Press.

Bryant, J. and Ellard, J. (2015) 'Hope as a form of agency in the future thinking of disenfranchised young people', *Journal of Youth Studies*, 18(4): 485–499.

Evans, K. (2011) '"Big Society" in the UK: A policy review', *Children & Society*, 25(2): 164–171.

Evans, K. and Furlong, A. (1997) 'Metaphors of youth transitions: Niches, pathways, trajectories or navigations, in: J. Bynner, L. Chisholm and A. Furlong (eds) *Youth, citizenship and social change in a European context*, Aldershot: Ashgate, pp.17–41.

Francis-Devine, B. (2019) *Youth unemployment statistics*, https://dera.ioe.ac.uk/34783/1/SN05871%20%284%29%20%28redacted%29.pdf

Fried, M. (2000) 'Continuities and discontinuities of place', *Journal of Environmental Psychology*, 20(3): 193–205.

Gilligan, R. (2000) 'Adversity, resilience and young people: The protective value of positive school and spare time experiences', *Children & Society*, 14(1): 37–47.

Halpern, R., Barker, G. and Mollard, W. (2000) 'Youth programs as alternative spaces to be: A study of neighborhood youth programs in Chicago's West Town', *Youth & Society*, 31(4): 469–506.

Hardgrove, A., Rootham, E. and McDowell, L. (2015) 'Possible selves in a precarious labour market: Youth, imagined futures, and transitions to work in the UK', *Geoforum*, 60: 163–171.

Hull, G. and Katz, L.M. (2006) 'Crafting an agentive self: Case studies of digital storytelling', *Research in the Teaching of English*, 41(1): 43–81.

Jeffrey, C. (2010) 'Geographies of children and youth 1: Eroding maps of life', *Progress in Human Geography*, 34(4): 496–505.

Jeffrey, C. and McDowell, L. (2004) 'Youth in a comparative perspective: Global change, local lives', *Youth and Society*, 36(2): 131–142.

KCC Live (2007) *Public sections of Hywel Evans' application to Ofcom for a Community Radio Licence on behalf of Mission Need Ltd and KCC Live*, Liverpool: KCC Live.

King, N., Madsen, E. R., Braverman, M., Paterson, C., and Yancey, A. K. (2008) 'Career decision-making: Perspectives of low-income urban youth', *Spaces for Difference: An Interdisciplinary Journal*, 1(1): 21–41.

Knowsley Council (2015) Child poverty and life chances strategy 2015–2018, https://www.knowsley.gov.uk/knowsleycouncil/media/Documents/liverpool-city-region-child-poverty-and-life-chances-strategy-refresh-2015–18.pdf

Lange, P. G. and Ito, M. (2010) 'Creative production', in: M. Ito, S. Baumer, M. Bittanti, R. Cody, B. Herr-Stephenson, H. Horst and L. Tripp (eds) *Hanging out, messing around, and geeking out*, Cambridge, MA: MIT Press, pp.243–293.

Lowndes, V. (2004) 'Getting on or getting by? Women, social capital and political participation', *The British Journal of Politics and International Relations*, 6(1): 45–64.

MacDonald, R. (2011) 'Youth transitions, unemployment and underemployment: Plus ça change, plus c'est la même chose?', *Journal of Sociology*, 47(4): 427–444.

Manzo, L. C., and Perkins, D. D. (2006) 'Finding common ground: The importance of place attachment to community participation and planning', *Journal of Planning Literature*, 20(4): 335–350.

Markus, H. and Nurius, P. (1986) 'Possible selves', *American Psychologist*, 41(9): 954–969.

Massey, D. (2005) *For space*, London: Sage.

McInerney, P. (2009) 'Toward a critical pedagogy of engagement for alienated youth: Insights from Freire and school-based research', *Critical Studies in Education*, 50(1): 23–35.

Miller, J., McAuliffe, L., Riaz, N., and Deuchar, R. (2015) 'Exploring youth's perceptions of the hidden practice of youth work in increasing social capital with young people considered NEET in Scotland', *Journal of Youth Studies*, 18(4): 468–484.

Morrow, V. and Richards, M. (1996) *Transitions to adulthood: A family matter?*, York: Joseph Rowntree Foundation and YPS.

Pimlott-Wilson, H. (2017) 'Individualising the future: The emotional geographies of neoliberal governance in young people's aspirations', *Area*, 49(3) 288–295.

Podkalicka, A. and Staley, J. (2009) 'YouthWorx Media: Creative media engagement for "at risk" young people', *Journal of Community, Citizen's and Third Sector Media and Communication*, 5: 2–8.

Prince, D. (2014) 'What about place? Considering the role of physical environment on youth imagining of future possible selves', *Journal of Youth Studies*, 17(6): 697–716.

Punch, S. (2002) 'Youth transitions and interdependent adult–child relations in rural Bolivia', *Journal of Rural Studies*, 18(2): 123–133.

Reay, D. (2004) ' "It's all becoming a habitus": Beyond the habitual use of habitus in educational research', *British Journal of Sociology of Education*, 25(4): 431–444.

Skelton, T. (2002) 'Research on youth transitions: Some critical interventions', in M. Cieslik and G. Pollock (eds) *Young people in risk society: The restructuring of youth identities and transitions in late modernity*, Aldershot: Ashgate, pp.100–116.

The Knowsley Partnership (2016) Knowsley children and young people's plan, https://www.knowsley.gov.uk/knowsleycouncil/media/Documents/Knowsley-Children-and-Young-Peoples-Plan-2017-20_1.pdf

Tolonen, T. (2008) 'Success, coping and social exclusion in transitions of young Finns', *Journal of Youth Studies*, 11(2): 233–249.

White, R. J. and Green, A. E. (2011) 'Opening up or closing down opportunities?: The role of social networks and attachment to place in informing young peoples' attitudes and access to training and employment', *Urban Studies*, 48(1): 41–60.

Wilkinson, C. (2017) 'Going "backstage": Observant participation in research with young people', *Children's Geographies*, 15(5): 614–620.

Woodman, D. (2011) 'Young people and the future multiple temporal orientations shaped in interaction with significant others', *Young*, 19(2): 111–128.

Worth, N. (2009) 'Understanding youth transition as "becoming": Identity, time and futurity', *Geoforum*, 40(6): 1050–1060.

15

Dependent subjects and financial inclusion: launching a credit union on a campus in Taiwan

Hao-Che Pei and Chiung-wen Chang

Introduction

In 2013, Jon Henley, correspondent for the *Guardian* newspaper, wrote about the unemployment crisis confronting young Europeans, and described 'a legion of young, often highly qualified people, entering a so-called job market that offers very few any hope of a job – let alone the kind they have been educated for' (Henley, 2019). This scene is not limited to Europe. According to Taiwan's Ministry of Education, 65.8% of people in their 20s and early 30s had degrees in 2014, but university graduates accounted for around one-third (34.1%) of all casual employment in the country – an increase of 41.7% over six years.[1] A series of financial reforms that favoured business conglomerates and the wealthy (Lin et al, 2011; Huang, 2014), together with the market-oriented expansion of higher-education institutions (Chan and Lin, 2015), have rendered a huge number of 'qualified youth' jobless over the last two decades. The growing concerns regarding the so-called 'crumbling generation' reflect the danger of Taiwan facing economic and demographic catastrophe[2] in the near future (Lin et al, 2011; Ku, 2017; Huang, 2014). Despite the dire warnings, those aged 18–22 who are currently studying at university and face a gloomy future have been largely overlooked so far.

This chapter focuses on Taiwan's college students who are vulnerable to diploma inflation and job uncertainty *before graduating*. A hike in tuition fees[3] is the basis of their financial predicament, since it often necessitates the taking on of student loans,[4] which in turn has a stifling effect on their future (Huang, 2010). But leaving student debt burdens aside, another reason for concern is the hardship that youngsters are facing during their student years, before they have even graduated. Living expenses, for example, are between 1.5 and 3 times the cost of annual tuition fees, depending on the university and location. Previously, around 60% of parents would cover their children's living expenses (Chou, 2007), but as the wealth gap in Taiwan grows ever wider, an increasing number of students are receiving less support from their families (Lin, 2012). Working as part-time assistants on university and college campuses used to be a useful way to supplement their income, but the availability of such work positions has fallen sharply over the last five years[5] (Pei, 2018). This has forced many students, especially the disadvantaged, to work in low-paid, part-time jobs.

Given this precarious nature of *studentship* and the various attempts at 'making a difference' (Fuller and Kitchin, 2004), we have been engaged in an action research project inspired by the multitude of collaborative endeavours undertaken to 'reinvigorate our economic imaginations and also to enact alternative economies' (Gibson-Graham, 2006a: ix; and see Gibson-Graham, 2006b; Roelvink et al, 2015). If an entire young generation in Taiwan is suffering from precarity and uncertainty, then we (both teachers and students) are under the obligation to deliberate on what kind of grassroots action we ought to take within campuses, instead of just waiting for so-called 'effective' governance.

With a special concern for the dilemma of financial exclusion faced by college students, we have been involved in an experimental project at the National Dong Hwa University (NDHU) in Taiwan. The project is linked to a cooperative discourse on mutual self-help through the launch of a campus-based credit union. Our initial motivation was to provide students with attainable access to revolving funds, so that they could avoid financial strain in a dignified way. However, we soon realised that student precarity is not simply due to financial constraints, even though it may seem so at first. There are also broader inequalities and barriers confronting them, fortified by a set of contradictory beliefs. One such inequality emanates from the global trend of neoliberal rhetoric that prioritises 'individualised responsibility for their future attainment', as Pimlott-Wilson (2017: 290) critically points out; another is related to the *belittling* attitudes towards 'the status of being a student' that are rooted in socio-cultural narratives specific to Taiwan. By drawing upon post-structuralist insights into politics (Gibson-Graham, 2008; Gibson-Graham, 2006b), the project entails a *deep* involvement in encouraging a 'new practice of the self' (Gibson-Graham, 2006a: xvi; Chatterton et al, 2007), rather than simply initiating an action to establish a cooperative-based association that supports students financially.

This chapter reports on our attempts to develop on-campus financial inclusion in Taiwan. We first take a critical look at the social embedding of students' economic experiences in order to identify how the student-subjects are culturally produced. Following this, we describe the experience of being involved in this project, and discuss the strategic value of campuses in promoting change. The chapter concludes by arguing that a critical process of resubjectivation is required for the young generation in Taiwan to reject the pre-determined position of dependent subject.

College students: an impotent subject of dependency?

In Taiwan, there is a tendency to equate college students, even though they are adults, with delicate and naive children who require pampering and instruction by their parents. This pre-set attitude, which is associated with paternalistic notions, is deeply rooted in Chinese patriarchal traditions. Such traditions are legitimised by the doctrine of Confucianism, which accentuates the supremacy of seniority and 'places the stress on the subordinate's duty to obey' (Hamilton, 1990: 93). Power and obedience are positional, rather than personal in nature (Chu, 1961), which renders a child's independent personality irrelevant (Lin and Wang, 1995). The legacy of patriarchy also underlines that 'individual behaviour is prescribed by the obligations of interlocking roles' (Heaney and Flam, 2015: 55), according to which parents should be kind, while children must display filial obedience. Therefore, although Chinese parents make the most of the financial decisions within the context of a family economy (Chu, 1961), they tend to take a benevolent attitude towards their children, no matter how old they are.

The seemingly benevolent narrative of 'it's for your own good' represents a form of parental domination over college students by incorporating their economic presence into a household economy both *emotionally* and *institutionally*. Benevolence represents parents' emotional enabling/limiting. It explains why a major part of student expenditure is paid off by parents, instead of by the students themselves. The paternalistic narrative is also reflected in institutional practices, in that eligibility criteria for all kinds of student allowances are based not on the applicants themselves but on their overall household income levels. As Sayer argues, 'most forms of symbolic domination or cultural misrecognition are accompanied by economic discrimination' (Sayer, 2001: 693). The paternalistic discourse propagates the subjectivity of college students – an impotent subject of dependency, and such hegemonic approaches then pre-determine their experience of subjection.

The claim that 'students don't need money' reflects a general discrimination against college students. The reality that college students have numerous financial needs: for example, to buy a new laptop for their research (a material need), or to take part in a graduation trip with their classmates (an emotional satisfaction) is categorically rejected. If necessary, they can 'go back home and ask for help'. Once no financial aid is available, they are given the advice to 'stop spending money if you don't have it'. This customary expression is not necessarily intended to advocate the virtues of thrift. Rather, it brushes students' desires and emotions aside apathetically.[6] To an extent, college students are deemed to play a negligible role in the economy because they contribute little to economic output. Consequently, they are asked to live frugally, while their austere experience is neglected.

College students can of course earn money themselves if they are on a tight budget. However, the workplace is another arena where they face multifaceted discrimination. In 2016, a 'wage map'[7] disclosed the wage levels for off-campus part-time jobs around the NDHU: at this point in time, wages were remarkably low, around NT$80 to NT$95 (around £1.73–£2.06) per hour, lower than the hourly minimum wage of NT$120 (around £2.60). The report soon became a sensation, prompting other students around Taiwan to conduct similar surveys,[8] all of which came to the same conclusion, namely that most college students in part-time jobs were significantly underpaid. Despite these disclosures, however, the reality for students has changed little; to date the Taiwanese public remains oblivious to the discriminatory conditions faced by most college students. A common excuse used by employers is that 'since they are students, there is no need to give so much'.[9] It is perceived that students do not need to maintain a family and their earnings are simply a supplement to their individual incomes. Moreover, there is a misconception that gaining experience is more important than receiving adequate pay. The wages may get cut arbitrarily because students *are* learning in the workplace. College students are thus even more marginalised in the workplace compared to other part-time workers.

College students as impotent subjects of dependency are divested of a voice in the overall economy, and therefore certain ambitions, emotions and energies specific to college students are largely disregarded. In their action research projects, Gibson-Graham provide post-structuralist insights into the way subjection can be *destabilised* so that economic possibilities can be opened up (Gibson-Graham, 2006b). They refer to the ethics of self-transformation involving 'a process of producing something beyond discursively enabled shifts in identity'

(Gibson-Graham, 2006a: xvi). Erasure is central to the subjection that college students experience. College students, despite their diversity in terms of socio-economic status, have common needs and share similar experiences. However, the identity of their subject appears invisible and ignorable in that they are inextricably attached to their families through the everyday practices of a paternalistic society. The self-transformation that college students ought to be engaged in is not to draw themselves out from their household in terms of their economic existence. This is unrealistic and unfeasible considering the actual situation of being a student, but what *is* worth attempting and attainable is for them to group themselves as one community, rather than as separate individuals. This is fundamental to the politics of *becoming*, by which civic engagement in terms of solidarity can be learned and carried out in order to bring about real change. The following section illustrates how we took a credit union as an institutional instrument to leverage the micro-political action of self-transformation at the NDHU.

In the action scenes

Credit unions are a cooperative financial institute whose members can borrow from a pooled deposit at fair interest rates. It was introduced to Taiwan in 1964 by Cardinal Paul Yu Pin, who was dedicated to poverty alleviation by helping people to save and to borrow more affordably based on the principle of 'people helping people' (Perin, 2013). Credit unions have played a significant role in making up the deficiency in financial services in peripheral areas – principally rural areas and regions with indigenous communities – for more than half a century. Yet, paradoxically, credit unions had been widely misunderstood as financially fraudulent organisations until the Credit Union Law was formally enacted in 1997 (Wu, 2011). According to the Law, the central governing authority for credit unions – the Ministry of the Interior (MOI) – has passed on this authority to a non-governmental organisation – the Credit Union League of the Republic of China (CULROC) (Yu, 1998).

The first time we[10] learned about credit unions was when we attended a CEDAW workshop[11] in December 2014. Given that credit unions not only provide financial services but also act as a vehicle for advancing financial literacy, they can be considered as an institutional leverage to accumulate assets – both tangible and intangible (Chang, 2014). Specifically, this form of cooperative-based association emphasises mutual aid among its members and economic democracy, and can deliver profound value in terms of collective action and autonomy for young people against the backdrop of disintegrating structures crushed by neoliberalism (Chang, 2017). Our core team initially comprised three graduates, two undergraduates and two teachers, but gradually some other staff members and alumni joined as well. Following extensive research and intensive discussions, we decided to initiate a credit union to promote financial inclusion at the NDHU. Our formal application was made in December 2015. In all, we produced three video clips and two sets of leaflets, designed a website, attended lobbying meetings, and immersed ourselves in the onerous duties of administering a complex organisation.[12]

In Taiwan, registering a credit union entails three steps.[13] The first is to define a common bond; that is, the members must have something in common (residence, occupation or association). In our case, the NDHU was taken as the axis of our common bond embracing students, faculty and alumni. Second, a *to-be-founded* credit union has to recruit more than 100 members and raise an amount of NT$1 million (approximately £24,379) at least.[14] Finally, all the preparatory procedures, including reaching the minimum limits in terms of membership and funds, need to be completed within six months[15] of applying. The last two requirements stood in the way of our opening our union. Up until that point, very few people had heard of credit unions in Taiwan, let alone taken part in one. It was therefore not an easy task to convince people (especially students) to join something about which they had no idea. Collecting such a large amount of funds from college students within a short period of time was even more challenging, considering their limited financial sources. Despite all these difficulties, however, the Dong Hwa Campus Credit Union (DHCCU) was officially launched in November 2016.[16] The challenges we encountered are described in the following section. Given that the experience of our engagement with this initiative was complicated, attention has been focused on our interactions with the authorities and with students, with a special regard to *inter-subjectivity*.

'Why don't you rookies just follow the existing rules?'

We had felt puzzled as to why credit unions were so unknown to the general public in Taiwan. A discussion of the reasons behind their relatively low popularity[17] is beyond the scope of this chapter; we shall focus instead on what we, a student-oriented group, experienced from the start of this project. We had sought advice from several senior officials of the CULROC in 2015 before making our application and were surprised by the warm reception. However, they all suggested that we join existing credit unions,[18] but we were determined to set up a new organisation, because we wanted the young students of the NDHU to be the top priority rather than subordinate to the needs and requirements of older members. Our concerns regarding (and insistence on) *self-subjectivity* were proven right.

First of all, the regulatory context in Taiwan is unfriendly towards young people. Besides the tough registration requirements, the managers of credit unions have to be at least 23 years old.[19] Undergraduates constitute the majority of the membership of the DHCCU, and most of them are under the age of 22. This age limit therefore deprives most of the student members of the chance to participate in the governance of the union, which could have enriched its capabilities and possibly boosted its tangible as well as intangible assets. It was also foreseeable that such a limit would cause a serious shortage of operational manpower. Therefore, before the preparatory work began, we endeavoured to negotiate with the CULROC to waive this specific restriction in the case of student-oriented groups such as ours. An experimental programme that asked for halving the minimum number of members and amount of capital, and lowering the age limit for managers to 20 years old[20] was proposed during a coordination meeting held in August 2015. An appeal was also made to the MOI – the central government authority – at the same time, but the responses we received were both bureaucratic and paternalistic, for example: 'cooperative forms of organisation on campus … according to the Civil Law, should be stewarded by adult members in order to avoid difficulties and suspicions regarding implementation' (email reply from a MOI official, 4 August 2015).

Nothing in this regard has changed thus far, even though the CULROC has repeatedly asserted that new blood is crucial for the development of credit unions.[21] In addition to institutional discrimination against youth, such a *routinist* attitude is the second element of the official approach that debases individual subjectivity. A debate over video conferencing goes to prove how the autonomy of an individual institute can be suppressed arbitrarily by routinism. Both the board of directors and the supervisory committee of each credit union have to convene a meeting on a monthly basis, according to the regulations. But a campus-based credit union needs to act in concert with the university's calendar. Members, including the directors and supervisors, may be away from the campus during vacations, in which case statutory meetings would not be possible. Our proposed solution to this problem was to conduct virtual meetings if physical ones were not possible, but even though this proposal had been officially voted through during our general meeting of members in January 2018, it was flatly rejected by the CULROC, with no room for negotiations. The reason cited for this rejection was conservative but ridiculous – one-third of credit union members in Taiwan are elderly and are unfamiliar with technical/video conferencing devices.

'Is this a new scam?'

It was not surprising that a great majority of Taiwanese students and faculty had no idea about credit unions, considering their low visibility.[22] This fact made 'education, training and information', one of the seven cooperative principles, even more crucial. A concerted effort was therefore made to translate non-commercially oriented financial knowledge into easily communicable ideas. Illustrated meetings, speeches and workshops were undertaken to introduce the concept of credit unions during the preparatory period. The workshops were particularly effective in explaining to students how a financial cooperative works, since they encouraged intensive group discussions[23] between the participants. But organising such workshops took up a lot of time, which was an issue given that we were all full-time students or faculty members, and our tight budget also presented difficulties.[24] Moreover, the relatively small audiences compounded the issues.

Conducting presentations in the classroom offered another way to publicise the project. We gave a total of 14 briefings between April and November 2015, each taking around 20 minutes to introduce the project and leaving around ten minutes for discussion. These presentations were conducted in collaboration with some teachers, who showed keen enthusiasm for the idea of promoting financial inclusion on campus. However, very few students were openly excited about participating in the credit union.[25] Common remarks that were heard in Professor K's class might explain this reticence. The issue of maintaining financial viability seemed uppermost in the students' minds, while some wanted to know what rates of interest they would get for deposits. When we stressed the fact that a credit union is committed to principles and people, not just profit generation, our initiative was then misunderstood as a charity:

> 'After my briefing, student X raised his hand and asked: "If
> a credit union charges loan interest, then how is it different

from a bank? How on earth are you going to help students?"'
(Field notes, 5 November 2015)

Besides the confusion regarding how credit unions differ from banks, some students had strong reservations about the concept of autonomous governance:

> 'Professor K made some remarks about how member-owned organisations operate on the basis of "one member, one vote". But student Y retorted "Saying that members having a voice in the decision-making is tantamount to saying people are the boss of the country, isn't it? Politicians always claim that the people are the boss, but actually they are the real holders of power." I tried to illustrate how members run a credit union collectively, but he started to do his own thing with a deprecating look on his face.' (Field notes, 5 November 2015)

Bringing the campus into full play

The various institutional and perceptional challenges that we faced demonstrated that our campus campaign had been stumbling along a bumpy road. As regards the CULROC, this was the first time that they had had to deal with an initiative that was campus-based, and they were not fully prepared to coordinate their work with a student-oriented union. The out-of-date rules, compounded by a hierarchical command structure, repressed the subjectivity of the youth. Whenever we asked for a modification of the rules that were impeding our operations, the CULROC just could not figure out 'why don't you rookies just follow the existing rules'. The supremacy of seniority was clearly at work again: that is, the DHCCU – a campus institute – was *a subject of disobedience* for the supervising body. The tension was palpable because we had challenged the label of 'an impotent subject of dependency' tagged upon the youth.

As regards the students themselves, many of them misconstrued financial literacy as an ability to obtain something lucrative, owing to their poor knowledge of finance. Besides, the controversy over the value proposition of democratic member-based control indicated the possibility that some students would rather stay *in situ* than actively engage,[26] simply because they had doubts about 'fake democracy'. These students tended to be prejudiced against radical new initiatives, and represented a *subject of self-restraint* when first learning about an alternative economic arrangement. In short, tensions emerged as a result of distrust towards the possibilities of seeking common goals.

Of more significance, our reflections on inter-subjectivity also led us to review our *self-positing* from a post-structuralist perspective (Cameron and Gibson, 2005). It is rightly stated that 'presupposing the rigidity of social roles and categories blind us to the possibilities of common ground and the potential for transformative dialogue' (Chatterton et al, 2007: 219). Truly, our experience of interacting with the authorities was frustrating, but we still placed a high value on the mission of our credit union – promoting financial wellbeing among students – even though its institutional mechanism appeared sluggish. We reconsidered what kind of constructive role a campus-based organisation could play in underpinning the credit union mission on a broader level, rather than simply struggling against the existing regulations with an oppositionist attitude. What a campus-based body can achieve is knowledge stimulation, and this meant that more students of vigour and creativity had to join us.

As already mentioned, the impact of our previous interventions was fairly limited, since we had been mostly concerned with inculcating the idea of advancing financial inclusion in the students. We failed to focus on the fact that an on-campus campaign as an action research project should be a collaborative process in which academia-based team members, students and various other agents all work together. Our engagement with the students seemed not so different from the paternalistic discourses whose purported aim was to protect youngsters from something deemed detrimental. Therefore, we changed our approach and re-orientated ourselves to act more as a facilitator, enabling students to think independently and participate to make 'a set of future-oriented possibilities' (Vieta, 2010: 4) in a way that suited them best. We also adjusted our engagement style by conceiving it as 'a spatial practice' by underlining the special socio-spatial features of a campus. In the next section are two examples that illustrate our new approach.

In business

The union currently offers various loan projects for members to borrow from the pooled deposit at low rates[27]. Some NT$950,000 (about £23,160) in total has been borrowed by the members (mostly students) since the union was funded. It gives student members alternative access to finance without checking overall household income levels or asking for parental consents.

The way in which the DHCCU operates is quite different from the *modus operandi* of other credit unions. Its volume of business is relatively low because of the limited membership, so our office hours are set for two days a week at specific times. The management of the DHCCU decided to recruit students as part-time employees[28] so that they could help run the business. This was partly because the DHCCU could not afford to hire personnel (due to its limited capital) and partly because we wanted to provide internship opportunities to our student members. For instance, Student J, who was studying in the Department of Accounting, was one of the union's accountants. The reason why he applied for the position was to acquire practical experience, as well as earn some money:

> 'I had an interview with an accounting firm ... these accountants consider that we undergraduates have little practical experience ... Although I'm not sure what the interviewers thought about this, [but] in my opinion, if [they] find someone ... who has been taken on as an accountant in a credit union, then [the guy] will get priority admission. This is because you have [experience in] the relevant background.' (Interview report by Student J, 10 January 2018)

The DHCCU is *a co-working space* where students can help build this *self-owned organisation* and put what they have learned into practice. Student F is another case in point. His ambition was to become an illustrator, and he required some opportunities to showcase his creativity. Therefore, we invited him to design some illustrations for our marketing campaign (Figure 15.1).

The comic-style leaflets caught the attention of a wide body of students and faculty members, and was a good opportunity for Student F to show his talents. Together with the feeling of achievement is the sense of belonging. It was highly gratifying for us to see that some student members had begun to take personal finance more seriously:

> 'I think it (the DHCCU) is a prudent organisation ... [I] found out about this organisation from teachers and peers. I thought we might try to do something. When [I] joined it ... [I] found it means business ... I attended a training

Figure 15.1: The DHCCU leaflets

seminar [and found] that those people were really working [in the credit union] ... all the members go to save. A great amount of funds circulate ... That's an atmosphere that has led me to reconsider the concepts of saving and monetary matters ... When I started saving [in the DHCCU], I didn't take it lightly, since it concerns money. [I] thought about what it actually is and then decided to learn [something about credit unions]. After gaining an understanding, [I] found it (the DHCCU) is innocent so far, and so [I shall] keep on.' (Interview report by Student R, 26 July 2017)

On courses

A basic way to represent a campus as a learning space for intellectual pursuits is to provide courses. Meanwhile, our concern had shifted from what to teach to how to learn about financial literacy. The Education Commission[29] of the DHCCU made an effort to design learning programmes in close collaboration with the Social Participation Office of the NDHU. With administrative support from the General Education Centre of the NDHU, in the spring semester of 2019 we offered undergraduates three electives: (1) Our Piggy Bank on Campus, (2) Self-reviewing Personal Finance, and (3) Doing Alternative Finance.

The first two were micro-courses run in a workshop format. In addition to introducing the concept of a credit union as a financial

Figure 15.2: Discussion session during a micro-course on self-reviewing personal finance

option to the students, we aimed to encourage students to ponder on their daily finances by making use of the ORID technique (see Figure 15.2).

The dynamic discussions inspired the students to review their personal economic situation and to consider how to navigate the financial system in a more effective way:

'The wage levels mentioned in the first half of the course were surprising to me 'cos I seldom took interest in financial news. This is the first time I became aware of [the fact that I would be] influenced by students' loans [and] interpersonal networks of the studentship. I think there are very few undergraduates who don't expect to become economically independent [and] to become a complete adult. Thus, [since I have] realised [how] the DHCCU operates, [I] intend to join it and [I hope to] make use of it when I have a need for funds, such as for doing fieldwork, buying [research] equipment, text books, and so on.' (Course feedback from Student D, 22 March 2019)

The third course was designed as an issue-centred learning programme. We intended to bring reality into the classroom by taking students out of the campus. With a focus on the practices of cooperative movements,

Figure 15.3: Visit to the Seed Co-operative

a two-day fieldtrip was arranged so that we could visit two newly-opened labour cooperatives[30] and one senior credit union[31] in Taipei (see Figure 15.3).

The visits were combined with brainstorming sessions involving three themes – worker autonomy, civil participation and mutual finance. For the first time in their lives, the students had the chance to talk with experienced cooperative operators face-to-face, and found that people who get involved with solidarity movements are typically 'romantic but pragmatic' (to use a phrase coined by the students). And what did they think about our own campus-based movement? The students held various opinions, but overall it was pleasing to see how they had begun to associate themselves with the credit union on different levels:

> 'A credit union can be one option. But I personally have a conservative concept of loans. While the idea of a credit union introduced during this visit might make me more open to the concept of loans, I still think that I [would] save money at the usual time for emergencies. Except for a mortgage or emergencies, I would save enough [money] and then buy it ... that's my attitude towards money. But if it's really necessary, a credit union can be considered.' (Course feedback from Student Z, 8 April 2019)

At the outset I took this course in a muddle and then joined [the DHCCU although I was] out of loop. For me, this institute visit is actually a member education programme. The credit union too is a sort of civil participation; I'm the individual to get involved with the affairs of the DHCCU community.' (Course feedback from Student L, 8 April 2019)

By defining the campus as a learning space for intellectual pursuits, we avoided providing dogmatic guidance in the participatory intervention. This allowed us to create an informative, creative and extensive milieu where the students could feel free to learn through active engagement, and the result was a palpable increase in their financial awareness, which in turn encouraged them to make positive changes in their lives.

Conclusion

This chapter revolved around the central concern that the talents cultivated in the Taiwanese higher education system are headed straight for economic deprivation. The financial burden imposed upon college students is partly because students are culturally assumed to be dependent upon their parents and partly that their financial right is institutionally subordinated to a household unit. With economic deterioration, an increasing number of college students in Taiwan receive less support from their family and have limited access to grants. Such a hardship forces the students to be stuck in part-time jobs on low pay which engage much of the students' time to study. The chapter illustrated a participatory action research in the context of a campus-based campaign for a credit union at the NDHU. The first campus-based credit union, the DHCCU, in Taiwan was initiated with the aim of supporting individuals to relieve students' financial strain. Although the DHCCU's scale remains much smaller than that in other unions, the financial services provided by the union conforms to the core values of financial inclusion and helps give back the right of decision-making to students in terms of financing.

It is noted that economic inequality is place-specific, and campaigners who wish to alleviate it have to look into the socio-cultural narratives where inequality is deeply embedded – in addition to facing the overwhelming might of neoliberalist globalisation. College students in Taiwan are labelled as an impotent subject of dependency, and therefore their financial experiences, aspirations and energies are largely ignored. Our engagement with the 'future in present', to use Cleaver's term

(1993), also encountered profound challenges over the four-year period of the union's operation, from the ingrained discourses of paternalism to passé institutional barriers. The self-empowerment on campus was impeded by out-of-date regulations and frustrated by students' inferior status when negotiating with supervisory institutes. The conventional constraints on the development of campus-based credit unions highlight the very caricature of youth discrimination. It, again, demonstrates that the student-subject is at the mercy of paternalistic narratives and its precarious nature is far beyond any financial dilemmas. In a sense, a latent challenge for the young generation in Taiwan to get past economic uncertainties is the youth-excluded conventions in various aspects that keep repressing the subjectivity of the youth, although it can be unwittingly.

Despite the many obstacles, representing the campus as a learning space has been acknowledged as an affirmative way to envisage alternative socio-economic futures. It was to readjust the engagement style by conceiving it as 'a spatial practice' after our reflecting on inter-subjectivity of the on-campus campaign from a post-structuralist perspective. The intellectual features of a campus were underlined to create an instructive milieu for students to imagine possibilities and to make changes. In its intention to make concessional loans to its members at affordable rates, the union endeavoured to further financial literacy in an innovative and dynamic way by collaborating with university administration. As its operation has been stabilising, the union also resumed its unfinished task of striving for youth-friendly regulations – although this part of the intervention is not discussed in this chapter. The on-campus project did work to advance financial inclusion and literacy on an organisational level. Besides, the idea and value of the politics of becoming that the project team is keen to disseminate have also been progressively accepted among students.

The project team made concerted efforts to engage with the practice of 'unite-for-good'. Yet, the union at present remains too underdeveloped to deal with the predicament of underpayment that many students meet. It is a much more complicated issue related to tendencies of neoliberalist atomisation in spheres of both macro-economy and higher education. Based on our experience, the critical point in dealing with the socio-economic perplexity of financial exclusion and economic discrimination, which students have been facing for years, is to be *self*-aware of economic marginalisation *collectively*. Indeed, the role that a campus-based credit union can play is to serve as an institutional lever to offer affordable financial services, as a resource hub to deliver appropriate financial knowledge to students, or even as a friendly partner to accompany those depressed students who are on a tight budget. However, in response to economic uncertainties, students have to act *in a group* to negotiate the issue of subjectivity by themselves, so that they can get a *conscious* foothold and confront the various inequalities that life throws at them.

Notes

[1] In Taiwan, official surveys of atypical employment began in 2008.

[2] Taiwan has the world's lowest fertility rate at 1.218 children per woman, according to the Fertility Rate by Country 2019 Report of the World Population Review (World Population Review, 2019).

[3] Between 1997 and 2006 there was a sharp increase of 42% in public university tuition fees and 14% in private university fees, which were already high (Chou, 2008), compared to a 7% increase in the consumer price index over the same period. Note that the growth rate has been held back by de-regulation since 2008 (Ding, 2014).

[4] Students from families with an annual income of NT$1.2 million or less (around £31,670) are eligible to apply for a concessional loan that is subsidised by the government (Ministry of Education, 2019).

[5] Annual wages for part-time assistants are basically fixed in every university. Two external factors have led to a reduction in on-campus job opportunities. One is the annual hike in the minimum wage (Department of Labour Standards and Equal Employment, 2019).The other is the increase in insurance costs because a new rule announced in 2015 stipulated that on-campus part-time workers have to be included in employment insurance and pension systems.

[6] One case we encountered is exemplary in this respect. A college student was given the 'suggestion' to give up his application for an outbound exchange programme by staff, since he was from a low-income household.

[7] It was released on 12 March 2016 by a self-organised student team from the NDHU (NDHU Student Labour Right Association, 2019).

[8] Another report was released 15 months later by student associations from ten universities. It revealed that up to 80% of employers were violating the Labour Law (Yu, 2019).

[9] This was stated by an actual employer, who was cited in the low-pay survey (Yu, 2019).

[10] Two of the authors of this chapter are the originators of the idea to launch this campus initiative, and both have been engaged in the cooperative campaign for many years.

[11] The workshop, held by the National Alliance of Women's Associations, was called to discuss the positive role of cooperatives in empowering rural women. CEDAW is short for 'Convention on the Elimination of All Forms of Discrimination against Women.'

[12] Additionally, certain academic works were also produced, including three essays (Chang, 2017; Pei, 2016; Pei, 2019) for public dissemination, five conference presentations, and one Master's dissertation (Pei, 2018).

13 The rules are based on the Regulations for the Establishment, Guidance, Management and Supervision of Credit Unions, which is formulated by the CULROC.

14 However, the maximum share of an individual member is limited to 10% of the total amount. The Law includes special concessions for indigenous people, who are allowed to organise a credit union with half the amount of members and capital.

15 An additional three months is allowed, if it is deemed necessary.

16 Eventually, the membership reached 128 individuals (with students accounting for 75% of the total, while faculty and alumni accounted for 20% and 5% respectively), and an amount of NT$1,065,608 was raised (the funds from the students were around 25% of the total).

17 The penetration rate in Taiwan has remained below 2% over the last two decades, reaching as low as 1.26%, compared to an average 9.09% globally (World Council of Credit Unions, 2019). The penetration rate measures credit union members as a proportion of the economically active population (in the 15–64 age group).

18 Soon afterwards, we realised that ageing is a major challenge facing credit unions in Taiwan. According to the CULROC, in 2018 credit union members aged 60 and above accounted for nearly one-third (29.19%) of all members nationwide.

19 This is based on the Regulations for the Election and Repudiation of Credit Unions, as formulated by the CULROC.

20 According to the Civil Law, majority in Taiwan is attained upon reaching the 20th year of age.

21 A particular source of frustration was the fact that two undergraduates, who had been keen to join the preparatory work, decided to withdraw from the project when the proposal was rejected. They felt that running a campus-based credit union would face many limitations due to the regulatory restrictions on youth participation.

22 An anonymous troll even spread a malicious slander through social media insinuating that the credit union was a pyramid scheme involving illegal fundraising.

23 They were the 'Union-for-Good' Workshop and the 'Co-Innovative Campus OST' Workshop, conducted using the World Café method and Open Space Technology respectively.

24 We acquired funding and technical support from some cooperative campaigners via interpersonal networks.

25 The briefings were arranged by the teachers, which may explain why some in the audiences appeared passive and somehow reluctant to speak (compared to those in the workshops and other meetings).

26 What we mean by this is not just becoming a passive member of the credit union but also getting involved in other civil movements and campaigns.

27 For example, the most favourable one is special for student members, by which students members can grant a loan up to NT$50,000 (about £1,219) at APR 1%.

28 In terms of the credit union's operations, three job positions have to be filled – cashier, accountant and secretary.

29 It is composed of one teacher and one graduate (both of whom are specialised in economic geography), as well as one alumnus who has graduated from the Department of Economics.

30 Both were founded by left-wing youngsters. One assembles a group of temporary cleaners who have been originally hired by a dispatching company to fight for labour rights, and the other is engaged in community empowerment in peripheral areas.

31 It is an occupation-based credit union set up in 1989 with more than NT$80 million funds.

References

Cameron, J. and Gibson, K. (2005) 'Participatory action research in a poststructuralist vein', *Geoforum*, 36: 315–331.

Chan, S.-J. and Lin, L.-W. (2015) 'Massification of higher education in Taiwan: Shifting pressure from admission to employment', *Higher Education Policy*, 28: 17–33.

Chang, C.-W. (2017) 'Why do universities require credit unions?', *Green Style*, 161: 22–23.

Chang, Y.-C. (2014) 'Elaborating on the relevance of credit unions to asset accumulation of economically disadvantaged families', *Cooperative Economy*, 122: 16–31.

Chatterton, P., Fuller, D. and Routledge, P. (2007) 'Relating action to activism: Theoretical and methodological reflections', in: S. Kindon, R. Pain and M. Kesby (eds) *Participatory action research approaches and methods: Connecting people, participation and place*, London: Routledge, pp.216–222.

Chou, C.-I. (2007) 'Beyond university tuition fees: A nation-wide on-line survey on university student living costs', *Journal of Education Research*, 154: 110–123.

Chou, C.-I. (2008) 'The impact of neo-liberalism on Taiwanese higher education', *International Perspectives on Education and Society*, 9: 297–311.

Chu, T.-T. (1961) *Law and society in traditional China*, Paris: Mouton.

Cleaver, H. (1993) 'Kropotkin, self-valorization and the crisis of Marxism', *Anarchist Studies*, 2: 1–34.

Department of Labour Standards and Equal Employment (2019) *The formulation and adjustment of basic wages*, https://www.mol.gov.tw/topic/3067/5990/13171/19154/

Ding, J.-C. (2014) 'Analysis of university tuition fees', *Taiwan Educational Review Monthly*, 3: 4–16.

Fuller, D. and Kitchin, R. (eds) (2004) *Radical theory/critical praxis: Making a difference beyond the academy?*, Victoria, BC: Praxis (e)Press.

Gibson-Graham, J. K. (2006a) *The end of capitalism (as we knew it): A feminist critique of political economy*, Minneapolis, MN: University of Minnesota Press.

Gibson-Graham, J. K. (ed) (2006b) *A postcapitalist politics*, Minneapolis, MN: University of Minnesota Press.

Gibson-Graham, J. K. (2008) 'Diverse economies: Performative practices for "other worlds"', *Progress in Human Geography*, 32(5): 613–632.

Hamilton, G. (1990) 'Patriarchy, patrimonialism and filial piety: A comparison of China and Western Europe', *British Journal of Sociology*, 41(1): 77–104.

Heaney, J. and Flam, H. (eds) (2015) *Power and emotion*, London: Routledge.

Henley, J. (2019) 'Young, qualified and jobless: plight of Europe's best-educated generation', *The Guardian*, https://www.theguardian.com/world/2013/jul/01/jobless-europe-young-qualified#comments

Huang, K.-Z. (2010) 'Student loans: Dreams or traps?', *Taiwan Panorama*, https://www.taiwan-panorama.com/Articles/Details?Guid=9c86bc53-d9fd-4055-bb7c-1597517deff0&CatId=2

Huang, Y.-K. (2014) 'Taiwan's dilemma under the onslaught of neoliberalism', *Global Hakka Studies*, 3: 230–244.

Hung, C.-S. (2014) 'The lost generation: Structural dilemmas in youth work', *Community Development Journal*, 146: 65–76.

Ku, Y.-W. (2017) 'Youth poverty and low pay: Phenomena and countermeasures', *New Society for Taiwan*, 52: 17–22.

Lin, C.-Y. (2012) 'The impact of a high university tuition policy on disadvantaged students in Taiwan', *Chinese Education and Society*, 45: 21–30.

Lin, W.-Y. and Wang, J.-W. (1995) 'Teaching styles of Chinese parents: Stern education or harsh education?', *Indigenous Psychological Research in Chinese Societies*, 3: 2–92.

Lin, Z.-H., Hong, J.-S., Li, J.-H., Wong, Z.-Q. and Chang, F.-Y. (2011) *The crumbling generation: Crises of conglomeration, pauperisation and less childisation*, Taipei: Taiwan Labour Front.

Ministry of Education (2019) *Senior high school and above student loans application guidelines*, http://edu.law.moe.gov.tw/LawContent.aspx?id=FL008654#lawmenu

NDHU Student Labour Right Association (2019) *NDHU Labour Movement*, https://www.facebook.com/ndhulabourmovement/

Pei, H.-C. (2016) 'A campus-based credit union: Making a wish for the future', *Cooperative Report*, 94: 12–16.

Pei, H.-C. (2018) *Self-cultivation of economic subjectivity on campus: A participatory action research of Dong Hwa Campus Credit Union*, Unpublished MA thesis, National Dong Hwa University.

Pei, H.-C. (2019) 'No way for the young to escape youth poverty: A solution from co-operative economy and a challenge from authority', Hualien City, Taiwan: National Dong Hwa University.

Perin, W. (2013) 'Credit union movement and development in our country', *New Century Forum*, 62: 54–63.

Pimlott-Wilson, H. (2017) 'Individualising the future: The emotional geographies of neoliberal governance in young people's aspirations', *Area*, 49(3): 288–295.

Roelvink, G., Martin, K. and Gibson-Graham, J. K. (eds) (2015) *Making other worlds possible: Performing diverse economies*, Minneapolis, MN: University of Minnesota Press.

Sayer, A. (2001) 'For a critical cultural political economy', *Antipode*, 33(4): 687–708.

Vieta, M. (2010) 'Editorial: The new cooperativism', *Affinities: A Journal of Radical Theory, Culture and Action*, 4: 1–11.

World Council of Credit Unions (2019) *World Council 2018 Annual Report*, http://www.woccu.org/about/annual_report/

World Population Review (2019) *Taiwan Population 2019*, http://worldpopulationreview.com/countries/taiwan-population/

Wu, C.-S. (2011) 'Church and society: Religious, ethnic and monetary networks of credit unions in Taiwan (1964–1997)', *Fu Jen Social Studies*, 1: 73–104.

Yu, R. (2019) '"Because they are students, there is no need to give too much": Two salary maps revealing how the unscrupulous bosses squeezed students', https://buzzorange.com/2017/07/26/college-student-low-paid

Yu, Y.-M. (1998) 'Problems of credit unions after institutionalization', *Credit Union Magazine*, 51: 2–5.

16

'If you think about the future you are just troubling yourself': uncertain futures among caregiving and non-caregiving youth in Zambia

Caroline Day

Introduction

The role of aspiration for youth in the Zambian context is an area that until recently has been greatly overlooked. Like many sub-Saharan African countries, a concern about young people's everyday lives and the challenges they face in the present (Evans, 2012; 2011; 2010; Evans and Becker, 2009; Ansell and Van Blerk, 2004; Becker et al, 2001), has meant little focus has been given to young people's views about their *futures*. Youth-centred policies were only introduced in Zambia in 1994. Focusing on the position of young people in society, such policies and associated movements attempt to outline the roles and responsibilities expected of these young people as they grow up into adulthood. They seek to ensure the development of a youth who is responsible, assertive and disciplined, seeing them as a resource for the future development of the country – one whose potential should be 'tapped' to ensure the Zambian economy continues to grow (MYSCD, 2015; 2006; 1994).

What is strikingly absent however, is any recognition of young people's individual aspirations, the ability of young people to decide their own future, and the need to provide adequate resources and funding to enable them to achieve this. Young people are expected to 'grow up to full adulthood in consonance with contemporary social, economic and political ideals and aspirations of the nation' (MSYCD, 1994: 1). This fails to recognise young people's own aspirations, outside of the wider goals of the country itself, which relate not only to growing up and getting by, but to being 'someone' one day too. The lack of consultation with young people about what their aspirations are, especially in light of the responsibilities they hold and the social and economic challenges they face, is the key motivation behind this chapter.

By addressing the ways in which Zambian youth view the future, particularly in relation to the education and employment opportunities they seek, this chapter further develops the dialogue surrounding the importance of being able to aspire. It argues that a better understanding of what youth want is key to formulating policies and programmes that can support young people to achieve their aspirations. However, it also acknowledges the challenges associated with this, and how for some the realisation of the hurdles that they need to overcome mean that they struggle to aspire, preferring to focus on the here-and-now, rather than looking towards something over which they feel they have no control.

Aspiration: a growing global agenda

Aspirations are defined as the wants, preferences, choices and calculations of an individual for their future that are multidimensional, many faceted and socially embedded (Copestake and Camfield, 2010; Appadurai, 2004). Appadurai (2004) describes how aspirations are never individual, but 'formed in interaction and in the thick of social life'. They derive from larger cultural norms (Appadurai, 2004) and are therefore formed against a broader changing social context (Leavy and Smith, 2010). Aspirations may be influenced by the socio-economic circumstances within which an individual lives, which impact on their capacity to aspire (Appadurai, 2004), as well as on their ability to achieve those aspirations. The aspirations of young people in the global North have increasingly become the focus of policy attention, particularly the assumed need to 'raise' aspirations as young people complete their transitions to adulthood (Pimlott-Wilson, 2011). This policy approach supports the notion of 'youth' as engaged in a process of becoming 'independent', 'responsible' and 'productive' adults (Potter et al, 2012) who need support to achieve their potential. Aspirations for 'a good life', equated with health and happiness, exist in all societies (Appadurai, 2004).

While what constitutes a 'good life' may vary across cultures and societies, aspirations for a good life are part of a system of ideas located in wider beliefs about life and how it should be lived before death, and about the nature and importance of possessions, material assets and social relationships. At a more local level aspirations are also the ideas held about marriage, work, leisure, respectability, friendship, health and virtue (Appadurai, 2004). Aspiration is described as an 'orientation to the future' (Brown, 2011) and therefore aspirations are highly related to the socially expected transitions that young people are expected to go through on their pathways to adulthood.

Dreams, hopes, desires and plans are all terms which are frequently conflated with and referred to as aspirations (Brown, 2011), yet each is argued to have a different meaning. Nilsen (1999) suggests that dreams are more abstract desires that are seldom rooted in time or space, hopes are more tangible, and plans are the most concrete form of approach to the future. Leavy and Smith (2010) refer to aspirations as being linked to expectations; both of which can increase or decrease according to young people's growing awareness of the possibilities and constraints of the world, as well as their own choices and experiences. The Cabinet Office Social Exclusion Taskforce in the UK, however, aligns aspiration with 'hopefulness' rather than 'expectation', stating 'aspirations are distinguishable from expectations; there is a difference between what people hope to achieve and what they expect to achieve' (2008: 8).

The role of aspiration in young people's lives is both personal and dynamic. Leavy and Smith (2010: 6) describe how 'aspirations may mean different things to different people and they are formed and develop in response to different environments and circumstances'. Aspirations can therefore be dependent on the experiences, choices and information available to an individual, as well as their awareness of their own abilities and the opportunities available to them. These factors are influenced by social class, gender, ethnicity, race and socio-economic status – higher levels of income for example correlate to higher aspirations (Morrison et al, 2008). Appadurai (2004) describes how the 'rich and powerful' have a more fully developed capacity to aspire, as they are more likely to have the 'possibilities', 'options' and 'material goods' available to them to make their aspirations happen (Appadurai, 2004).

High aspirations and a positive outlook have been identified as important for young people experiencing adversity (Newman, 2002). Evans's (2012a) study of orphaned young people living in child and youth headed households in Tanzania and Uganda, found that having aspirations for the future had a significant influence on their resilience and capabilities. Young people caring for parents or relatives with HIV, or who had lost parents because of HIV, often had high aspirations for both the completion of their education and their ability to gain a 'good job' to support themselves and their siblings in the future (Evans and

Becker, 2009). In contrast, those who had limited resources available to them having lost valuable assets such as land and who were unable to attend school, had low aspirations and expressed a sense of hopelessness about the future (Evans, 2012a). Research on resilience contends that when youth believe that they have some control over their lives and environment, they also have healthy aspirations and are motivated to achieve (Werner and Smith, 1989).

It is young people experiencing adversity, however, who are often the most likely to identify a range of barriers that might prevent them from fulfilling their future ambitions. Young caregivers in Warren's (2005) study, for example, cited a lack of money, a lack of qualifications and the need to look after family members as preventing them from thinking about and preparing for the future. Similarly Ibrahim (2011) highlights how poverty is associated with the failure of aspirations due to powerlessness and vulnerability. Appadurai describes how it is not that those experiencing poverty cannot 'wish, want, need, plan or aspire' (2004: 69), but that poverty reduces the circumstances in which these practices can occur, and therefore the capacity for them to happen. So while youth in Zambia recognise that they might not be able to achieve their capabilities, it does not mean that they do not have aspirations that they wish to fulfil (Day, 2015; Ibrahim, 2011). This is particularly important to acknowledge when considering those who have significant caregiving responsibilities for disabled or chronically ill parents and relatives. One day those responsibilities may be gone and the opportunity to develop their own identity and be something other than a caregiver is important to recognise and believe in.

There is, however, also an acknowledged 'aspiration attainment gap' where high aspirations are not necessarily associated with positive outcomes (Leavy and Smith, 2010). Chant and Jones (2005: 193) discuss how many young people affected by poverty in Gambia express 'over-idealised and/or improbable career aspirations given the nature and level of their educational and skill profiles and prospects'. Nwagwu (1976: 115) described how students in Nigeria and Kenya would maintain high aspirations for their future employment based on the desire to occupy positions that would gain them respect in society and achieve high standards of living when their aspirations 'neither reflect the employment opportunities and the supply and demand nature of the labour market, nor the socio-economic conditions and development levels of their countries'.

Where literature on aspirations in Africa is available it tends to focus on 'aspirations failure' (Bernard et al, 2011) and young people being 'afraid to aspire' (Ibrahim, 2011). 'Fatalism' and 'hopelessness' is equated with the situation of many young Africans. There is an acknowledged crisis between aspirations and outcomes as a result of unequal global partnerships and the impact on education, employment and other ideals sought after by African youth. Aspirations can reflect the extent to which people feel that they have control over their future (Bernard et al, 2008). Yet those who grow up in poverty are constrained because of their socio-economic circumstances. They are in effect in an aspiration 'trap' (Heifetz and Minelli, 2006).

Researching young caregivers in Zambia

This chapter discusses the findings of qualitative research between 2011 and 2016 over multiple research visits to Zambia that investigated the transitions to adulthood of young people with and without a caregiving responsibility for a sick or disabled parent or relative (Bowlby and Day, 2018; Day, 2017; 2016; 2014; Day and Evans, 2015). Recognising the tendency in research to focus on children, and those under the age of 18, the research sought to recognise that many *youth* are also living in households in which 'adults are either not present or not fully functioning, in terms of providing material, practical and/or emotional support for children and young people' (Payne, 2012: 294). The study therefore explored how caregiving may impact on older youth's lifecourse transitions and imagined futures in the global South, building on the work of scholars such as Evans (2012a; 2012b).

The young people who participated in the research were aged between 14 and 30 years old. This accounted not only for internationally recognised definitions of youth (UN, 2019) but local definitions too as the Zambian government defines 'youth' as young people between the ages of 18 and 35 (MSYCD, 2006). Pilot research revealed that few people identified themselves as 'youth' after the age of 30 as they were usually employed, married and had children. The age of 30 was therefore used as the upper age limit, while the slightly lower age limit was used in recognition that many young people have significant responsibilities at a much younger age than age-based understandings of transitions assume.

The research was conducted with 35 young people (aged 14–30 years); comprising 15 young people who were caring for a chronically sick or disabled parent or relative (nine female, six male) and 20 who did not have specific caring responsibilities for a family member (nine female, 11 male). Five young people cared for their sick or disabled mother, two were caring for their brother, two for their grandmother and two for their uncle, while others cared for their father, grandfather, sister, aunt and niece. Several young people were also responsible for other family members who were not sick or disabled but still needed financial support and emotional guidance, such as younger siblings, nieces and nephews. When information about illness or disability was volunteered, four family members were reported to have HIV-related illnesses, although the chronic illness of several other family members was also likely to be HIV-related. Other conditions reported included stroke, blindness, spina bifida, cerebral palsy and hydrocephalus, epilepsy and amputation. Many young people had witnessed the death of parents or family members earlier in their lives, often from HIV-related illnesses. Purposive sampling techniques were used to identify the research participants, aided by the support of two key community based organisations. The research used a combination of semi-structured interviews and life mapping methods to capture the stories and opinions of the young people involved (see Day and Evans, 2015; Day 2014; 2016; 2017). The life-maps acted as both reflections on the past, as well as being a 'future-oriented' drawing exercise (Daum, 2019) to allow the young people to articulate how they looked towards the future and the key events that they hoped would take place.

Young people's aspirations, hopes and dreams

For young people in Zambia, aspirations are inextricably linked with their transitions to adulthood, revolving around the markers of adulthood such as education, employment and marriage. However, youth transitions have become increasingly 'fuzzy' (Day and Evans, 2015; Calves et al, 2009) as young people's trajectories 'are characterised by delays, interruptions, incompletions, false starts, chance opportunities, reversals, adverse events and interactions' (Locke and te Lintelo, 2012: 783). While it is recognised that the ability to look forward, plan and dream is itself a form of resilience that helps young people cope with the 'critical moments' (Thomson et al, 2002) in their lives that occur outside their control, young Zambians also have to be realistic about what is achievable in increasingly challenging times.

The young people in the study showed significant differences in how far into the future they were willing, or able, to look, plan or hope for when they talked about their aspirations, particularly based on whether or not they were caregiving. While those without a caregiving responsibility were happy to talk about events that could happen five, ten, twenty or more years in the future, those with caregiving responsibilities were often more hesitant to do so, focusing on their immediate futures over the coming weeks and months, the day to day responsibilities they had and the short-term needs of their families, which they often prioritised over their own needs. Many of the young caregivers therefore, only looked a few years ahead. The exceptions to this were the young people who were not 'caregiving', but still had significant responsibilities within their households to provide for their families. These young people were also hesitant to have too many aspirations and hopes for the future as they wanted to concentrate on their current challenges and not set themselves up to fail.

Overall, the majority of non-caregiving young people were far clearer about what they hoped might happen in their lives and the direction they wanted their futures to take. Those caregiving, however, lived with daily uncertainty, especially in relation to those they were caring for. Needing to focus on day to day care routines, earning a livelihood and, for those still in education, attending school, they focused on the short-term needs of themselves and their families. This echoes findings from Evans and Becker's (2009) study in which young people expressed experiencing uncertainty about their futures. Young people expressed apprehension when thinking about the future because they knew that it was unlikely that they would achieve their long-term aspirations. Chisala (caregiver, aged 30) when I interviewed her commented, "it's difficult because we don't know each day what comes. We know only for that day. We wouldn't know for tomorrow." This did not mean that caregivers had no aspirations, however, but their responsibilities changed the way they perceived life and their expectations of what it could offer. This was often represented in the types of aspirations they had and the fact that supporting their family was usually prioritised ahead of aspirations for themselves. We need to recognise, therefore, the unpredictability of social and environmental changes, which can destabilise the conventional notions of life transitions as directional, highlighting the precarity and unpredictability of lives in transition, especially for young people in the global South (Horschelmann, 2011).

Faith and religion played an important part in young people's perceptions of, and aspirations for, their futures. The young caregivers particularly talked about their futures in relation to God and their religious affiliations offered a great deal of support to them. All the young people saw their lives as being linked to 'God's will'. Placing responsibility with God for the events that had occurred in their lives so far helped them to justify why they had experienced adversities. They felt that God had given them these challenges for a reason and it was now their responsibility to see them through. In a similar vein, many of my participants placed their future hopes and aspirations 'in God's hands' as He would decide what should happen next in their lives. Aspirations and having a faith gave the young people hope for the future, while not having a faith was seen as reducing the chances of their aspirations coming to fruition.

Hearing young people talk about their aspirations for the future and seeing – perhaps unrealistically – how high many of them wanted to aim, often contrasted with the beliefs aired within local communities and sometimes organisations. Such members often thought that young people had no aspirations, were not taking their lives seriously or planning for the future – only living for today. It would be understandable that if young people cannot see a future or do not believe in it then maybe such an attitude would become a form of coping mechanism. Growing up expecting poor health, no money and no job they could quite easily focus on living for now. Thus such youth may well exist but within this study almost all the young people had aspirations of some kind – including completing their education, to which I now turn.

Completing education

As across much of sub-Saharan Africa, young people in Zambia are under increasing pressure to obtain a good education in order to obtain employment and make successful transitions to adulthood (Day and Evans, 2015). The cost of education, particularly secondary education, as well as the social challenges affecting young people means that schooling is often hard to complete. Only five young people in the study had completed Grade 12, the equivalent of completing secondary school, and 20 were unable to attend school at the time of the research. The young people all aspired to complete their education, or return to school if they were not attending. Thomas (non-caregiving, aged 23) when completing his lifemap for the future and discussing the key transitions he hoped would happen, described how he wanted to "get back to school and complete my Grade 12 and study medicine", while Gregson (non-caregiving, aged 18), also on his lifemap, wrote "I am happy because 2011 is the year I will be writing my Grade 9 examinations, so I keep on studying so that I can pass and go on to Grade 10." A good education was perceived as more likely to attract sponsorship for further higher level study, particularly from the government who could offer bursaries for gifted students or opportunities into state supported careers such as nursing, as well as from wealthy family members or benefactors.

Jeffrey (2010) highlights how education is highly valued by young people in different global contexts as it offers some social opportunities and can promote social mobility, yet ties them ever more tightly into systems of inequality. Certainly the young people in the study were aware that many of the barriers to education which they had already experienced would continue in the future and hinder their aspirations to complete school. Education, particularly at secondary level, was a financial challenge for many young people for a multitude of reasons. Almost all the young people had experienced breaks in their education when they could not afford to attend school, and 19 of those currently not attending school cited 'lack of money' as the main reason. Unfortunately this was a challenge that was likely to remain for the majority of young people, in the short term at least, and they planned to undertake casual informal work in order to 'raise the fees' in order to go back. Many of them were also still hanging on to the notion of the elusive 'sponsor' who would 'take them back to school'. This could be a family member, friend, boyfriend, NGO or wealthy benefactor. Samantha (non-caregiving, aged 19) when interviewed described how she wanted to find a 'sponsor' and was aware that this had happened for other young people through the church. She commented, "if I was to find someone to sponsor me I would like to go back to school again. Like here, sometimes people from church come here and sponsor people."

While many of the young people wanted to pursue further education, none of them expected this to be a direct transition following secondary school and therefore planned to work first in order to raise the money to study further. Mary (caregiving, aged 14), for example, told me she planned to work for a local wig-making company to save the money for her course. Esther (non-caregiving, aged 20) was working as a hairdresser but said she still hoped to return to school. Even those from more financially stable families who had received financial support from either immediate or extended family members to support them in going to school, did not expect to receive the same kind of support to pay for their university education. For example, Eric's father, a consultant employed by the government and who had himself studied for a degree in South Africa, had paid for Eric's education up to Grade 12. Eric (non-caregiving, aged 21) was now working as a 'bus boy' to raise the money which he hoped would enable him to study auto-engineering at university. He told me in his interview that he did not expect his father to offer him any support towards this.

While the young people in my study were very aware of the challenges that they faced in accessing education currently, and of those that they would face in the future, they also aspired to adapt their lives and routines to ensure that they could continue education. Betty (caregiving, aged 14), for example, who told me in her interview that she was caring for her sick mother, her three younger siblings and was pregnant, knew that if/when she could go back to school she would do night classes so that she could still work during the day and take care of her child. Abigail (caregiving, aged 21) also wanted to study at night school so that she could stay home to care for her disabled brother during the day. After creating her lifemap for the future, she commented, "the school which I will like to go back to is night school. At the moment the school for day I wouldn't manage. At least night school where I go in the evening." Night classes offered an alternative way for young people to gain qualifications if they had not achieved high enough grades or had enough money to pay to attend secondary education during the day. Classes were usually offered by NGOs or community schools. Many young people, however, were aware that they might not be able to return to school and had alternative aspirations if they could not complete their education. These are discussed in further detail later in the chapter.

A small number of young people recognised that, because of their age and their responsibilities, it was too late for them to re-engage with education and so they had to focus on their lives now. Tasila (caregiving, aged 20), for instance, told me that she thought that education was no longer an option. She was caring for her disabled mother, male partner, child and siblings. Her priority was to provide for her family and to meet their daily needs. She wanted to work instead to raise the money to buy some land and build their own house. Her educational aspirations were now focused on her son. She hoped that she would soon be able to pay for him to attend nursery and hoped that he would eventually go to college. Generally, the young people wanted to use their educational opportunities to improve their employment opportunities, although many recognised the limitations associated with this and the need to think more flexibly about how to achieve their dreams, as I will discuss next.

Employment and career aspirations

Having a job, earning an income and being financially stable were key to young people's notions of being an 'adult'. One of the most discussed aspirations therefore was the desire for young people to find some sort of employment, be it in a career sense in the future, or in terms of finding local, short-term work. Almost all the young people were already engaging in some form of employment in order to contribute to their households, to raise the fees for their education, or to pay their rent and bills if they were living alone. Most of this work was informal, casual and low paid (Gough et al, 2013). It was done either alongside their education or sometimes instead of attending school. Young people often showed great initiative and actively sought such opportunities to support themselves and their families (Day, 2017; Gough et al, 2016). Employment was also viewed as a significant part of their futures and in the long term was seen as the key way in which young men, particularly, would be able to afford a house and a wife and family. It was therefore considered a necessary socially expected transition that should take place on their journey to adulthood (Bowlby et al, 1998).

Aspirations were often high among the young people, and almost all of them wanted jobs that had potential for personal and career development, whether they were caregiving or not. A significant number of the jobs aspired to required the young people to have not just Grade 12 education, but higher education in a college or university – doctors, accountants, journalists, engineers and teachers were all mentioned. Whether a young person was caregiving or not did have some impact on young people's career choices. Fewer young male caregivers, for example, sought highly skilled jobs such as medicine, teaching and accountancy, while more of them opted for the military (a government supported career which could offer guaranteed employment). More young female caregivers wanted to be teachers compared to those not caregiving (another government supported career), while only one wanted to be a nurse compared to five of the non-caregiving young women. This suggests that having a caring responsibility at home did not encourage young women to aspire to careers that also required caregiving, but maybe instead towards something removed from their caring responsibilities and therefore different from their home experience. This finding contradicts those in Evans and Becker's (2009) study which found that young people who were caring for a sick parent or relative were more likely to aspire to work in caring professions in the future, as doctors or healthcare professionals, for example, motivated by their desire to help and care for people.

While aspirations were generally high, there was also a common recognition that these might not be achievable. Many of the young people recognised that their preferred jobs depended on their ability to return to and complete secondary school, as well as potentially pursue higher education. This supports research by Chant and Jones (2005) in Ghana in which they found that young people expressed over-idealised and improbable career aspirations in relation to their skills and the level of education they could achieve. For that reason alone, it was highly probable that few of the young people would ever achieve their aspirations and were already living in the knowledge that if secure, paid employment was a marker of adulthood, this would be very hard for them to achieve.

As outlined earlier, education was important to all the young people. Those currently in school described completing Grade 12 as their priority, while those out of school at the time of the research and who hadn't completed Grade 12, all aspired to return. However, despite this aspiration, education was not seen as a panacea, and it was widely recognised among the young people, their relatives and professionals that even with an education finding employment was difficult, if not impossible. Achieving a Grade 12 certificate was no longer a guarantee of employment and the young people who had completed Grade 12, such as Albert (non-caregiving, aged 24), were unhappy with the lack of opportunities that reaching even this stage had for them. He told me when I interviewed him:

'It was immediately after I finished school, the year after I completed [Grade 12], yes, I was looking for a job and I find one job in town. I was working there but the difficult part was that we were getting very small salary of which we were not managing to buy everything that we needed.'

In recognition of this, the majority of young people had a 'back-up plan' or an alternative occupation in mind that they could do in the future if they could not continue their studies and therefore achieve their aspired profession. The most common was 'doing business' which could involve selling vegetables or charcoal in the market, along the roadside or outside their house, or setting up a grocery stall or shop. The other types of jobs the young people aspired to engage in were working as a maid (for girls), or a mini-bus driver or brick-layer (for boys). Albert, for example, described while completing his lifemap, how if he failed to go back to school he would become a mini-bus driver. He commented, "maybe when I don't go back to school I will just do driving so that I just look for a job". Domestic, driving and building work was perceived as being relatively easy to secure, however, the increasing emphasis on qualifications in these professions, particularly the completion of Grade 12 at school, meant they might not be as easy to obtain as some young people thought.

Casual, informal work was also seen as being a good way of earning money on an interim basis. Even if the young people were in school and hoping to complete Grade 12, they planned to do business or obtain a driving job while they waited for their Grade 12 results (which could take many months) and to raise money which would enable them to study at college. Josphat (caregiving, aged 17), for example, told me, "I would want, when I finish school, to do some short work [part-time jobs] … so I would want to do [that] such that I raise money for college or university." Others aspired to run a business alongside having a more regular form of employment. Rose (non caregiving, aged 22) described how she did not want to rely on a salary where she only got paid at the end of the month, but wanted to be doing something 'for herself' also. Alongside qualifying as a nurse, she hoped to set up a boutique that she could operate around her hospital shifts. She saw this as an investment for her future, as well as indulging her passions for fashion and business.

Interestingly, more of the young men generally described having no set ambitions and being unclear about what they wanted to do in the future. Those caregiving related this to the level of responsibility they currently had and preferred to focus on their current situation rather than worry about the future. However, those who were not caring for someone who was sick or disabled, often still had a great deal of responsibility to support their families, providing an income rather than going to school. Blackson (non-caregiving, aged 16) had not been in school since the age of 12 when his father died. He told me, after I asked him why he had not indicated any plans for the future on his lifemap, that he did not want to think about what he could achieve in the next week, let alone in the future, and described making plans as "troubling yourself". He had no employment aspirations, saying that he looked for work when he needed it.

Caregiving young people described how they did not like talking about the future with their relatives as not only did they find it difficult to look ahead when the future was often uncertain, but their relatives found this difficult too. All the young people however, aspired to be able to continue looking after their families. Getting a 'good job' was the way they believed that they could achieve the financial security they did not currently have. In line with Appadurai's (2004) research they wanted to ensure their parents/relatives would live a 'good life', and a 'better life' than they were currently living, with access to resources such as suitable accommodation and the medical help they required.

Conclusion

This chapter has explored the young people's future transitions discussed in relation to their aspirations for the future. It emphasised the importance of recognising young people's hopes and dreams and the fact that they want to look towards the future, rather than continue to focus, as much of the recent literature has, on their daily experiences and challenges (Evans, 2012b; 2011; 2010; Evans and Becker, 2009; Ansell and Van Blerk, 2004; Becker et al, 2001). Increasingly, policy has concerned itself with ensuring that young people become 'independent', 'responsible' and 'productive' adults (Potter et al, 2012). Few studies in Africa, however, have actually asked young people what they want to achieve in the future and looked at their ability within the wider socio-economic climate to achieve this.

The study identified that aspirations for the future featured in all the young people's lives. Such aspirations were also generally high and almost all the young people had an ideal of what they would like to do in the future, reporting career goals that would almost all require higher level education to achieve. This was despite the fact that few of the young people had completed secondary education, many were no longer attending school and those that were attending school had often experienced in the past, or were currently experiencing, many disruptions to their school attendance and attainment.

Young people's aspirations were rarely based on personal hopes and dreams, but were centred on their wider roles and responsibilities. Ultimately, young people (both male and female and from rural and urban areas) aspired to care for their siblings and relatives through the economic empowerment achieved by completing education and gaining employment. Family obligations to care for those older and younger, in line with the intergenerational contract (Collard, 2000), were still very much a part of both young men and young women's aspirations for the future.

The study highlights, however, how for any young person there is often a huge gap between what is dream and what is available in reality. *Having* aspirations, and *achieving* aspirations, are not necessarily the same thing. Veenhoven (2000) describes this as potentiality and actuality: what are aspired life chances and what are actually achievable life results. Young people's aspirations were often highly optimistic, often far beyond their current, and potential future opportunities and, for most, unachievable. Within another space, place and time where young people had better access to financial, educational and emotional resources, their aspirations could be possible to achieve. But within their current situation there were too many barriers to overcome. Many of the young people were aware of this and knew it was unlikely they would become the doctors, teachers and accountants that they dreamed of, yet still they had this dream. There is a need, therefore, to examine what role aspirations have in a young person's life and whether they are useful. To have aspirations is acknowledged as a form of resilience (Newman, 2002), but at what point do dreams turn to despondency when the restraints of financial difficulties, lack of education or limited employment opportunities take over, alongside the realisation that in reality there is nothing to aim for other than just surviving on a day to day basis?

Abbink (2005) suggests that the overwhelming majority of young people in sub-Saharan Africa do not hold their futures in their own hands, as population growth and scarce resources mean that young people remain dependent and powerless with their social mobility blocked. I would disagree with this in that young people in Africa are resourceful, resilient, dynamic and opportunistic, carving out opportunities when they need them. They are, however, facing increasingly difficult socio-economic times where the wider challenges of unemployment, poverty and caregiving increasingly dictate what they are able to achieve. The youth in Zambia were hardworking and astute, with very clear ideas about what they would like to do with their lives and how their lives related to those around them. What they lacked, however, were the opportunities, the resources and the skills to reach their potential.

To close, this chapter calls for further research on the role of aspiration within young people's transitions to adulthood, particularly among those with significant responsibilities at home such as caregiving. It calls for further analysis of the value of aspiration and usefulness of aspirations in understanding young people's hopes for the future, as well as for more research into the impact of failed aspirations within wider social and political contexts. There is a need to look at what it is that really inspires young people's imaginations of the future as they grow up, and the role of both governmental and non-governmental institutions in shaping young people's aspirations and providing the opportunities to achieve them.

Acknowledgements

Thanks go to the University of Reading PhD studentship, the Royal Geographical Society (with the Institute of British Geographers) Slawson Award and the University of Portsmouth for financial support for the research.

References

Abbink, J. (2005) 'Being young in Africa: The politics of despair and renewal', in: J. Abbink and I. van Kessel (eds) *Vanguard or vandals: Youth, politics and conflict in Africa*, Leiden: Brill, pp.1–33.

Ansell, N. and van Blerk, L. (2004) 'Children's migration as a household/family strategy: coping with AIDS in Lesotho and Malawi', *Journal of South African Studies*, 30(3): 673–690.

Appadurai, A. (2004) 'The capacity to aspire: Culture and the terms of recognition', in: V. Rao and M. Walton (eds) *Culture and public action*, Stanford, CA: Stanford University Press, pp.59–84.

Becker, S., Dearden, C. and Aldridge, J. (2001) 'Children's labour of love? Young carers and care work', in: P. Mizen, C. Pole and A. Bolton (eds) *Hidden hands: International perspectives on children's work and labour*, London: Routledge, pp.70–87.

Bernard, T., Taffesse, A. S. and Dercon, S. (2008) *Aspirations failure and well-being outcomes in Ethiopia: Towards an empirical exploration*, London: Department for International Development.

Bernard, T., Dercon, S. and Tafesse, A. S. 0. (2011) *Beyond fatalism: An empirical exploration of self-efficacy and aspirations failure in Ethiopia*, CSAE Working Paper 2011-03, Oxford: Centre for the Study of African Economies, University of Oxford.

Bowlby, S. and Day, C. (2018) 'Emotions, disclosures and reflexivity: Reflections on interviewing young people in Zambia and women in midlife in the UK', in: T. Loughran and D. Mannay (eds) *Emotion and the researcher: Sites, subjectivities and relationships*, Bingley: Emerald, pp.127–142.

Bowlby S., Lloyd-Evans S. and Mohammad R. (1998) 'The workplace. Becoming a paid worker: Images and identity', in: T. Skelton and G. Valentine (eds) *Cool places: Geographies of youth cultures*, London: Routledge, pp.229–248.

Brown, G. (2011) 'Emotional geographies of young people's aspirations for adult life', *Children's Geographies*, 9(1): 7–22.

Cabinet Office Social Exclusion Taskforce (2008) *Aspiration and attainment amongst young people in deprived communities: analysis and discussion paper*, London: Department of Communities and Local Government/Department for Children, Schools and Families.

Calves, A. E., Bozon, M. and Kuepie, M. (2009) 'Transition to adulthood: Rethinking the definition and analysis of first-time events', in: P. Antoine and E. Lalivre, E. (eds) *Fuzzy states and complex trajectories: Observation, modelization and interpretation of life histories*, Paris: INED., pp.121–125.

Chant, S. and Jones, G. A. (2005) 'Youth, gender and livelihoods in West Africa: Perspectives from Ghana and the Gambia', *Children's Geographies*, 3(2): 185–199.

Collard, D. (2000) 'Generational transfers and the generational bargain', *Journal of International Development*, 12(4): 453–462.

Copestake, J. and Camfield, L. (2010) 'Measuring multidimensional aspiration gaps: A means to understanding cultural aspects of poverty', *Development Policy Review*, 28(5): 617–633.

Daum, T. (2019) 'Of bulls and bulbs: Aspirations, opinions and perceptions of rural adolescents and youth in Zambia', *Development in Practice*, 29(7). 882–897.

Day, C. (2014) 'Giving the vulnerable a voice: Ethical considerations when conducting research with children and young people', in: J. Lunn (ed) *Fieldwork in the global South: Ethical challenges and dilemmas*, London: Routledge, pp.192–205.

Day, C. (2017) 'Education and employment transitions: The experiences of young people with caring responsibilities in Zambia', in: T. Abede, J. Waters and T. Skelton (eds) *Labouring and learning*, Singapore: Springer, pp.385–409.

Day, C. and Evans, R. (2015) 'Caring responsibilities, change and transitions in young people's family lives in Zambia', *Journal of Comparative Family Studies*, 46 (1): 137–152.

Evans, R. (2010) 'Children's caring roles and responsibilities within the family in Africa', *Geography Compass*, 4(10): 1477–1496.

Evans, R. (2011) '"We are managing our own lives …": Life transitions and care in sibling-headed households affected by AIDS in Tanzania and Uganda', *Area*, 43(4): 384–396.

Evans, R. (2012a) 'Safeguarding inheritance and enhancing the resilience of orphaned young people living in child-and youth-headed households in Tanzania and Uganda', *African Journal of AIDS Research*, 11(3): 177–189

Evans, R. (2012b) 'Sibling caringscapes: Time-space practices of caring within youth-headed households in Tanzania and Uganda', *Geoforum*, 43: 824–835.

Evans, R. and Becker, S. (2009) *Children caring for parents with HIV and AIDS: Global issues and policy responses*, Bristol: Policy Press.

Gough, K. V., Langevang T. and Owusu, G. (2013) 'Youth employment in a globalising world', Special issue of *International Development Planning Review*, 35(2): 91–102.

Gough, K. V., Chigunta, F. and Langevang, T. (2016) 'Expanding the scales and domains of insecurity: Youth employment in urban Zambia', *Environment and Planning A*, 48(2): 348–366.

Heifetz, A. and Minelli, E. (2006) *Aspiration traps*, Brescia: Dipartimento di Scienze Economiche Discussion Paper

Hörschelmann, K. (2011) 'Theorising life transitions: geographical perspectives', *Area*, 43: 378–383.

Ibrahim, S. (2011) *Poverty, aspirations and wellbeing: Afraid to aspire and unable to reach a better life – voices from Egypt*, Manchester: Brooks World Poverty Institute Working Paper.

Jeffrey, C. (2010) 'Geographies of children and youth I: Eroding maps of life', *Progress in Human Geography*, 34(4): 496–505.

Leavy, J. and Smith, S. (2010) *Future farmers: Youth aspirations, expectations and life choices*, Brighton: Future Agricultures Consortium.

Locke, C. and te Lintelo, D. (2012) 'Young Zambians "waiting" for opportunities and "working towards" living well: Lifecourse and aspirations in youth transitions', *Journal of International Development*, 24(6): 777–794.

Morrison Gutman, L. and Akerman, R. (2008) *Determinants of aspirations*, London: Centre for Research on the Wider Benefits of Learning.

MSYCD (Ministry of Sport, Youth and Child Development) (1994) *National youth policy*, Lusaka: MSYCD.

MSYCD (Ministry of Sport, Youth and Child Development) (2006) *National youth policy*, Lusaka: MSYCD.

MSYCD (Ministry of Sport, Youth and Child Development) (2015) *National youth policy*, Lusaka: MSYCD.

Newman, T. (2002) *Promoting resilience: A review of effective strategies for child care services.* Exeter: Centre for Evidence-Based Social Services.

Nilsen, A. (1999) 'Where is the future? Time and space as categories in analyses in young people's image of the future', *Innovation*, 12(2): 175–194.

Nwagwu, N. A. (1976) 'The vocational aspirations and expectations of African students', *Journal of Vocational Education and Training*, 28(71): 111–115.

Payne, R. (2012) 'Agents of support: Intra-generational relationships and the role of agency in the support networks of child-headed households in Zambia', *Children's Geographies*, 10(3): 293–306.

Pimlott-Wilson, H. (2011) 'The role of familial habitus in shaping children's views of their future employment', *Children's Geographies*, 9(1): 111–118.

Potter, R., Conway, D., Evans, R. and Lloyd-Evans, S. (2012) *Key concepts in development geography*, London: Sage.

Thomson, R., Bell, R. Holland, J., Henderson, S., McGrellis, S. and Sharpe, S. (2002) 'Critical moments: Choice, chance and opportunity in young people's narratives of transition', *Sociology*, 36(2): 335–354.

United Nations (2019) *Youth*, https://www.un.org/en/sections/issues-depth/youth-0/index.html

Veenhoven, R. (2000) 'The four qualities of life: Ordering concepts and measures of the good life', *Journal of Happiness Studies*, 1: 1–39.

Warren, J. (2005) 'Carers: How the lives of young carers differ from those of young non-carers and how their efforts sometimes go unsupported', *Research Matters*, 19: 5–10.

Werner, E. E., and Smith, R. S. (1989) *Vulnerable but invincible: A longitudinal study of resilient children and youth*, New York: McGraw-Hill.

17

Conclusions and futures

Helena Pimlott-Wilson, Sarah Marie Hall and John Horton

Introduction

Children, young people and families in hard times

This book set out to illuminate the personal, everyday effects of hard times for children, young people and families in diverse global contexts. In this concluding chapter, we begin by outlining the contribution of the three Parts of the book and their constituent chapters to our understanding of the hard times which interlace with the lives of children, youth and families. Our focus on 'hard times' aims to shed light on all manner of structural inequalities, longstanding exclusions and power imbalances which are being constituted or intensified by neoliberalisations, austerities and economic crises. Elucidating the implications of these complexly relational, hurtful and deeply affecting moments leads us to reflect on the opportunities and prospects for socially-differentiated children and young people getting by and growing up in hard times. In bringing together neoliberalisations, austerities and economic crises, we recognise how these processes are lumped together, materially and spatially (Katz, 2004; 2018) and in people's everyday experiences. Drawing the collection to a close, we consider further directions for research which is sensitive to the interrelations between broadscale political-economic shifts and locally-scaled, personally inflected inequalities.

Examining hard times: a collection

Divided into three key Parts, the collection began with an exploration of the transformative impacts of hard times for children, youth and families at the sharp end of neoliberalisms, austerities and economic crises. Drawing on work from diverse international contexts, Part 1 explored the transformations which play out unevenly at personal, familial and local scales as a result of political-economic processes.

The chapters detail how hard times impinge on the discursive norms and deeply-rooted social inequalities which pervade the lives of children, youth and families. In Part 2 of the book, our contributors sketch out the ways in which the contours of hard times intersect with axes of social difference to produce new or intensified forms of poverty and inequality. The chapters outline how alongside experiences of precarity and marginalisation, social ties and moral responsibilities are being refashioned, moderated or entrenched in the lives of children, youth and families. Heteropatriarchal familial norms, intergenerational obligations, discourses of normative childhoods and politics of poverty coalesce with marginality and inequalities, constituting variegated experiences of hard times. In Part 3, our contributors elucidate how, in negotiating marginality and inequality, children and young people look towards their futures. Across diverse global contexts, the chapters highlight the role of social bonds between the individual and others at the familial, community and institutional scales in working through and going beyond current hardships. In the collection, there are examples of the hopeful, affirmative ways in which people are living in and through neoliberalisms, austerities and economic crises but also the entrenched inequalities and harms rooted in these hard times.

In analysing the challenging and deeply affecting situations through which children, youth and families live, the discussions within the preceding chapters make a case for further exploration of the interplay between broad scale political-economic processes and the lived, experienced and personal scale of daily life. Through consideration of the everyday lived-in and lived-through nature of hard times, the collection underscores the imperative to explore the peopling of these processes, the differential forms and potentials of young people's agency across time/space and 'their role in the reproduction of, as well as resistance to, socio-spatial inequalities' (Holloway et al, 2019: 462). Illuminating personal, relational and emotional accounts of neoliberalisms, austerities and economic crises brings the effects of deep cuts to services and welfare, employment insecurity, educational marketisation and the proliferation of debt into sharp relief (Hall, 2016; 2017; 2018; Hitchen, 2016; Horton, 2016). Hard times matter and by attending to the relational experiences of diverse children, youth and families, readers can appreciate how they live-with and live-through these moments, the parallels and differences in daily lives, and how experiences of inequality, poverty and marginality are intensified. This multiscalar approach enables us to grasp the complex interplay between lived experiences and deeper problematics of hard times, bringing into focus the liminal spaces where both the transformative and mundane occur (Pimlott-Wilson and Hall, 2017).

Possibilities for getting by and growing up

In the collection, readers encountered first-hand accounts of neoliberalism, marketisation, austerities and economic crises impinging on the ability of children and young people in diverse contexts to 'get by' on a daily basis. The chapters herein recount the effects of 'hard times' in their various contextual guises, with children and young people 'getting by': going on with their everyday lives which are touched by incursions from broader socio-economic and political change, getting by in often difficult (yet rather differentiated) circumstances. Whether that is navigating for-profit educational establishments (Larsson and Bengtsson, Chapter 2), engaging in collective action in response to debt (Pei and Chang, Chapter 15) or embracing uncertainty in order to support themselves and their families (Aufseeser, Chapter 3; Day, Chapter 16; Johnson and West, Chapter 8), the collection uncovers the manifestation of hard times in young people's lifeworlds.

In an age of uncertainty, children, young people and families are demonstrating the ability to withstand and adapt to stress at a time when services and opportunities are disintegrating. Through her work with young people responding to rapid economic change in the 1980s and 1990s in the USA and Sudan, Katz (2004) draws a distinction between resistance, resilience and reworking. In facing difficult circumstances, she suggests resilience involves people managing the conditions of their everyday lives and keeping their communities afloat. In more recent times, the concept of resilience has been critiqued for emphasising individual and community responses to economic, social and environmental insecurity over state responsibilities (Harrison, 2013; Hall, 2016). For some, 'resilience' is central to the dominance and continuation of status quo neoliberal ideology, whereby citizens pragmatically adapt to crises and withstand resultant hardships (Diprose, 2014). Notwithstanding the damage caused by hard times and the difficulties faced by people in their efforts to get by, resilience does not imply passivity on the part of individuals and communities, nor negate state culpability. Rather, it recognises the ability of people and places to endure and adapt to the ongoing, lived and hidden impacts of hard times. Some suggest resilience can establish the foundations for incremental change and creativity (Katz, 2004; DeVerteuil, 2015; DeVerteuil and Golubchikov, 2016) whereas among others, enduring the harms and anxieties induced by drawn out, multifaceted hard times and structural inequalities can manifest in weariness and inertia (Wilkinson and Ortega-Alcázar, 2019). While not a passive act, getting by in times of profound uncertainty and deepening inequality reduces the capacity of children, youth and families to flourish.

Throughout the collection, the tenacity of respondents in the face of diverse hard times comes to the fore. Young people are not simply passive, weathering the effects of hard times but rather have the capacity to act (Horton et al, 2008; Jeffrey, 2012; Harrison, 2013; Honwana, 2014). There are a number of instances in the collection of young people who are optimistic for their own future possibilities, navigating inequalities and socio-economic transformations as they remain hopeful despite inequalities and hardships. In Chapter 5, Denise Goerisch discusses institutional structures in the USA which normalise debt and thus fail to recognise the financial pressures and determination of low-income young people caught within the wider web of their family's economic circumstances. In Chapter 4, Lee-Caldararo recounts the bodily experiences of sleepless youth which arise from highly competitive neoliberal education systems in South Korea. Education is considered to facilitate the enterprising neoliberal future-orientated citizen to obtain employment and thus bolstering national economies, even though research suggests that increased educational levels are not being met by corresponding employment opportunities (Jeffrey, 2010a; Gough et al, 2013; McEvoy-Levy, 2014). Government rhetoric in diverse parts of the world positions education as a route to self-sufficiency (Jenson and St Martin, 2006) yet the collection demonstrates clear inequalities in access and quality (see chapters by Aufseeser, Chapter 3; and Johnson and West, Chapter 8). Nonetheless, throughout the collection, there are reports of children, young people and families getting by with ingenuity and pragmatism in an attempt to mitigate the deleterious impacts of inequities and marginalisation at the everyday scale.

Getting by, whether a quiet resignation (Hitchen, 2016) or steady on-going endurance (Wilkinson and Ortega-Alcázar, 2019), enables children, young people and their families to negotiate and manage uncertain futures in sub-optimal conditions. The onus is placed on young people to navigate and rewrite their biographies in response to hard times in order to survive, yet the capacity to do so is marred by social inequality and the varying magnitude of obstacles which individuals face. This sense of liminality, on the threshold of simply 'enough' (Ingleby and Randalls, 2019) undercuts young people's possibilities. Living through hard times and 'getting by' is not enough and children, young people and their families cannot continually be expected to bounce back from challenging circumstances. Rather as critical social scientists, we suggest the social and economic realities of young people should allow them to do more than simply 'get by' and instead, we call for action which seeks to reduce poverty, inequalities and marginalisation, supporting the creation of conditions whereby they can thrive.

Chapters in this collection have explored the difficult circumstances under which many children and young people get by in their everyday lives. Our approach in the book has been to acknowledge the significance of the current lived experiences of children and young people in the everyday while also recognising that temporarily matters, as the future is implicated in the hard times experienced now (Henderson et al, 2007). This bringing together of both the everyday 'getting by' with 'growing up', the links between 'being and becoming' (Uprichard, 2008), draws attention to the fact that 'our experiences as children, and memories of this period, can shape who we become' (Valentine, 2003: 39). In many of the chapters, expectations of children and young people as 'becoming' something other than they are now are highlighted, whether this stems from institutions, the state, wider family or young people themselves. Their experiences of 'getting by' in the here and now are thus significant for their 'growing up', particularly when they are etched with difficulty. Experiences of growing up through hard times resonate through the lifecourse, as cuts to public services limit the facilities available to young people (Wilkinson, Chapter 14); experiences of employment precarity influence masculine norms and role models for young men (Kelly, Chapter 11); and contemporary experiences of indebtedness mean that some young people have to curtail their university education, leaving an imprint on future career prospects (Goerisch, Chapter 5). Through a simultaneous focus on the ways in which children and young people actively reconstruct their lives in the here and now, while also looking at their hopes for the future, the collection illuminates 'how youth are able to move, what they seek to move towards and the ways external forces seek to shape their movements' (Christiansen et al, 2006: 16). With the COVID-19 pandemic precipitating a global economic slowdown, external constraints will affect current experiences and future plans. In the present moment, young people and women are at greatest risk of joblessness and poverty, with the effects of the pandemic likely to disrupt a whole generation (OECD, 2020; ILO, 2020a). Getting by in times of prolonged economic, social and political uncertainty leaves a mark on the lives of some young people who are facing a future where their prospects for social mobility are significantly worse than their parents (McDowell, 2017).

Young people are under pressure to take responsibility and provide for themselves in order to achieve deep-rooted social markers of adulthood and align with neoliberal expectations of success and self-reliant responsible citizenship (MacLeavy, 2008; Raco, 2009). Normative understandings of linear transitions have been subject to critique, particular in contexts where notions of childhood, youth and adulthood are fluid and the certitude of predictable life stages is eroded by socioeconomic change (Valentine, 2003; Langevang, 2008; van Blerk, 2008; Worth, 2009; Brown et al, 2012; McEvoy-Levy, 2014). Regardless of pervasive insecurity, neoliberal governance continues to tie citizenship with individual responsibility and instructs young people to internalise uncertainty in diverse contexts (Katz, 2004; Evans, 2008; Cairns, 2013; Pimlott-Wilson, 2017). Prevailing social norms construct a linear pathway to adulthood (Hopkins, 2006), as adulthood and citizenship remain closely tied to the achievement of financial independence. Neat linear pathways through education, employment, leaving home and towards financial independence can be disrupted by young people themselves and/or the socio-economic circumstances in which they are located (Holdsworth and Morgan, 2005; Gough et al, 2013; Honwana, 2014). Rearrangement of the pathway, such as returning to the childhood home, is becoming increasingly commonplace, but represents a reversal of the traditional cycle, diminishing an individual's identification as an adult in some contexts (Arnett, 2004; Tomaszczyk and Worth, 2018). Young people thus face a paradox, as opportunities and expectations are simultaneously broadened and constrained (Berlant, 2007; Honwana, 2014; McEvoy-Levy, 2014), complicating the achievement of these social markers and leading to protracted and non-linear transitions (Jeffrey, 2010b; Hörschelmann, 2018).

At a time of complexity, examples in this collection suggest that the association between economic provision and adulthood has not lost its normative force, acting as a benchmark for young people, governments and institutions (McDowell, 2003; McEvoy-Levy, 2014). At an individual level, it is important to recognise that the life course and 'growing up' are non-linear, yet persistent societal prescriptions complicate transitions at a time of significant political-economic change (Schwiter, 2011). Growing up can thus be fraught with unpredictability, which presents both challenges and opportunities for children and young people. The collection of chapters here demonstrated this complexity for young people who continue to hope that they will secure a job, support themselves and often also their family. In Colombia, Marzi (Chapter 13) elucidates inequalities and discrimination rooted in class, race, gender and place affecting young people. Despite these intersecting constraints, young people remain hopeful and sought opportunities for social mobility. In Zambia, Day (Chapter 16) articulates government expectations of self-sufficiency placed on young people who live in a context where a lack of opportunities and resources stifles their potential. She illustrates that in a wider socio-economic climate infused with complexity, young people are intricately linked to family through webs of caring relations and responsibility yet feel unable to achieve their aspirations to provide across the generations. In a context of global economic uncertainty and constrained local opportunities, young people from different cultural contexts aim to secure social markers associated with emergent adulthood.

What is concerning about the contemporary moment is that 'hard times' create uncertainty for young people who are increasingly reliant on a transformed labour market to achieve socially-sanctioned markers of success but also their own hopes. The entanglement of austerities, neoliberalisms and economic crises thus makes achieving desired and normative outcomes complex as failures of the market and state become internalised as personal failures, overlooking the socio-economic barriers which limit the achievement of such milestones (Holloway and Pimlott-Wilson, 2011; Pimlott-Wilson, 2017). As discussed in the postscript to Chapter 1, the implications of the unfolding COVID-19 pandemic are only just emerging at the time of writing, yet indications suggest that the crisis is having a disproportionate effect on youth employment (ILO, 2020b; 2020a). Long-lasting wage losses and competition for fewer jobs are set to constrain young people, who generally occupy less secure jobs and are highly represented among workers in industries most affected by the pandemic (OECD, 2020). Across the EU, one in three young people work in the three sectors most disrupted by COVID-19 (wholesale, retail and accommodation and food) (Balate, 2020) and one in six young people aged 18–24 globally have stopped working since the start of the pandemic (ILO, 2020a). Young people have also experienced severe disruptions to education and training, with those in lower-income countries hit hardest (ILO, 2020a). The combined effect of fewer job vacancies, increased competition for jobs and disrupted education means that school-to-work transitions are more arduous for some young people (ILO, 2020c). While public narratives may suggest that 'we're all in this together', the disproportionate impacts of COVID-19 on diverse young people and their families lay bare deep social disparities at a variety of scales (Bruzelius and Ratzmann, 2020). Structural inequalities combined with the multifaceted effects of hard times mean that the gap between promises and realities for young people in neoliberal societies is expanding (Berlant, 2007; McEvoy-Levy, 2014; Hörschelmann, 2018; ILO, 2020d). By bringing together the diverse voices and agencies of children and young people from different international contexts at this particular moment in the book, readers can see that experiences of hardship and growing up are multidimensional, complex and ongoing.

Looking ahead in uncertain times

Neoliberalisms, austerities and economic crises are multiscalar in nature (Pimlott-Wilson and Hall, 2017) and the analyses presented in the preceding chapters bring into conversation micro-geographies with macro issues (Ansell, 2009; Holt, 2010). In the collection, contributions have noted the everyday experiences of hard times as relational, influenced by the complex scaling of global, national, regional, community, household and individual issues. Exploring the interplay between broadscale political-economic processes and the lived, experienced and personal scale of daily life acknowledges the wider social structures that shape the lives of respondents (Gallacher and Gallagher, 2008) and the agentic role of children, young people and families in (re)producing and challenging socio-spatial inequalities (Holloway et al, 2019). We argue that further work exploring the spatially-contingent nature of hard times can inform analysis and the interrogation of these processes, as well as the possibilities for transformation. Indeed, this approach seeks to move away from an 'overly narrow focus on children's micro-worlds' (Holloway, 2014: 387) to recognise the connections between broadscale processes and everyday lived realities. Attending to the intersections of the private and mundane with global, 'spectacular' subjects of study can provide valuable insights to the ongoing, gradual erosion of daily life (Pain, 2014) and more hopeful, transformative possibilities.

Focusing on individual and community solutions to problems rooted in neoliberalisms, austerities and economic crisis which are exacerbated by social inequity recognises that incremental change may be possible (Katz, 2004; DeVerteuil, 2015). This shifting of responsibility from the state to the individual comes at the cost of overburdening everyday lives, as individuals are tasked with adapting to the precarious existence in which they find themselves, privatising the problems experienced

(McEvoy-Leavy, 2014). Yet this also provides space for more hopeful futures, to recognise the possibilities of apparently mundane sites as key contexts for social transformation in hard times (Wilson, 2013; Honwana, 2014; DeVerteuil and Golubchikov, 2016). With a multiscalar lens, it is possible to both focus in on the ways hard times play out in the everyday realities of children, young people and their families in place, while also scaling up our attention to question and actively address the injustices of neoliberalisms, austerities and economic crisis (Pimlott-Wilson and Hall, 2017).

In the collection, the ability to 'get by', and how this manifests in daily life, is shaped by structural inequalities and deep-rooted social norms and stereotypes. Social norms may be becoming less relevant in regulating individual life courses in contemporary socialites (Tosi, 2017). Individuals have agency over their pathways and readers have witnessed how young people contest and rework social norms associated with childhood and adulthood as the liminal space of daily life shifts their ability (and desire) to align with entrenched ideals (McEvoy-Levy, 2014). Yet the spectre of these unwritten rules of behaviour continues to resonate, even when hard times make conformity increasingly difficult and individuals choose to resist them. In Chapter 7, Piggot reveals how household circumstances entwine with patriarchal norms and neoliberalism to affect experiences of poverty, inequality and marginality for women within families. Lehtonen and Breslow demonstrate the interplay between social constructions of childhood and deficit parenthood in UK media and policy discourses, with issues of power, dependency and poverty in order to justify austerity measures (Chapter 9). In Chapter 11, Kelly highlights the interplay between immigration and employment precarity, which in turn undermines notions of masculinity among Filipino-Canadian men. Aufseeser draws attention to normative understandings of childhood in Peru, which construct children as vulnerable and in need of protection (Chapter 3). This framing of childhood jars with everyday realities, as children migrate in order to secure employment to support their families and access education. Individuals therefore (re)negotiate idealised neoliberal subject positions and socially-sanctioned notions of childhood, youth, parenting and gender in the face of multiple risks, challenges and changing social circumstances (Armstrong, 2006; Raco, 2009; Holloway and Pimlott-Wilson, 2012). We observe a problematic interplay between hard times and prevailing social norms which pervade government policy, community and intergenerational relations. Examples from the collection suggest that these are changing more slowly than the everyday realities in which children and youth get by and grow up, necessitating further attention in the context of shifting socio-economic and political realities.

The home environment is a locus for policy attention and a confluence where external insecurities are felt through intergenerational relations (Hopkins et al 2019). Hard times are experienced and contested through webs of inter- and intra-generational relations, intensifying and compounding deeply-rooted inequalities (Hall, 2016; 2017; 2018; Horton, 2016; McDowell, 2017; Stenning, 2020). As we write, the on-going challenges of the COVID-19 pandemic are exposing the centrality of familial and community connections as years of austerity measures have hollowed out public services (see Flesher Fominaya, 2020). Cuts to public funding following previous crises have left women's employment in the healthcare and education sectors more exposed than in the past, and social distancing measures have had a large impact on sectors with high female employment shares (ILO, 2020b). In the UK, ethnic inequalities are manifest through both occupational exposure to infection and economic vulnerability under lockdown restrictions (Platt and Warwick, 2020). Families already struggling with broader insecurities are asymmetrically impacted by coronavirus, worsening labour market and housing insecurities (Gustafsson and McCurdy, 2020; Pouliakas and Branka, 2020). While saving lives, lockdown has caused distress for families, as domestic violence escalates, children are deprived of education (compounding educational inequalities) and the social services on which those with disabilities rely come under threat (ILO, 2020b). The experiences of children, youth, the household and family in hard times are interconnected and thus further research is required to explore the interaction between the different scalar processes, social expectations and familial relations at play. Attending further to the lives of children and young people within broader circuits of influence, including (but not limited to) the family, friendships, peer groups and neighbourhoods, while recognising the role of the state, social norms and economic processes in their lifecourse provides a fuller picture of getting by and growing up. By looking inward at the distinct yet interrelated ways in which broadscale social processes play out in the lives of children, young people and their families, we can further explore the contingent nature of socio-economic shifts and the mundane, socially-diverse experiences of hard times.

References

Ansell, N. (2009) 'Childhood and the politics of scale: Descaling children's geographies?', *Progress in Human Geography*, 33(2): 190–209.

Armstrong, J. (2006) 'Beyond "juggling" and "flexibility": Classed and gendered experiences of combining employment and motherhood', *Sociological Research Online*, 11(2), http://www.socresonline.org.uk/11/2/armstrong.html

Arnett, J. (2004) *Emerging adulthood: The winding road from the late teens through the twenties*, Oxford: Oxford University Press.

Balate, F. (2020) *Generation L: How COVID-19 affect young people's jobs and what we can do about it*, OECD Forum, 15 July, https://www.oecd-forum.org/posts/generation-l-how-covid-19-affects-young-people-s-jobs-and-what-we-can-do-about-it

Berlant, L. (2007) 'Cruel optimism: On Marx, loss and the senses', *New Formations*, 63(winter): 33–51.

Brown, G., Kraftl, P., Pickerill, J., and Upton, C. (2012) 'Holding the future together: towards a theorisation of the spaces and times of transition', *Environment and Planning A*, 44(7): 1607–1623.

Bruzelius, C. and Ratzmann, N. (2020) *The social consequences of Covid-19 for vulnerable migrant groups in Germany*, London: London School of Economics and Political Science, https://blogs.lse.ac.uk/socialpolicy/2020/04/30/the-social-consequences-of-covid-19-for-vulnerable-migrant-groups-in-germany/

Cairns, K. (2013) 'The subject of neoliberal affects: Rural youth envision their futures', *The Canadian Geographer*, 57(3): 337–344.

Christiansen, C., Utas, M. and Vigh, H. E. (2006) 'Introduction: Navigating youth, generating adulthood', in: C. Christiansen, M. Utas and H. E. Vigh (eds) *Navigating youth, generating adulthood: Social becoming in an African context*, Uppsala, The Nordic Africa Institute, pp.9–28.

DeVerteuil, G. (2015) *Resilience in the post-welfare inner city: Voluntary sector geographies in London, Los Angeles and Sydney*, Bristol: Policy Press.

DeVerteuil, G. and Golubchikov, O. (2016) 'Can resilience be redeemed? Resilience as a metaphor for change, not against change', *City*, 20(1): 143–151.

Diprose, K. (2014) 'Resilience is futile', *Soundings*, 58: 44–56.

Evans, B. (2008) 'Geographies of youth/young people', *Geography Compass*, 2(5): 1659–1680.

Flesher Fominaya, C. (2020) *How austerity measures hurt the Covid-19 response*, Oxford University Blog, https://blog.oup.com/2020/04/how-austerity-measures-hurt-the-covid-19-response/

Gallacher, L. A. and Gallagher, M. (2008) 'Methodological immaturity in childhood research: Thinking through "participatory methods"', *Childhood*, 15: 499–516.

Gough, K. V., Langevang, T., and Owusu, G. (2013) 'Youth employment in a globalising world', *International Development Planning Review*, 35(2): 91–102.

Gustafsson, M. and McCurdy, C. (2020) *Risky business: Economic impacts of the coronavirus crisis on different groups of workers*, Resolution Foundation, April, https://www.resolutionfoundation.org/app/uploads/2019/10/Risky-business.pdf

Hall, S. M. (2016) 'Everyday family experiences of the financial crisis: Getting by in the recent economic recession', *Journal of Economic Geography*, 16(2): 305–330.

Hall, S. M. (2017) 'Personal, relational and intimate geographies of austerity: Ethical and empirical considerations', *Area*, 49(3): 303–310.

Hall, S. M. (2018) 'The personal is political: Feminist geographies of/in austerity', *Geoforum*, https://doi.org/10.1016/j.geoforum.2018.04.010

Harrison, E. (2013) 'Bouncing back? Recession, resilience and everyday lives', *Critical Social Policy*, 33(1): 97–113.

Henderson, S., Holland, J., McGrellis, S., Sharpe, S. and Thomson, R. (2007) *Inventing adulthoods: A biographical approach to youth transitions*, London: Sage.

Hitchen, E. (2016) 'Living and feeling the austere', *New Formations*, 87: 102–118.

Holdsworth, C. and Morgan, D. (2005) *Transitions in context: Leaving home, independence and adulthood*, Buckingham: Open University Press.

Holloway, S. L. (2014) 'Changing children's geographies', *Children's Geographies*, 12(4): 377–392.

Holloway, S. L. and Pimlott-Wilson, H. (2011) 'Geographies of children, youth an families: Defining achievements, debating the agenda', in: L. Holt (ed) *Geographies of children and young people: An international perspective*, London: Routledge, pp.9–24.

Holloway, S. L. and Pimlott-Wilson, H. (2012) 'Neoliberalism, policy localisation and idealised subjects: A case study of educational restructuring in England', *Transactions of the Institute of British Geographers*, 37(4): 639–654.

Holloway, S. L., Holt, L. and Mills, S. (2019) 'Questions of agency: Capacity, subjectivity, spatiality and temporaloty', *Progress in Human Geograpy*, 43(3): 458–477.

Holt, L. (2010) 'Geographies of children and young people: Disentangling the socio-spatial contexts of young people across the globalizing world', in: L. Holt (ed) *Geographies of children and young people: An International Perspective*, London: Routledge, pp.1–9.

Honwana, A. (2014) 'Waithood: Youth transitions and social change. Response to Syed Mansoob Murshed', In: D. Foeken, T. Dietz, L. de Haan and L. Johnson (eds) *Development and equity: An interdisciplinary exploration by ten scholars from Africa, Asia and Latin America*, Leiden: Brill, pp.28–40.

Hopkins, P. E. (2006) 'Youth transitions and going to university: The perceptions of students attending a geography summer school access programme', *Area*, 38(3): 240–247.

Hopkins, P., Hörschelmann, K., Benwell, M. C. and Studemeyer, C. (2019) 'Young people's everyday landscapes of security and insecurity', *Social & Cultural Geography*, 20(4): 435–444.

Hörschelmann, K. (2018) 'Unbound emotional geographies of youth transitions', *Geographica Helvetica*, 73, 31–42.

Horton, J. (2016) 'Anticipating service withdrawal: Young people in spaces of neoliberalisation, austerity and economic crisis', *Transactions of the Institute of British Geographers*, 41(4): 349–362.

Horton, J., Kraftl, P. and Tucker, F. (2008) 'The challenges of "children's geographies": A reaffirmation', *Children's Geographies*, 6(4): 37–41.

ILO (International Labour Office) (2020a) *Youth and COVID-19: Impacts on jobs, education, right and mental well-being*, Geneva, https://www.ilo.org/wcmsp5/groups/public/---ed_emp/documents/publication/wcms_753026.pdf

ILO (International Labour Office) (2020b) *ILO monitor: COVID-19 and the world of work* (4th edn), Geneva, https://www.ilo.org/wcmsp5/groups/public/@dgreports/@dcomm/documents/briefingnote/wcms_745963.pdf

ILO (International Labour Office) (2020c) *Preventing exlusion from the labour market: Tackling the COVID-19 youth employment crisis*, Policy Brief, May, Geneva, https://www.ilo.org/wcmsp5/groups/public/---ed_emp/documents/publication/wcms_746031.pdf

ILO (International Labour Office) (2020d) *Global employment trends for youth 2020: Technology and the future of jobs*, Geneva, https://www.ilo.org/wcmsp5/groups/public/---dgreports/---dcomm/---publ/documents/publication/wcms_737648.pdf

Ingleby, M. and Randalls, S. (2019) (eds) *Just enough: The history, culture and politics of sufficiency*, Basingstoke: Palgrave Macmillan.

Jeffrey, C. (2010a) 'Timepass: Youth, class and time among unemployed men in India', *American Ethnologist*, 37(3): 465–481.

Jeffrey, C. (2010b) 'Geographies of children and youth. I: Eroding maps of life', *Progress in Human Geography*, 34(4): 495–505.

Jeffrey, C. (2012) 'Geographies of children and youth. II: Global youth agency', *Progress in Human Geography*, 36(2): 245–253.

Jenson, J. and St Martin, D. (2006) *Building blocks for a new social architecture: The LEGO™ paradigm of an active society*, http://www.cccg.umontreal.ca/pdf/Jenson%20and%20Saint-Martin-Policy%20and%20Politics%203.pdf

Kallio, K. P. and Mills, S. (2016) 'Editorial: Geographies of children and young people's politics, citizenship, and rights', in: K. P. Kallio, S. Mills and T. Skelton (eds) *Politics, citizenship and rights*, Singapore: Springer, pp.ix–xviii.

Katz, C. (2004) *Growing up global: Economic restructuring and children's everyday lives*, Minneapolis, MN: University of Minnesota Press.

Katz, C. (2018) 'The angel of geography: Superman, Tiger Mother, aspiration management, and the child as waste', *Progress in Human Geography*, 42(5): 723–740.

Langevang, T. (2008) ' "We are managing!" Uncertain paths to respectable adulthoods in Accra, Ghana', *Geoforum*, 39(6): 2039–2047.

MacLeavy, J. (2008) 'Neoliberalising subjects: The legacy of New Labour's construction of social exclusion in local governance', *Geoforum*, 39(5): 1657–1666.

McDowell, L. (2003) *Redundant masculinities? Employment change and white working class youth*, Oxford: Blackwell.

McDowell, L. (2017) 'Youth, children and families in austere times: Change, politics and a new gender contract', *Area*, 49(3): 311–316.

McEvoy-Levy, S. (2014) 'Stuck in circulation: Children, "waithood" and the conflict narratives of Israelis and Palestinians', *Children's Geographies*, 12(3): 312–326.

OECD (2020) *Young people and women hit hard by jobs crisis*, http://www.oecd.org/about/civil-society/youth/

Pain, R. (2014) 'Everyday terrorism: Connecting domestic violence and global terrorism', *Progress in Human Geography*, 38: 531–550.

Pimlott-Wilson, H. (2017) 'Individualising the future: The emotional geographies of neoliberal governance in young people's aspirations', *Area*, 49(3): 288–295.

Pimlott-Wilson, H. and Hall, S. M. (2017) 'Everyday experiences of economic change: Repositioning geographies of children, youth and families', *Area*, 49(3): 258–265.

Platt, L. and Warwick, R. (2020) *Are some ethnic groups more vulnerable to COVID-19 than others?*, Institute for Fiscal Studies, May, https://www.ifs.org.uk/inequality/chapter/are-some-ethnic-groups-more-vulnerable-to-COVID-19-than-others/

Pouliakas, K. and Branka, J. (2020) *EU jobs at highest risk of COVID-19 social distancing: Is the pandemic exacerbating the labour market divide?*, Luxembourg: Publications Office of the European Union, Cedefop working paper 1, http://data.europa.eu/doi/10.2801/968483

Raco, M. (2009) 'From expectations to aspirations: State modernisation, urban policy, and the existential politics of welfare in the UK', *Political Geography*, 28(7): 436–444.

Schwiter, K. (2011) 'Anticipating the transition to parenthood: The contribution of Foucaultian discourse analysis to understanding life-course patterns', *Area*, 43(4): 397–404.

Stenning, A. (2020) 'Feeling the squeeze: Towards a psychosocial geography of austerity in low-to-middle income families', *Geoforum*, 110(10): 200–210.

Tomaszczyk, A. C. and Worth, N. (2018) 'Boomeranging home: Understanding why millennials live with parents in Toronto, Canada', *Social and Cultural Geography*, DOI: 10.1080/14649365.2018.1535088

Tosi, M. (2017) 'Age norms, family relationships, and home-leaving in Italy', *Demographic Research*, 36: 281–306.

Uprichard, E. (2008) 'Children as "being and becomings": Children, childhood and temporality', *Children and Society*, 22(4): 303–313.

Valentine, G. (1995) 'Angels and devils: Moral landscapes of childhood', *Environment and Planning D: Society and Space*, 14(5): 581–599.

Valentine, G. (2003) 'Boundary crossings: Transitions from childhood to adulthood', *Children's Geographies*, 1(1): 37–52.

Van Blerk, L. (2008) 'Poverty, migration and sex work: Youth transitions in Ethiopia', *Area*, 40(2): 245–253.

Wilkinson, E. and Ortega-Alcázar, I. (2019) 'The right to be weary? Endurance and exhaustion in austere times', *Transactions of the Institute of British Geographers*, 44(1): 155–167.

Wilson, H. F. (2013) 'Collective life: Parents, playground encounters and the multicultural city', *Social and Cultural Geography*, 14(6): 625–648

Worth, N. (2009) 'Understanding youth transition as "becoming": Identity, time and futurity', *Geoforum*, 40(6): 1050–1060.

Index

Note: Page numbers in *italic* type refer to figures; those in **bold** type refer to tables.